Social
Experimentation
and
Public
Policymaking

David Greenberg, Donna Linksz,
and Marvin Mandell

Social Experimentation

and

Public Policymaking

THE URBAN INSTITUTE PRESS
Washington, D.C.

THE URBAN INSTITUTE PRESS
2100 M Street, NW
Washington, DC 20037

Library of Congress Cataloging in Publication Data

Greenberg, David H.
  Social experimentation and public policymaking / David Greenberg, Donna Linksz, and Marvin Mandell.
    p. cm.
Includes bibliographical references (p.) and index.
    ISBN 0-87766-711-X (pbk.)
    1. United States—Social policy—20th century—Case studies. 2. Evaluation research (Social action programs)—United States—Case studies. I. Linksz, Donna. II. Mandell, Marvin. III. Title.
  HN57.G693 2003
  361.6'1'0973—dc21

                                                                                    2003002253

ISBN 0-87766-711-X (paper, alk. paper)

Printed in the United States of America

THE URBAN INSTITUTE is a nonprofit, nonpartisan policy research and educational organization established in Washington, D.C., in 1968. Its staff investigates the social, economic, and governance problems confronting the nation and evaluates the public and private means to alleviate them. The Institute disseminates its research findings through publications, its web site, the media, seminars, and forums.

Through work that ranges from broad conceptual studies to administrative and technical assistance, Institute researchers contribute to the stock of knowledge available to guide decisionmaking in the public interest.

Conclusions or opinions expressed in Institute publications are those of the authors and do not necessarily reflect the views of officers or trustees of the Institute, advisory groups, or any organizations that provide financial support to the Institute.

To our families for their support

Contents

Preface ix

PART I: Conceptual Foundations

1 Introduction 3

2 Social Experimentation 11

3 Conceptual Framework and Methodology 45

PART II: Case Studies

4 The RAND Health Insurance Experiment 67

5 The Nursing Home Incentive Reimbursement
Experiment 89

6 The Income Maintenance Experiments 111

7 The Unemployment Insurance
   Bonus Experiments 165

8 The Welfare-to-Work Experiments 211

PART III: Conclusions

9 The Dissemination and Use of Experiments in
   State Policymaking 273

10 Lessons from the Case Studies 297

References 313

About the Authors 327

Index 329

Preface

In social experiments, the effects of a proposed change in social policy are examined by first randomly assigning individuals, households, or organizations to either a treatment group that is covered by the policy of interest or a comparison group that is not. The groups are then compared in terms of outcomes of interest—for example, earnings, receipt of welfare payments, or health status. Such experiments represent a very powerful means of estimating the impacts of social policies and programs. Indeed, millions of dollars have been and continue to be spent on social experiments, and the rationale for funding them is that they will improve policymaking.

Interestingly, however, the role that social experiments play in policymaking is not well understood. This makes it very difficult to, for example, assess whether the return from social experiments is worth the substantial resources required to conduct them. Hence, we set out to examine why social experiments are conducted, whether they are used in making public policy and, if they are, how. Our analysis is based in large part on five detailed case studies of previously completed social experiments. These case studies are augmented by a survey of state policymakers we conducted that examined the dissemination and use of findings from three other social experiments. We believe the analysis presented sheds important light on the general issues of the usefulness of policy research and the more specific issues of how useful social experiments are for policy purposes, the circumstances under which they are likely to be most useful, and whether their usefulness can be enhanced.

In writing this book, we had several potential audiences in mind. Perhaps the most obvious readers are program evaluators interested in whether and how their efforts are used in the policy process. Another obvious audience is staff in government agencies and foundations that fund policy research, as well as public officials who propose policy changes and their staffs. In addition, academics who read and contribute to the knowledge utilization literature should find this book of considerable interest. Finally, we hope that students who are enrolled in a wide range of programs, including public administration, public policy, health policy, and social work, will benefit from reading the book.

We are very grateful for the financial support that we received from the Robert Wood Johnson Foundation to conduct much of the research on which this book is based. We also want to express our appreciation to the many colleagues who helped us out in a variety of ways. Matt Onstott was a major contributor to the survey that forms the basis of chapter 9. In several places we borrow heavily from Greenberg and Shroder's *Digest of Social Experiments* (1997). Hence, we are heavily indebted to Mark Shroder. We also wish to thank colleagues who commented on various chapters in the book, including Michael Barth, Judith Gueron, Robert Moffitt, William Prosser, and Philip Robins. Finally, and especially, we wish to thank the many individuals who took time out from very busy schedules to participate in interviews and surveys that form the basis of our analysis. Without their cooperation, this book could not have been written. Of course, the responsibility for any errors that remain lies with us.

PART I:
Conceptual
Foundations

1

Introduction

I t is almost tautological to say that policy research is intended to improve decisions made in the public policy arena. It is not at all obvious, however, that this mission is actually accomplished. Indeed, those conducting policy research often wonder if their efforts are used by policymakers in the manner intended, or used at all.

In this book, we examine the connection between a very specific form of policy research—randomized social experiments—and the policy process. Social experimentation has been part of the public policy landscape since the 1960s when Heather Ross, for her doctoral dissertation research, proposed and helped implement the New Jersey Income Maintenance Experiment with funding from the Office of Economic Opportunity.[1] Since then, more than 200 randomized field experiments, which have probably cost more than $1 billion (Greenberg and Robins 1986) to conduct and evaluate, have been initiated as pilots to test various proposed changes in social programs. Moreover, use of this evaluation technique, usually referred to as "social experimentation," has accelerated in recent years (Greenberg, Shroder, and Onstott 1999). Although varying greatly in size, budget, focus, and area of interest, social experiments can be characterized as incorporating four common components (Greenberg and Shroder 1997, 4):

- Individuals, families, or organizations are randomly assigned to treatment and control groups. The groups should then differ from each other by chance alone.

3

- Members of each of the randomly assigned groups receive distinct treatments. The random assignment process, rather than the participants or program staff, determines which treatment each individual, family, or organization receives. Treatment group members face changes in economic incentives, opportunities, or constraints, while members of the control group face no change in the status quo.
- Data are obtained on outcomes of interest—for example, welfare payments, Medicaid utilization, receipt of training and employment services, unemployment insurance receipt, earnings, and health status.
- Comparisons are made of outcomes of interest across the randomly assigned groups, using techniques of statistical inference.

This characterization of "social experiments" is deliberately narrow, as it excludes numerous evaluations of social programs that did not use random assignment, randomized trials that do not seek to measure market or fiscal outcomes (e.g., tests of alternative courtroom or police procedures or clinical tests of health care or teaching techniques), or trials that do not test policy interventions (e.g., fair housing audits or experiments conducted in laboratories by social scientists to investigate behavioral responses to various stimuli). Thus, the emphasis in this book is on field tests of social policies that change economic incentives or constraints and that are evaluated by random assignment and (at least partially) in terms of effects on economic outcomes. Sometimes these field tests are called "economic experiments," although we will use the term "social experiments" throughout this book to emphasize their focus on social policies that are evaluated through random assignment.

During the period from the late 1960s through the 1990s, social experiments ranged from large, lengthy, and costly projects (e.g., the income maintenance experiments) to more modest demonstrations (e.g., job-finding clubs) (Greenberg and Shroder 1997). Whereas many of the experiments focused on examining social welfare policies targeted to low-income populations, some tested programs that addressed problems in such areas as criminal justice, substance abuse, mental impairment, and health insurance. Begun in an atmosphere that was optimistic about the ability of social science research to enlighten public policy deliberations and improve policy decisions, the experiments were justified as an appropriate means for gathering information needed to accomplish these ends.

Objectives of the Research

Understanding the connection between social experiments and the policy process is critical for several reasons. For one, millions of dollars have been spent on them and continue to be spent. The justification made for funding social experiments is almost always an anticipated improvement in policymaking. Social experimentation has become a major, if not the most important, method for evaluating proposed changes in many areas of public policy. Therefore it seems appropriate to ask whether its payoff is worth the substantial efforts it requires. At the same time, to judge the success of social experiments properly, it is important that policymakers, funders of social experiments, the public, and those who conduct social experiments establish appropriate and realistic standards and expectations. The absence of such standards and expectations is likely to lead either to cynicism or to investment on the basis of blind faith. Understanding the connection between social experiments and the policy process can contribute to the establishment of realistic standards and expectations for judging the social gains from experiments. Finally, understanding this connection may provide important insights into ways to increase the social gains from experimentation.

We examine three specific aspects of the connection between social experiments and the policy process. (1) What are the reasons for conducting the social experiments? Our goal here is to understand and describe the process leading to the decision whether or not to conduct social experiments. What do those involved in initiating social experiments hope to accomplish? Why is experimentation rather than other means (for example, case studies, statistical inferences using multiple regression, or simulation) used to accomplish these ends? (2) What is the impact of findings from experiments on subsequent policy deliberation? In what ways, if any, do they exert an influence on policy choices? (3) What factors account for variations in the types and amount of influence that social experiments exert on policy choices?

For each of these questions, there are a variety of possible answers. One set of such answers might be termed the "classical" view. The classical explanation of the decision to conduct a social experiment is an essentially rational paradigm, in which the expected value of the information provided by a social experiment is computed, and a social experiment is conducted if and only if this expected value exceeds the expected costs of conducting that experiment. The classical view of the way social experiments influence the policy process is centered on what we and others term "concrete-substantive use." By this we mean that research findings directly and decisively influence specific policy decisions, thereby resulting in policies being adopted that otherwise would not be. The picture here is of a key decisionmaker, say a cabinet secretary or legislator, reaching a decision largely on the basis of the results of a social experiment. Finally, in the classical view, variations in the types and amount of influence that social experiments exert on policy choices are purely a function of scientific quality.

The classical view, at least at first blush, is very appealing. It is consistent with Progressive ideas of good government. Unfortunately, the classical view is rarely, if ever, consistent with empirical reality. For example, it is difficult to meet in practice the conditions necessary to compute a priori the expected value of the information provided by a social experiment. There is also a wide range of influences on policy choices—some of which are widely viewed as legitimate, others not. Hence, "concrete-substantive use" is both rare and perhaps less desirable than it might be initially viewed as being. Rather, a variety of different types of uses, which are more subtle and less direct than concrete-substantive use, also occur. Similarly, a variety of factors affect the manner and extent to which a given social experiment influences policy choices. Some of the factors pertain to the design and conduct of the experiment, as well as the ways in which its results are communicated, whereas others pertain to the characteristics of the policy environment into which results of experiments are inserted.

In part due to recognition of the limitations to the classical view, several alternative theories and hypotheses have arisen on the connection between social experiments and public policy. These are found particularly in the knowledge utilization and the decision theory literatures. In this book we integrate the theories and hypotheses into a unified, comprehensive framework. That framework is then used as a lens through which to examine the relationship between a number of different previously conducted social experiments and the policy process. Moreover, based on our empirical data, we assess the adequacy of competing characterizations of the relationship between social experiments and the policy process and suggest some directions for further refining the hypotheses and concepts that are embedded within our conceptual framework.

Our Research Approach

Although social experimentation has now become commonplace, relatively little systematic inquiry into the relationship between social experiments and the policy process has been undertaken. Hence, knowledge about the connection between social experiments (or, more generally, policy research) on the one hand and public policymaking on the other remains elusive. In this book, we aim to fill the gap. Our primary mechanism for doing so is five in-depth case studies, each of which focuses on a social experiment or a group of closely related social experiments. Two of these (the RAND Health Insurance Experiment and the Nursing Home Incentive Reimbursement Experiment) focus on an area of great public concern: the quality and cost of health care. The other three (the Income Maintenance Experiments, the Unemployment Insurance Bonus Experiments, and the Welfare-to-Work Experiments) are from the field of income security, the policy area that has been subjected most frequently to social experimentation. All five case studies involve randomized field tests of social policy that meet the criteria listed earlier for a social or economic experiment.

The experiments included in the case studies were run within a specific city or county or several cities or counties, rather than conducted throughout the entire state or country. However, they tested policies that are under the jurisdiction of the federal government and (in the case of the nursing home, unemployment bonus, and welfare-to-work experiments) state governments, but not local governments. Thus, we focus on the use of lessons from these experiments at the federal and state levels, but not at the local level.

The experiments for four of the case studies were selected because they are among the most prominent social experiments ever conducted. As documented in the case studies, they were large, highly publicized, and conducted in multiple sites located throughout the country. Consequently, they were well known to both the research and policy communities. A priori, it seemed to us that the probability that findings from these experiments would be used in the policy process was substantially higher than that for most other social experiments. Thus, it seemed likely that if evidence existed that conducting social experiments is useful, it would be found among these experiments. For contrast, we also selected one experiment that was small, limited to a single site, and known to relatively few individuals—the Nursing Home Incentive

Reimbursement Experiment. Many social experiments have been conducted that are similar to the Nursing Home Incentive Reimbursement Experiment in these respects. Our expectation was that little use is likely to be made of the results of such experiments.

Conceptual Framework for the Research

The case studies of these experiments use a common conceptual framework adopted from the knowledge utilization and decision theory literatures. Nearly all previous empirical studies contained in the knowledge utilization literature are either case studies of individual pieces of policy research or surveys that look at policy research in general. The case studies are typically limited in their ability to draw generalizable conclusions, because each case study examines only one policy study. Because the policy studies examined in different case studies tend to differ greatly from one another, the case studies fail to build upon one another. In the surveys, respondents are commonly asked if research findings have influenced policy decisions they have made, but no particular set of research findings or policy issues is specified. Consequently, because of the overgenerality of the questions they pose to respondents, the surveys assume a degree of homogeneity that does not exist among research and policy issues. Because the case studies presented in this book focus on a specific type of research—social experimentation—in which individual studies are based on a core of common elements, they partly overcome these shortcomings. In particular, by exploiting the fact that there is considerable homogeneity across social experiments, multiple case studies, each focusing on different experiments, can increase the generalizability of the conclusions drawn.

The knowledge utilization and decision theory literatures offer explanations and conceptual frameworks for the different ways in which knowledge is used in the policymaking process. These explanations and frameworks have typically been developed by looking at policy research as a general topic, rather than by looking at specific policies or specific pieces of research. Although such generalizations are provocative and intriguing, there has been little systematic effort to test their validity. This study specifically uses the five case studies of social experiments as empirical data to test models of research use.

The cases, two health-related and three from the field of income security, are sufficiently varied that they increase the generalizability of the conclusions drawn from them. At the same time, each is specific enough that key players in the policymaking and research processes in these two policy areas can be asked to focus on the use of specific experimental results, rather than on policy research in general.

The case studies consist of in-depth analyses of the process surrounding each of the social experiments that are examined:

- Why the experiments were undertaken. The origins of the experiments, decisions that led to running them, and environmental context in which the decisions were made.
- The range of use of findings from the experiments. In part, that was determined by key players such as researchers involved in the experiments, policymakers involved in the debate about the issues addressed by the experiments and in subsequent implementation of policies that potentially could have been influenced by the experimental results, and social thinkers whose views might have been influenced by the experiments.
- Factors influencing whether and how the experiments were used. Such factors include the characteristics of the experiments themselves and the policy environment after findings from the experiments were available.

Organization of This Book

This book begins by providing background information on social experimentation. Thus, chapter 2 first presents an overview of the history of social experiments since they began in the late 1960s and then examines trends in social experimentation over time. Chapter 3 discusses the relevant knowledge utilization and the decisionmaking literature and describes a conceptual framework that is drawn from that literature and used in conducting the case studies. The chapter also describes the methodology used in collecting information for the five case studies.

Chapters 4 through 8 present the five case studies themselves. Relying on a common conceptual framework, each of these chapters examines the origins of the experiment or set of experiments covered by the chapter; describes the experiment(s); summarizes key findings from the experiment(s); and, most important for this work, uses the conceptual framework developed in chapter 3 to examine the effects of the experiment(s) on policy.

Chapter 9 augments the five case studies by examining the dissemination and use of findings from three recent social experiments, each of which tested a welfare-to-work program in a different state. The chapter examines whether state welfare officials learn about findings from experiments conducted in other states and, if they do, how they learn of the findings and whether and how they use that information for policy-making in their own states.

Finally, we end (chapter 10) with inferences and conclusions that are drawn across the case studies. Specifically, we assess whether lessons from the case studies can be applied to other situations and circumstances. We focus particularly on the implications of the case studies for circumstances in which the payoff from conducting social experiments is greatest, the utility of experiments for policy purposes, and means of enhancing their usefulness. We also draw some conclusions about whether the knowledge utilization and decision theory literatures provide a useful conceptual framework for examining the origins of social experiments and their role in the policy process.

NOTE

1. Telephone interview conducted with Heather Ross on December 2, 1994.

2

Social Experimentation

The evaluation of various social programs and policies receives considerable attention. A major component of program and policy evaluation concerns the program's or policy's effects on outcomes of targeted individuals, an effort that is called *impact analysis*. Social experimentation has evolved as a major form of impact analysis. In this chapter, we discuss the ways social experiments can be used to measure the effects of current and proposed government social programs, the reasons they are often (but not always) superior to alternative methods for doing this, and some of the limitations of social experiments.[1] Following that, we present a short historical sketch of the development of random assignment experimentation in general and *social* experimentation in particular. We then present summary descriptive information on all the known social experiments conducted to date and examine trends in social experimentation.

Social Experiments As an Approach to Impact Analysis

Impact analysis of a social program almost always involves some sort of comparison. For example, in assessing a proposal for a new government program (for instance, financial incentives intended to encourage recipients of unemployment compensation to find jobs more quickly), one almost automatically makes a comparison with what would happen if the innovation were not adopted. Similarly in evaluating an existing program (say, a government-funded training program for the unemployed), one tends to compare the program with what the world would look like if it were eliminated.

These hypothetical alternatives with which existing programs are compared are often referred to as *counterfactuals*. Counterfactuals are required to answer the "what if" questions that evaluation inevitably poses: What if we eliminate program X, or adopt program Y, or implement program U instead of program V? Answers to such questions typically require estimates of differences in *outcomes* between the current environment and the counterfactual environment, differences that are often referred to as *policy impacts*. To illustrate: If it takes unemployment compensation recipients an average of 10 weeks to find jobs in the absence of financial incentives designed to encourage them to find new jobs and an average of only 8 weeks with the incentives, one policy impact of the innovation is the difference between those two outcomes—a two-week reduction in the average length of unemployment.

A variety of approaches for impact analysis have been devised. Most rely upon the use of treatment and comparison groups with impacts measured as differences in outcomes between the two. One particularly attractive approach to estimating program impacts is *social experimentation*. The essence of social experimentation is the random assignment of human subjects to at least two groups, one eligible to participate in the program of concern, the other not.

Various means of impact analysis other than random assignment are also available. The most obvious of these nonexperimental approaches is to compare persons who choose to participate in a particular program that is being evaluated with persons who do not participate, with the participants constituting the "treatment group" and the nonparticipants the "comparison group." The least sophisticated version of this approach consists of selecting the comparison group from among persons who initially applied for program benefits, but for one reason or another did not actually participate. A more sophisticated version involves drawing a comparison group from among persons sampled in national micro-data sets (for example, the Current Population Survey) by statistically matching those persons with members of the treatment group to make the two groups as comparable as possible. Yet another approach, a so-called saturation design, is to implement a program sitewide in selected locations and then compare the program sites with similar sites that do not have the program.

As compared with its alternatives, social experimentation has several advantages and disadvantages.[2] The most commonly cited advantage of social experimentation is that random assignment, if correctly carried out, ensures that the treatment and control groups will differ only in terms of eligibility for the evaluated program, except by chance alone. Hence, the argument goes, a high degree of *internal validity*[3] is usually assured when social experiments are used to estimate program impacts. In contrast, internal validity is frequently problematic when other approaches are employed. Of particular concern is *selection bias* when nonequivalent control group designs are employed. That is, if an individual can choose whether a policy intervention will or will not apply to himself, then the people who select treatment A will differ from those who choose treatment B in ways that are both observable and unobservable. The same thing is true if program administrators make the choice for individuals, rather than the individuals making the choices for themselves.[4]

If individuals in treatment and comparison groups differ only in ways that are observable (for example, in education level), then the analyst can, in principle, adjust for them when researching outcomes.[5] However, absent random assignment, individuals in treatment groups are also likely to differ from those in comparison groups in unobservable ways. Moreover, the same unobserved factors that influence which group they are in are also likely to influence outcomes. It then becomes difficult to adjust statistically for differences between the two groups. Consider a training program, for example, for which the impact of central interest is the program's effect on earnings. Perhaps persons who enter the program are more motivated than are persons who do not, but (as is typically the case) the nonexperimental data being used provide no information on differences in motivation. If so, it might be incorrectly concluded that higher average earnings received by members of the treatment group than by members of the comparison group result from the training when, in fact, they really result from greater motivation on the part of the trainees.

This illustration suggests one mechanism by which selection bias might occur in using nonexperimental data to measure program impacts, and it is not difficult to imagine others. Not surprisingly, therefore, there have been a number of attempts to develop statistical techniques to adjust for selection biases (see, for example, Dehejia and Wahba 1999; Heckman and Hotz 1989; and Heckman et al. 1998). So far, unfortunately, findings from a number of different studies suggest that the success of these techniques is limited (Fraker and Maynard 1987; Friedlander and Robins 1995; LaLonde 1986; and LaLonde and Maynard 1987).

Although social experiments have important strengths, in many cases they also have significant weaknesses. Those weaknesses may explain, at least in part, why numerous impact analyses have been conducted that have been based on nonexperimental, rather than experimental, comparisons. One significant disadvantage of experiments is particularly germane when conducting an impact analysis of a social program that has existed for some time. As a result of random assignment, people who have traditionally qualified for services under this program would now be denied them. This may generate considerable political resistance to using random assignment. Moreover, nonexperimental comparisons often can rely on already existing data on persons who have previously participated in the program and persons who have not to obtain impact estimates. Obtaining the data needed to make an experimental comparison may, in contrast, require considerable delay and expense. Policymakers may not want to wait until all this is completed to find out if a particular program works. Consequently, alternatives to social experiments that use existing data may be used to obtain impact estimates more quickly.[6]

In addition, it is rarely feasible to use social experiments to evaluate programs that have impacts that must be measured at the neighborhood or community level—for example, preventive medicine and crime prevention programs—rather than at the individual level.

Impact analyses are also subject to concerns of *external validity*—that is, the extent to which impact estimates are applicable to types of individuals other than those on whom they are based, or to other places and other time periods. For example, differences in timing imply that social attitudes, governmental institutional arrangements, the business cycle, the relative demand for unskilled and skilled labor, the rate of inflation, and other relevant factors may vary from what they were when the impacts were estimated. Different locations may result in dissimilarities in age, sex, racial, or ethnic mixes; social attitudes; state and local governmental institutions; industrial mixes; and numerous other factors. Although many concerns about external validity exist whether or not experimental or nonexperimental designs are employed, in some cases random assignment exacerbates them.

In addition, impact estimates frequently are limited to relatively few geographic areas. Because the sites are rarely selected randomly,[7] the external validity of the evaluations can be questioned (see Heckman 1992; Heckman and Smith 1995; and Hotz 1992). Difficulties in obtaining a representative sample of program sites are especially acute where the cooperation of local administrators is essential. However, the degree to which site selectivity translates into bias in the results of an impact analysis has not been empirically demonstrated.[8]

The small scale at which proposed innovations to social programs are often tested[9] raises additional concerns about external validity. Manski and Garfinkel (1992) and Garfinkel, Manski, and Michalopoulos (1992), for example, suggest that an important aspect of some policy innovations intended for widespread adaptation is that they cause changes in community attitudes and norms; these, in turn, result in feedback effects that influence the innovation's success. They further suggest that program success depends on information diffusion to potential participants. They argue that feedback effects and information diffusion will not occur unless the innovation is adopted on a large scale and, hence, will be missed by small-scale tests. Potentially important marketwide effects may also not occur in small-scale tests. For example, training programs could affect the level of wages in a community. They might also affect the number of employers in a community if enough workers receive the training to induce firms to move into the area. Little is usually known about the importance of feedback, information diffusion, and market effects. Thus, one can do little more than speculate about whether small-scale tests of social policies are seriously biased because they do not allow such effects to occur.

It has also been argued that participants in small-scale demonstrations may not be representative of individuals who would participate in ongoing, full-scale programs (see Heckman 1992; Heckman and Smith 1995; and Manski 1995). This could result from of the lack of the information diffusion that would occur in a full-scale program, the reluctance of some individuals to subject themselves to random assignment, resource constraints in full-scale programs that result in program administrators restricting participants to persons meeting certain criteria, and numerous other reasons.

An additional external validity issue concerns *entry effects* (see Moffitt 1996). For example, if only unemployed persons or persons with incomes below certain thresholds are eligible for a training program, and the services provided by the program are perceived as beneficial, some ineligibles may leave their jobs or otherwise reduce their incomes to qualify. On the other hand, if programs are perceived as burdensome, individuals might try to avoid them. For example, some individuals who qualify for transfers and who otherwise might have received them might decide not to apply for them to avoid having to participate in a welfare-to-work program. Measuring entry effects in a random assignment context requires that ineligibles be included in the evaluation sample, and, because of cost considerations, this has virtually never been done.[10] It is sometimes possible, however, to estimate entry effects nonexperimentally by using a site saturation design (see Chang 1996; Johnson, Klepinger, and Dong 1994; Schiller and Brasher 1993; and Wissoker and Watts 1994).

Types of Social Experiments

Two types of social experiments can be distinguished. The first, which are referred to as *response surface experiments,* are those that are designed in a way that permits estimation of the effects of small variations in the parameters of the program being tested (e.g., variations in program tax rates and guarantee levels in the case of the income maintenance experiments and in insurance copayment rates in the case of the RAND Health Insurance Experiment). Once obtained, estimates of responses to these parameters can, at least in principle, be used to project the effects of any program that has the same basic features of the one experimentally tested, even if the specific values of the program parameters differ. The four income maintenance experiments and the RAND Health Insurance Experiment are examples of this type of social experiment.

In contrast with response surface experiments, most social experiments permit only *black box* assessments of the efficacy of the tested policy intervention. Only limited information is provided on the way changes in the design of the program tested would affect the impact of the program. This problem is sometimes compounded by the fact that some black box experiments provide different randomly selected groups of individuals with different combinations of services and incentives (e.g., job training *and* child care assistance *and* job search assistance) to determine whether outcomes (for example, postprogram earnings) differ among the groups. Only limited information is typically provided on the degree to which these impacts can be attributed to specific components of the packages of services. The response surface technique has greater appeal to professional economists, but it often is not possible in practice to implement an intervention in a way that permits estimation of the effects of variations in a particular set of parameter values.

Process Analysis and Cost-Benefit Analysis

Impact analyses are often supplemented by *process analyses* as well as by *cost-benefit analyses*. Process analysis (which is also sometimes called implementation analysis) simply entails learning as much as possible about how a program that is being evaluated in a social experiment actually operates and the environment in which it operates. For example, in the case of an evaluation that is being used to evaluate a training program, a process analysis might involve learning about the bureaucracy set up to run the program, the types of people who receive the training, the length of time they remain in training, the services they receive, the economic environment they will face when they complete the training, the way decisions are made on what sort of people receive what sorts of services, and the availability of alternative training programs.

For policy purposes, it is often important to determine not only whether a program being tested in a social experiment has positive impacts, but also whether the effects can be obtained cost-effectively. The most comprehensive way of doing this is through cost-benefit analysis, which is part of many, but far from all, social experiments. In the simplest terms, the objective of cost-benefit analysis is to determine whether the benefits of an existing or proposed government program less the program's cost are positive or negative. Thus, in conducting a cost-benefit analysis of a social program, all the benefits from the program would be summed, all the costs would be summed, and then the total benefits would be compared to the total costs to ascertain whether the program results in a net gain (i.e., positive net social benefits) or loss to society (negative net social benefits) as a whole:

TOTAL SOCIAL BENEFITS − TOTAL SOCIAL COSTS = NET SOCIAL BENEFIT

History

As indicated, the essence of social experimentation is the random assignment of human subjects to at least two groups to examine the effects of social policies. This concept did not occur all at once, but evolved over time. The idea of comparing a treatment group with a control group came first and was firmly established by 19th-century pioneers of medical and biological research. For example, in one classic experiment, Louis Pasteur divided a flock of sheep into two groups, a treatment group and a control group. The treatment group was injected with attenuated material from other animals that had died of anthrax, so that they could development immunity, but the control group was not. Both groups were then injected with anthrax-infected matter. None of the treatment group sheep became sick, whereas all of the control group sheep died.

If Pasteur's results had been less dramatic, critics might have claimed that for some reason the control group was more anthrax-vulnerable than the treatment group. Over time, in fact, the charge that controls were "inadequate" became commonplace, as it was recognized that no treatment group was ever identical with the control group. This realization stimulated development of the concept of randomization, which, like many other fundamental statistical tools, was conceived by Ronald Fisher.[11] Fisher pointed out that no two groups could ever be identical because each individual organism, test tube, soil sample, and so forth would vary slightly from every other. Therefore, the researcher's task was to allocate cases among groups in such a manner that the mechanism used was not related to the issue being studied. Allocation by pure chance (a coin flip, a table of random numbers) achieved that result. Based on this concept, random assignment experiments came into widespread use in many areas of research—medicine and agriculture, for example—by the end of the first half of the 20th century.

Social experimentation, however, did not come about until the late 1960s when Heather Ross, a Massachusetts Institute of Technology (MIT) graduate student in economics, developed the idea of conducting an income maintenance experiment as her Ph.D. dissertation research and wrote a proposal to the federal government to obtain funding. As described in some detail in chapter 6, Ross's idea was quickly implemented in the form of the New Jersey Income Maintenance Experiment, which was initiated in 1968 and is widely considered the first social experiment.[12]

Since the New Jersey experiment, numerous additional social experiments have been conducted and many more continue to be initiated. Before examining social experiments that have been conducted and the way they have evolved over the past three decades or so, it will be helpful to consider briefly the broader context of this historical period, particularly what presidents held office, what their general stance was on health and welfare policies, and what major initiatives were undertaken in those areas.

The Historical Context

The period 1962–96 started with a major push to expand the role of government in health and welfare policy. President Lyndon B. Johnson declared "unconditional war on poverty" in his 1964 State of the Union address (Haveman 1987, 3). Later that year, the Economic Opportunity Act was passed. In addition to creating a series of new social programs aimed at reducing poverty, the act created the Office of Economic Opportunity (OEO). As we shall see below, in its relatively short existence the OEO played a major role in the rise of social experiments. In addition, Medicare and Medicaid were enacted in 1965.

The push to expand the role of government in health and welfare policy was short-lived. Fink and Graham (1998, 3) identify 1968—the year that the New Jersey Income Maintenance Experiment was initiated—as "the watershed date in postwar American political history." At a minimum, the 1968 election marked a turning point in the further expansion of government programs. Several factors contributed to waning support for further expansion of government-sponsored social programs, including the collapse of the New Deal coalition and slower economic growth. Consequently, beginning with President Richard M. Nixon in 1969, presidential administrations placed considerable emphasis on either controlling or reducing the scope and cost of government.

Light (1999, 70) asked 126 White House staff members from presidential administrations from Presidents John F. Kennedy to Jimmy Carter "to name the most important domestic programs of their respective administrations." Welfare reform was mentioned prominently by staff members from both the Nixon and Carter administrations. A handful (28 percent) of staff members from the Carter administration identified "hospital cost containment," but not national health insurance, as an important domestic issue. Staff members from both the Nixon and Ford administrations did not mention health in any form.

Welfare reform was identified as an important domestic issue by 75 percent of staff members from the Nixon administration—more than any other domestic issue cited. Upon his election, Nixon appointed a transition task force on the issue. Light (1999, 76–77) argues that the prominence of welfare reform on the Nixon domestic policy agenda was, in large part, due to its potential to make a historic mark. In any case, in August 1969, Nixon's Family Assistance Plan (FAP) was introduced to Congress. Although Nixon and his advisers advocated FAP's adoption over the next three years (Lynn and Whitman 1981, 25), as discussed in chapter 6, it never succeeded legislatively.

National health insurance does not appear to have been a priority for President Nixon during his first term. In 1974, however, he introduced a plan for comprehensive national insurance. Light (1999, 129) attributes this to an attempt to "direct attention away from Watergate" and "salvage Nixon's crippled presidency."

President Gerald Ford, Nixon's successor, repeated Nixon's request for a national health plan immediately upon assuming office. However, he did not pursue it vigorously and dropped the proposal six months later because of economic pressures. The Ford administration also conducted internal deliberations about welfare reform. However, in light of their lack of political capital at the time, the Ford administration chose to wait to pursue welfare reform until after the 1976 election (Light 1999, 129).

Jimmy Carter's election in 1976 followed eight years of Republican administrations. Although liberals at the time hoped that this would enable them "to pick up where they had left off in the Great Society era," this was not to be the case (Leuchtenburg 1998, 11). President Carter was a "centrist, [who] . . . straddle[d] both liberal and conservative positions" (7). The reason, in part, was Carter's own predilections and temperament. It was also partly the new nature of the electorate. Finally (although this can be viewed as the result, not the cause, of Carter's centrist positions), a combination of inflation and economic stagnation and the resultant poor condition of the federal budget created limits to the ability of the Carter administration to pursue an ambitious agenda in such issues as welfare reform or national health insurance.

To be sure, welfare reform was a major theme in Carter's 1976 election campaign. In addition, Carter pledged his support for national health insurance in his 1976 campaign. However, Carter also pledged to balance the federal budget by 1980 (Light 1999, 136). This latter issue substantially affected the way Carter approached both welfare reform and national health insurance. Although welfare reform was identified as a priority when he assumed office, Carter insisted upon a plan that would result in minimal, if any, increases in costs to the federal government. Carter's welfare reform plan—the Program for Better Jobs and Income—was introduced in August 1977. As discussed in chapter 6, this reform proposal was abandoned in mid-1978. A less ambitious welfare reform was introduced in May 1979, but it too was ultimately defeated (Patterson 1998).

The pressure to control the federal deficit also resulted in the issue of national health insurance being put on hold early in the Carter administration and replaced with an emphasis on hospital cost containment (Light 1999, 74–75, 136–37). However, pressures associated with Carter's upcoming reelection campaign—namely, the potential candidacy of Senator Edward Kennedy, a staunch supporter of national health insurance, and the need to retain the electoral support of organized labor—resulted in the reemergence of national health insurance late in the Carter administration. As discussed in chapter 4, this culminated in June 1979 in Carter presenting a proposal for national health insurance, albeit a far less ambitious one than that outlined in his 1976 campaign (74–75).

Haveman (1987, 3) identifies the election of President Reagan in 1980 as the end of the postwar "liberal era" of federal social policy. Whereas Nixon and Carter sought to *control* welfare rolls and costs, Reagan sought to *reduce* welfare rolls and costs (Danziger 2001, 143). These commitments were based on both practical grounds and "an altered social philosophy embedded in the nation's federal social expenditure programs" (Meyer 1986, 76). Central to this social philosophy was the argument that welfare programs fostered dependence.

During the Reagan administration, two pieces of legislation significantly modified the Aid to Families with Dependent Children (AFDC) program. One of these, the Omnibus Budget Reconciliation Act of 1981 (OBRA 1981), was enacted early in the Reagan administration, whereas the other, the Family Support Act (FSA) of 1988, was enacted at the end of the Reagan administration.

OBRA 1981 included numerous provisions that modified the AFDC program, primarily in terms of changes in benefit calculations and eligibility criteria. Those changes resulted in the removal of nearly 14 percent of all beneficiaries from the AFDC rolls by early 1983. Among them were more than 400,000 working recipients (Danziger 2001, 144; Meyer 1986, 86). OBRA 1981 also stimulated the welfare-to-work experiments discussed in chapters 8 and 9.

The FSA, which, as detailed in chapter 8, was strongly influenced by findings from the welfare-to-work experiments, resulted in significant changes in the nation's welfare system. Foremost among them was greater focus on moving welfare recipients into regular jobs through encouraging AFDC recipients to participate in training, education, subsidized private sector jobs, public service jobs, and job search assistance. In addition, the FSA extended the length of time families leaving the AFDC rolls could continue to remain eligible for Medicaid and child care subsidies,[13] once again to encourage recipients to leave welfare and take jobs. The FSA also tightened federal provisions for the awarding and collection of child support for custodial single parents. Finally, the FSA required all states to participate in the AFDC-Unemployed Parent (AFDC-U) program. This program allowed two-parent families in which the father was unemployed to receive AFDC benefits under certain restrictive circumstances. Before the FSA mandate, state participation in this program was optional and only about half the states took part.

The Reagan administration's interest in reducing the cost of and dependence on social programs probably also contributed to an interest in innovative policy changes in the nation's unemployment compensation system. One result of this interest was a series of experiments, which are described in chapter 7, that tested financial incentives as one way to encourage unemployment compensation claimants to take jobs more quickly.

Efforts to expand health insurance coverage were largely absent from political agendas during the Reagan-Bush years. This lack of attention is reflected in the lack of media coverage of this issue.

> Media coverage of health care reform was almost nonexistent through the 1980s. Between 1980 and 1990, for example, three of the most widely read national newspapers—the *Christian Science Monitor, New York Times,* and *Wall Street Journal*—together ran a total of forty stories on health care reform insurance. . . . [I]n four [of those years], there was no coverage of the issue whatsoever. (Hacker 1997, 21)

Health insurance coverage reentered the political spotlight during the 1991 special U.S. Senate election campaign in Pennsylvania between Harris Wofford and Richard Thornburgh. During the 1992 presidential campaign, Bill Clinton made comprehensive health care reform a major issue. He also pledged to "end welfare as we know it." Comprehensive health care reform became his top domestic priority upon assuming office, with welfare reform not far behind. One of his first actions upon becoming president was to create a special task force, chaired by Hillary Rodham Clinton, to develop a reform plan. The plan was outlined in a speech before a joint session of Congress in September 1992 (Hacker 1997), but went nowhere.

Upon assuming office in 1993, President Clinton also appointed several nationally known welfare experts to key positions at the U.S. Department of Health and Human Services and instructed them to develop a welfare reform plan. The plan that ultimately emerged in 1994, the Work and Responsibility Act, was a clear departure from the existing system. One of its key provisions was a two-year lifetime limit on AFDC, after which the heads of AFDC families would be required to participate in a newly established WORK program to receive any additional assistance. The legislation also would have increased participation in the Job Opportunities and Basic Skills (JOBS) Training Program among those who had not reached the two-year limit in an attempt to minimize the number of AFDC households that reached the limit. JOBS also was to focus more strongly on immediate job entry. Moreover, to encourage employment among those below the two-year limit, any months in which the head of the household worked at least 20 hours per week at a regular job would not be counted against the limit.

Congress never seriously considered the Work and Responsibility Act, and the November 1994 congressional elections, in which the Republicans achieved majorities in both houses of Congress, sealed the fate of this proposal. However, in 1995 Congress, which was now Republican dominated, passed major welfare reform legislation, the Personal Responsibility Act. President Clinton then vetoed this legislation. The next year similar legislation, renamed the Personal Responsibility and Work Opportunity Reconciliation Act (PRWORA), was again passed by Congress, but this time with sufficient modifications to win the votes of many Democrats in Congress, as well as presidential approval.

PRWORA represented a clear break with previous welfare policy. It completely replaced the AFDC program with block grants to the states called Temporary Assistance for Needy Families (TANF). It also for the first time legislated time limits on welfare receipt. Three separate time limits were included in the legislation, the most prominent of which is that states are prohibited from using federal block grant funds to provide cash benefits to families who have accumulated a lifetime total of five years of TANF assistance, whether consecutive or not.[14] PRWORA also included strong incentives to states to induce those receiving TANF benefits to engage in work-related activities, including subsidized or unsubsidized employment, job training and vocational education, and job search.

Characteristics of Previously Conducted Social Experiments

This section provides summary descriptive information about the characteristics of previous social experiments that have been conducted and examines changes in social experimentation over time.[15] The data reported in this section were extracted from the *Digest of Social Experiments* (Greenberg and Shroder 1997) and pertain to social experiments that were completed by the end of 1996.[16] The *Digest* provides two- to three-page summaries of a total of 143 completed social experiments.[17] It also provides brief summary information on an additional 74 experiments that had been initiated by the end of 1996 but were not yet complete. All but four of the experiments were conducted within the United States.

Although some social experiments are relatively small and obscure, Greenberg and Shroder (1997) made extensive efforts to uncover as many experiments as possible and have probably missed relatively few. Experiments were included in the *Digest* only if they met the definition of social experiments that can be found in chapter 1. Thus, like the experiments covered by the case studies presented in this book, the included experiments were all random-assignment field tests of social policies; the tested program confronted the treatment group with different economic incentives, or constraints; and the evaluation of the experimental treatment measured program effects on market or fiscal outcomes.

In examining trends in social experimentation, we will use a chronology of social experiments developed by Greenberg and Robins (1986). The authors suggest that social experimentation has gone through three distinct "eras": Era I (1962–74), in which elaborate, lengthy, costly experiments were used to test fundamental changes in social policies; Era II (1975–82), in which modest experiments were used to test incremental changes in policies—for example, modifications in existing programs; and Era III (1983 and beyond), in which experiments that are typically less costly than those of Era I, but much larger than those of Era II, were administered by state and local government agencies and used to test changes in existing programs.

Figure 2.1 indicates the number of social experiments initiated each year between 1962 and 1996. This figure includes both those experiments that are complete and those that were still ongoing at the end of 1997. Except when explicitly indicated otherwise, the remaining statistics presented in this section are based on only the 143 experiments that were completed by the end of 1996 and summarized in Greenberg and Shroder (1997).

As can be seen from figure 2.1, relatively modest numbers of new experiments were started each year until the mid-1970s, when the number increased substantially. The number of experiments that were begun each year escalated again during the early 1980s; and although the figures have varied from year to year since then, the use of random assignment experiments to test social programs has continued to increase. In terms of the three eras mentioned above, an average of 1.9 experiments began each year in Era I (1962–74), 6.5 experiments per year started in Era II (1975–82), and 9.7 experiments per year began in Era III (1983–96).

Target Groups

The subjects of social experiments are drawn from a target population— persons, families, or organizations at which the tested policy is aimed. The programs tested in different social experiments were aimed at vari-

Figure 2.1. *Number of Experiments Begun, by Year*

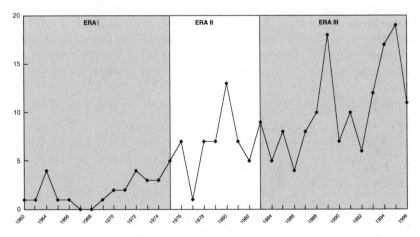

ous types of target groups. Table 2.1 allocates the 143 social experiments completed by the end of 1996 to target group categories. The category to which the experiment in question should be assigned was usually clear, although judgment was sometimes required. For example, experiments that tested programs that were directed at both young and old unemployed workers were categorized as targeted at the unemployed, whereas an experimentally tested program that was aimed solely at unemployed young people was classified as targeted at youth. Two experiments tested programs that were directed at persons in several target group categories and thus could not be assigned to a single category.

The most striking implication of table 2.1 is that most social experiment test programs are targeted at persons or families who are somehow disadvantaged, particularly in terms of having low incomes. For example, nearly one-half of the 143 previously completed social experiments tested programs that targeted public assistance recipients or other low-income families. Sixty percent of these tested programs targeted recipients of AFDC, a politically unpopular program that over the period covered by the table was the major cash transfer program for the poor in

Table 2.1. *Target Group, by Era*
(Percentage in each category)

	Era I 1962–74 ($n = 21$)	Era II 1975–82 ($n = 52$)	Era III 1983–96 ($n = 70$)	Total ($n = 143$)
Public assistance				
AFDC	0.0	26.9	40.0	29.4
Other	0.0	7.7	5.7	5.6
Low-income families	38.1	3.8	14.3	14.0
Youth	0.0	17.3	11.4	11.9
Unemployed	14.3	5.8	18.6	13.3
Health problems[a]	42.9	25.0	5.7	18.2
Charged/convicted	4.8	5.8	0.0	2.8
Taxpayers	0.0	0.0	1.4	0.7
Electricity	0.0	5.8	1.4	2.8
Multiple groups	0.0	1.9	1.4	1.4

Note: AFDC = Aid to Families with Dependent Children.
a. Includes frail elderly, substance abusers, mentally ill, and general health care users.

the United States. In addition, almost all the experimentally tested programs for youths were limited to young people from low-income families. Without a strong policy interest in the poor, it is evident that far fewer social experiments would be conducted. Most of the remaining experiments have tested programs that might also be viewed as directed at the disadvantaged—for example, the unemployed and persons with major health problems (17 of the 26 experiments in the latter category tested programs for the frail elderly).

In one respect, the focus of social experiments on the disadvantaged is unsurprising. Many social programs, both tested and untested, are directed at relieving the special problems of persons facing low incomes, unemployment, or poor health. Nonetheless, the scarcity of experiments involving the middle class is striking. For the dozens of experiments in transfer policy, there has been only one that has focused on tax policy. There have been a few Medicaid experiments, but none for Medicare. There have been a few tests for Supplemental Security Income recipients, but none for Social Security recipients. The government has tested innovations in Food Stamps, but not in farm subsidies.

It is important not to overstate this tendency, however. There have been experiments testing middle-class sensitivity to time-varying electricity pricing and to copayments and deductibles for health insurance. Moreover, experiments have been conducted on such nonimpoverished parties as employers and health care agencies. Nonetheless, it is evident that there is a much stronger tendency to evaluate rigorously programs that affect resource allocations to the disadvantaged than programs that are aimed at the rest of society. Perhaps this is because the disadvantaged have the least political power. As will be documented later, with rare exceptions social experiments are funded by governmental agencies. There may be greater hesitancy on the part of governmental agencies to make the nondisadvantaged the subjects of social experiments than the disadvantaged.

Types of Programs Tested

Types of Interventions

Table 2.2 shows the various interventions (that is, types of treatments) that have been tested by social experiments. The total number of interventions displayed in the table (293) is more than double the number of

Table 2.2. *Type of Intervention, by Era*
(Number of interventions in each category)

Intervention	Era I 1962–74 ($n = 21$)	Era II 1975–82 ($n = 52$)	Era III 1983–96 ($n = 70$)	Total ($n = 143$)
Education and training				
Preschool	2	0	0	2
Basic education/ABE/GED	2	1	14	17
Prevocational/vocational	2	2	11	15
Life skills/social and emotional/family skills	0	0	6	6
Postsecondary	0	0	2	2
Work experience/OJT	1	12	19	32
Education subsidy	0	1	1	2
Incentive bonus to participate	0	0	5	5
Other/unspecified education and training	0	0	11	11
Obtaining employment				
Job placement	1	5	1	7
Job search assistance	2	13	18	33
Job clubs	2	8	2	12
Other services	0	3	10	13
Wage subsidy	0	10	4	14
Employer tax credit	0	1	0	1
Bonus for employment	1	4	5	10
Child care	1	0	3	4
Income transfers				
Guaranteed income	4	2	0	6
Housing assistance	1	1	4	6
AFDC monthly reporting	0	3	0	3
Changes in AFDC benefit rules	0	0	5	5
Food stamp cashout	0	0	4	4
Tax system				
Tax compliance	0	0	1	1
Health				
Home health care	6	8	3	17

Table 2.2. *Continued*
(Number of interventions in each category)

Intervention	Era I 1962–74 (*n* = 21)	Era II 1975–82 (*n* = 52)	Era III 1983–96 (*n* = 70)	Total (*n* = 143)
Health insurance				
cost-sharing rates	1	0	1	2
Nursing home incentive				
payments	0	1	0	1
Incentive to immunize				
children	0	1	0	1
Electricity				
Electricity rate structure[a]	0	3	1	4
Information and counseling				
Case management	4	9	19	32
Counseling	1	12	9	22
Mentoring	0	0	3	3
Total	**31**	**100**	**162**	**293**

Notes: ABE = Adult basic education; AFDC = Aid to Families with Dependent Children; GED = general equivalency diploma; OJT = on-the-job training.

a. Perhaps as many as eight additional experiments that tested changes in electricity rates were not summarized by Greenberg and Shroder (1997).

completed (1996) experiments (143) because many experiments have tested several different treatments. For example, the Seattle-Denver Income Maintenance Experiment tested income guarantees, educational subsidies, and counseling, while numerous experiments have tested programs that provide various combinations of training, work experience (that is, temporary placement at government or nonprofit agencies), counseling, and assistance in finding a job. Sometimes, as with the Seattle-Denver Income Maintenance Experiment, the experiment is designed in a manner that allows the impact of each program component to be separately measured; but more often the components are combined into a package and only their combined impact can be measured.

Perhaps the most interesting implication of table 2.2 is that the great bulk of interventions tested by social experiments have been directed at labor markets. These interventions are aimed at increasing the potential earnings of persons in treatment groups through education and training or at getting them into jobs in the first place.[18] The testing of treatments that provide education, training, and work experience appears to have undergone an especially rapid growth between Eras II and III. Because, as previously indicated, the target populations of most social experiments consist of low-income or otherwise disadvantaged persons, it would appear that most of the interventions tested by social experiments are intended to increase the self-sufficiency of the disadvantaged.

The types of impacts that social experiments measure also demonstrate their concentration on labor markets. For example, the effects of the experimental treatment on either employment status or earnings or both were used as impact measures in 71 percent of the 143 completed experiments on which we have information. Moreover, the use of these impact measures grew from 60 percent in Era I to 63 percent in Era II to 81 percent in Era III. The next most prominently used impact measure has been the effect of the experimental treatment on welfare payments. However, this impact measure was rarely used when impacts on employment or earnings were not also used.

The third most commonly used type of impact measure has been the effect of experimental interventions on health status and health care usage. One or both of these measures were used in 16 percent of the 143 experiments. However, the importance of those two measures has declined substantially over time, falling from 32 percent in Era I to 21 percent in Era II and to 7 percent in Era III.

Voluntary versus Mandatory Policies

The types of programs tested in social experiments can be usefully divided into voluntary and mandatory programs. Experimental tests of both types of programs raise important, although somewhat different, ethical issues.

Under experiments that test voluntary programs, individuals first volunteer to participate in the experiments and then are assigned randomly to a treatment or control group. In keeping with this assignment process, the experimental treatment is not expected to make members of the treatment group worse off for having volunteered, but they may be better off— for example, as a result of being eligible to participate in a transfer program or having access to certain services. Thus, the major ethical issue that arises is the denial of the treatment to members of the control group.

Most mandatory programs apply to obligations imposed on public assistance or unemployment compensation recipients in exchange for receiving their benefits. For example, in some social experiments, welfare recipients who have been randomly assigned to a treatment group are required to work off their grant in a community service job as a condition of maintaining welfare eligibility. Consequently, an ethical issue in conducting these experiments is that members of the control group are able to escape the obligation imposed by the tested program, but members of the treatment group are not, and thus the program might make them worse off.

The denial of benefits or services to members of control groups in experimental tests of voluntary programs was an important source of resistance to social experimentation well into the 1980s and probably served to retard its growth. As increasing numbers of experimental programs have been conducted, however, this resistance has tended to disappear. The resistance to experimental tests of mandatory programs was even stronger, although it too has faded over the years. Thus, none of the Era I social experiments tested mandatory programs, while almost 20 percent of the Era II experiments did so. During Era III, this percentage more than doubled, as over 40 percent of the completed social experiments initiated during this period tested mandatory programs.

Tests of New Programs versus Changes in Existing Programs

An important literature distinguishes between proposals to introduce new programs, perhaps to replace existing programs, and proposals to modify existing programs through incremental changes (for example, see Baumgartner and Jones 1993). In particular, this literature suggests that political support can usually be more readily obtained for incremental changes in existing programs than for new programs, especially those that would replace existing programs.

Social experiments have tested both proposed new programs, some of which would replace existing programs if adopted, and incremental changes to existing programs. In addition, random assignment has occasionally been used to assess the effectiveness of existing programs.

In practice, it is sometimes difficult to make clear distinctions among these three types of experiments. For our purposes, we classify experiments as being used to assess existing programs if the treatment tested is one that already exists. We categorize experiments as testing incremental changes to existing programs if the tested policy modifies the provisions of or adds a new component to an already existing program, but leaves the basic program intact. Finally, we classify experiments as testing new programs if the tested program is not run under an existing program, but stands on its own, perhaps as an alternative to an existing program. Thus, if existing welfare offices provide a new type of job search service to public assistance recipients, then the new service would be classified as an incremental policy. But if new offices were established to provide job search services to unemployed persons, some of whom currently receive transfer benefits and some of whom do not, then the change would be classified as a new program.

During Era I, over 80 percent of all the social experiments that were initiated tested new programs. Some of the programs, if implemented nationally in the United States, would have resulted in fundamental changes in social policy—for example, by guaranteeing incomes, by providing large housing subsidies for the poor, and by making supported work programs for disadvantaged workers widely available. In contrast to Era I, a little over one-third of the completed social experiments initiated during Era II and only one-quarter of those begun during Era III tested new programs.

Over time, therefore, social experiments have been used increasingly to test incremental changes to existing programs, rather than to test new programs. This trend almost certainly can be partially attributed to an increasingly conservative political climate and the declining availability of public funds to invest in potentially expensive new social programs. Indeed, many of the incremental changes that have been tested by social experiments are modest in nature. Others, however, have tested policies that significantly modify existing programs—for example, by requiring that public assistance recipients participate in either training or work programs in exchange for their benefits.

Of the 143 completed social experiments in our sample, only three have been used to assess the effectiveness of already existing programs, and all three were conducted fairly recently during Era III. The apparent reluctance to use random assignment to evaluate existing programs may arise because members of control groups must be denied services to which they previously have had access and because groups or individuals have a stake in the continued existence of programs that experiments may seem to threaten.

Experimental Designs

Response Surface versus Black Box

Earlier in this chapter, we drew a distinction between response surface and black box experiments. As the reader may recall, response parameter experiments are feasible only when the programs being tested can be defined in terms of policy parameters—for example, tax or subsidy rates, prices, or amounts of income transfers—that can be varied more or less continuously. As table 2.2 indicates, however, most social experiments have instead tested services or combinations of services—for example, training, work experience, job search assistance, home health care—that can be varied only in discrete lumps, if at all. Thus, of the 143 completed experiments for which we have information, only 12 were of the response surface type.[19] Six of them were initiated in Era I, four in Era II, and only two in Era III. Several of the response surface experiments are the subject of case studies presented in this book—specifically, the RAND Health Insurance Experiment, the income maintenance experiments, and the unemployment insurance bonus experiments.

Size of Experiments

Table 2.3 reports the percentage size distributions, means, and medians for the samples used in social experiments in each of the three eras.[20] In preparing this table, members of both treatment and control groups were included in the sample population. The table is based on the 140 completed social experiments for which we have the necessary data. In all but six of these experiments, sample observations consisted of either individuals or families. One very small experiment had a sample that consisted of 36 nursing homes and a second had a sample of 47 health care agencies. In the four remaining social experiments, the sample observations were individual firms. These social experiments were not necessarily small; the largest had a sample of 1,089 firms.

Table 2.3 has two obvious implications. First, the samples that have been used in social experiments have varied enormously in size, ranging from under 100 to well over 10,000. Just under half of all the previously completed social experiments on which we had data had samples under 1,000. Second, it is evident that the scale of social experiments, at least as reflected by the size of the samples they use, has greatly increased over

Table 2.3. *Sample Size, by Era*
(Percentage in each category)

	Era I 1962–74 ($n = 21$)	Era II 1975–82 ($n = 50$)	Era III 1983–96 ($n = 69$)	Total ($n = 140$)
< 200	42.0	10.0	17.4	18.6
200–499	19.0	24.0	10.1	16.4
500–999	9.5	22.0	11.6	15.0
1,000–1,999	14.3	18.0	7.2	12.1
2,000–4,999	9.5	12.0	21.7	16.4
5,000–9,999	4.8	6.0	8.7	7.1
≥ 10,000	0.0	8.0	23.1	14.3
Median	401	870	2,312 (2,259[a])	1,010
Mean	1,093	2,741	10,226 (6,054[a])	6,183

Note: a. Excludes two Wisconsin experiments that each had samples of 150,000.

time. The increase in the percentage of experiments with samples of over 10,000 is especially notable.[21]

The increasingly large sample size that has been used in social experiments appears attributable to a number of trends that have made social experiments less expensive to conduct, a change that has resulted in freeing up funds for larger samples.

1. The programs tested in some experiments have provided costly income or in-kind transfers or intensive services to treatment group members. Some of the Era I social experiments such as the RAND Health Insurance Experiment, the National Supported Work Demonstration, the Housing Allowance Demand, and the four income maintenance experiments are especially notable in this respect. Other experiments, especially those of recent vintage, have, in contrast, tested quite inexpensive programs and policies—for example, help in searching for a job or replacing food stamps with cash payments.

2. Some experiments use data from expensive surveys administered to the sample population. Others rely entirely on administrative data, which are collected by government agencies for other purposes and are relatively inexpensive to obtain and process—for example, state

welfare agency records of transfer payments and earnings data that employers are required to report to state unemployment compensation agencies. Most Era I experiments tended to depend mainly on survey information, whereas Era II and III experiments have relied more on existing administrative records.

3. The complexity of experimental designs, at least as indicated by the number of treatment groups, has declined. Two or more treatment groups, each of which received different sets of financial incentives or services, were not uncommon in Eras I and II. Indeed, the proportion of experiments with only two randomly assigned groups (one treatment and one control) was just over half the total in Eras I and II, but has grown to more than 80 percent in Era III. This partly reflects the declining popularity of response-surface designs,[22] but may also partially reflect the needs of funding agencies. More complex designs are more difficult to explain to busy officials who have no technical training. As the field of social experimentation developed, there appears to have been a growing attempt to increase the use of findings by making them more readily understood. This is reflected by enhanced efforts at the dissemination of findings, for example, but may have also resulted in less complex experimental designs.

4. The number of months over which data are collected on members of treatment and control groups has fallen over time. Specifically, the median Era I experiment collected data on participants for nearly five years after random assignment began. The median Era II experiment completed data collection less than two and a half years after the first intake, and the median Era III experiment stopped gathering follow-up data at a little less than three years. This trend results partly because, as indicated above, the tested treatments are often less complex today than they were in Era I. Moreover, many of the more recent experiments test interventions, such as training programs, from which long-term effects are likely only if short-term effects also occur. There has also been considerable effort to analyze experimental data more quickly to reduce costs and make findings available while they are still relevant.

5. The programs tested in most social experiments have been administered from offices that were already established to serve the target populations of these programs—for example, public assistance and unemployment compensation agencies. Only 34 of the 143

completed social experiments on which we have data have tested programs that were administered by offices established especially for this purpose. However, in almost two-thirds of the experiments initiated during Era I, offices were established specifically to administer the programs being tested. In contrast, during Eras II and III, offices specifically established to initiate tests administered only 27 percent and 8 percent, respectively, of the completed experiments. The administrative costs of experimentally tested programs operated from existing offices are considerably lower than those of programs managed out of specially established offices. In fact, some recent experiments in existing public assistance offices involved easily implemented changes in benefit computations or administrative procedures that did not even require the hiring of additional workers.

The Use of Process Analysis and Cost-Benefit Analysis

As mentioned earlier in the chapter, impact analyses are always conducted with data from social experiments; but, in addition, process analyses and attempts to compare impacts with costs are also frequently part of social experiments. Indeed, some sort of process analysis was conducted in more than 80 percent of the 143 completed social experiments for which we have data, and during Era III the figure increased to just below 95 percent. However, many different activities qualify as process analysis. Thus, although the process analyses associated with many social experiments, especially the more recent ones, are extensive, others involve little more than a few interviews with the individuals responsible for administering the experimental treatment.

Attempts to compare impacts with costs have been made in slightly fewer than half of completed social experiments on which we have data. Over time, however, such analyses have become increasingly frequent. For example, cost-impact comparisons were part of the analysis in only 27 percent of the social experiments conducted during Era I and in only 40 percent of the experiments conducted during Era II, but such comparisons were made in 60 percent of the completed Era III experiments. Most of the cost-impact comparisons involved formal cost-benefit analyses—that is, there was an attempt to measure as many benefits and costs in monetary terms as possible and then to compare the benefits received by all members of society to the costs incurred by all members of society. In some instances, however, less extensive analyses were conducted. For example, the analysis might be limited to a simple comparison between government expenditures on a particular treatment and government savings resulting from reductions in transfer payment outlays.

Funding Sources for Social Experiments

Table 2.4 lists the funding sources for the 143 completed social experiments for which we have information. The table makes it evident that to date the major funding source for social experiments has been the federal government. It was the sole source of funding for 57 percent of the social experiments represented in the table and helped to fund an additional 16 percent in combination with other levels of government or nongovernmental organizations. Although playing a much smaller role than the federal government, state governments have also been an important source of funding. They were the sole source of funding for 18 percent of the experiments represented in the table and contributed to the funding of an additional 11 percent.[23] Nongovernmental organi-

Table 2.4. *Funding Source, by Era*
(Percentage in each category)

	Era I 1962–74 (n = 21)	Era II 1975–82 (n = 52)	Era III 1983–96 (n = 70)	Total (n = 143)
Federal	57.1	73.1	45.7	57.3
State	14.3	7.7	25.7	17.5
Local	0.0	2.0	0.0	0.7
NGO	0.0	7.7	5.7	5.6
Federal/state	4.8	2.0	1.4	2.1
Federal/local	4.8	2.0	0.0	1.4
Federal/NGO	9.5	0.0	8.6	5.6
State/NGO	0.0	0.0	2.9	1.4
Federal/state/NGO	9.5	3.8	8.6	7.0
Private	0.0	2.0	1.4	1.4

Note: NGO = nongovernmental organization.

zations (NGOs), most of which are nonprofit foundations, also have had a significant role in funding social experiments, having contributed to the funding of 20 percent of the experiments represented in the table. So far, local governments have played a negligible role in the funding of social experiments and for-profit corporations have funded only two experiments—both of them by electric utilities.

Table 2.4 indicates that the role of the federal government in funding social experiments, although still dominant, has diminished somewhat over time, whereas that of state governments has grown. The federal government was involved in funding more than 80 percent of the completed social experiments initiated during Eras I and II, but in only 64 percent of the completed experiments initiated during Era III. Offsetting the declining role of the federal government, state involvement in funding social experiments has grown from 18 percent of all the completed experiments begun during Eras I and II to almost 40 percent of the completed experiments initiated during Era III.

Location of Experimental Sites

Greenberg and Shroder (1997) found only one completed social experiment that took place outside of North America: an unemployment-counseling program in the Netherlands. In addition, there has been one completed experiment and there are two ongoing experiments in Canada. The remaining experiments that are included in Greenberg and Shroder (1997) have all been conducted in the United States. The U.S. hegemony in the field of social experimentation seems clear.

The explanation for this is not obvious. However, certain features of American governance have undoubtedly encouraged policy evaluations in general and social experimentation in particular. One is the separation of powers between the federal and state governments: Federal funds for particular programs may be used with considerable discretion by the states, and this fact has encouraged the view that the states should literally be the laboratories of democracy. A second is the system of checks and balances at the federal level: an important policy innovation must obtain the agreement of both houses of Congress and the president. Sponsors of some proposed reforms may find the other house or the other branch of government unalterably opposed to nationwide change this year but willing to consider demonstrations. The United States is the only developed country with both strong subnational governments and a strong separation of powers between the legislative and executive branches, and the combination has probably contributed to the interest in experimentation for policy purposes.

Nongovernmental organizations also have some responsibility for the higher level of U.S. activity. Large private national foundations, notably Ford and Rockefeller, have funded social experiments either in whole or in part, and local foundations have (less consistently) provided partial support for demonstrations in their areas of interest. No other developed country has a nonprofit, nongovernmental, nonreligious sector with comparable resources and social policy interests.

The separation of powers and the participation of foundations undoubtedly do not fully explain the striking difference in social experimentation between the United States and the rest of the world. The historic backgrounds, social policies, and philosophies of the other developed countries differ in many ways from those of the United States. Those differences almost certainly have some connection with the apparent lack of interest in experimental methods in other nations.

The map of experiments within the United States is partly the map of tolerance to policy innovation and social research. As previously indicated, most recent social experiments have been run through existing local agencies. This means that the funder accepts the agency as a competent administrator, and the agency accepts the experiment as a legitimate intrusion on its ordinary business. This combination of admitted competence and admitted legitimacy is not universal.[24] Moreover, government funding agencies would rather avoid experiments in areas where a senator, representative, mayor, or other major political figure is loudly opposed.

To examine the geographic distribution of social experiments in the United States, the number of completed experiments conducted in each state was determined. A state was counted only once for each experiment located within its boundaries regardless of the number of experimental sites. For example, the Virginia Employment Services Program was operated in 11 different counties, but Virginia was given credit for one experiment. For experiments conducted in more than one state, such as the Seattle-Denver Income Maintenance Experiment, each state was counted once.

The major conclusion from this exercise is that social experimentation in the Unites States is widespread. All but two states (Alaska and Idaho) had served as the site of an experiment by the end of 1996. New York provided sites for 27 completed experiments; California for 26 experiments; Illinois and Pennsylvania for 19 experiments each; Ohio for 16 experiments; and Florida, Massachusetts, Texas, and Washington for 13 experiments each. With the possible exceptions of Massachusetts and Washington, this list is hardly surprising as the remaining seven states are the most populous in the country. As a crude control for population size, we divided the number of times each state provided experimental sites by the state's population in 1995. The eight highest ranked states in terms of the number of times serving as the site of an experiment per capita are the District of Columbia (which provided sites for 4 experiments), Maine (4), Colorado (10), Delaware (2), Nebraska (5), Rhode Island (3), Washington (13), and Arizona (7). Only Washington appears in both lists. Indeed, after controlling for population size, New York, California, Illinois, and Pennsylvania rank 23rd, 30th, 19th, and 22nd, respectively.

Evaluators

Social experiments are increasingly evaluated by a few organizations. The industry leaders are Abt Associates, the Manpower Demonstration Research Corporation (MDRC), and Mathematica Policy Research (MPR), which are denoted hereafter as the Big Three.

Table 2.5 charts market shares over time.[25] A firm or agency is given credit for each experiment for which it served as the primary evaluator.[26]

The Big Three performed just under half the completed Era III experiments, and had contracted as of late 1996 for a little less than 45 percent of the ongoing experiments. Moreover, the experiments these firms evaluate tend to be among the larger and more prominent ones. The Institute for Research on Poverty (IRP) at the University of Wisconsin[27] and the Vera Institute of Justice were significant members of the industry in Eras I and II, but since then they have apparently exited the industry. Some large, prominent social science firms, such as the Urban Institute, the RAND Corporation, SRI International, and Battelle Memorial Institute either have played no role in social experimentation or have been the primary evaluators of only one or two experiments.[28]

Researchers with academic affiliations compose much of the fringe of the industry. Small demonstrations will sometimes employ one or a few

Table 2.5. *Market Share, by Era*
(Percentage of experiments evaluated)

	Era I 1962–74 (n = 21)	Era II 1975–82 (n = 52)	Era III 1983–96 (n = 70)	Ongoing 1989–97 (n = 65[a])
Big Three	11.9	28.8	47.1	44.6
Abt	4.8	4.8	17.1	18.5
MDRC	0.0	11.5	15.8	12.3
MPR	7.1	12.5	14.3	13.8
Vera Institute	4.8	5.8	0.0	0.0
IRP	11.9	1.0	0.0	0.0
RAND	4.8	1.9	1.4	0.0
SRI International	4.8	0.0	1.4	0.0
Government agencies	4.8	8.6	10.0	4.6
Academic	16.7	23.1	18.6	29.2
Others	40.5	30.8	21.4	21.5

Note: Columns may not total 100 percent because of rounding.
IRP = Institute for Research and Poverty; MDRC = Manpower Demonstration Research Corporation; MPR = Mathematica Policy Research, Inc.; RAND = RAND Corporation.
a. Excludes 9 experiments for which the evaluator had not yet been determined.

academic researchers for the evaluation, or a contractor may obtain an academic researcher's consulting services for a specialized role in a major project. An academic researcher may also use grants to initiate a small experiment. Government evaluators are usually the employees of state employment or welfare departments that are running the experiments being evaluated; it is uncommon for those evaluators to participate in more than one experiment. The "others" category consists mainly of private sector firms (such as Deloitte and Touche, Berkeley Planning Associates, and Maximus) that have been the primary evaluators of only one or two experiments.[29]

NOTES

1. Detailed discussions of these topics can be found in Boruch (1997) and Orr (1998).
2. For a fuller discussion of the relative advantages and disadvantages of social experimentation, see Burtless (1995) and Heckman and Smith (1995).

3. The term *internal validity* refers to whether the measured difference in outcomes between the treatment and control groups can be appropriately attributed to the evaluated program.

4. This is also the situation with comparisons across sites that have and have not implemented a program, if, as is usually the case, the decision on whether to adopt the innovation was made locally. For example, the sites may differ in terms of local economic conditions and population characteristics.

5. In practice, even observable differences may interact nonlinearly with treatment, and the analyst may fail to adjust for them correctly.

6. In contrast with evaluations of already existing programs, when used in evaluations of new and pilot programs, experimental approaches not only offer superior internal validity but also are similar to nonexperimental approaches in time and cost requirements.

7. Note that this refers to selecting sites randomly from the population of potential sites, not to a saturation design in which sites are assigned randomly to program and control status.

8. The standard argument is that only sites operating superior programs will acquiesce to an evaluation. However, there may be only minimal correlation between local operators' self-appraisals and the results of a rigorous third-party evaluation. Indeed, even when sites are self-selected, estimated impacts are typically modest, suggesting that any site selection bias is not large enough to lead to an unwarranted expansion of a program in response to inflated impact estimates. Nevertheless, the fact remains that biases of unknown magnitude may arise from management difference among self-selected sites.

9. Although most social experiments have operated on a small scale, there is no inherent reason why they must be run in this way. For example, in some experiments, all members of the target population within a particular geographic area except a small group of randomly selected controls are eligible to receive program services.

10. An exception is the Self-Sufficiency Project evaluation, a recently completed random assignment experiment that was conducted in Canada (Berlin et al. 1998). The entry effects that were measured in this experiment were small.

11. The concept appeared initially in a 1925 book by Fisher, *Statistical Methods for Research Workers,* and then was fully elaborated in his 1935 book, *The Design of Experiments.* It also seems to have been conceived independently of Fisher, and slightly earlier, by W. A. McCall (1923).

12. Strictly speaking, about half a dozen social experiments preceded the New Jersey Income Maintenance Experiment. The earliest of these, the Perry Preschool Project, was initiated in 1962. These very early experiments were all small relative to the New Jersey experiment, and their design did not require the same level of technical innovation. With the possible exception of the Perry Preschool Project, they never captured the attention of social scientists and policymakers. The Perry Preschool Project has received considerable attention, but much of this attention occurred after adult earnings data were available for the preschool children in the study sample, many years after both the Perry Preschool Project and the New Jersey experiment were initiated.

13. This continued eligibility for Medicaid and child care subsidies is commonly referred to as transitional benefits.

14. However, states are permitted to exempt up to 20 percent of their caseloads from this provision. States are allowed to reduce the length of each of the three time limits if they so choose.

15. Much of the material presented in this section previously appeared in Greenberg, Shroder, and Onstott (1999).

16. We are indebted to Matthew Onstott for compiling these data for us.

17. Perhaps as many as a dozen experiments have been conducted to test behavioral responses to changes in electricity rate structures. However, Greenberg and Shroder (1997) were able to obtain sufficient information to summarize only four. Consequently, the remaining electricity rate experiments are not included in the statistics presented in this section.

18. Most of the interventions that involved case management or counseling were also employment-oriented. Case management often provided a one-stop source of information about various social services, including training programs, that unemployment compensation claimants or welfare recipients might use, while counselors often provided guidance and support to persons who were looking for a job or enrolled in training. In addition, all five of the interventions listed under "changes in AFDC benefit rules" involved attempts to increase the incentives of AFDC recipients to seek or retain employment.

19. As mentioned previously, Greenberg and Shroder (1997) were unable to obtain information on as many as eight experiments that tested variations in electricity pricing structures. Several of the experiments were probably of the response surface type.

20. It would have been useful also to have compared the costs of social experiments. Unfortunately, cost information was unavailable to Greenberg and Shroder (1997) for many experiments. In some instances, the cost records that were needed were no longer accessible or could not be located. In other cases, an experiment was part of a larger research project, and costs were not separately allocated to the experimental and nonexperimental parts of the research. Even when cost data are available, it is not entirely clear which items should be included in costs. For example, should the cost of providing the treatment be counted, or just the cost required by the evaluation? Even if this question can be resolved in principle, in practice the two types of costs cannot be separated from one another for some experiments, whereas, for others, evaluation costs are available but the cost of providing the treatment is not. The latter situation often occurs in the case of experiments administered through existing government agencies. In such cases, the cost of the experimental treatment may be difficult to separate from other costs incurred by the agency.

21. Table 2.3 includes two recently completed experiments in Wisconsin that involved fairly important changes in the computation of benefits available to AFDC recipients. The changes were made for 90 percent of the state's caseload, and the remaining 10 percent of the caseload was randomly assigned to the control group. Thus, the data analysis for both experiments, which relied entirely on administrative data files, was conducted on the state's entire caseload of about 150,000 families.

22. By definition, response surface experiments must have multiple treatment groups. Thus, 1 of the 12 response surface experiments had four treatment groups (plus a control group), 2 had five, 3 had six, and the remaining 6 had eight or more treatment groups.

23. Even when states are listed in table 2.4 as the sole funders of social experiments, they were often at least partially reimbursed by the federal government.

24. This does not matter if an agency is created specifically to administer the experiment, but, as indicated earlier in the chapter, that has seldom happened in recent years.

25. A major problem in showing the changes in market share is in deciding how to measure the market. The unit of analysis we have used is a single experiment, however large or complex. Revenues per experiment, as we noted earlier, are not always available or meaningful for this purpose. The experiments could be weighted by the size of the sample. However, that would have given unwarranted importance to Deloitte and Touche, an accounting firm brought in to report on impacts at the end of two Wisconsin welfare experiments that feature enormous samples even though the firm had not had any previous role in the design or implementation of these experiments.

26. There were a few experiments in which two evaluation firms were more or less equally important. In such cases, each firm is given half credit in computing the market share.

27. As discussed in chapter 6, IRP was responsible for designing and evaluating the New Jersey Experiment, while MPR administered the experiment and collected the evaluation data. Thus, together, they may be considered the industry founders.

28. The Battelle Memorial Institute has been the primary evaluator of only one social experiment, but has been a subcontractor on over half a dozen experiments.

29. Some of these firms also have served as subcontractors on other social experiments.

3

Conceptual Framework and Methodology

As noted in chapter 1, the key questions we address in this book include the following:

- Why are social experiments conducted?
- In what ways, if any, do they exert an influence on policy choices?
- What factors account for variations in the types and amount of influence social experiments exert on policy choices?

To respond to these questions, we employ a conceptual framework that includes four components. The first consists of several competing characterizations of the process leading to the decision whether or not to undertake research. Those characterizations are drawn largely from the literature on decisionmaking in general and organizational decisionmaking in particular. The remaining three components are drawn primarily from the knowledge utilization literature mentioned in chapter 1.

The conceptual framework guides the case studies found in the following five chapters of this book. The case studies are, in turn, used to test the validity of each of the four components. In this chapter, we describe the conceptual framework and the methods used in conducting the case studies.

When Are Experiments Conducted?

The first component of our conceptual framework consists of several competing characterizations of the process leading to the decision whether or not to conduct social experiments. The traditional characterization of this process is that the decision to conduct a social experiment is made according to an essentially rational paradigm. That is, the expected value of the information provided by a social experiment is computed, and a social experiment is conducted if and only if the expected value exceeds the expected costs of conducting that experiment.[1]

Although appealing, the requirements of this model are stringent. For one thing, the model requires that findings from an experiment be intended to aid a specific policy decision (Feldman 1989, 80). In addition, in deciding to conduct the experiment, decisionmakers must expect that the analysis will be completed *before* the policy decision is made and that the policy alternatives tested are similar to those that will be considered in the policy process.

In short, making a decision whether to conduct a social experiment based on the rational paradigm requires a predictable and orderly policy environment. In actuality, however, the policy environment is typically fluid and volatile. Such matters as the issues that will be on the agenda at a particular time, the forms those issues will take, and the alternatives to be seriously considered are extremely unpredictable (see, for example, Kingdon 1984; March and Olsen 1976; and Weiss 1980). The difficulty of predicting these matters casts doubts upon the usefulness of the rational paradigm for making decisions about the conduct of any type of policy research, but especially social experiments, as there is generally a considerable amount of time between the decision to conduct a social experiment and the availability of findings.

Nonetheless, although the requirements of the rational model may not be met in practice and consequently findings from experiments may not be used in a manner consistent with the paradigm, expectations that these conditions will be met may still provide the basis on which the decision is made to undertake social experiments. Furthermore, the decision to initiate some experiments might be based essentially on less demanding variants of the rational paradigm than the rather pure form described above. For example, decisionmakers who are responsible for determining whether to adopt a proposed policy innovation may specify that a small-scale experimental pilot test be conducted first so that they have better information on which to base their decision. Alternatively, it may be anticipated that if an experiment demonstrates convincingly that an idea really works, it will then generate the political support needed to place it on the policy agenda and, ultimately, to adopt it. In other words, the expectation is that a convincing experimental test of a policy will itself engender an appropriate response.

An alternative characterization of the decision to undertake social experiment is what we label inventory creation. The characterization is largely that of Feldman (1989, 92–96), who argued that the unpredictability of the policy environment makes it impossible to specify when and for what issues policymakers will seek research results. She suggests that policy research be viewed as creating inventories of information for future policymaking situations that are unspecified at the time the information creation process begins. This argument implies that a social experiment simply adds another item to the information inventory—one that should help reduce uncertainty about alternatives—just in case a pertinent policy issue is actively considered.

Although not based on the decision-theoretic calculations of the rational paradigm, this explanation still focuses on the value of the products of social experiments. In general, the inventory creation explanation appears more applicable to low-cost experiments than to expensive experiments. It seems implausible that analysts or policymakers would be willing or able to invest large amounts of resources in an activity that has only a limited probability of ever being called upon for guidance.

Another set of possible explanations of the decision to conduct a social experiment focuses not on the anticipated future products of the experiment, but instead on the benefits from the process of designing and conducting the experiment, benefits that begin to accrue as soon as the process begins. A traditional and rather cynical version of this explanation claims that experiments are conducted to replace real action with symbolic action and thereby serve as an inherently conservative force. Such a strategy could backfire, however. Social experiments provide rigorous tests of policies. The experimental data might eventually demonstrate that the tested policy actually works and, consequently, might ultimately result in its adoption. Because policymakers presumably know this, it seems unlikely that most experiments are initiated to avoid adopting a particular policy.

Perhaps a more interesting variant of the set of explanations that focus on the benefits from the process of designing and conducting the experiment, rather than on the anticipated future products of the experiment, is that experiments represent an attempt to influence the policy-making agenda. For example, an experiment may be a means for keeping alive a policy innovation for which adequate political support does not yet exist with the hope that such support will materialize in the future. This explanation implies that social experiments serve as a (modest) force for change by increasing the likelihood of the innovative policy alternatives ever appearing on a future political agenda. Conducting social experiments provides an extra impetus for the inclusion of the tested alternatives on the agenda at the time the results become available, at least if the findings are generally supportive of the tested innovation. This argument further implies that political negotiation will proceed in parallel with the process of designing and conducting the experiment. Hence, a political agreement might very well be reached before the results of the experiment are available, in which case any impact those results have on policy deliberations would be icing on the cake, but not essential.

Policy Effects of Experiments

The second component of the conceptual framework is based on a reformulation of Whiteman's (1985) typology of the diverse ways findings from policy research can potentially be used. Whereas Whiteman employed a two-dimensional typology, as did Greenberg and Mandell (1991), the taxonomy employed here has three dimensions.

The first dimension of our taxonomy distinguishes between concrete utilization—situations in which research findings influence specific policy decisions—and conceptual utilization—situations in which research findings influence the general intellectual orientations (worldviews) of policy actors.

The second dimension is a continuum that characterizes the scope of use. Whiteman (1985) referred to this dimension as the substantive–elaborative utilization dimension. Alternatively, it might be labeled the core–periphery dimension. At one end of the continuum are substantive uses—cases in which research findings influence the core of either specific policy decisions or general intellectual orientations. (Using Whiteman's terms, these cases would be referred to as concrete-substantive and conceptual-substantive use, respectively.) At the other end of the continuum are elaborative uses—cases in which research findings influence relatively narrow and peripheral elements of either specific policy decisions (concrete-elaborative) or general intellectual orientations (conceptual-elaborative), the cores of which are established independently of the research.

The final dimension of our taxonomy distinguishes between formative and persuasive/advocacy use (see Majone 1989, chapter 2).[2] Formative utilization refers to situations in which individuals use research to establish their positions. Persuasive/advocacy use refers to the use of research findings to advocate already established positions.

Dividing each dimension into a dichotomy, the typology allows for eight types of use. For example, if individuals use research to help establish the core of a specific policy position, formative-concrete-substantive use would be said to occur. On the other hand, the use of research to advocate already established positions on relatively narrow and peripheral elements of a general intellectual orientation would be labeled persuasive/advocacy-conceptual-elaborative utilization. The eight-cell typology is illustrated in figure 3.1.

The taxonomy just described is useful for conceptual purposes. It indicates that research in general and social experiments in particular can potentially be used in numerous different ways. This is important because social experiments typically are launched with the expectation

Figure 3.1. *Typology of Research Use*

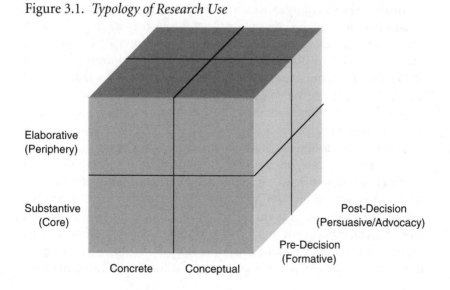

that formative-concrete-substantive utilization will occur. The taxonomy suggests that even if such utilization does not take place, the seven other types of use could occur and hence should not be overlooked. However, although useful conceptually, it is extremely difficult in practice to apply the taxonomy to empirical data such as those gathered in our case studies. There are several reasons for this difficulty.

First, there are problems with definitions. For example, it is sometimes difficult to determine exactly where to draw the line between a substantive use and an elaborative use. Because the prior positions of policymakers are not always known, it is also not always clear whether formative or persuasive/advocacy use has occurred. More important, what counts as "a use" is often not obvious. For example, does a finding from an experiment that is used in a similar manner in 50 different states count as 1 use or 50? Similarly, if findings from an experiment persuade a number of policymakers to change their position, have these been one use or many?

Second, it is virtually impossible to uncover every instance of use of any research, social experiments included. Moreover, examples of concrete use are probably more readily discovered than examples of conceptual uses. Similarly, substantive use is probably more apparent than elaborative use. Thus, whether one cell in the taxonomy contains more items than another is not very meaningful.

Third, the categories in taxonomy are usually presumed to be mutually exclusive and collectively exhaustive. The knowledge utilization literature to date has followed this convention. That is, any instance of use is placed in only one category (see Berg et al. 1978; Boeckmann 1976; Greenberg and Mandell 1991; Pelz 1978; and Whiteman 1985). However, although the categories in our typology are collectively exhaustive, they are not mutually exclusive. The complexity of research use probably makes it impossible to develop mutually exclusive categories. Thus, the previous literature has probably proceeded from an incorrect premise.

One reason it is difficult, if not impossible, to develop mutually exclusive research use categories is that different persons can use the same findings in different ways. For example, use of information at congressional hearings can be both formative and persuasive. Members of the executive branch, such as the secretary of labor, can use information from a social experiment to justify a previous decision to propose legislation. This is advocacy utilization. However, members of Congress at those same hearings can use the same information in a formative fashion as they work to decide whether to enact the legislation. Thus, persuasive/advocacy and formative use have both occurred.

The boundary between conceptual and concrete use is also sometimes blurred. Whereas use of experimental results in formulating specific policy proposals would seem to be concrete, those proposals may ultimately color the policy landscape, rather than be enacted. Although those making a proposal may desire specific action, the ultimate result may be a contribution to the ongoing process of filling in the policy landscape and refining its contours. This is especially true of testimony before congressional committees. Whereas advocates attempt to use research findings to engender action, in practice the immediate effect may be more to enlighten. This, in turn, may result in new and different policy proposals later. Thus, the concrete-conceptual dichotomy blurs from player to player and over time.

The dynamics of research use also make it difficult to develop categories that are mutually exclusive. Categories tend to be most useful in static situations, as any specific instance of research use is best viewed as a snapshot occurring at a specific point in time. But policymaking is usually a process, not an event. It is in constant flux, changing with time. This fact has important implications for interpreting findings from our case studies. Each of the core studies generates a "story" about the use of the results of the experiment being examined. Each story evolved over time. As it did, it typically wove its way through several cells of the taxonomy, much as a river might wind its way through several states. For example, changes in worldviews that are associated with conceptual use might influence specific policy decision in the future. In other words, formative-conceptual-substantive use might lead to formative-concrete-substantive use and formative-conceptual-elaborative use might lead to formative-concrete-elaborative use. Thus, one use generates others.

In conducting the case studies for this book, we discovered numerous examples of research use. Using our best judgment, we have placed each example in one or more of the eight cells in our typology (see chapters 4–8). The points just made strongly suggest that this exercise should be viewed as no more than illustrative. Others may define what constitutes "a use" differently than we did. Furthermore, we undoubtedly missed many instances of research utilization. And other instances should be placed in cells additional to the ones to which they were assigned. In our view, therefore, the exercise is most useful for illustrating the variety of ways in which findings from social experiments have been used. It is also useful for determining whether certain cells are empty or nearly empty. In other words, the exercise can be appropriately used for assessing whether there are certain ways in which findings from social experiments are never or only rarely used. It can also be used to examine whether the empty or nearly empty cells seem to differ among different types of experiments (see chapter 10). This information may have implications for funding decisions about experiments.

Utilization Factors

The third and fourth components of our conceptual framework consist of two sets of factors that the knowledge utilization literature suggests should affect the ways in which a given social experiment is used and the amount of influence it exerts on policy choices. The first set of factors refers to key characteristics of the social experiment. Although the exact list differs somewhat from author to author, the factors most commonly mentioned seem to fall into one of the following five categories: (1) definitiveness, (2) timeliness, (3) communicability and visibility, (4) generalizability, and (5) relevance. The second set of factors pertains to the characteristics of the policy environment into which results of experiments are inserted. Weiss's (1983) I-I-I (Ideology-Interests-Information) framework seems valuable in understanding these factors.

Definitiveness

Definitiveness refers to the certainty associated with key findings from a research project. Definitiveness is influenced by several considerations, including

- the extent to which findings are ambiguous (for example, an effect that is large, but not statistically significant);
- the extent to which the research is subject to scrutiny (i.e., to attacks on its methodological quality);
- the extent of debate among researchers over the validity of the findings;[3]
- the extent to which the findings threaten potential users' goals or imply that change is needed in the current activities of potential users;[4]

- the opinions of potential users toward research in general;[5] and
- the characteristics of those who produced the research (Bozeman 1986, 531; Coursey 1990; Leviton and Hughes 1981, 540; Mandell 1989, 45).

In the case of social experiments, some of the factors just listed are under the control of funding agencies. For example, a large research sample can increase the chances of obtaining statistically significant results. Also, hiring researchers with strong reputations makes it more likely that findings will be viewed as valid. Once a decision is made to undertake a particular experiment, however, little can be done to control some of the other factors—for example, the opinions of potential users about research and whether the findings threaten the goals of those persons.

At first glance, it might appear that research findings based on a random-assignment social experiment would result in more definitive findings than findings based on nonexperimental techniques. After all, an experimental research design is less vulnerable to methodological criticism than alternative designs and is also readily understood by policymakers. Indeed, John Ziman, a physicist, has suggested that "a good experiment is a powerful piece of rhetoric; it has the ability to persuade the most obdurate and skeptical mind to accept a new idea. . ." (Majone 1989, 30–31).

Empirical findings on the relationship between the scientific quality of research and its use, however, are inconsistent and conflicting (see Beyer and Trice 1982, 610; Mandell and Sauter 1984). Moreover, careful examination of the factors previously listed suggests that potential users do not necessarily view findings from social experiments as more definite than findings from nonexperimental research. For example, experimental findings are not necessarily less ambiguous in nature (see Heckman and Smith 1995) than nonexperimental findings or less likely to contradict expectations. In addition, in the case of large-scale social experiments, their very size and importance may attract both scrutiny and reanalysis of the experimental data.

Moreover, some social experiments are poorly implemented. For example, some members of the treatment group do not receive components of the program being tested in the manner intended, or some members of the control group do receive the tested program although they were not supposed to. Fortunately, none of the experiments examined in the case studies described in this book seem to have had serious implementation problems. If they had, this probably would have reduced the chances that they would have affected policy.

Timeliness

Research findings are timely, and thus more likely to be used, if they reach decisionmakers when, to use John Kingdon's (1984) term, "policy windows" are open (i.e., when decisions are actually being made). Because conceptual uses are relatively independent of time frames associated with specific decisions, timeliness is more important for concrete than for conceptual uses (Leviton and Hughes 1981, 525; Weiss 1984, 181). In stressing the importance of timeliness in congressional decisionmaking, Weiss (1987, 106) has suggested that, to be used, "policy analysis probably needs to get into the pipeline while general approaches to legislation are still being considered. . . . By the time congressional committees begin action on specific bills, the determining conceptual premises have usually started to set." Similarly, James Coleman (1979) argued that the greatest source of incompatibility between research and policy might be the fact that policy decisions have time schedules that often conflict with the time schedules of research.

In part, the importance of timeliness depends on how long policy windows remain open and how often they reopen. It also depends on whether decisionmakers use inventories of previously conducted research (Feldman 1989) or only newly available results. This, in turn, depends on whether findings from the older research continue to be viewed as relevant to current policy concerns, an issue we take up later.

Relative to other research, social experiments would appear to be at a particular disadvantage regarding timeliness. By the time an experiment is designed and implemented, the treatment administered, and the data analyzed, several years can easily pass. To mention an extreme example, one that is discussed further in chapter 6, the Seattle-Denver Income Maintenance Experiment was initiated in 1970, preliminary results began to be available in 1976, and the final report was not published until 1983.[6] Perhaps more typically, the San Diego Job Search and Work Experience Demonstration, one of the earliest and more prominent of the welfare-to-work experiments (described in chapter 8), began in 1982, but the final report was not published until February 1986.

Although these time lags are certainly lengthy, problems of timeliness associated with social experiments may not be as severe as sometimes supposed. As suggested, social experiments themselves can help open policy windows by exerting influence on the political agenda. Moreover, as mentioned, policy windows sometimes reopen. For example, there were important similarities in the Nixon and Carter administrations' welfare reform proposals, and findings from the income maintenance experiments were applicable to both. Furthermore, some policy concepts germinate sufficiently slowly that experimental findings are available before they reach the policy agenda.

Communication and Visibility

It seems self-evident that the more decisionmakers are aware of research findings and the better they understand them, the greater the likelihood of the research being used. Social experiments would appear to enjoy an important inherent advantage over other types of social science research in this respect. Their findings can be reported in simple comparisons of differences between members of randomly assigned groups, statistics that are readily communicated to and understood by nontechnicians (see Mundel 1985, 254). It also seems apparent that large-scale social experiments or similar experiments run in a number of different sites have an advantage in visibility over small experiments run in only one site. In referring to highly visible experiments, Aaron (1985, 276) suggests that "the fact that [they] are political events would appear to give them a great advantage." Indeed, findings from the more visible social experiments are frequently reported by the news media.

The literature on utilization, however, suggests that communication and visibility do not depend only on characteristics inherent in the type of research being conducted. They also depend on dissemination efforts by those conducting the research and by others, a topic taken up in detail in chapter 9. Dissemination efforts may not occur if researchers do not take the initiative (Beyer and Trice 1982, 602; Mandell 1988). Even if such efforts are undertaken, however, their effectiveness depends upon the characteristics of presentation—for example, how long the presentation is (decisionmakers face severe time and energy constraints), whether it is written or oral, how clear it is, and whether jargon is used (Cox 1977; Mintzberg 1971; Sproull and Larkey 1979; Weiss 1984). Dissemination may also be facilitated by the existence of what Heclo (1978) has called an "issue network"—a group of researchers and policy analysts who focus on the issues being addressed by the experiment and who interact frequently with one another.

Just as the dissemination effort on the part of researchers may affect use, so may advocacy by users. The literature suggests that the advocacy of research results by one or more key individuals may be crucial to the concrete use of the findings (Leviton and Hughes 1981, 541–42; Weiss 1984). It is also sometimes suggested that utilization may be enhanced if potential users participate in the research (Beyer and Trice 1982, 607; Bryk 1983; Mandell 1984), as occurs in the case of a social experiment run through existing administrative offices. Advocacy, of course, is only likely if the findings help promote the key individuals' goals.

Generalizability

Generalizability refers to whether research findings can be applied to different periods or places. Thus, basic theoretical research is typically more generalizable than highly applied empirical research. In the context of social experimentation, an important related issue is whether the findings are relevant to policies that differ somewhat from the ones directly tested. As should be apparent, the more generalizable a particular piece of research is, everything else equal, the more likely it is to be used.

It is arguable that generalizability is increased when a social experiment permits estimation of response surface parameters. (See chapter 2 for the distinction between black box experiments and response surface experiments.) In such cases, parameters estimated from the experiment can be incorporated into microsimulation models (see Betson and Greenberg 1983; Citro and Hanushek 1991; and Haveman 1987, chapter 10). These models, which are discussed in chapters 4, 6, 7, and 8, are based on micro-data on large representative samples of the nation's households. Microsimulation models have, for example, been used to predict the effects and costs of substantial changes in the nation's welfare system and the nation's health care system. Thus, microsimulation potentially allows findings from an experiment to be extrapolated to the nation as a whole and to programs other than those directly tested in the experiment. By permitting this, microsimulation can became a bridge between the experiment and concrete policy use. However, the importance of this bridge should not be exaggerated. Microsimulation is complex, easily subjected to technical criticism that tends to undermine its definitiveness, and difficult to describe in a readily accessible form to policymakers.

A lack of generalizability of experimental findings from black box experiments may sometimes lead to further experiments. For example, suppose an experiment is initially conducted in one site and yields results that are suggestive and promising. Whether the findings can be applied elsewhere may be unclear. One possible response to this situation is to attempt to replicate the initial experiment in additional sites in an effort to obtain more generalizable results.

Relevance

Relevance concerns whether the needs of decisionmakers are met by the research (Leviton and Hughes 1981, 527). Research that meets decisionmakers' needs is obviously more likely to be used. The knowledge utilization literature suggests that research that focuses on variables that can be manipulated by policy decisions, as social experiments do, tends to be viewed as more useful to policymakers (Beyer and Trice 1982, 613). Moreover, as Leviton and Hughes (537) have suggested, "Evaluation [such as social experiments] differs from some other social research in that users are usually aware of the relevance of evaluations to policies and programs."

The Policy Environment: Ideology, Interests, and Information

The knowledge utilization literature suggests that the policy effects of findings from social experiments will be influenced by the characteristics of the policy environment. Moreover, it seems plausible that the characteristics of the policy environment will affect whether or not particular experiments are undertaken. The fourth component of our conceptual framework, therefore, concerns the characteristics of the policy environment and their influence on the decision to conduct social experiments and on the policy utilization of findings from experiments.

The starting point for this component is Weiss's (1983) I-I-I (Ideology-Interests-Information) model. The central premise of this model is that "the policy positions taken by policy actors are the resultant of . . . the interplay of ideology, interests, and information. . ." (221). Ideology, as Weiss uses it, "encompasses . . . principles, values, [and] political orientation. At its core are ethical and moral values" (224). Weiss defines interests "primarily in terms of self-interest" (224). Information is descriptive in nature, defined as policy actors' "sense of the current state of affairs, the relative seriousness of problems, [and] why things happen as they do"

(225). Weiss points out that ideology and interests are typically only weakly affected by research findings, if they are affected at all, and that research is only one of several competing sources of information used by policymakers. Other sources include direct experience, craft lore, media reports, formal and informal organizational channels, and interest groups.

An important hypothesis that Weiss (1983, 243) derives from the I-I-I framework is that the greater the internal consistency among ideologies, interests, and information from sources other than research, the less research results are used. Using Weiss's model, we have developed a somewhat different hypothesis: Although I-I-I consistency tends to reduce the likelihood of concrete-substantive use being made of social experiments, it does not affect concrete-elaborative use or the various forms of conceptual use (Greenberg and Mandell 1991). Thus, our hypothesis provides one potential explanation of where in the research utilization typology described earlier in the chapter various social experiments are most likely to fit.

Jenkins-Smith (1990, 91) expands on the I-I-I framework in two significant ways. First, he suggests that inconsistency among ideology, interests, and information from sources other than research influences not only the effects of research on policy, but also the decision to conduct the research in the first place.[7] Second, Jenkins-Smith identifies two additional factors that plausibly affect the provision and the use of policy research: whether the issue at hand is analytically tractable, and what the nature of the forum in which analysis is employed is. When examining the decision whether or not to conduct a social experiment, we believe it is important to view the first of these factors in both absolute and relative terms. That is, in addition to looking at whether a social experiment can potentially provide useful information about important elements of the issue, it is also important to consider the merits of social experimentation relative to other forms of evaluation.

Some of the factors discussed are dynamic in nature. For example, ideology, interests, and relevance may change over time as the political environment evolves. Moreover, the various factors interact and influence one another. Timeliness, for example, helps determine relevance. In addition, in using research for advocacy purposes, "relevance" is often defined to apply only to those results that conform to the position that the users already hold, a position that presumably is at least partially based on their ideology and interests (Beyer and Trice 1982, 612–13).

Methodology

The conceptual framework described provides a way of organizing empirical data regarding the conduct of social experiments and their impact on policymaking. As indicated in chapter 1, the empirical data come from five case studies of social experiments. Two of these (the RAND Health Insurance Experiment and the Nursing Home Incentive Reimbursement Experiment) are health-related and three (the income maintenance experiments, the unemployment insurance bonus experiments, and the welfare-to-work experiments) are in the field of income security. These five case studies are supplemented, in chapter 9, by a study of the dissemination of findings from three recent social experiments that were targeted at the welfare population: California's Greater Avenues for Independence, New York's Child Assistance Program, and Florida's Project Independence. We examine how findings from these experiments, all of which were conducted in one state, were disseminated to other states, and whether and how this information was used.

Case studies can take on a range of strategies, usually falling into exploratory, descriptive, and explanatory categories. This book focuses on the descriptive (what happened leading up to the experiments we study and subsequent to their completion) and explanatory (why did events, activities, and use occur or fail to occur).

Somewhat similar, but not identical, methodologies were used in conducting the five case studies. Data were gathered through document analysis and interviews. In the case of the RAND Health Insurance Experiment, the income maintenance experiments, and the welfare-to-work experiments, the interviews were semistructured. Some interviews were conducted in person and others were conducted on the telephone. In the case of the Nursing Home Incentive Reimbursement Experiment and the unemployment insurance bonus experiments, the interviews were structured and were all conducted by telephone. In those two case studies, the interviews were supplemented by surveys mailed to potential users of the experimental results. A structured telephone survey also was used in conducting the research on dissemination that is described in chapter 9.

The following subsections provide a general discussion of each of the methods that we used to obtain data. Details that are specific to the individual case studies appear in the chapters describing the studies.

Document Analysis

As part of the research, an attempt was made to locate as many documents that were pertinent to the study experiments as possible. The goals of the document search were to find

- a history of the experiments;
- examples of use of the results of the experiments;
- descriptions of issues surrounding decisions on whether and how to conduct the experiments;
- characteristics of the experiments that affected their definitiveness, timeliness, communication and visibility, generalizability, and relevance; and
- characteristics of the decisionmakers and the policy environment that affected their use.

The references used for the document analysis included primary sources (government documents and technical reports chronicling the conducting of the experiments and the reporting of findings from them) and secondary sources that refer to the experiments. Such documents were almost always available to us because the experiments we studied were all government funded.

The number of documents that pertain to each of the experiments we studied varies enormously. However, reports exist for all the experiments that describe the processes involved in implementing them and findings from them. In addition, references to the experiments often appear in congressional testimony, the popular press, scholarly books, and journal articles.

Interviews

Structured or semistructured interviews were conducted with individuals who fell into one or more of the following four groups:

- **Researchers:** persons who were involved in the conduct and analysis of the experiments included in the case studies.
- **Sponsors:** employees of the government agency or agencies that funded the experiments. These persons were involved in setting up, monitoring, or running the experiments.

- **Policymakers:** elected or appointed officials in government at the federal or state levels, and their staffs. These persons held government positions at the time that the experiments were initiated, while they were being conducted, or at the time that the results became known; and they were in a position to influence policies germane to the experiments.
- **Research brokers:** people who channel research findings to policymakers. Included in this category are individuals who summarized the results of the experiments in congressional testimony, at conferences and meetings, or in newsletters; and persons who have publicized the findings in books and articles.

The instrument used in conducting the interviews was tailored to each respondent, depending on the group or groups to which he or she belonged and the specific experiment or experiments about which he or she was being asked. If it appeared to us that an experiment about which we were asking might have provided pertinent information on a policy or program proposal that had reached the policy agenda, respondents were specifically queried on whether the experiment had played any role in considerations of the proposal.

As many interviews as possible were conducted in person, with the remaining interviews conducted by telephone. Notes were taken of responses during all the interviews. In addition, the in-person interviews were taped. Using these sources, a report of each interview was written. These reports were used as a major source in writing the case study chapters.

Each of the interviews covered a subset of the following topics, with the selected topics determined on the basis of our judgment on the sort of information the respondent could best provide:

- Social and political reasons for conducting the experiments
- The process leading to the decision to conduct the experiments
- The original goals of the experiments
- Design issues, including site selection, the design of the tested treatment, time frame, ethical concerns, and implementation concerns
- Key findings from the experiments and their influence on views and policy
- Utilization factors: the definitiveness, timeliness, communication, generalizability, and relevance of findings from the experiments

- Respondents' ideology, interests, and information context
- The role played or not played in the policy process by the experiments, and the reasons
- The ways in which findings from the experiments were disseminated
- Identification of additional relevant documents
- Identification of additional key individuals

The elapse of time between the experiments and the interviews resulted in a problem conducting the interviews. Respondents were often being asked questions they had not thought about for a very long time. Although this was a problem in all the case studies, it was especially serious for the older experiments such as the income maintenance experiments and the RAND Health Insurance Experiment. The problem was partially overcome by jogging the memories of respondents by mentioning a few facts concerning the experiment about which they were being asked. As they began talking, respondents usually found that they remembered more than they anticipated.

Survey

As previously mentioned, a mail survey was used as part of the process of conducting case studies of the Nursing Home Incentive Reimbursement Experiment and the unemployment insurance bonus experiments. The survey was mailed to all state unemployment insurance administrators and all state nursing home regulators and state Medicaid directors. The survey was used to obtain several types of information:

- Current policy as it relates to the issues studied in the experiments;
- Respondents' knowledge of findings from the experiments;
- The way respondents learned of the experiments;
- Any attention given to results from the experiments in policy deliberations that occurred during informal discussions, meetings, and legislative hearings;
- Important state-level issues in unemployment insurance and in nursing home reimbursement; and
- The question of whether the findings of the experiments supported or corroborated existing values or ideology.

Survey respondents also were asked to identify items for the document analysis portion of the case studies. Further, they were asked to provide the names and telephone numbers of others who might be able to identify additional documents or furnish further information for the use of results from the experiments.

The survey instrument was almost identical for the Nursing Home Incentives Reimbursement and the unemployment insurance bonus case studies. They were pilot-tested with the help, respectively, of the nursing home regulator and the executive director of employment services in Maryland. The Department of Labor provided a list of the appropriate unemployment insurance administrators in the 50 states and the District of Columbia. A survey was sent to each UI administrator. The nursing home regulator in Maryland provided a list of her counterparts across the country, and the U.S. Health Care Financing Agency provided a list of all state Medicaid directors. A survey was sent to each state director of nursing home regulation and then to Medicaid directors for states that did not respond to the first mailing.[8] Each survey included a self-addressed stamped envelope.

Of the 51 surveys mailed to unemployment insurance directors, 50 were returned, a 98 percent return rate. Only Kansas failed to reply. Of the 51 surveys sent to the state nursing home regulators and/or Medicaid directors, responses were received from 44 states, an 86 percent return rate. Only Arizona, Washington, the District of Columbia, Hawaii, Kentucky, Mississippi, and South Dakota failed to respond.

NOTES

1. For details on this model, see Burtless (1995, 82); Burtless and Orr (1986); Gramlich (1981, 172–75); Orr (1998, part 2: 1); Stafford (1979); and Thompson (1982).

2. We are indebted to Larry Orr for suggesting these labels.

3. Such debate tends to demystify the technical expertise of researchers (Sabatier 1978, 409).

4. On the basis of cognitive dissonance theory, Sabatier (1978, 410) suggests that such threats will reduce use because "information that does not conform to policy predispositions will be ignored or distorted by the decisionmaker."

5. Leviton and Hughes (1981, 540) note that there is evidence, for example, that doctors are more receptive to research than lawyers (also see Bozeman 1986, 531).

6. Indeed, important findings from this experiment continued to appear even after 1983. For example, a major reanalysis of the effects of the Seattle-Denver treatment on marital stability, one that purported to overturn the findings appearing in the final

report, was not published until two decades after work on the experiment first began (Cain and Wissoker 1990).

7. Jenkins-Smith uses terminology that differs from Weiss's. Specifically, he refers to conflict on the "core elements of belief systems," rather than to inconsistency among ideology, interests, and information. However, the two concepts are essentially equivalent. In Jenkins-Smith's formulation, conflict can occur either within individual policy actors or among different policy actors. Jenkins-Smith also suggests that "it is in the mid-range of conflict—where some incentive exists to mobilize resources for analysis yet change in belief systems would be tolerable—that the results of (policy) analysis could be expected to affect the beliefs of those in the policy elite. Low-level conflict would be expected to draw little analytical attention, and when conflict is high, analysis will tend to be deployed primarily as a political tool to promote, justify and defend a predetermined policy position" (1990, 172).

8. In some states, the state nursing home regulator was inappropriate for such a survey.

PART II:
Case Studies

4

The RAND Health
Insurance Experiment

The RAND Health Insurance Experiment (HIE) was one of the largest and most ambitious randomized social experiments ever fielded. Although the initial cost estimates were considerably lower, the total cost of the experiment was $136 million (in 1984 dollars) (Greenberg and Shroder 1997). One key objective of the HIE was estimating the effects of varying levels of cost sharing on the use of medical services and health outcomes. Another key objective was comparing the use of medical services and health outcomes for those enrolled in the prepaid group practice with the use of medical services and health outcomes for those enrolled in fee-for-service plans (Newhouse and the Insurance Experiment Group 1993, 5). The first findings of the HIE were published in 1981 (Newhouse et al. 1981), although findings were informally available somewhat earlier.

Description

Design

Participants in the HIE were drawn from six sites across the country (Dayton, Ohio; Seattle, Washington; Fitchburg and Leominster, Massachusetts; Franklin County, Massachusetts; Charleston, South Carolina; and Georgetown County, South Carolina). The six sites "were intended to represent the United States along several dimensions," including city size, region, and waiting times for an appointment with a primary care physician (intended as a measure of delivery-system capacity). In addition, the designers of the experiment "wanted both northern and southern sites . . . and at least one site had to have a well-established HMO" (Newhouse and the Insurance Experiment Group 1993, 15–17). The first participants were enrolled in 1974, and data collection continued through 1982. Some participants were enrolled for three years and others for five.

Two sets of outcome variables were of primary concern in the RAND Health Insurance Experiment. The first was the use of and expenditures on medical, dental, and mental health services. The second set of outcome variables of primary concern was health outcomes, such as health status and patient satisfaction.

The HIE was a "response surface experiment." Participants were randomly assigned to 1 of 14 fee-for-service insurance plans or to a staff-model HMO (the Group Health Cooperative of Puget Sound in Seattle). None of the different insurance plans corresponded directly to specific national health insurance plans that were being considered at the time by policymakers. A total of approximately 2,000 families, representing 7,708 individuals, participated in the HIE. Of the 7,708 individuals, 5,816 were assigned to 1 of the 14 fee-for-service insurance plans and the remaining 1,892 to the prepaid group practice (Newhouse and the Insurance Experiment Group 1993, 16).

The 14 fee-for-service insurance plans varied in the coinsurance rate and maximum dollar expenditure (MDE).[1] One of the fee-for-service plans, labeled the "Free Care Plan," had zero coinsurance (and therefore no out-of-pocket expenditures). There were 3 plans in which the coinsurance rate was 25 percent. These plans differed from each other in terms of the MDEs. Specifically, in one of the plans, the MDE was 5 percent of family income or $1,000, whichever was less. In another, the MDE was 10 percent of family income or $1,000, whichever was less. In the third plan with 25 percent coinsurance, the MDE was 15 percent of family income or $1,000, whichever was less. Three other plans combined a coinsurance rate of 50 percent with maximum dollar expenditures of 5 percent, 10 percent, or 15 percent of family income, respectively, or $1,000, if it was less. Three other plans were created by combining a coinsurance rate of 95 percent with three different MDEs (5 percent, 10 percent, or 15 percent of family income, or $1,000, if it was less). Three other fee-for-service plans were labeled "25/50 plans." These plans combined a 50 percent coinsurance rate for outpatient mental health and dental services and a 25 percent coinsurance rate for all other services, combined with three different MDEs (5 percent, 10 percent, or 15 percent of family income, or $1,000, if it was less). The final fee-for-service plan was labeled the "Individual Deductible Plan." That plan had 95 percent coinsurance for outpatient services and zero coinsurance for inpatient services along with an MDE of $150 per person or $450 per family, whichever was less.

The characteristics of the 14 fee-for-service plans were as follows:

1. Zero coinsurance (and therefore no out-of-pocket expenditures); termed "free care"
2. 25 percent coinsurance and MDE of 5 percent of family income or $1,000, whichever was less
3. 25 percent coinsurance and MDE of 10 percent of family income or $1,000, whichever was less
4. 25 percent coinsurance and MDE of 15 percent of family income or $1,000, whichever was less
5. 50 percent coinsurance and MDE of 5 percent of family income or $1,000, whichever was less
6. 50 percent coinsurance and MDE of 10 percent of family income or $1,000, whichever was less
7. 50 percent coinsurance and MDE of 15 percent of family income or $1,000, whichever was less
8. 95 percent coinsurance and MDE of 5 percent of family income or $1,000, whichever was less
9. 95 percent coinsurance and MDE of 10 percent of family income or $1,000, whichever was less
10. 95 percent coinsurance and MDE of 15 percent of family income or $1,000, whichever was less
11. 25 percent coinsurance for all services except outpatient mental health and dental, which were subject to 50 percent coinsurance; and MDE of 5 percent of family income or $1,000, whichever was less
12. 25 percent coinsurance for all services except outpatient mental health and dental, which were subject to 50 percent coinsurance; and MDE of 10 percent of family income or $1,000, whichever was less

13. 25 percent coinsurance for all services except outpatient mental health and dental, which were subject to 50 percent coinsurance; and MDE of 15 percent of family income or $1,000, whichever was less
14. 95 percent coinsurance and MDE of $150 per person, subject to a maximum of $450 per family; this plan is called the "Individual Deductible" plan

For purposes of analyzing the effects of varying levels of cost-sharing, the plans were grouped into five categories, namely

1. the free care plan;
2. plans with 25 percent coinsurance for medical services, regardless of the amount of the MDE (thus, the 25/50 plans were included here);
3. plans with 50 percent coinsurance for medical services, regardless of the amount of the MDE;
4. plans with 95 percent coinsurance for medical services and family (as opposed to individual) MDEs, regardless of the amount of the MDE; and
5. the "Individual Deductible" plan (Newhouse and the Insurance Experiment Group 1993, 32).

To compare the use of medical services and health outcomes for those enrolled in prepaid group practice with the use of medical services and health outcomes for those enrolled in fee-for-service plans, those randomly assigned to the staff model HMO were compared either to participants enrolled in the free-care plan in Seattle or to fee-for-service participants assigned to cost-sharing plans in Seattle (263).

A number of innovative design features were incorporated into the HIE. First, rather than simple random assignment, the Finite Selection Model was used for assigning families to the different plans. This model "can be regarded as a special case and a major extension of the Conlisk-Watts model," which was used in the income maintenance experiments (Newhouse and the Insurance Experiment Group 1993, 419). Second, a method of side payments, referred to as Participation Incentive (PI) payments, was developed to "guarantee that no one would become financially worse off as a result of participation in the [HIE]" (12). In addition to the ethical reasons for providing them, PIs were intended to ensure that refusal rates were independent of the experimental plan to which families were assigned. Although not completely successful in that refusal of the offer did turn out to be about the plan, the PIs did succeed to the extent that the differential refusal rates among plans "did not generally lead to detectable bias" (313). Third, a "Completion Bonus," which was intended to counter the potential incentive to leave the experiment prematurely, was provided (408).

Estimation Methodology

Newhouse and his colleagues note that medical expenditures are not normally distributed. Therefore, to produce more precise and robust estimates of the effects of health insurance, the RAND team developed a four-equation model. The first two equations are probit models. In the first of these, the dependent variable is whether the individual received *any* medical service during the year. The second probit model estimates the probability of an individual having at least one inpatient stay, conditional on the person having used some medical service during the year. The remaining two equations are linear regressions in which the dependent variable is the logarithm of total annual medical expenses. One of the linear regressions is estimated for those individuals who have nonzero outpatient services, but no inpatient stays, whereas the other is estimated for those individuals who have at least one inpatient stay. In the latter model, the dependent variable includes both outpatient and inpatient expenses (Newhouse and the Insurance Experiment Group 1993, 36).

Key Findings

In general terms, the HIE found that cost sharing reduces consumption of medical services without having substantial negative effects on health status. More specifically, among the most important findings on the effect of cost sharing on use were these:

1. Expenditures for families in the plans with 95 percent coinsurance and family MDEs were about 30 percent lower than for the families that received free care (i.e., expenditures for those in the free plan were 45 percent higher than for those in plan with 95 percent coinsurance and family MDEs).
2. Expenditures in the HMO group were 28 percent lower than for the families that received free care.

The HIE also showed that the health effects of cost sharing on health status were generally negligible. One exception to this was that free care resulted in lower blood pressure among the poor who had hypertension at the start of the experiment. In addition, free care resulted in better dental health and improved vision correction, particularly among the poor. Finally, free care resulted in better outcomes for poor children with anemia.

Origins of the Experiment

Several possible explanations of the decision to conduct randomized social experiments were discussed in chapter 3. These include the rational model, the inventory model, and a model that focuses on the benefits to be gained from the process of conducting a randomized social experiment rather than from the information produced by the experiment. In particular, this process can replace real with symbolic action. Alternatively, it can keep alive innovative policy alternatives for which adequate support cannot be obtained immediately.

The RAND Health Insurance Experiment can be viewed as the result of an almost random intersection of several forces. First, in 1972, a group of RAND researchers (including Joseph Newhouse, Charles Phelps, and Tom Rockwell) submitted an unsolicited proposal to the Office of Economic Opportunity (OEO) that involved using existing databases to examine how people would react to various levels of copayments. Second, at approximately the same time, Larry Orr, a key member of the OEO research staff, was interacting extensively with staff from the Office of the Assistant Secretary for Planning and Evaluation (ASPE) in the U.S. Department of Health, Education, and Welfare on the Nixon Family Assistance Plan (FAP). As a result of his involvement with ASPE on FAP, Orr became involved with attempts to reform Medicaid in response to congressional concern about the "Medicaid notch."[2] He was struck by how little was known about the issue of "the effect of health insurance on the use of medical care (and therefore the cost of medical care) and by the extent to which health policy analysts subscribed to the belief that first dollar coverage was essential" (Orr interview). Although those two factors were instrumental in OEO becoming involved in a health insurance study, two other related factors strongly influenced the decision to field an experiment rather than simply fund the nonexperimental research.

First, as discussed in chapter 2, the Office of Planning, Research, and Evaluation of OEO was a pioneer in fielding large-scale social experiments. By 1972, it was a natural part of office staffers' mindset to think of using experiments to examine a variety of questions. Second, by 1972 the New Jersey and Rural Income Maintenance Experiments that OEO was sponsoring were beginning to wind down. There was an interest on the part of those in the OEO, as one interviewee told us, in "initiating another large, visible project, preferably an experiment." Further, the funds required to do so were available.

Given those forces, OEO decided to fund the original RAND proposal and also encouraged the RAND team to design an experiment to study the effect of health insurance on the use of medical care. The RAND team designed such an experiment. OEO then went forward with a formal competition for who should undertake a more detailed design and the actual conduct of the experiment. A consortium consisting of RAND and Mathematica Policy Research won that competition and work on the experiment began.

In early 1973, however, OEO was dismantled and sponsorship of the HIE was transferred to the Department of Health, Education, and Welfare (HEW) and placed in the Office of the Assistant Secretary for Planning and Evaluation, who at the time was William Morrill. The transition was neither smooth nor automatic. Morrill convened a department-wide review group, headed by Stuart Altman, to "assess the value of the experiment and to determine if it warranted HEW sponsorship" (memo from Morrill). Included in the review process was a review of the proposed experiment by six prominent consultants. Several of the consultants, along with representatives of various bureaus within HEW, expressed strong reservations on continuation of the HIE. Opponents of continuing the HIE raised two main arguments. The first was that because of its high costs, the HIE would displace important nonexperimental research pertaining to health policy. The second argument was that the HIE did not fit well with the policy process in two senses. First, the insurance plans included in the HIE did not correspond directly to the policy options being considered by Congress at the time. Second, it was widely believed that some kind of national health insurance plan would be enacted well before the HIE results would be available.

HIE supporters did not dispute the argument that the HIE would not contribute much to the apparently impending decisions on national health insurance. They did, however, argue that whatever national health insurance was initially adopted would subsequently be modified and that the HIE would provide information that would be useful in making those modifications. Others echoed the need for information to help guide future modifications of whatever plan would be initially enacted. For example, in the February 1975 issue of the magazine *Consumer Reports,* Consumers' Union expressed concern about including cost sharing in a national health plan. They also argued that if copayments were initially included in a national health insurance (NHI) plan, they should be eliminated once it is shown that they "deter persons from seeking needed care" (cited in Bowler, Kudrle, and Marmor 1977). Ultimately, Casper Weinberger, the secretary of HEW, decided to continue the HIE, albeit with a somewhat reduced scope. At that time it was estimated that the HIE would cost $30–35 million, rather than $50 million.

This history has several implications for possible explanations of the decision to conduct randomized social experiments. First, nothing in the history of the HIE suggests that it was undertaken either to substitute symbolic for real action or to keep alive an innovative policy alternative for which adequate support could not be obtained immediately. The history of the HIE also provides no support for the rational model. Although national health insurance was high on the policy agenda in the early 1970s, even supporters of the HIE recognized that it would not contribute much to the decision about national health insurance that was widely believed to be imminent. The response on the part of proponents of the HIE to criticism raised by opponents suggests support for Feldman's "inventory" model. One of our interviewees stated it this way:

> Health insurance issues were at the forefront of social policy debate at the time. There was a general awareness of the need for this kind of information, even though it was pretty clear we didn't know what we were going to do with it once the results came in. But this was also an age when we were committing to going to the moon without even a clue about how we would get there. We figured that once we start down the path, we would work out the technology and I think to some extent the same thing is true here.

While the history of the HIE fits best with the inventory model, it also highlights an inadequacy of this model. The inventory model, like the rational model, stresses the demand for information on the part of policymakers. However, the history of the HIE highlights the importance of "supply-side push." In particular, the unsolicited proposal submitted by RAND to OEO was a key factor in bringing the HIE into existence. In addition, organizational factors within OEO were critical ingredients in the decision to field the HIE. Had the OEO been abolished in, say, 1970, it appears unlikely that the HIE would have been fielded, even though the value of adding to the inventory of information pertinent to health policy would presumably have been the same. Similarly, assuming that OEO was not abolished earlier, had the RAND group submitted its proposal to OEO in 1970, it is much less likely that the HIE would have been fielded. That is, the perceived need to add to the inventory of information on the elasticity of demand for medical care was a necessary, but not sufficient, condition for initiation of the HIE.

Two additional organizational factors appear to have been essential for the HIE to be initiated. First, OEO viewed the opportunity costs of the HIE as being much lower than HEW (the potential alternative birthplace of the HIE) did in 1972 or than OEO itself might have earlier. HEW was greatly concerned about the nonexperimental research that the HIE would displace, but OEO was in the process of winding down the income maintenance experiments that they had sponsored. There was little in the OEO research portfolio that the HIE displaced and, indeed, it is not inconceivable that the HIE represented an important source of protection for a substantial portion of the OEO research budget. The second key organizational factor is the credibility attached to randomized social experiments. Opponents of the HIE within HEW did not view the experiment as substantially reducing the range of estimates of possible effects of cost sharing. In contrast, OEO supporters of the HIE, because of their previous experience with the income maintenance experiments, were much more optimistic about the extent to which the HIE would increase the credibility and precision of such estimates.

Policy Impacts of the Experiment

Ginzburg and Ostrow (1994) note that the issue of national health insurance has been on the agenda of various U.S. presidents as far back as Theodore Roosevelt, who included a variant of national health insurance in his election platform in 1912. The first formal proposal for national health insurance from the executive branch was advanced by President Truman (Aaron 1996, 2). Following the enactment of Medicare and Medicaid in the mid-1960s, it was widely believed that universal national health insurance was imminent. The early and mid-1970s saw the introduction of numerous proposals for national health insurance. For example, President Nixon presented a plan for comprehensive national health insurance in 1974 (Light 1999, 129). Members of Congress, including Senators Edward Kennedy, Russell Long, and Abraham Ribicoff and Representatives Wilbur Mills and Martha Griffiths, introduced many other proposals for national health insurance. One of the major differences among these plans was the extent of cost sharing (i.e., out-of-pocket payment at the time of use).

None of the national health insurance proposals introduced during the Nixon and Ford administrations were enacted. However, national health insurance continued to be an issue during the 1976 presidential campaign and Jimmy Carter pledged support for national health insurance during his campaign (Light 1999, 136; Ginzburg and Ostrow 1994). Despite these campaign promises, the issue of national health insurance was put on hold during the first few years of the Carter administration. However, in the spring of 1979, President Carter did present a proposal for a national health insurance plan (Light 1999, 136).

The Carter Health Plan

Cost estimation for the Carter health plan was conducted by a modeling group that included staff from the Office of the Deputy Assistant Secretary for Planning and Evaluation/Health, staff from Medicare (SSA/HCFA) and the Office of the Actuary, and outside consultants. Karen Davis, who was deputy assistant secretary for planning and evaluation/health, led the effort. The primary model the team used to estimate the cost of national health insurance options was a microsimulation model referred to as the National Health Insurance Model. The model produced two profiles—a Present Law Profile and a Future Law Profile (FLPM). The former contained "baseline data concerning the use and financing of" health services, while the latter produced "estimates of how health care financing will change under a proposed NHI program" (U.S. Department of Health and Human Services [HHS], Office of the Assistant Secretary for Planning and Evaluation 1981, 3).

The estimates produced by the FLPM reflected both transferred costs (i.e., cost changes based on existing utilization patterns) and new costs associated with "induced" services (i.e., "changes in utilization due to changes in the out-of-pocket cost to consumers for newly covered beneficiaries and services") (HHS, Office of the Assistant Secretary for Planning and Evaluation 1981, 12). A key element in estimating induced services, of course, is the price elasticity of demand for services. The HIE was intended to provide just such estimates. However, results from the RAND Health Insurance Experiment were not available until after the bulk of the analysis of the Carter health plan was completed (Davis interview; Lave interview). Rather, in the National Health Insurance Model "Econometric studies and *natural* experiments" [emphasis added] were used "to give an idea of the possible range of the elasticities for various medical services. The point estimates for the specific parameters in the model were chosen in such a manner to be consistent with independent actuarial estimates of the change in aggregate expenditures that would occur" (HHS 1981, 12).

The Clinton Health Care Plan

Following the defeat of the Carter health plan in Congress in November 1979, national health insurance did not occupy a major place on the national agenda again until the early 1990s. Health care reform is widely credited as a major factor in Senator Harris Wofford's 1991 victory in a special election in Pennsylvania. During the 1992 presidential campaign, health reform was a major issue. Immediately after being inaugurated, President Clinton appointed a 12-member task force, chaired by Mrs. Clinton, to oversee development of a health care reform proposal. An advisory group that consisted of over 500 experts, headed by Ira Magaziner, supported this task force. The advisory group was divided into a series of "working groups" (Hacker 1997, 122–29).

One of the key working groups was the Premium Estimation Group. Ken Thorpe, who was deputy assistant secretary for health policy, headed it. Representatives of the Health Care Financing Administration (HCFA), Agency for Health Care Policy and Research (AHCPR), the Office of the Assistant Secretary for Planning and Evaluation (ASPE), and the Office of Management and Budget (OMB) also participated in this working group (Waldo interview). The group's main role was to estimate premiums and other financial consequences of different types of benefits packages. The estimates were based on two microsimulation models: the SPAM model, which had been developed by HCFA, and the AHSIM model, which had been developed by AHCPR. Specifically, as reported by two of our interviewees, during the first three months or so of the Clinton administration the Premium Estimation Group met virtually daily. At each meeting, a benefits package was defined. The HCFA representatives (using SPAM) and the AHCPR group (using AHSIM) would then return to their offices and produce estimates of the costs and premiums associated with the plan. The group would then meet again the next day and share the numbers. Generally the estimates produced by the two models agreed. When they did not agree, the group would attempt to determine why. In many instances the differences were attributable to a mistake (e.g., programming error) by one or the other group.

The HIE strongly influenced both the SPAM and AHSIM models. We consider the AHSIM model first.

Development of the AHSIM model began in 1990–91, during the administration of President George H. W. Bush, although it was not called AHSIM at the time.[3] It was originally focused on tax policies because that was the thrust of what the Bush administration wanted to do. The outlines of a fairly sophisticated microsimulation model were in place by the summer of 1992. As the 1992 presidential election drew near, it became evident to those at AHCPR that Governor Clinton was going to be elected and that health care reform was going to be one of his administration's first major pushes. At that point, work on the model accelerated and AHCPR analysts began to modify the model to make it suitable to analyze the types of proposals that they expected a Clinton administration to develop.

In the AHSIM model, the population was divided into groups that were defined by demographic characteristics, health conditions, and broad categories of insurance coverage (Medicaid, commercial insurance, and so forth). An econometric model was used to predict the level and mix of health expenditures for individuals in each category. That econometric model was based directly on the ones that had been developed by RAND to analyze the HIE. Specifically, in the AHSIM model, a probit model was used to predict the probability of *any* health expenditures for each type of individual. Ten different categories of health services were then identified. For each category of health services, another probit model was then used to predict the probability that each type of individual would have nonzero expenditures in that category of health services, given that there were nonzero expenditures for health services as a whole. Finally, a series of 10 log-linear regression models was used to predict the expenditures of each type of individual for each category of health services, conditional on nonzero spending for that service. Thus, the model produced estimates of this form: "Individuals with a particular set of health conditions and demographic characteristics who have a particular generic type of insurance coverage will have the following average expenditures in each of ten categories of health services." Data from the 1987 NMES survey, a large (approximately 35,000 individuals), nationally representative household survey, were used to estimate the parameters of the model.

The estimates produced by the econometric portion of the AHSIM model were based on the average cost-sharing provisions for the category of health insurance of concern. That is, they did not account for variations in cost sharing within categories of plans. To account for the difference between the average cost-sharing provisions of plans within each category and the actual cost-sharing provisions contained in the alternative being modeled, a series of adjustment factors that were taken directly from the empirical estimates provided by the HIE were employed. Specifically, as related by one of our interviewees, who was a key figure at AHCPR:

> [One of the AHCPR analysts] had a series of spreadsheets on her computer. She had taken the results of the HIE and using the information about how expenditures varied based upon different levels of coinsurance and deductibles, she developed adjustment factors that would correspond to different benefit package parameters. What she would then say is: "This is based on an average deductible and coinsurance rate that's known from the NMES data. That puts them about here on the scale. Given what we know from [the HIE] we know that if we raise the deductible from $100 to $250 the probability of any expenditure will be reduced by [some amount] and we know that the impact of the increase on the deductible on the conditional expenditures will be [some amount]." So when a new insurance package would come in, we would essentially go to her and she would go into her office and come back and announce what the adjustment factors were. We would then take those adjustment factors and put them into the premium calculation model and combine them with the econometric model.

The decision to use the HIE results to compute these adjustment factors is noteworthy. Our AHCPR interviewee asserted that "if we hadn't had the elasticities from the HIE, we might have been able to estimate something from NMES, which was the only other data source that even came close to the HIE. [Indeed], if we at AHCPR thought NMES was up to the task, we would have used it, for good solid bureaucratic reasons." Thus, the HIE estimates were viewed as the best available estimates.

The SPAM (Special Policy Analysis Model) was developed during the late 1980s. The model was developed by the Actuarial Research Corporation under a contract from the Office of the Actuary of HCFA. The main purpose of the model is to predict the costs of various health insurance reform proposals. To predict the effect of various health insurance policy reforms, the SPAM model first imputes estimated health expenditures to the uninsured that are derived from the distribution of health expenditures for (roughly) equivalent persons who are currently insured. It then adjusts health expenditures for both the currently insured and those who would be newly covered due to changes in the nature of coverage (i.e., types of services covered and level of deductibles and coinsurance rates).

The procedure used in the SPAM to adjust health expenditures for the currently insured and those who would be newly covered because of changes in the nature of coverage is similar to the procedure used in the National Health Insurance Model during the Carter administration to estimate "induced" services to create the Future Law Profile. As part of this procedure, a series of induction factors is required. The developers of SPAM obtained the induction factors by "speaking to knowledgeable industry people [primarily actuaries] and asking them to provide a subjective estimate of the induction factors" (Waldo interview). The model developers then synthesized these subjective estimates and selected one from somewhere in the middle of the distribution.

The HIE results influenced the induction factors in two related ways. First, they may have influenced the perceptions of industry people who provided subjective estimates of the induction factors. Waldo believes that those providing subjective estimates relied on some combination of the experience of the plans they worked for and the HIE results, with the former having a somewhat larger weight, but with the weight assigned to the HIE results being far from negligible. Second, in selecting estimates of the induction factors from among the subjective estimates obtained from knowledgeable industry people, the model developers were aware of the HIE results and selected a number that they believed to be consistent with the HIE results, as well as with the subjective estimates provided with the actuaries they consulted. Thus, although the HIE results are not directly incorporated into the SPAM, the HIE results were incorporated in the SPAM implicitly through the insurance effect parameters.

In summary, then, the HIE influenced estimates of premiums produced by the Premium Estimation Group. The structure of the AHSIM model was based directly on econometric work that had been done as part of the HIE. In addition, the elasticities of the demand for health care estimated by the HIE were used in the AHSIM model to estimate how deductibles and copayments would affect utilization and expenditures. The primary influence of the HIE on the SPAM model was in the subjective estimates of insurance effect parameters provided by the actuaries consulted and in the synthesis of those parameters by the model developers. Given the influence of the HIE on the estimates of premiums produced by the Premium Estimation Group, the next question is how these premium estimates influenced the policy process.

The basic structure contained in the Clinton plan—"managed competition"—had been established before the inauguration and hence before the production of the estimates produced by the Premium Estimation Group (see Hacker 1997, 119). Thus, it appears unlikely that the premium estimates had predecision concrete substantive use. However, there is considerable evidence that they had considerable predecision concrete elaborative use as well as predecision enlightenment elaborative use within the development of the Clinton health plan.

Even with the basic structure of the Clinton health plan in place, a number of issues remained to be resolved by the Clinton task force. The estimates produced by the Premium Estimation Group were influential in resolving those issues. Ken Thorpe (1996, 175), who as noted above headed the Premium Estimation Group, has written that "Within the administration, financial estimates of the costs and savings of the president's plan served as important inputs into the final formulation of the Health Security Act." Another member of the Premium Estimation Group told us:

> My sense is that the numbers [produced by the Premium Estimation Team] were most important early on in the process in trying to sort through some of the issues. They at least served as the basis for defining the policy issues that needed to be addressed [in the design of the plan]. . . . A meeting [was held] at the White House in which a debate took place between . . . Len Nichols and Atul Gawande. Basically, it was the health policy types and the economists debating the scope of the proposal. Should this be a comprehensive benefits package or should it be a catastrophic package? The models were really important in helping both sides understand what the implications of that decision would be. The numbers were brought to bear in that meeting.

Enlightenment

The HIE appears to have had several important enlightenment effects. In terms of direct policy impacts, before the HIE it was unclear whether various forms of cost sharing should be included in health insurance policies. Largely as result of the HIE, health policy experts have reached a consensus—though still not unanimity—that cost sharing is, on balance, a desirable feature of health plans and that any health insurance policy must include them. This consensus has evolved in the context of a general predisposition toward health plans that incorporate cost sharing rather than in the context of evaluating a specific health plan. Hence, it is a conceptual-elaborative impact.

In addition to affecting beliefs among policymakers, the HIE had significant impacts on the beliefs of health economists and other health services researchers. The most significant impact in this regard concerned the effects of various forms of copayments. As one of our interviewees explained:

> The HIE changed the mindset of a lot of people and it changed some fundamental beliefs of the impacts of deductibles, coinsurance, and the like. In the 1970s a lot of people didn't believe that if you changed deductibles or coinsurance it affected utilization or expenditures. I think the HIE managed to demonstrate that this wasn't true.

In Fuchs's (1993, 171) words, the HIE "conclusively demonstrated that the 'general law of demand' applies to medical care as well as to wheat and widgets." Another impact the HIE had on the beliefs of health economists and other health services researchers was the result that, in the words of one of our interviewees, "copayments affect the probability of nonzero expenditures (both overall and in certain categories), but not the amount of expenditures given that they are nonzero."

The HIE has also had significant effects on the methodological tools available to health services researchers. Those effects fall into two main categories. The first is the structure of econometric models. The Office of Technology Assessment (U.S. Congress, Office of Technology Assessment 1994, 126–27) noted that "the [multi]-part model of utilization [was] made standard after the RAND Health Insurance Experiment." For example, the structure of the AHSIM model, which as discussed above was one of the major models used to estimate costs of different variations of the Clinton health plan, followed directly from the modeling approach that was developed by RAND in analyzing the HIE. As one of our interviewees put it:

> The HIE drove a lot of methodological work among health economists and it was really that work that provided the intellectual foundation for a lot of what we were able to do. . . . I don't think the health economists would have been able or comfortable generating the kinds of estimates that we did during health care reform if we hadn't had the experience of the HIE to back up what we were doing. It would have been an actuarial activity only. Actuarial and economic methods are

very similar, but there is a huge gulf in terms of the language and the nuances of the methodology. [If there hadn't been the methodological work,] we would have found a different way to [produce estimates]; we never would have dropped out. But we would have had a much more difficult time developing an econometric model than we did.

The second area in which the HIE has made significant methodological contributions to health services research is the conceptualization and measurement of health. As part of the HIE, RAND researchers, led by Robert Brook, John Ware, and Kathleen Lohr, developed a series of measures of health status. Five types of measures were developed, namely: general health status, which included physical, mental, and social health; physiologic health; health habits; prevalence of symptoms and disability days; and risk of dying from any cause related to various risk factors (Newhouse and Insurance Experiment Group 1993, 183). These measures have been widely used in subsequent studies by researchers both within and external to RAND. Brandon (1995, 1058) observes that this work played a central role in "the rapid advances of impact and quality studies during the last decade."

Utilization Factors

Timeliness

The HIE was initiated during a time when national health insurance (NHI) proposals were "flying fast and furious." However, activity on NHI waned at almost the same time the results of the HIE became available. Before President Clinton, the last president who paid serious attention to NHI was Carter. At the time of the Carter activity, only preliminary results from the HIE were available. By the time the HIE was completed, NHI no longer occupied a prominent place on the policy agenda (i.e., during the Reagan-Bush years).

Of course, NHI regained a prominent place on the policy agenda during Clinton's first term. However, by that time, the HIE results were based on data that had been collected between 10 and 18 years earlier. Of particular concern in that regard were the changes that had occurred in the health care marketplace, such as the introduction of features typical of managed care (e.g., utilization review, requirements for second opinion) into virtually all health insurance plans. As one of our interviewees pointed out, "The NMES data were criticized because they were old and yet [the HIE data] were even older. . . . Moreover, they were really very limited in terms of the ability to look at HMO activities." These considerations resulted in reservations about the validity of the HIE estimates in the context of developing the Clinton health plan. Still, despite these imperfections, the HIE estimates were used to compute the adjustment factors in the AHSIM model. One of our interviewees succinctly summarized the reasons for this:

> Everyone involved in the process (CBO, CRS, OMB, Cutler, Nichols, and Thorpe) understood that the RAND data were the best data that we had on elasticities. They persuaded Magaziner. If you just had taken a health actuary off the street and said "How do you do this?" they would have gone immediately to the RAND data. It was part of the culture. [In addition], because it had information about behavior outside the "normal" range of premiums, we were able to get a much better handle on what would happen. We could look at catastrophic packages [for example]. There really aren't that many catastrophic insurance plans out there which you would observe from the NMES data.

Relevance

It was generally impossible to apply the HIE results directly to predicting impacts of policy proposal for national health insurance. As noted above, none of the different insurance plans included in the HIE corresponded directly to specific national health insurance plans that were being considered at the time by policymakers. In general, policy proposals for national health insurance have been more complicated than the stylized plans included in the HIE. The differences between NHI proposals and the HIE treatments, moreover, have increased over the years. Rather, the results were incorporated into microsimulation models and the like.

To some extent, the relevance of the HIE results has further decreased over the years because of the increasing importance of managed care, with its emphasis on rationing services by providers and giving incentives to providers as opposed to consumers. However, cost sharing on the part of consumers of care remains an important means of controlling utilization. Newhouse (interview) argues that the two techniques (rationing of services by providers or by giving incentives to providers and incentives to consumers) are complementary. "Demand-side cost sharing, the HIE showed, affects the number of treated episodes but has very modest effects on cost per episode, while supply-side incentives are likely to affect cost per episode to a much greater degree."

Communication and Visibility

Results were widely disseminated in conventional academic outlets (journal articles and book chapters), as well as RAND reports. All told, over 300 RAND reports, journal articles, and book chapters were based on the HIE. This wide dissemination in academic outlets resulted in the HIE results attaining an extraordinarily high profile in the academic world. Brandon (1995) notes that the paper in which the findings from the HIE on the effect of cost sharing on use of medical services were first reported, Newhouse et al. 1981, has been cited 171 times in the scientific literature and 248 times in the social sciences literature. The paper in which the findings about the effect of cost sharing on health outcomes were first reported, Brook et al. 1983, has been cited 151 times in the scientific literature and 181 times in the social sciences literature.

Dissemination to the policy community occurred through several means in addition to the academic outlets described above. The sponsoring agency (initially OEO and later DHEW) received regular reports during the time that the experiment was actually being conducted. These reports were generally accompanied by a briefing within the sponsoring agency. In addition, results of the experiment were presented in congressional testimony. Finally, when major articles based on the HIE appeared, a press release was typically prepared and a briefing held for HHS and congressional staff.

Generalizability

As noted above, the HIE was set up as a response-surface experiment. Although this might have reduced relevance, particularly in the short run, it potentially increased generalizability by enabling analysts to estimate demand elasticity parameters. Those parameter estimates could then be incorporated into microsimulation models used to predict the impacts of health insurance plans other than those that were actually included in the experiment.

However, there are several potential challenges to the generalizability of the HIE. Perhaps the most obvious is the representativeness of the six sites selected. The sites were not randomly selected; rather they were a purposive sample that, as noted above, were chosen to be representative in a variety of dimensions. The results did not differ among the six sites in which the HIE was fielded. Moreover, the characteristics of the experiment's sample were similar to national averages (Newhouse and the Insurance Experiment Group 1993, 367). A second set of potential challenges to the generalizability of the HIE concerns changes in the health care system that occurred since 1974–82 (when the HIE was conducted). Perhaps the strongest potential challenge to the generalizability of the HIE stems from its relatively small scale. The HIE did not provide health insurance to a substantial portion of the population in any of the experimental sites. Indeed, in the site with the highest proportion of the population enrolled, less than two percent of the population was enrolled in the HIE (369). Making one of the HIE plans universal might have several effects that would reduce the validity of the HIE results, including the greater (or lesser) importance of nonprice rationing and increased physician-induced demand.

Definitiveness

There was relatively little controversy on the findings of the HIE. The results on the effects of cost sharing on the use of services were rarely challenged. The primary challenge was based on the generalizability of the results, as discussed above. Ironically, the fact that NHI no longer occupied a prominent place on the policy agenda by the time the HIE was completed might have contributed to the definitiveness of the results. Neuberg (1995, 893) suggests that this enabled the RAND researchers "to finish the work in political tranquility."

The results on the effects of cost sharing on health outcomes generated somewhat more controversy. The prevailing interpretation of the HIE results is that, with some relatively narrow exceptions, the health risks of cost sharing are minimal (Newhouse and the Insurance Experiment Group 1993, 339). However, critics, such as David Mechanic, a noted health sociologist, argued that this prevailing interpretation pays too little attention to results that showed that "decreased utilization from cost sharing affects to a similar degree both the use of appropriate or highly effective care and that of inappropriate or rarely effective care" (Rasell 1995, 1165; also see Eden 1994; Mechanic 1993, 99). These results, critics argue, suggest a contradiction. It seems inevitable that reduction in the use of necessary and effective care would have harmful effects on health status. They argued that cost sharing would, in fact, present more substantial risks to health status than the HIE results indicate, but that because of factors such as small sample size and insensitive measures of health status, these were not detected by the experiment. These criticisms, however, were not widely voiced.

Ideology, Interests, and Other Information in the Policy Environment

At the time that planning for the HIE began, a major concern was increasing access to medical care. Many viewed this as the logical outgrowth of the rapid expansion of private health insurance during the 1940s and 1950s and the enactment of Medicare and Medicaid in 1965. As noted above, numerous proposals for national health insurance were introduced in the early to mid-1970s. In addition, of course, President Clinton introduced an ambitious health plan early in his first term. Yet none of these proposals were enacted. Consistent with Weiss's I-I-I framework, this lack of action, however, can be traced more to ideology, interests, and other information than the information provided by the HIE.

Interests have played a significant role in the absence of major changes in health care financing over the past three decades. Aaron (1991, 2) suggests that, in the 1970s and early 1980s, major interest groups (business, organized labor, physicians, hospitals, suppliers of pharmaceuticals and medical equipment, insurance companies, and the insured) "all were more or less satisfied with the status quo." Although this might have changed during the late 1980s and early 1990s, major reform proposals generally failed to satisfy the self-interests of all or even a majority of major interest groups. As Atul Gawande, a Clinton health advisor, noted in a memorandum written immediately following Clinton's election:

> Getting health reform passed will be enormously difficult. We are at great risk of defeat. As you know, health reform involves restructuring spending in a sector that occupies 15 percent of our economy. We will have to take on extremely powerful and entrenched interests, and navigate through a deeply divided Congress (and that's just Democrats) (Johnson and Broder 1996, 94).

Ideology has also played a significant role in decisions about health care financing. During the 1970s, liberals frequently advocated national health insurance on the basis of "rights," at the same time conservatives frequently employed Cold War–type labels in opposing certain proposals. Hacker (1997, 167) contends that "the first and most obvious reason [that the Clinton health plan was centered around 'managed competition' rather than 'play-or-pay'] was ideological. Clinton was . . . a New Democrat who had cast off the philosophical shackles of his old-style 'tax-and-spend' brethren." Opposition to the Clinton health plan also was strongly rooted in ideology. Arguments raised by opponents of the Clinton health plan centered around the themes of the related threats of expanding bureaucracies, "government-run medicine," limiting consumer choice, and interfering in doctor-patient relationships (see Johnson and Broder 1996, 191; U.S. Congress, Congressional Budget Office [CBO] 1993).

NOTES

1. The coinsurance rate represents the fraction of charges paid by the participant. The maximum dollar expenditure represents an upper limit on family out-of-pocket expenditures during a given year.

2. The "Medicaid notch" referred to the fact that households that qualified for means-tested cash assistance also qualified for Medicaid, but that if their earnings went above the eligibility line for cash assistance, they also lost their Medicaid benefits.

3. Unless otherwise noted, information about the AHSIM model is drawn from an interview with a key figure at AHCPR.

5

The Nursing Home Incentive Reimbursement Experiment

In the early 1980s, there was concern over both Medicaid costs and the growing need for, but limited access to, skilled nursing facilities for those patients receiving Medicaid coverage and requiring long-term care. A U.S. Government Accounting Office (GAO) report (1983) to the Subcommittee on Health and the Environment of the House Committee on Energy and Commerce noted that there were "gaps in basic data on program differences across the States, the use of and need for services nationally, and the actual number of hospitalized patients awaiting nursing home beds . . . [which] . . . undermine[d] efforts to predict the effects of policy changes on Medicaid expenditures and on the provision of nursing home care to the Nation's elderly." In response, the National Center for Health Services Research and Health Care Technology Assessment (NCHSR)[1] of the Public Health Service initiated the Long-Term Care Studies Program. As part of that program, NCHSR helped fund a social experiment, the Nursing Home Incentive Reimbursement Experiment.

The purpose of the experiment was to test the use of bonuses as incentives to change nursing home behavior in three areas: admission of patients requiring heavy care, improvement in patient health outcomes, and discharges of patients to lower-cost facilities. There had been reluctance at the state level to undertake programs that incorporated economic incentives because of concern that such programs would increase costs without necessarily engendering offsetting benefits (Thorburn and Meiners 1986, 4). The experiment was designed, in part, to determine whether this reluctance was well placed.

Because costs were rising for medical care in general and for skilled nursing facilities in particular, cost containment concerns in the states led to ceilings on the amount of Medicaid paid to facilities. The ceilings on reimbursement for the care of a patient affected the case mix at nursing homes; heavy care patients required more costly treatments. Thus, nursing homes, facing a ceiling on their income, preferred to take in patients requiring less care who were less costly to maintain. Those nursing homes also had little motivation to discharge patients who were less expensive to care for in favor of those needing more care, again for reasons of cost. To offset such behavior on the part of nursing homes, a few states had tried schemes that paid differing amounts of reimbursement for different levels of care. However, there was a lack of evidence about the effectiveness of such incentive systems. The Nursing Home Incentive Reimbursement Experiment was designed to address that issue.

This chapter will describe the experiment's characteristics and findings, examine its origins, and provide an analysis of the utilization of findings from the experiment.

Description

The National Center for Health Services Research and Health Care Technology Assessment, a department of the Public Health Service, sponsored the Nursing Home Incentive Reimbursement Experiment in cooperation with the Health Care Financing Administration. The research sample for the experiment was 36 proprietary, Medicaid-certified nursing homes in San Diego County. The experiment was run during the early 1980s.

The treatment tested by the experiment was intended to improve the access of Medicaid patients to long-term care and to improve their health without increasing overall health costs. The tested treatment consisted of a reimbursement incentive program designed to encourage skilled nursing facilities to achieve the following specific goals:

- To encourage nursing homes to admit highly dependent Medicaid residents who might otherwise be hospitalized inappropriately;

- To improve the nature of the care provided by the nursing home by setting target outcome goals for specific patients and by establishing formal treatment plans for achieving these goals; and
- To encourage more appropriate discharges by encouraging institutions to provide case-management services and by paying additional sums in situations in which discharge resulted from improved care (Jones and Meiners 1986, 2).

The 36 nursing homes had a combined Medicaid clientele of 3,600 residents. Beginning in November 1980, and for the next six months, baseline data were collected on the patients and the nursing homes. Then the nursing homes were randomly assigned to either the treatment group or a control group. For the next two years, the nursing homes assigned to the treatment group were eligible for incentive payments if they met certain conditions described below. The control group nursing homes proceeded, as before, without benefit of incentive bonuses. At the treatment group nursing homes, an outside contractor performed staff training, data collection, authorization of incentive payments, and supervision of the experiment. Both groups of nursing homes remained responsible for all decisions involving admissions, care, assessment, and discharges.

The Incentive Scheme

The incentive payments had the following four characteristics:

- *Admission incentive payments* were made on the basis of a classification of residents system, which awarded larger payments for patients requiring greater care.
- *Outcome incentive payments* were made for patients who achieved previously approved health care goals.
- *Discharge incentive payments* were made for residents who were discharged and remained at a lower, less costly level of care for 90 days.
- The incentive payments were in addition to regular Medicaid reimbursements that were made to the nursing homes.

At the time the experiment was initiated, Medicaid reimbursement rates were typically flat daily rates for all patients, regardless of each patient's needs or the costs they engendered. The admission incentive payments were designed to compensate for the extra time required for heavy care patients. They were calculated using mean times for each required activity, which were obtained from the baseline data collected for the experiment, and a wage, which was computed using a weighted mean of the skills required for the service to be delivered. Each patient was classified into one of five levels on the basis of the type of nursing care needed (Types A through E). Incentives were then based on the marginal cost for each level of care relative to that required for the third level (Type C), allowing for a 5 percent profit (Meiners et al. 1985, 13). The profit component was adopted to provide an incentive for the additional staffing and management activities required by the experimental treatment (Weissert et al. 1983, 45). Type A patients were predicted to stay in the nursing homes less than the required 90 days and thus were ignored for purposes of computing admission incentive payments. Types D and E patients were judged to require heavy care. Thus, incentive payments were received for caring for such patients. As Type B patients were assumed to need no special nursing care, dollars were subtracted from the positive payments made for Types D and E "to offset the implicit overpayment in the actual Medicaid payment rate and to balance the incentive system" (Meiners et al. 1985, 6–7). The facility received the admission incentive fee only if a patient's condition improved. If the patient deteriorated, his or her original classification type held and the facility did not receive the admission incentive payment.

The outcome incentive payment also was based on a composite of the skills required to deliver the needed services and the time required to accomplish the outcome goals. The payment rates were adjusted upward to compensate for the error rate (50 percent[2]) anticipated in predicting how successful patients would be in attaining the outcomes projected for them. Facilities dedicated staff and time to attaining outcome goals, impeded by the somewhat vague criteria and diagnoses that were used for assigning specific goals to patients.

The discharge incentive payment was based on vacant bed costs and staff efforts to plan, coordinate, and follow up discharges. Differing rates were established based on a facility's number of beds, using Medicaid bed rates that were in effect at the start of the study. The payment covered up to a maximum of 10 days for a vacant bed after discharge and up to a maximum of 40 hours for staff time.

Two design issues about the reimbursement determinations were raised after the fact. First there was almost a 50 percent error rate in determining who should be classified as a Type A patient and thus excluded from the incentive plan. Second, the complexity of trying to reimburse on the basis of patient-specific, case-mix characteristics led to incorrect assumptions as a result of less homogeneity in patient characteristics than was ideal for administering the rate structure (Meiners et al. 1985, 14).

As just seen, the treatment tested by the experiment was separate incentives that were intended to encourage three distinct outcomes: (1) more admission of heavy care patients; (2) improved patient health status; and (3) patient discharge to lower-cost care. This, in turn, generated three distinct sets of research hypothesis that were tested through the experiment. These hypotheses are briefly discussed next.

Admissions

The research hypotheses for the admissions component of the experiment were

- A higher proportion of severely dependent patients will be admitted to treatment group homes compared with control group homes.
- The average hospital length of stay of geriatric patients with specified conditions will decline over time in the study area.
- Costs of admission payments, their administration, and patient assessments associated with them will be offset through reduced medical or Medi-Cal[3] hospital payments (Weissert et al. 1983, 44).

Taken together, the hypotheses imply that encouraging nursing home facilities to admit patients who no longer needed hospital care would reduce hospital length of stay. The hypotheses further imply that the amount saved as a result of these shorter hospital stays would exceed the incentive payments and incentive costs, thereby generating net cost savings for taxpayers.

Patient Health Status

The hope was that the health status of patients in nursing homes would improve because, as a result of the incentives, they would be more likely to receive necessary care than to be warehoused. Thus, the research hypothesis for the outcomes portion of the experiment was this: "Among residents in the home when the study begins and among newly admitted residents, a lower rate of deterioration will be experienced over time in physical and mental functioning and contentment, both in cross-sectional comparison of treatment with control group patients, and in time-series analysis of the treatment group alone" (Weissert et al. 1983, 44).

Discharge Rates

Under the existing system, nursing facilities had little motivation to discharge less dependent patients in favor of more dependent patients. Thus, the discharge component of the experiment used economic incentives to encourage nursing homes to move patients to lower, less expensive levels of care. A further hope was that by freeing up beds, the discharge part of the experiment would facilitate the admission of more severely dependent patients. Two research hypotheses were tested in the discharge component of the evaluation:

- The length of nursing home stay among certain minimally disabled patients . . . who are admitted during the study will be shorter in the treatment group than in the control group.
- Costs of the discharge incentive payments, their administration and patient assessments associated with them . . . will be offset through reduced Medi-Cal or Medicare hospital payments (Weissert et al. 1983, 44).

Origins of the Experiment

In the 1980s, the National Center for Health Services Research and Health Care Technology Assessment (NCHSR) undertook a research program to examine the problems that arise in providing care for the chronically ill and the policy issues that surround provision of this care, particularly in nursing homes. Those problems were becoming increasingly serious for several related reasons. Because of technological improvements in medical care, life expectancy was increasing. Consequently, there was a corresponding increase in the incidence of chronic diseases. At this time, however, the reimbursements received by for-profit nursing homes for private patients were higher than those for Medicaid patients. Moreover, such facilities were not motivated to provide care for heavily dependent Medicaid patients, as the cost of caring for such persons exceeded the reimbursement rate. Thus, nursing home access was an issue for Medicaid patients requiring heavy care. Nursing homes also had little incentive to provide more than as little care as possible because doing so would simply reduce their profits. In addition, states were facing rising costs for Medicaid and wished to cap expenses and so, through regulation, limited the number of nursing home beds available. With an insufficient supply of beds for Medicaid patients and the reluctance of nursing homes to admit Medicaid patients needing heavy care, such patients had to seek care in hospitals. As hospitals that specialize in acute care are more costly than nursing facilities, the result was inefficient utilization of existing facilities for the chronically ill (Norton 1992, 106).

The Nursing Home Incentive Reimbursement Experiment addressed those concerns by testing alternatives to the system in use in the early 1980s. "The point of the experiment was to encourage facilities to do things they were not previously doing" (Thorburn and Meiners 1986, 10) to improve the quality and "appropriateness of nursing home care" (Meiners et al. 1985, 5). Thorburn and Meiners suggest that the experiment could provide information on the following issues:

- the size and sources of expenditures for long-term care,
- the feasibility of alternative financing and reimbursement strategies,
- the cost and economic implications of informal support systems, and
- the economic and social implications of alternative health care and living arrangements (1986, 2).

The experiment was designed to test the proposition that the structuring of reimbursement could affect the quality of care by rewarding positive outcomes. "The underlying premise of the experiment was that reimbursement or financial incentives were sufficient tools to facilitate improved patient care" (Thorburn and Meiners 1986, 10). These financial incentives were seen as an alternative to regulatory activity. In keeping with this, Weissert, who designed the experiment, wanted to test the hypothesis that while others thought nursing home operators were "bad people," the operators were only doing what they were paid to do. If the incentive payments rewarded alternative behavior, that behavior would change (telephone interview, May 2, 1996).

In certain respects, the decision to undertake the Nursing Home Incentive Reimbursement Experiment appears consistent with the rational model described in chapter 3. Based on the published and spoken comments of those involved in the research, the experiment was a rational response to the perceived need by the Health Care Financing Administration (HCFA) to seek out information with which to make policy decisions. HCFA joined forces with NCHSR to promote research activities that would help "construct a model . . . of the long-term health care delivery, reimbursement, and financing systems to provide . . . direction for . . . public policy making" (Hamm, Kickham, and Cutler 1985, 170). The experiment was one of those activities. It was conducted in an atmosphere that increasingly accorded importance to research in health policy (Fox 1990, 484). The rational model predicts this approach to decisionmaking. Additionally, according to Mark Meiners, the Nursing Home Incentive Reimbursement Experiment was initiated in 1980 because "back then the sense was that experimentation is a better way to go" (telephone interview, March 5, 1996). Meiners echoes the sentiments of others involved in social experimentation.[4]

Although in certain respects initiating the nursing home experiment is consistent with the rational model, a better case can be made that the primary motivation was, as Feldman suggests, creating an inventory of information. The motivation for NCHSR's existence was to build such an inventory and to suggest ways in which policy could be improved by the information such an inventory provided. Rather than a specific policy proposal fueling a specific experiment, the agency and HCFA set up a series of investigations to "present information useful to those making administrative or policy decisions on matters related to long-term care or the general problem of health care for the elderly" (Jones and Meiners 1986, 2). Thus, the work of NCHSR and HCFA, including their sponsorship of the Nursing Home Incentive Reimbursement Experiment, is best viewed as building an inventory of information in the hope that it will eventually support decisionmaking.

Design Issues

Choice of Location

Several issues affected the site selection. First, researchers thought that the experiment should be conducted in a small enough area for factors affecting internal validity to be uniform. As the San Diego Standard Metropolitan Statistical Area (SMSA) was located entirely in one state,

state policies affecting health care would be constant. Second, there were no other SMSAs within easy driving distance of the San Diego SMSA. Thus, there were no available nursing facilities, other than those in the experiment; that fact ensured "a clear focus on the local health facility industry" (Meiners et al. 1985, 6). Third, the California Department of Health Services and the California Association of Health Facilities were interested in the study and supportive of its implementation. At a more personal level, William Weissert, who had the major responsibility at NCHSR for implementing the experiment, indicated in an interview that about half a dozen cities met his criteria. Finally the choice came down to Baltimore and San Diego. As he lived near Baltimore, Weissert thought that San Diego would be a more interesting place in which to spend time (telephone interview, May 2, 1996).

Target Group of Interest

The unit of analysis used in the experiment was for-profit nursing homes, which make up the majority of nursing facilities that admitted Medicaid patients.[5] The assumption was that such facilities were more likely to respond to economic incentives than were nonprofit nursing homes. Only facilities that were classified as skilled nursing facilities (SNF) and admitted Medicaid (Medi-Cal) patients were considered. A key motivation for conducting the experiment was to determine if financial incentives could result in Medicaid savings.

Mark Meiners, one of the evaluators of the experiment, felt that the design of the admissions component of the experiment would have been improved had more effort been made to target heavy care patients (telephone interview, March 5, 1996). In his view, too few such patients were identified for the effect of incentive payments on admitting heavy care patients to be detectable.

Outcome goals were established for patients upon admission once the level of care that they needed was determined.[6] Because there is "no consensus as to what quality care is or should be" (Thorburn and Meiners 1986, 4), the focus of the evaluation was on determining whether the economic incentives provided by the experimental treatment affected the accomplishment of the goals. Thus, 90 days after the outcome goals were established the patient's condition was assessed to determine whether the goals had been met and an incentive payment to the facility should be made. For purposes of the evaluation, patients at the control facilities were also assigned goals and assessed at the end of 90 days to learn if their goals were attained. No incentive payments were made to the control facilities, however.

The discharge component of the experiment focused on two types of patients: those who needed "moderate to heavy" care and who would require residence in a nursing home for more than 90 days; and those who met Medicaid criteria for discharge, but who had other barriers (e.g., psychological or financial) to their placement in a lower-level-of-care situation.

Period of Treatment

The incentive payments were offered for two years, following a six-month period during which baseline data were collected on the nursing homes and their patients. Although this may have seemed like a long time frame, it may not, in fact, have been long enough to allow the nursing homes in the treatment group to fully implement necessary changes in their procedures, staffing, and organization. According to Meiners, the facilities "didn't seem to gear up and take the incentive system seriously" (telephone interview, March 5, 1996). For example, "Only half of the experimental facilities prepared discharge plans" (Jones and Meiners 1986, 7). The patient care requirements were also a barrier to participation by the nursing facilities in the discharge incentive component of the experiment. The experimenters attribute this to "the reluctance of the facility staff to set a goal which might not be achieved, to the resistance of some staff members to complete the required paperwork, and to the perception of the facility staff that the process was too complex" (10).

Because of the limited duration of the experiment, there were few opportunities to make the sorts of adjustments that occur in ongoing, fully implemented programs. As some of the subgroups of patients assigned to various outcome goals were small, a longer treatment period also would have increased the sample sizes used in making comparisons between the treatment and the control facilities.

Barriers to Participation: Voluntariness

Of the 41 proprietary nursing homes in San Diego County that were eligible for the experiment, only 36 chose to participate. The experimental incentive payments were based on only those Medicaid patients who were expected to stay in one of the participating nursing homes for at least 90 days. Shorter-term patients were excluded because nursing home access was not a problem for them. Moreover, they did not fit the chronic care pattern that the experimental treatment was designed to modify. They also did not need special intervention for early discharge.

Patients who were already in residence at the control facilities at the time the experiment was initiated were excluded from the outcome component of the experiment. Only those admitted during the treatment period were eligible. At the treatment facilities, in contrast, patients who were admitted to the facilities before the beginning of the experiment were eligible to participate in the outcomes portion of the experiment. The nursing home staff determined who could participate in the discharge component of the experiment. Potentially eligible patients included both persons who already resided at the facilities at the beginning of the experiment and persons admitted during the first year of treatment (May 1981 through April 1982).

Consent for participation was required, either from the patients themselves or from their legal guardians. Because of this requirement, 34 percent of the Medicaid patients at the treatment facilities and 37 percent of the Medicaid patients at the control facilities were eliminated from the sample used in the analysis (Thorburn and Meiners 1986). The evaluators did not indicate whether they thought that this resulted in any bias.

Participation in the outcomes and discharge components of the experiment was further complicated by a requirement that patients first be nominated to participate by the nursing homes and then be approved and followed by nurses on the research team. Both stages of this process required an assessment of how well a patient met the eligibility criteria and of whether there was a reasonable probability that the patient would attain his or her outcome goal or be discharged and then assigned to a lower-level care facility. When patients were admitted, assessment of the level of care needed was also based on the judgment of the research nurses. Disagreements did occur among the nurses, but data were not maintained on their frequency.

Private-Pay Patients

Because Medicaid patients account for only a portion of the supply side of the market, incentives provided under Medicaid could be offset by responses by private-pay patients:

If there is an abundance of private-pay patients willing and able to pay a premium for access to the limited supply of nursing home beds, incentive reimbursement can only be expected to increase access for heavy care, public-pay patients if they produce competitive profits. . . . "The reimbursement rates for heavy care, public-pay patients must reflect the profit opportunities in the private-pay market." (Meiners et al. 1985, 14–15)

The evaluators noted that because of the dearth of data on private-pay patients it was not obvious where reimbursement incentives to encourage utilization of nursing homes by Medicaid patients should be set.

Summary of Findings

The experimental results do not make a strong case either for or against nursing home incentive payments. Neither the health outcomes nor the discharge incentive payments had statistically significant effects. Only the admissions incentive payments had a statistically significant impact; they apparently had the desired effect of increasing the admission of heavy care patients to nursing homes.

No statistically significant differences were found in patient outcomes between treatment and control facilities. That is, the lump sum incentive payments did not result in improved patient outcomes. One possible reason for this is that incentive payments did not increase the number of patients assigned to those goals that required the most intensive care services to attain. Indeed, experimental facilities nominated fewer patients for such goals than did control facilities.

The results suggest that the discharge incentive payment was inadequate to "encourage the experimental facilities to identify their patients for possible discharge, but that the incentive payment did increase the likelihood of the experimental facilities following through on placing appropriate discharge candidates in a lower level of care" (Jones and Meiners 1986, 6). In other words, only a few facilities were motivated by the incentive payments to put extra efforts into discharge work and follow-up, but these nursing homes had a "reasonably good expectation of success" (9).

The experiment resulted in statistically significant effects on admissions: heavy care patients in the Type E group were admitted in greater numbers than would have been the case in the absence of incentives; and fewer of the lowest cost, long-staying patients were admitted. How-

Each group should also prepare a 2 page maximum Summary Memorandum with answers to the questions above.

Group Assignments

Wednesday Nov. 12:

Health Insurance Experiment (Chap. 4)—Groups 1 & 2

Nursing Home Reimbursement Experiment (Chap. 5)—Groups 3 & 4

Friday Nov. 14:

Unemployment Insurance Bonus Experiment (Chap. 7)—Groups 5 & 6

Welfare to Work Experiments (Chap. 8)—Groups 7 & 8

Social Experimentation and Public Policymaking by D. Greenberg et al. explores the relatively new practice of gathering the data necessary for rational policymaking from designed and controlled social experiments. In class we will examine the practice in general terms (Ch. 1-3) and I will go over the first major experiment of this type ever undertaken—the income maintenance experiments (Ch. 6). I have divided the remaining experiments discussed in the book among the policy groups and each group should be prepared to present to the class their analysis of the following questions. You should plan on a presentation of no more than 20 minutes. As before not all groups will present in class but each group should be prepared to do so. (If you don't present you can keep the group that also does "your" experiment honest with your insightful questions!)

Audience: Policy Makers responsible for decisions in your policy area

Content:

1.   What is the policy being tested?
2.   What are the specific questions being addressed?
3.   How is the experiment structured?
4.   What are the results?

ever, providing incentive payments to encourage admission of Type D patients did not have a statistically significant effect. Only a small portion of eligible facilities responded to the incentive plan, and the response was modest among these facilities. Thus, the results were positive for the admissions incentive program, but success was limited to the relatively small number of patients who were in the heaviest care group.

Policy Effects of Experiments—Typology of Research Use

For reasons discussed later, an examination of documents, hearings, interviews, and the mailed survey suggests that use of findings from the nursing home incentive experiment was minimal. Consequently, as shown immediately below, examples could be found for only three of the eight cells in the typology and then there is only one entry in each cell:

	Concrete	Conceptual
Formative		
Elaborative	0	1
Substantive	1	1
Persuasive/Advocacy		
Elaborative	0	0
Substantive	0	0

Formative-Concrete-Substantive

This cell pertains to examples of use in which research findings are used to make specific policy decisions at the core of policy. According to William Weissert, the NCHSR official who designed and implemented the experiment, the State of Maryland wished to adopt an incentive system for nursing homes in the early 1980s. The state hired Applied Management Science, the firm that was Weissert's contractor in the San Diego experiment, and this firm used the scheme they had designed for the experiment as the basis for the incentive plan implemented in Maryland.[7]

One possible reason that only one example of concrete use of findings from the San Diego experiment could be found is that federal legislation has impeded the adoption of incentive reimbursement plans for nursing homes (Burman 1994). The Boren Amendment to the Social Security

Act requires that Medicaid reimbursements use a cost method but allows states "freedom in developing and implementing reimbursement methodologies that would promote an efficient and economical delivery of hospital and nursing facility services" (60). This legislation would appear to encourage implementing bonuses, but in practice it resulted in considerable litigation by providers who have challenged state methodologies for calculating reimbursements. This, in turn, discouraged states from adopting bonus schemes. Thus, its effect has been exactly the opposite of its intent.

Formative-Conceptual-Elaborative

This category covers use in which the opinions and views of policymakers are influenced or the policy community enlightened, but at the periphery, rather than at the core. Both William Weissert and Mark Meiners, the researchers on the project, believe that the findings influenced subsequent research.[8] The experiment preceded HCFA's implementation of resource utilization groups. These groups categorize patients according to the level of care they need and determine adjusted levels of reimbursement by case mix. Meiners claims that the resource utilization group demonstrations that HCFA ran in the late 1980s were stimulated by the San Diego experiment (telephone interview, March 5, 1996). It is a matter of conjecture whether these approaches to nursing home care were directly influenced by the San Diego Experiment or were merely part of the same policy environment that motivated conducting the experiment. At best, the effect of the experiment was to contribute to the discussion.

Formative-Conceptual-Substantive

This cell pertains to examples of use that influence the policy environment and policymakers' opinions or views on the basic outline of specific policies. In our survey, only Wisconsin indicated that it has a bonus system for admitting patients who require above average care *and* that it had considered the San Diego results in devising its system. Wisconsin respondents did not indicate, however, that these results actually influenced the design of Wisconsin's system. A number of other states have rate systems that could technically be called bonuses for admitting heavy care patients or for higher levels of care: Alabama,

Delaware, Maine, Maryland, New York, Oregon,[9] Pennsylvania, Texas, Utah, and West Virginia. None of the Medicaid directors that we surveyed in these states, however, had previously heard of the San Diego experiment.

Utilization Factors

The conceptual framework proposed in chapter 3 contains two sets of factors that affect the type and amount of influence that the results of social experiments have on policy deliberations. The first set pertains to the characteristics of the research itself and the second to the characteristics of the policy environment.

Definitiveness

The San Diego experiment was conducted in an era when "the sense was" that experimentation was "a better way to go" (telephone interview, Mark Meiners, March 5, 1996). However, relative to the other social experiments examined in this book, the nursing home experiment was small. In addition, unlike the income maintenance, welfare-to-work, and UI bonus experiments, there was no replication. Moreover, the results were not conclusive. Or, as Meiners said, not "super-wow in terms of changing the world." The findings neither threatened other interests nor were they counterintuitive. They just were not notable enough to stimulate state Medicaid directors to agitate for change.

When interviewed, however, Weissert argued that this is attributable to a simplistic analysis of the data that did not lead to conclusive results. And, in fact, when Norton (1992) later conducted a reanalysis of the data, he obtained more positive findings. It is impossible to say whether the results would have gotten more use if they had been more conclusive. There were other factors that militated against use as discussed below. Moreover, Norton's findings appear to have received little notice.

Timeliness

Use of results from the San Diego Experiment may have been overshadowed by other policy concerns. When the experimental findings became available in the mid-1980s, welfare reform issues dominated the federal policy agenda. Proponents of health care reform did not expend much political capital on long-term care. Moreover, to the extent health issues were considered, home health care options were the mode of choice for reforming long-term care. The major policy goals were to control costs by keeping nursing home enrollments down, provide standards for long-term care, and encourage people to obtain private insurance. Thus increasing Medicaid expenditures on nursing homes through incentive payments was an unlikely policy option. Instead, Prospective Payment Systems (PPS), a program where an attempt is made to base payments on projections of actual costs, became Congress' preferred method for reimbursement of nursing homes (U.S. Congress, House Ways and Means Committee 1993).

At the state level, the major policy shift in the mid-1980s was in the direction of case-mix systems (Swan et al. 1993), not toward further reimbursement of nursing homes. Although the goals of a case-mix system would appear to be addressed by findings from an experiment for admission of heavy care patients, the plans actually adopted relied on regulation, not economic incentives, to accomplish their objectives. Similarly, concern with patient outcomes, another issue that was addressed by the experiment, was not dealt with through incentives, but by regulation in the Nursing Home Reform Act of the Omnibus Budget Reconciliation Act of 1987 (U.S. Congress House Select Committee on Aging 1986; U.S. Congress Senate Finance Committee 1987, 1990).

Weissert claims that the story on the results of the experiment is not over (telephone interview, May 2, 1996). He believes that the experiment was "ahead of the curve." The policy environment was not ready at the time. Needs assessment of patients was not done until 1987, and not every state has mandated case-mix systems, which are an expensive innovation that ultimately may meet with political resistance.

Communication and Visibility

Journal articles are one means of affecting the policy universe. They enlighten the policy community and sometimes suggest solutions to policy issues. One example is Edward Norton's reanalysis of the results of the San Diego experiment, which is mentioned above. Norton reported his findings in a 1992 article in the *Journal of Health Economics* in which he attempted (so far unsuccessfully) to influence consideration of bonuses as a method of addressing health costs.

Rosko, Broyles, and Aaronson (1987) examined existing policy options for addressing issues arising in the nursing home industry, and they used the San Diego experiment as an example of one possible option. In contrast to Norton, they asserted that the incentive scheme tested in the San Diego experiment "failed to exert a significant effect" (695).

Other articles have also either focused on or mentioned the San Diego experiment:

Three NCHSR reports: *Nursing Home Discharges: The Results of an Incentive Reimbursement Experiment; Nursing Home Admissions: The Results of an Incentive Reimbursement Experiment;* and *Nursing Home Patient Outcomes: The Results of an Incentive Reimbursement Experiment.*

"Case Mix Reimbursement for Nursing Homes," by Robert Schlenker, in the *Journal of Health Politics, Policy and Law.*

"Care for the Chronically Ill: Nursing Home Incentive Payment Experiment," by William Weissert et al., in *Health Care Financing Review.*

"Comparing Case-Mix Systems for Nursing Home Payment," by Brant Fries, in *Health Care Financing Review.*

"Nursing Home Resident Assessment and Case-Mix Classification: Cross-National Perspectives," by Clauser and Fries in *Health Care Financing Review.*

Long-Term Care: Principles, Programs, and Policies, by Kane and Kane, under access issues.

Long-Term Care, Perspectives from Research and Demonstrations, chapter XVIII, by Cotterill (edited by Vogel and Palmer).

"Case-Mix Payment for Nursing Home Care: Lessons from Maryland," by Feder and Scanlon in the *Journal of Health Politics, Policy and Law.*

The authors of these articles suggest that the findings on using incentives to affect the admission of patients needing heavy care support the need for a case-mix approach to nursing home care for Medicaid patients. Except for the articles from NCHSR and the one by Weissert et al., however, these articles merely mention the San Diego experiment as one of a number of research projects that have addressed long-term care issues. Moreover, most of the articles focus on relying on regulation, rather than on economic incentives, to affect the case mix.

When interviewed, both Weissert and Meiners indicated that the San Diego results were published by NCHSR as reports that have a short shelf life. After that, with the exception of the Weissert et al. article, there was little further effort to publicize these findings. Weissert hypothesized that those who remained at NCHSR did not have his enthusiasm for the experiment.[10] Thus, there was "no entrepreneurial work done"—that is, no one at NCHSR played the role of research broker (telephone interview, May 2, 1996).

Meiners indicated that findings from the experiment were sent to the states and to policymakers working on case-mix reimbursement issues. However, in the survey conducted for this research, Medicaid directors in only California, Indiana, Montana, Massachusetts, and Wisconsin indicated that they had heard of the experiment (and then only "vaguely"). Two respondents guessed that the sources of their information were probably the *Health Care Financing Review* or the *Journal of Health Economics*.[11] One respondent even indicated that he had asked around among his colleagues, and none of them had heard of the experiment either.

One additional source of published information should be noted. In 1985, a book was published, *Long-Term Care: Perspectives from Research and Demonstrations,* which described the study as under way. Actually it was completed by then, but the results were not yet available. One of the purposes of the book was to catalog pertinent research, mostly sponsored by HCFA, and list findings from that research that might be valuable in policy deliberations. However, the experiment was only one of many research projects listed and did not receive major emphasis.

To summarize, the nursing home experiment was invisible when compared with most of the other social experiments examined in this book. Its smaller scale, less than conclusive results, black box nature, loss of a research broker after Weissert left NCHSR, and lack of replication meant that it was little discussed in policy circles and resulted in little information being fed into the policy process.

Generalizability

As indicated in chapter 2, response surface experiments are fairly generalizable. However, the San Diego experiment was a black box experiment. Hence, strictly speaking, its results are limited to the treatment tested. There was no range of bonuses tested and no variety in qualifications for the bonuses. There was only one bonus level per qualifying condition. Thus, the results are difficult to apply to programs other than the specific one tested. Moreover, the small sample size used in the experiment may also have reduced its generalizability.

Weissert wondered whether confounding problems with the control group might also have affected the experiment's generalizability. The experiment was conducted countywide in a closed market. By paying some nursing homes (the treatment facilities) to admit heavy care patients, the experiment reduced social pressure on control group homes to make the "socially responsible choice" to admit that type of patient (telephone interview, May 2, 1996). Therefore, any measured difference between the two groups may have been inflated.

One of the NCHSR reports notes that because the experiment was short-term its generalizability may be threatened:

> The information flow generated by discussions among interest groups, in the mass media, and in specialized industry publications is much more limited than would occur if the change were permanent and widespread. An experiment that affects nursing home behavior for an entire year is viewed as a long-term commitment by the research organization. To the participants, however, it may seem of very brief duration and there may be reluctance to make staffing, policy, and organizational changes which could affect their environment long after the experiment is concluded. Also, there are few opportunities in an experiment to make small adjustments and to monitor the results, whereas repeated fine tuning of reimbursement formulas is always a possibility with ongoing programs. (Meiners et al. 1985, 5–6)

If the experiment had lasted five years, this would be a less valid criticism.

Relevance

Results must fit into the policy environment at the time they are available if the relevance condition is to be met. At the time findings from the Nursing Home Incentive Reimbursement Experiment became available, community-based health care and home health care, rather than long-term institutional care, were the major options being considered for reducing costs within overall health care reform. Consequently, using federal dollars for these purposes, rather than for increasing reimbursements to nursing homes, was the focus of congressional hearings. In a national survey of state Medicaid payment policies, the incentives policies that were listed dealt with efficiency measures, occupancy rates, quality-of-care measures, and AIDS care; but not with nursing home reimbursement (Buchanan, Madel, and Persons 1991). Although quality-of-care measures appear germane to patient outcomes, they really are applied more to inputs required for patient care such as licensing and certification than to outcomes.

The survey respondents indicated that many of the issues that were important to the designers of the experiment—for example, access to nursing home care for Medicaid patients, cost containment, incentives for providers who meet quality-of-care regulations, and adequate reimbursement for patients requiring a high level of care—were important to them as well.[12]

Ideology, Interests, and Other Information in the Policy Environment

Weiss's I-I-I scheme hypothesizes that new information will be used only if it is compatible with previously existing information on the issue and with the (self-) interest and ideology of the policymaker.

The nursing home experiment produced results about a treatment that was outside the mainstream of thought at the time. As Meiners indicated, "There was nothing out there before this experiment" (telephone interview, March 5, 1996). The information did not supplement an existing body of similar knowledge, adding to the information base, the way other social experiments did.

With anecdotal evidence backed up by an Institute of Medicine study on nursing home regulation (U.S. Congress, House Select Committee on Aging 1986), public sentiment (read "ideology") preferred government regulation of nursing homes to incentive systems. Indeed, when the White House proposed deregulating nursing homes, Congress blocked that effort. An emphasis on regulation, coupled with cost-containment concerns, was not conducive to adopting a policy (bonuses) that would have thrown more money at the problem of obtaining an appropriate case mix. Even Weissert suggested that a case-mix adjustment system would need to be implemented before bonuses could be adopted (telephone interview, May 2, 1996). In times when the added expense for bonuses goes against the dominant themes of deficit reduction and cost containment, ideology[13] and interest work against policymakers accepting such incentives. Although 19 states did implement some form of case-mix system (Buchanan et al. 1991), those systems tended to rely on regulations that required nursing homes to admit heavy care patients, thereby rendering the use of bonus incentives moot.[14] One survey respondent even indicated that because information about bonuses was not in his information base, he had to find other ways to solve the problems that the experiment addressed: "The industry is not really interested in the offer [of bonuses]."

Overall, it seems that the lack of awareness of the experiment, coupled with the absence of other information about incentive reimbursements and an ideological interest in decreasing government spending, worked together to prevent the introduction of nursing home bonus plans into public policy deliberations.

NOTES

1. Now called the Agency for Healthcare Research and Quality.

2. This figure came from an earlier study (Weissert et al. 1983, 48). Assessment teams, including a physician, predicted patient functioning at the end of three months after a thorough examination of patients by the team. The error rate in that prediction process was around 50 percent, about as effective as tossing a coin.

3. Medi-Cal is the name of California's Medicaid program.

4. For example, see comments of Robert Spiegelman and Steve Wandner on the unemployment insurance bonus experiments in chapter 7.

5. As indicated in chapter 2, this is unusual. In most social experiments, the unit of analysis is the individual or the family.

6. Nurses on the research team used the eligibility criteria for the activities of daily living (ADL) tasks in establishing outcome goals. The ADL criteria are widely used measures for evaluating a patient's functional status. They were useful for developing outcome goals because accomplishment of the ADL tasks marked success in reducing a patient's dependence.

7. Weissert himself only discovered this when he became engaged in conversation with state health officials after he spoke at a meeting at the University of Maryland at Baltimore.

8. Weissert now hypothesizes that in contrast to an unregulated environment, cost reimbursement is not feasible in a regulated environment because "you can't figure out marginal cost . . . in a regulated environment." He believes that it would be better for nursing homes to bid on patient care or for the government to set the level of reimbursement without regulating the number of beds. Then costs could be determined in a market environment. Weissert views the failure of the experiment to show significant impacts as a challenge to the notion of cost reimbursement (telephone interview, May 2, 1996).

9. Oregon conducted its own bonus demonstration in the late 1980s. The tested program offered bonuses for improved quality on certain indicators. It was discontinued as a result of budget cuts after it failed to demonstrate that the quality of care had been improved.

10. Weissert conceived, designed, and implemented the experiment but left NCHSR before the experiment was completed.

11. They show remarkable recall because articles mentioning the experiment were actually published in these two sources—one in 1983 and the other in 1992.

12. In fact, in at least one instance, the survey that we conducted may have served as an unintended communication tool. One respondent, while not having previously heard of the experiment, learned of it through the survey and indicated that its results were "relevant to the case mix reimbursement system we are now developing." The experiment was relevant in the sense that its results added to the tool kit of policymakers looking for alternatives to regulation. However, the mood of the times was toward further regulation.

13. Ideology may affect political interest. For example, decisionmakers who perceive that the mood of their constituency is against spending, an ideological concern, may decide that it is in their political best interest to move in that direction.

14. This conclusion was suggested by the survey of state nursing home administrators.

6

The Income Maintenance Experiments

The beginning of social experimentation in this country, as mentioned in chapter 2, is usually traced to the income maintenance experiments (IMEs). These experiments were initiated over a quarter of a century ago and most of the analysis of them was completed over a decade ago. Indeed, as a result, many of the individuals we interviewed had some difficulty in recalling details about them and their use in the policy process.

There were four IMEs in all: the New Jersey Income Maintenance Experiment, which took place in four small cities in New Jersey and a small city in Pennsylvania; the Rural Income Maintenance Experiment, which took place in a rural county in North Carolina and two rural counties in Iowa; the Gary (Indiana) Experiment; and the Seattle-Denver Income Maintenance (or SIME/DIME) Experiment.[1] Some major characteristics of each of the experiments are summarized in table 6.1.

The federal government sponsored all four of the IMEs. State and local governments did not play a major role in either launching or operating them. As table 6.1 indicates, the New Jersey and Rural Income Maintenance Experiments were initiated earlier and were somewhat smaller than the Gary Income Maintenance Experiment and much smaller than the Seattle-Denver Income Maintenance Experiment. The two earlier experiments were launched by the Office of Economic Opportunity (OEO), whereas the two later IMEs were initiated by the Office of the

Table 6.1. *Background Data on the Income Maintenance Experiments*

	New Jersey	Rural	Gary	Seattle-Denver
Sponsor	OEO	OEO	DHEW through the State of Indiana	DHEW through the states of Washington and Colorado
Locations	Trenton, Paterson, Passaic, and Jersey City, N.J.; and Scranton, Pa.	Dublin County, N.C.; and Pocahontas and Calhoun Counties, Iowa	Gary, Ind.	Seattle, Wash.; and Denver, Colo.
Period of fieldwork	1968–72	1969–73	1971–75	1971–78[a]
Experiment duration (years)	3	3	3	3 (71%), 5 (25%), and 20 (4%)
Final report issued	1973	1976	1980	1983
Principal contractors	IRP and MPR	IRP	Indiana University and MPR	SRI and MPR
Sample size (families)	1,357	809	1,799	4,800
Control families	40%	54%	43%	43%
Sample racial/ethnic composition	black (37%) white (32%) Hispanic (31%)	black (35%) white (65%)	black (100%)	black (43%) white (39%) Hispanic (18%)

	Two-parent (100%)	Two-parent (85%) and single-parent (15%)	Two-parent (41%) and single-parent (59%)	Two-parent (61%) and single-parent (39%)
Family types studied				
Benefit levels tested (percent of FPL)	50, 75, 100, and 125	50, 75, and 100	77 and 101	90, 116, and 135
Tax rates tested (percent)	30, 50, and 70	30, 50, and 70	40 and 60	50, 70, and 80[b]
Income truncation (percent of FPL)	150	150	240[c]	325
Other treatments	None	None	Day care subsidies and social service referrals	Counseling and educational subsidies
Cost ($millions)	$8.4	$5.5	$20.3	$77.5

Source: General Accounting Office 1981.

Notes: DHEW = U.S. Department of Health, Education, and Welfare; FPL = federal poverty level; IRP = Institute for Research on Poverty; MPR = Mathematica Policy Research, Inc.; OEO = Office of Economic Opportunity; SRI = SRI International.

a. About 200 families were originally to receive experimental benefit payments through 1991. However, this portion of the sample was discontinued in 1980.

b. Experiment tested four tax rates: two constant rates, 50 and 70 percent; and two rates, 70 and 80 percent, which declined by 2.5 percent for each $1,000 of income.

c. A small fraction of the sample had incomes above this limit.

Assistant Secretary of Planning and Evaluation (OASPE) in the Department of Health, Education, and Welfare (DHEW),[2] now the Department of Health and Human Services.

All four of the income maintenance experiments (IMEs) were designed to test variants of the negative income tax program (NIT), a program that had been proposed as a replacement for the existing welfare system. Briefly, a negative income tax program would provide an income "guarantee," which would increase with family size, to a household that has no other source of income. Under the program, the household's income could not fall below the guarantee, but program benefits would be reduced by a predetermined fraction of each dollar of earnings or income from nonprogram sources that the household received. This fraction is called the "program benefit-reduction rate" or the "program tax rate." At the point at which nonprogram income times the program tax rate just equaled the guarantee, the "program breakeven point," the household would no longer qualify for NIT benefits. Thus, the higher the guarantee or the lower the tax rate, the higher the program breakeven point. As the breakeven rose, households with increasing amounts of nonprogram income qualified for program benefits. Consequently, the program breakeven was a key policy variable because it determined the number of households eligible for program benefits.

At the time the income maintenance experiments were initiated, the NIT had great appeal to many economists and policy analysts with a spectrum of political beliefs. For example, two economists who subsequently became Nobel Prize winners separately proposed an NIT: James Tobin (1965), a liberal, and Milton Friedman (1962), a conservative. In 1968, 1,200 economists signed a petition supporting an NIT.

Economists and other policy analysts believed that implementation of an NIT would allow the then-existing patchwork of inconsistent public assistance programs to be replaced by a single integrated system. Of particular interest to some economists, including Friedman, was the fact that recipients under the then-existing public assistance system faced extremely high benefit-reduction rates that were thought to discourage work effort. An NIT appeared to be as efficient a means as possible for redistributing income to and providing a safety net for the poor, while minimizing intrusion in existing markets. For example, it was hoped that reducing the benefit-reduction rate facing current public assistance recipients would encourage the recipients to work more. Moreover, many analysts thought, perhaps naively, that an NIT could be operated similarly to the positive tax system and possibly even be administered by the Internal Revenue Service, thereby allowing much of the elaborate and intrusive administrative apparatus associated with the welfare system to be dismantled. Finally, and perhaps most important to many economists such as Tobin, benefits would be determined solely on the basis of "need" (i.e., income). Thus, an NIT would provide for horizontal equity by allowing all households whose incomes fall below the program breakeven to participate. This contrasted with the welfare system at the time the IMEs began, a system in which very few two-parent households were eligible for benefits.[3] Indeed, most participants in the then-existing system, as today, were households headed by single mothers.

The notion of allowing all households whose income fell below the breakeven to participate was appealing on equity grounds. Moreover, by excluding most intact households, it was thought that the then-existing welfare system promoted family splitting and that an NIT would eliminate those incentives. However, the possibility of extending a guaranteed income to households headed by able-bodied males raised concern that many of those persons would reduce their hours of work and possibly withdraw from the workforce entirely. The IMEs were designed to test that possibility because they allowed the hours worked by fathers in families assigned to the experimental groups—and, hence, eligible to participate in one of the NIT plans being tested—to be compared with the hours worked by fathers in control families. In addition, the Gary experiment also tested day care subsidies and the Seattle-Denver experiment also tested education subsidies to see whether provision of the subsidies might partially mitigate any adverse effects on work incentives engendered by the NIT. Finally, the Seattle-Denver Income Maintenance Experiment also provided counseling for all those eligible for the education subsidies and for a randomly selected group of families who were not eligible for subsidies.

Why Were the Income Maintenance Experiments Undertaken?

Although it seemed to early supporters of the NIT concept that the major obstacle to adoption of the program was uncertainty about its effect on the work incentives of recipients in two-parent households, little information existed that could be used to make inferences about the size of the effects.[4] NIT supporters thought that the effects were likely to be small, but also believed that without credible evidence demonstrating that this was indeed the case, the political acceptance needed to implement the program was unlikely to be obtained.

Thus, it was thought that results from the IMEs about the effects of an NIT on work effort would influence the policy process. However, although the central experimental outcome of interest was the effect of NITs on hours worked, it was always anticipated that something would be learned from the IMEs about other issues of interest, such as the administrative feasibility of an NIT, the effects of an NIT on consumption and savings behavior, and the effects of an NIT on family stability. And indeed, as discussed later, findings from the IMEs did provide information about these additional issues. Nevertheless, the income maintenance experiments were not designed with the other issues in mind. The focus was always on the effects on the work effort of participants. As Michael Barth, an economist who joined OEO's research staff during the year between the time the New Jersey and the Rural Income Maintenance Experiments were launched, told us, if work effort had not been an issue, "the experiments would never have been done."[5]

Even though the IMEs were intended to influence the policy process, there is little evidence that at the time these experiments were launched much explicit consideration was given to precisely how this would occur. To see this, consider the four alternate explanations described in chapter 3 of the decision to conduct social experiments.

The first of these explanations is the variant of the rational paradigm that posits that research is undertaken to influence specific policy decisions. As discussed in chapter 3, this explanation requires an expectation that information from the experiment will be available before the policy decision that it is to influence is made. This condition was clearly not met by any of the four IMEs. In August 1969, President Nixon proposed his Family Assistance Program (FAP), the first major attempt to implement an NIT-like program. Although the New Jersey and Rural experiments were initiated before Nixon's FAP proposal, the later Gary and Seattle-Denver Income Maintenance Experiments were launched after FAP was proposed. None of the four experiments was completed before congressional consideration of the proposal. As will be described later, findings from the IMEs were available by the time welfare reform proposals subsequent to FAP were made, but those involved in initiating the experiments did not know, indeed could not know, when these proposals would be considered.

A second explanation of the reasons experiments are conducted is to create an inventory of information for future, but unspecified, policy-making situations. It was expected that each of the four IMEs would be expensive, costing in the millions of dollars.[6] It seems implausible that investments of this size would have been made for the mere possibility that the IMEs would be used. Moreover, as already pointed out, the expectation on the part of those who launched these experiments was that they would remove what they perceived as the major obstacle to adoption of an NIT: concern over the effects of such a program on work effort. Thus, the policymaking situation addressed by the IMEs was well specified.

A third explanation is that social experiments are conducted to substitute symbolic actions for difficult political decisions. Although that explanation may appeal to cynics, there is no evidence that it pertains to the IMEs. Those who initiated the experiments were enthusiastic about replacing the existing welfare system with a negative income tax. Moreover, they did not view themselves as the ones who had to make the ultimate political decision; instead, the president and the members of Congress were perceived as those who would use the experimental results to reach a decision.

A fourth explanation, one that is another variant of the rational paradigm, is that social experiments provide important information to decisionmakers and they will make effective use of this information. That explanation implies that those launching the IMEs assumed that if the experiments demonstrated that an NIT program is a good idea, such a program would be placed on the policy agenda and adopted once findings from the IMEs became available. It also suggests that those who decided to undertake the IMEs viewed welfare reform as a long-term issue to which information provided by the IMEs, whenever it became available, would make a major contribution. Of the four explanations of the reason the IMEs were undertaken, this one seems most consistent with the facts.

More specifically, the launching of the income maintenance experiments appears to have been premised on four largely implicit assumptions on the part of those sponsoring them:

1. Concern over the potential effects of NIT on the hours of work of two-parent households is the major obstacle to adoption of an NIT.
2. Findings from the experiments would probably demonstrate that these effects are small.

3. A finding of small effects on hours would place the NIT on the policy agenda and result in its being politically accepted.
4. Detailed information from the IMEs would result in a better NIT by helping policymakers select the optimal combination of tax rates and guarantee levels.

Although those who launched the IMEs appear to have embraced these assumptions and initiated the experiments on the basis of their presumed validity, with benefit of hindsight the soundness of each can be questioned, some more than others. The evidence on the assumptions will be detailed later in this chapter, so only a brief summary is provided here. (1) There were obstacles to the passage of an NIT that were probably more important than the program's potential effects on hours of work. Given those obstacles, it is doubtful that this program would have found sufficient political support regardless of the outcome of the IMEs. (2) Findings from the experiments, although clearly demonstrating that NIT effects on hours of work in two-parent households are not large, suggested that they are not negligible either. (3) NIT-like programs were placed on the policy agenda several times and received serious consideration. However, this appears to have resulted not from findings from the IMEs, but (at least in part) because strong supporters of the concept remained in key staff positions within the executive branch. (4) Findings from the IMEs did play an important role in designing the NIT-like plans that were considered. However, these proposals did not secure legislative success. In addition, as more recent welfare reform proposals have increasingly diverged from the NIT concept, the IME findings have become increasingly less relevant.

Origin of the Income Maintenance Experiments

In 1966, an MIT graduate student in economics, Heather Ross, was beginning work on her dissertation as a thesis-writing fellow at the Brookings Institution in Washington, D.C. Ross was frustrated that inferences on the way low-income persons responded to transfer payments could not be readily drawn from existing data. She was also concerned by the unsubstantiated anecdotes about welfare recipients that were sometimes promulgated by politicians. She wished to collect data that could be used to determine what poor people would actually do if they were provided money. Would they work less? Would they quit work altogether? How would they spend the additional money? To answer such questions, she proposed that a random assignment experiment be conducted.

To fund the project, Ross wrote a proposal in 1967 to OEO, which had a staff of social scientists who were strongly sympathetic to the NIT concept. Indeed, OEO had already conducted design work on NIT-type programs, and Sergeant Shriver, the director of OEO, had endorsed the concept. Ross's proposal to conduct an experiment appealed to Shriver and other NIT supporters as an opportunity to prove that an NIT works. Consequently, as Ross puts it, she ended up with a "$5 million thesis," which at the time was an extraordinary amount of funds for a single social science research project.

OEO assigned Mathematica Policy Research, Inc., a Princeton, N.J., research firm, responsibility for random assignment, running the pilot NIT programs, and collecting data. The Institute for Research on Poverty at the University of Wisconsin was selected to conduct the evaluation. Although Ross had originally proposed Washington, D.C., as a test site, partially because of Mathematica's location, OEO decided to locate the project in New Jersey. To increase the number of white families in the sample, a later decision was made to add Scranton, Pa., to the four New Jersey sites (Trenton, Paterson, Passaic, and Jersey City), as most of the poor persons in the New Jersey sites were black.

As indicated in chapter 2, the importance of the germination of Heather Ross's idea, the New Jersey experiment, as a landmark in social science research is difficult to overstate. Although the technique of randomly assigning individuals for purposes of clinical health trials had been used for years, the New Jersey Income Maintenance Experiment was the first prominent example of use of this technique to test social programs. Other social experiments, including additional IMEs, followed fairly quickly.

The first of the additional IMEs was the Rural Income Maintenance Experiment. Researchers at OEO viewed that experiment as a natural companion to the New Jersey Income Maintenance Experiment. Whereas the latter focused on urban areas, many of the poor in the 1960s resided in rural areas. From both a policy and a political perspective, it seemed important to examine the effects of an NIT on the rural poor. Moreover, administering an NIT to low-income farmers seemed to pose special problems that could be explored through a rural experiment. For example, measuring income for purposes of determining NIT benefit levels is much more difficult for farmers than for wage earners. As with the New Jersey Income Maintenance Experiment, principal responsibility for operating and evaluating the Rural Income Maintenance Experiment resided with Mathematica and the Institute for Research on Poverty, respectively.

OEO initiated the first two IMEs, but by the late 1960s DHEW was coming under both internal and external pressure to launch social experiments of its own. DHEW had responsibility for running the major public assistance program of the 1960s, Aid to Families with Dependent Children (AFDC). Not surprisingly, given the general dissatisfaction with the existing welfare system, the staff of the Office of the Assistant Secretary for Planning and Evaluation (OASPE), the central analytical office within DHEW, was already studying alternatives to the existing system at the time the New Jersey and Rural Income Maintenance Experiments were launched. Those alternatives included NITs, as well as other programs such as demogrants.[7] As part of this effort, DHEW asked the Institute for Research on Poverty to develop a research agenda in the income maintenance area. As might have been anticipated, given its involvement with the New Jersey Income Maintenance Experiment at the time, the Institute responded, in part, by outlining a menu of social experiments, including income maintenance experiments (Orr, Hollister, and Lefrowitz 1971). At around the same time, the Department of Housing and Urban Development was receiving local proposals for the Model Cities demonstrations, some of which incorporated income maintenance schemes. Ultimately, DHEW took over responsibility for conducting these demonstrations, and the demonstrations themselves evolved into experimental tests of NITs.

Although an interest in social experiments had clearly germinated at DHEW by the late 1960s, the New Jersey and Rural Income Maintenance Experiments were already under way. Thus, one might ask why the agency felt it necessary to launch additional tests of NITs. One reason was that DHEW thought that it could learn from OEO's experience and do it better. Specifically, the agency wanted to test experimental components that were not being tested in the earlier experiments—day care and educational subsidies. In fact, the possibility of testing alternatives to the existing welfare system other than an NIT—for example, child allowances (a demogrant) or various combinations of services—was also considered. In addition, DHEW had ample funds to run experiments with larger samples than those available to the earlier two experiments. Finally, it seemed desirable to test responses to an NIT in other parts of the country. Indeed, as New Jersey had an exceptionally generous existing AFDC program, it was thought by staff at OASPE to be an atypical state.[8]

Another important reason that DHEW initiated additional experiments was that it was the responsible federal agency for income maintenance. As Jody Allen, who was on the OASPE staff at the time, put it, the feeling was that "DHEW ought to be in this business. After all, it was their program." This feeling of proprietorship and competitiveness with OEO was almost certainly given additional impetus by U.S. Representative Melvin Laird of Wisconsin, a prominent member of the DHEW appropriations committee, who in committee hearings in 1968 stated (Joint Economic Committee 1968 as cited in Williams 1972, 157):

> I am very interested in the [New Jersey experiment] which is being financed by the OEO through the Poverty Institute at the University of Wisconsin. I think that we should watch the results of this project very carefully, because I see in the year 1975 a tremendous welfare bill as far as this country is concerned if we continue along the present program level. . . . I had felt that the Social Security Administration should really finance this study and that it should have been done in the Department of Health, Education, and Welfare. They were very slow in moving. So, I commend OEO for going forward with this study. I believe that this study is most important.

Thus, by the late 1960s, DHEW was clearly under both internal and external pressure to initiate experiments of its own. However, in August 1969 President Nixon proposed his Family Assistance Program (FAP). Although planning for the Seattle-Denver and Gary Income Maintenance Experiments was under way by then, it was obvious that findings from these experiments could not possibly be available in time to influence the legislative decision on FAP. Nonetheless, plans for the Seattle-Denver and Gary Income Maintenance Experiments proceeded without interruption. One reason was that DHEW thought that these experiments, which tested a variety of specific NIT plans, would provide information on the optimal NIT guarantee and tax rate. Thus, if FAP won legislative approval—an outcome that was far from certain—this information could be used to modify the program appropriately after it was put into place. Interestingly, Nixon's FAP proposal also locked DHEW into testing NITs. As previously indicated, the department had earlier considered testing a variety of other alternatives to the existing welfare system. However, after 1969, testing policies that differed in structure from the president's proposal would have raised serious political questions.

The Seattle-Denver Income Maintenance Experiment differed from the New Jersey and the Rural Income Maintenance Experiments in that research firms competed to operate and evaluate the experiment. The State of Washington issued a "Request for Proposals" in 1969 and selected a joint proposal by SRI and Mathematica from among the four they received. In this arrangement, Mathematica once again had responsibility for field administration, while SRI was responsible for evaluating the experimental data.

The Gary Income Maintenance Experiment was initially operated out of Indiana University. Unlike the other experiments, which were dominated by economists, sociologists initially conducted the Gary Income Maintenance Experiment. There was considerable dissatisfaction with them at DHEW, however; in 1974 Ken Kehrer, an economist, was given major responsibility for the experiment. Shortly thereafter fieldwork on the experiment ended, Mathematica won a competition to conduct the analysis of the experimental data, and Kehrer and a few others who were already involved with the experiment moved from Indiana University to Mathematica.

Findings from the Income Maintenance Experiments

The income maintenance experiments (IMEs) probably engendered the most voluminous literature of any of the social experiments—over six shelf-feet of books, journal articles, and reports. In keeping with the initial goals of the experiments, much, although far from all, of the literature is concerned with the effects of the experimental NITs on the number of hours worked. In this section, we briefly summarize some of the more important findings from the IMEs, giving particular emphasis to those that are pertinent to the issue of whether the IMEs affected policymaking. Given the extensive literature on the IMEs, we obviously do little more than scratch the surface here. For greater detail, the reader is referred to various summary reports that are available on the four IMEs.[9]

Effects on Hours of Work

Both common sense and economic theory suggest that an NIT program, or at least one that is more generous than the existing welfare system, will cause those who are eligible for benefits to work less. There are two reasons for this. First, by increasing family income, NIT payments make work less necessary. Economists refer to this as an "income effect." Second, the program tax rate reduces the reward for each hour of work. For example, under an NIT with a 50 percent tax rate, a worker whose employer pays him or her $5.00 per hour retains only $2.50. This presumably reduces the worker's incentive to work through what economists call a "substitution effect."

Thus, those who initiated the IMEs anticipated that the experimental NITs would cause reductions in hours worked. The question the experiments were designed to answer is how large these reductions would be. The most straightforward way in which the experimental data were used to address this question was to compute differences between the average annual hours worked by members of the treatment groups and the average annual hours worked by members of the control groups. Estimates of such experimental-control differences were made for each of the IMEs, usually after first statistically adjusting for differences between the experimental and control groups caused by random chance and the process used to assign families between the experimental and control categories. Burtless (1986) has computed weighted averages of these estimates for the four IMEs, with the weights reflecting the relative size of the samples in the four experiments. Burtless's weighted averages indicate that husbands in the treatment group worked 119 hours per year (7 percent) less than their control counterparts, wives 93 hours (17 percent) less, and female family heads 113 hours (17 percent) less.[10] Separate estimates of experimental-control differences for each of the four IMEs and for subgroups within each IME were also typically negative.

These findings were pretty much what those involved in the IMEs anticipated: negative but, relative to the 2,000 hours worked by a full-time, year-round worker, not especially large. As Albert Rees (Rees and Watts 1977, 5, 31), one of the editors of the New Jersey experiment's final report, wrote:

> The researchers all expected from the outset that the payment of substantial amounts of unearned income to poor families would reduce the amount of labor they supplied, though not by very large amounts. . . . In general the estimated effects of the experimental treatment on labor supply are in accord with our expectations.

The findings for husbands were considered especially reassuring. There was no evidence that an NIT would cause large numbers of these persons to withdraw from the workforce, the major policy issue at the onset of the IMEs. Instead, further analysis of data from the IMEs seemed to suggest that although NITs cause substantial reductions in the employment of a small number of men, most men respond little, if at all (Moffitt and Kehrer 1981, 131–33).

Nevertheless, as the following example developed by Burtless (1986, 28) illustrates, the reductions in hours that are implied by the IMEs, although modest, had political and cost implications that were far too striking to be dismissed by advocates of NITs:

> In the Seattle-Denver experiment . . . eligible two-parent families received transfer payments that were $2,700 larger than the nonexperimental payments sent to members of the control group. The combined earnings reduction of husbands and wives in the Seattle-Denver experiment [due to their reduction in hours] was almost $1,800. . . . The average tax rate of the Seattle-Denver plans was about 50 percent, implying that the $1,800 earnings reduction caused payments to be $900 above what they would have been in the absence of a work effort response. Thus, one-third of the net transfer cost of the Seattle-Denver plan was due to the reductions in reported earnings among participants. Another way to interpret the same set of figures is to say that the experiment spent nearly $2,700 on transfers and succeeded in raising the incomes of two-parent families by only $900.[11]

Although the simple experimental-control comparisons just discussed provide a valuable way to use data from the IMEs to examine information on work effort, they are not the only way. A second approach involves using the experimental data to estimate income and substitution effects. These estimates are important for two reasons.

First, as previously discussed, NITs are expected to reduce hours of work through both income and substitution effects. Other types of transfer programs also engender these effects. Thus, if data from the IMEs can be used to obtain estimates of income and substitution effects, these estimates, in turn, can be used in simulations to predict how transfer programs that were not directly tested by the IMEs would change the number of hours worked by recipients. These predictions of effects on hours are not only of policy interest themselves, but, as Burtless's illustration for the Seattle-Denver experiment implies, they are needed to make accurate predictions of program budgetary costs.

Second, for many years before the IMEs, economists had conducted nonexperimental research on labor supply—that is, on how changes in wage rates, tax rates, income, and other factors affect the number of hours people work. For example, based on various pieces of evidence, economists believed that the hours of work of adult males were unresponsive to changes in wage rates and that the hours of work of adult females were considerably more responsive. This, in turn, suggested to economists that a reduction in net wage rates caused by an increase in tax rates probably would not cause much of a change in the hours worked by men but might in the hours worked by women. Much of the nonexperimental research on labor supply had been framed in terms of income and substitution effects. By providing evidence on the empirical magnitude of those effects, therefore, the IMEs could make an important scientific contribution. In particular, at the time the IMEs were conducted, existing nonexperimental estimates of income and substitution effects varied considerably and there was some question about their reliability. Thus, the IMEs could reduce uncertainty about the magnitude of these effects.

A substantial number of different studies have produced estimates of income and substitution effects based on data from the IMEs. Those estimates can be usefully compared to the even larger number of studies that have produced estimates based on nonexperimental data, most of which were obtained from household surveys.[12] Four important conclusions may be drawn from these comparisons.

1. Findings based on both experimental and nonexperimental data are consistent with economic theory: most indicate that increases in income (holding wage rates constant) tend to reduce hours of work and that increases in wage rates (holding income constant) tend to increase hours of work.

2. Estimates based on the IME data reinforce evidence from nonexperimental data that suggests that the labor supply of women is more responsive to changes in wage rates and tax rates than the labor supply of men.

3. On average, experimental estimates of income and substitution effects for both men and women are smaller than nonexperimental estimates. In other words, estimates from the IME data imply that labor supply responses to changes in work incentives are smaller than might be believed if one were to rely solely on estimates from the nonexperimental data.

4. There is considerably less variation in income and substitution estimates based on IME data than in estimates based on nonexperimental data. That fact suggests that the IMEs substantially reduced the degree of uncertainty about labor supply responses to changes in income, wage rates, and tax rates. Thus, as Harold Watts, the director of research on the New Jersey Income Maintenance

Experiment, suggested to us, the experimental labor supply findings "narrowed the range of responsible beliefs on the part of
serious scholars."

As previously mentioned, early advocates of NITs had thought that by
reducing benefit-reduction rates facing *current* recipients of public assistance, such persons might actually be encouraged to increase their work
effort. However, to the best of our knowledge, a separate analysis of the
effect of lowering the benefit-reduction rates facing current public assistance recipients was never undertaken with the IME data.[13] One possible reason was concern over the adverse effects on the hours of work of
two-parent families who would be added to the public assistance rolls
under an NIT. That concern came to swamp interest in the possibility
that current recipients, who were mostly from one-parent families,
might work more. Thus, by the time the required data were available for
analysis from the IMEs, the latter possibility was no longer being used to
argue in favor of an NIT. One implication of nonuse of the IMEs to analyze the effects of changes in benefit-reduction rates on current welfare
recipients is that the experiments have contributed little to recent proposals to reduce benefit-reduction rates in existing welfare programs.

Effects on Marital Stability

The findings from the IMEs on the effects of NITs on hours worked were
pretty much what was anticipated, but the experimental findings on the
way NITs affect marital stability came as a real surprise. At the time the
IMEs were initiated, it was widely believed that the existing welfare system tended to destabilize marriage because two-parent families were
rarely eligible for AFDC; when they were it was under highly restricted
circumstances. Thus, it seemed possible, although compelling evidence
was lacking, that some fathers might leave the family unit so that the
remaining family could become eligible for AFDC. Inasmuch as eligibility for an NIT depends only on income, the belief was that replacing
the existing welfare system with such a program would enhance marital
stability.

Findings from the New Jersey, Rural, and Gary experiments were generally inconclusive on the effects of the experimental NITs on marital
stability. Sometimes they suggested small reductions in marital dissolution and sometimes small increases, but the estimated effects were rarely

statistically significant. However, contrary to expectations, findings from the Seattle-Denver experiment indicated that the experimental NIT increased marital dissolution rates for both blacks and whites by over 40 percent during the experimental period. Moreover, those estimated effects were strongly statistically significant. The estimated effects for Hispanics were also positive, but much smaller in magnitude and statistically insignificant.[14]

One possible explanation for the surprising Seattle-Denver findings is that they resulted from an "independence effect." That is, the experimental plans provided a source of alternative financial support to women who might wish to leave unhappy marriages, support that was substantially higher than that which could potentially be received by their control counterparts under the existing welfare system. Moreover, unlike most of their control counterparts, married women in the Seattle-Denver treatment group were already enrolled in a transfer program, namely, the experimental NIT. They were presumably well aware of the benefits that they would receive should their marriages dissolve. Therefore, they would not have to spend the time and go to the trouble of entering the welfare system.

The original marital stability analysis for the Seattle-Denver experiment was conducted during the mid- and late 1970s by sociologists at SRI International. During the late 1980s, economists at the Institute for Research on Poverty conducted a reanalysis of the Seattle-Denver data. On the basis of the reanalysis, they concluded that the experimental NITs that were tested in the Seattle-Denver experiment had virtually no effect on marital stability (see Cain and Wissoker 1990). The reasons for the differences between the original analysis and the reanalysis are highly technical and need not concern us here. Suffice to say that both sets of findings have their supporters and both remain controversial among social scientists. However, this episode suggests two important points that are germane to the policy use of the marital stability findings from the IMEs. First, results from the reanalysis were not available until more than a decade after the initial findings were released.[15] Thus, the initial Seattle-Denver findings had the policy floor to themselves for a long time. Second, there is no evidence from the IMEs, including findings from the reanalysis, that supports the original expectation that NIT programs would tend to enhance marital stability. The most favorable inference that one can make on the basis of the reanalysis of the IME data is that there would be no effect.

Other Effects

Data from the IMEs were used to examine a large number of topics in addition to NIT effects on hours of work and marital stability (see sidebar). With few exceptions, these findings attracted little notice at the time they were reported and, based on our interviews, seem virtually forgotten today. One reason is that the IMEs were expressly designed to

---

Some examples of findings from studies appear below:

- Although consumption levels were higher in the presence of NIT payments, consumption patterns were similar to consumption patterns in the absence of the payments.
- Evidence from the Gary and Seattle-Denver experiments indicates that NIT programs increased home ownership.
- Health status did not seem to improve as a result of the increased income provided by the experimental NITs.
- Evidence from the Gary experiment suggests that NIT programs reduce the incidence of low-weight births among the poor. However, a study based on data from the Seattle-Denver experiment did not support this finding.
- An analysis of data from the Rural experiment found evidence of small nutritional improvements for members of the treatment group in North Carolina, but not in Iowa.
- Evidence from the New Jersey, Gary, and Seattle-Denver experiments suggests that although NIT programs reduce hours worked by youths, this is roughly offset by increases in their schooling.
- Data from the Rural and Gary experiments imply that participation in NIT programs improves the performance of children in the lower grades on standardized tests.
- Relative to controls, there were substantial increases in migration by members of the Seattle-Denver experimental group.
- Findings from the Seattle-Denver experiment suggest that participants in the experimental NIT plans were more likely to use day care purchased on the market and less likely to use family day care than their control group counterparts.

examine the effect of NITs on hours worked and most of the data collection and research efforts were in keeping with this objective. The studies on which the findings listed above are based were treated a bit like poor relatives. The experiments really were not designed to study most of these issues, and they received a relatively small share of survey and research resources. A second reason is that, unlike the original Seattle-Denver finding on marital stability, most of the findings listed above are unsurprising and did not present a challenge to the NIT concept. For example, a finding that additional income received as a result of an NIT was mostly expended on alcohol and drugs would probably have received considerable attention, but the actual findings that consumption patterns were not much influenced by the NIT receipts did not.

One additional finding from the IMEs was surprising. The Seattle-Denver experiment provided 50 percent subsidies for the direct cost of job-related training (i.e., tuition, fees, books, transportation, and child care) to a randomly selected subgroup and 100 percent subsidies for the same purpose to another randomly selected subgroup. Individuals were given considerable freedom to select the type of training they wished. Evidence from studies of the effects of these subsidies indicated that they substantially increased the amount of training and education received by persons who were eligible for them, but failed to increase the earnings of those persons. Indeed, the experimental evidence indicated that the earnings of husbands and female heads of single-parent households decreased during both the subsidy period (that is, while the training was presumably taking place) and the year after the subsidy ended (Dickinson and West 1983). Whereas the decrease during the earlier period can, perhaps, be attributed to reductions in work hours while undertaking training, the reduction in the later period is less readily explained.

These findings, although unexpected, attracted little attention, perhaps because subsidized training that allows low-income individuals to select the type of training they receive was not on the policy agenda at the time experimental findings on the effects of such a program became available. Had the findings for the program been strongly positive, it is conceivable that it might have been put on the policy agenda. But as the findings were negative, both they and the tested program were quickly forgotten.

The IMEs provided policy-relevant information on one additional topic. At the time the experiments were initiated, welfare benefits for each month were computed on the basis of projections of income and family expenses during the following month. In addition, although welfare recipients were supposed to inform their caseworkers of changes in their circumstances that affected their benefit eligibility, there was no systematic way of ensuring that they would do this. As a result, benefit amounts were seldom adjusted until formal redetermination occurred, usually every six months or longer. Consequently, benefit amounts were frequently in error.

The IMEs, in contrast, collected income and expense information each month and then used this information to determine benefits for each family during the following month, an approach that is referred to as monthly reporting and retrospective accounting. Although the IMEs were not designed in a manner that permitted a conclusive assessment of monthly reporting and retrospective accounting, they did demonstrate that the approach was administratively feasible.[16] Because the approach appeared to offer a promising way to reduce errors in the determination of benefit amounts, several social experiments were subsequently run specifically to test monthly reporting and retrospective accounting. Based in part on favorable early findings from the first of these experiments, which indicated substantial reductions in total benefit payments (see Williams 1979), Congress required states throughout the country to use retrospective accounting and monthly reporting in administering AFDC and food stamps. The findings in subsequent studies were much less favorable, however, implying much smaller and typically statistically insignificant benefit savings (Burghardt 1982; Hamilton 1985). Consequently, Congress later revised the law to provide the states greater flexibility.

Use of Findings from the Income Maintenance Experiments

The IMEs did not play the pivotal role in policymaking originally envisioned for them. A negative income tax program was not implemented as a result of findings from these experiments; nor, as will be seen, were the experiments decisive in keeping an NIT from being implemented. Nevertheless, the IMEs did exert an important influence in a number of spheres. Those effects, however, were considerably less dramatic and more subtle than was initially foreseen. In this section, we describe these effects. We also discuss the reasons the IMEs were not a more critical determinant of welfare policy.

Effects on Other Social Experiments

The IMEs were the first prominent social experiments. As previously discussed, they directly stimulated experiments on the use of monthly accounting in administering welfare. In addition, they provided the model used in designing the Housing Allowance Demand Experiment, probably the most expensive random assignment experiment ever conducted. More generally, the IMEs did much to popularize the idea of using social experiments as a major tool for evaluating social policy. At the time the IMEs were initiated, there was considerable resistance to the use of control groups in assessing social programs because it meant that some individuals would be denied benefits or services. The IMEs helped lead to greater acceptance of the use of control groups by establishing a precedent for denial of benefits or services through random assignment and by demonstrating the importance of having reliable control groups for policy analysis. Much was also learned from the IMEs about how to conduct social experiments and communicate findings from them to the policy community.[17] In addition, there were technological spillover effects: statistical tools that were developed or refined for purposes of analyzing the IME data were later used in analyzing nonexperimental data.

Effects on Research and Policy Analyses

Over the years, estimates of behavioral parameters from the experiments, especially estimates of income and substitution effects on labor supply, have been incorporated into numerous policy analyses and published articles. Typically, the parameters have been used to estimate the behavioral effects of existing policies and to predict the effects of policy proposals.

Effects on Conceptual Views

If social experiments are to influence policymaking, they must first influence the views of decisionmakers. They can do this either by changing existing views or by reinforcing them. In general, as previously indicated, findings from the IMEs on hours of work had the latter effect, findings on marital stability had the former effect, and most other findings had little influence at all.

To recapitulate, labor supply findings from the IMEs reinforced the view of economists that responses to changes in wage rates and income are small among males (perhaps even smaller than many initially thought) and are somewhat larger among women (although again perhaps smaller than initially thought). In keeping with this, the experiments demonstrated that an NIT would cause only modest reductions in hours of work and, in particular, would not result in large numbers of men withdrawing from the workforce. Although the findings were consistent with the initial expectations of those who supported NITs, there is little evidence that they changed the views of those who did not support NITs. Moreover, as will be seen, the IMEs undercut the position of NIT supporters. They demonstrated that the reductions in hours of work were sufficiently large to have potential effects on the government's budget and on the effectiveness of transfer programs in raising incomes. These effects could not be ignored in designing welfare reform initiatives.

The IME marital stability findings did change the views of some. At a minimum, it was no longer possible to argue that adoption of an NIT would enhance marital stability. As Senator Daniel Patrick Moynihan, the Senate's leading expert on welfare issues, stated during congressional hearings in 1978, the findings suggested that an NIT, "far from strengthening family ties, might weaken them. . . . Ten years ago, we expected quite different outcomes from these tests" (quoted by the GAO 1981, 15). On a more intellectual level, although the concept of an independence effect was introduced into the academic literature well before the IMEs began (see Goode 1966, for example), the experimental findings provided some empirical evidence that such effects might actually exist[18] and helped drive home their potential importance to social scientists, especially economists.

It would appear, therefore, that both the labor supply and the marital stability findings from the experiments were used conceptually. However, research findings that change prevailing views, such as the IME marital stability results, tend to be credited with having more "influence" than findings that reinforce prevailing views, such as the IME labor supply results. This need not be the case. Whether views are changed or reinforced depends, in part, on what the findings are, something that cannot be known with certainty in advance. In either case, there is conceptual use. For example, if the marital stability findings had implied that NITs strengthen marriages and the labor supply findings suggested that NITs greatly reduce hours of work, both sets of findings might still have influenced opinions. If so, both would still have been used conceptually. We turn next to whether either set of findings was used concretely, that is, to influence specific policy decisions.

Effects on Welfare Administration

In developing the rules for running the IMEs, much was learned about the practical operation of welfare programs. Specifically, as previously described, the IMEs played a major role in helping initiate the use of more frequent reporting and the retrospective accounting periods in administering welfare programs. It is important to recognize, however, that this had little to do with the classical experimental design used in the IMEs. What was critical was that the IMEs demonstrated that monthly reporting and retrospective accounting, two ideas that seemed good on paper, could be successfully implemented. Rigorously testing the ideas remained for other social experiments.

Effects on Welfare Reform Initiatives

Since the IMEs were initiated, there have been numerous proposals to modify the nation's welfare system. In this subsection, we look at the more important of the proposals and examine the role the IMEs played in formulating each and in determining whether or not it was ultimately adopted. The examination will show that the IMEs played a major role in designing one of the proposals but probably were not pivotal in determining the legislative outcome of any.

A hint about why can be found in the 1968 statement of Representative Melvin Laird of Wisconsin from which we quoted earlier. Part of Laird's statement bears repeating: "I think that we should watch the results of this project [the New Jersey Experiment] very carefully, because I see in the year 1975 a tremendous welfare bill as far as this country is concerned if we continue along the present program level. . . ."

Laird went on to indicate that welfare costs would rise because the size of the welfare rolls was likely to increase dramatically. Assuming that the views of Laird, a moderate Republican who was soon to become President Nixon's Secretary of Defense, were similar to those of other members of Congress, his statement did not bode well for either the role of the experimental findings in the policy process or the fate of the NIT program being tested by the IMEs. It said nothing about the effects of NITs on hours of work, the very thing the New Jersey experiment and the other IMEs were designed to measure; but was instead mainly concerned with growing welfare rolls and welfare costs, issues the IMEs did not really address. Indeed, the NIT program tested by the IMEs, if implemented nationally, would almost surely have increased both the welfare rolls and welfare costs by greatly expanding the number of two-parent households eligible for welfare.

NIXON'S FAMILY ASSISTANCE PLAN

In a televised address on August 8, 1969, President Nixon proposed a welfare reform plan that would guarantee an annual income to every American family of $500 for each parent and $300 for each child (approximately $2,000 and $1,200, respectively, in current prices). Thus, a family of four with no other income would have been eligible for $1,600 (or about $6,400 in current prices) under the proposed program. Earnings in excess of $720 were to be subject to a 50 percent tax rate. This program, which was called the Family Assistance Plan (FAP), was similar to the negative income tax program envisioned by the designers of the IMEs.[19] FAP and the IMEs also used similar procedures for administering payments to beneficiaries—for example, monthly reporting and annual accounting periods.

Findings from the IMEs about work incentives and other behavioral effects could not have contributed to the design of FAP, as no such findings were yet available at the time Nixon made his announcement. Indeed, by the time reliable findings were available, FAP was no longer under serious political consideration. However, Daniel Patrick Moynihan, a White House aide who played a major role in persuading Nixon to propose FAP, was well aware of the existence of the New Jersey experiment and may have found the fact that an experimental NIT had been successfully implemented reassuring. Moreover, staff members from OEO and DHEW who were involved in the IMEs were drawn upon to help in the FAP design work. Hence, it is not surprising that administratively the design of FAP had much in common with the experimental plans tested in the IMEs. Moreover, data from the New Jersey experiment were used to examine the cost implications of alternative approaches to income reporting and accounting periods and findings from these analyses were incorporated into the design of FAP (Storey 1973).

Although FAP passed in the House of Representatives, the Senate subsequently rejected it.[20] The IMEs probably played little role in the ultimate failure of FAP. This is not surprising. The experiments were not complete when FAP was debated in Congress. Moreover, with or without information from IMEs, FAP probably did not have the support it needed in the Senate. Michael Stern, the former Senate Finance Committee staffer who was responsible for welfare issues, asserts that at the time FAP was being considered, and for a long time thereafter, the Senate consisted of three roughly equally divided groups—those who favored the NIT approach,[21] those who wanted to keep the welfare rolls from expanding and therefore favored a work-oriented approach,[22] and those who did not favor either approach. Given this situation, as Stern points out, it was impossible to obtain a consensus for any approach to welfare reform.

The fact that FAP could not muster a majority in the Senate might have been anticipated. As detailed by Coyle and Wildavsky (1986), there simply was not much of a political constituency for FAP. Polls around the time consistently showed that the voting public was overwhelmingly against plans that would provide income guarantees, although there was considerable support for programs that would provide food or jobs to those in need. The polls further showed that even among low-income persons, support for income guarantees was tepid. Indeed, as Coyle and Wildavsky discuss, organizations that represented AFDC recipients opposed FAP because it would reduce the payments received by many of these persons and possibly subject them to a work test. Low-income two-parent families, many of whom would be better off under FAP, simply did not have much of a political voice.[23]

Interestingly, although the IMEs seem to have had little influence on the Senate's decision on FAP, supporters of FAP used early findings from the New Jersey experiment to argue in its favor. Under strong pressure from a variety of sources, including Daniel Patrick Moynihan, the Institute for Research on Poverty released very rudimentary results for this experiment.[24] The Institute's report (Watts 1970, 38–39) concluded:

> The main impression left after a review of these crude analyses is that the experimental treatment has induced no dramatic or remarkable responses on the part of the families. The data are weak at this point, and so we can only expect to detect large effects with any confidence. Consequently, the only prudent conclusion at this point is that no convincing evidence of differences between control and experimental families has been found. . . . But to the extent that differences appear between control and experimental families they are generally in favor of *greater* work effort for experimentals [emphasis in original].

Despite the carefully stated caveats, backers of FAP seized upon these preliminary findings, especially to emphasize the possibility that the program could conceivably increase work effort. As previously indicated, however, the early findings for New Jersey, which were declared "premature" by the General Accounting Office, were, in fact, misleading; later analyses of IME data clearly showed that NIT-type programs result in reductions in hours of work. The early New Jersey findings were discussed in meetings between congressional staff and the researchers working on the experiment and also in closed sessions of the Senate Finance Committee. However, they were not mentioned much in the congressional hearings and floor debates (Coyle and Wildavsky 1986, 179). Any debating points that FAP supporters might have gained from the early New Jersey findings were quickly neutralized by opponents who could point to the fact that the analysis was based on preliminary and incomplete data that still contained numerous coding errors. Moreover, the early New Jersey findings may have focused more attention on the *possibility* that FAP might reduce hours of work than the issue would have otherwise received.[25]

THE INCOME SUPPLEMENT PROGRAM

In 1973, toward the end of the Nixon administration, a second welfare reform proposal was developed under the general direction of Casper Weinberger, who was then Secretary of the Department of Health, Education, and Welfare. This plan, the Income Supplement Program (ISP), leaned even more in the direction of a pure NIT than FAP had. For example, unlike the case with FAP, single individuals and childless couples were eligible for benefits. ISP did contain a work test provision, however.

At the time ISP was developed, completed findings from the New Jersey experiment, but not the other three IMEs, were available. Upon being briefed on the New Jersey findings, Secretary Weinberger was convinced that the reductions in hours of work that would result from ISP would be modest. The DHEW publication detailing the proposal also argues that the New Jersey findings imply relatively small effects on work effort (U.S. Department of Health, Education, and Welfare 1974, 13–14). However, White House Chief of Staff Alexander Haig killed ISP in 1974 for reasons having nothing to do with the IMEs; the Nixon presidency was embroiled in the Watergate scandal.

CARTER'S PROGRAM FOR BETTER JOBS AND INCOME

On August 6, 1977, President Jimmy Carter announced a welfare reform proposal, the Program for Better Jobs and Income (PBJI). This proposal, which was quite complex, contained several separate components. One component was a cash assistance plan that, examined in isolation, is similar to an NIT. It provided a guaranteed income to all families with children and reduced benefits as earnings increased. Like FAP, but unlike ISP, it excluded childless couples and single individuals from the benefits. A second program component would have divided families with children into two groups: those that contain an adult expected to work (essentially, families with at least one able-bodied adult and, in the case of one-parent families, no children under 7) and those that do not contain an adult expected to work. Families in the latter group were simply eligible for cash assistance; but those in the former group were expected to obtain employment within eight weeks of becoming eligible for cash assistance. If they did not, then their cash assistance would be substantially reduced. To ensure that they could actually obtain employment, however, PBJI specified that the government would provide public service jobs that paid the minimum wage if a five-week period of supervised job search failed to yield a regular job. Thus, unlike FAP and ISP, PBJI was not a pure cash assistance, NIT-like program. Instead, it combined an income guarantee with a work requirement backed up by a job guarantee.

In this subsection, we first describe how this program design came to be adopted and the role that the IMEs played in this. We then consider whether the IMEs influenced how the program fared politically.

The role of the IMEs in designing PBJI. At the time PBJI was being developed, the analyses of data from the New Jersey and Rural experiments were complete; and although the analyses of the data from the Gary and Seattle-Denver experiments were still incomplete, those analyses were fairly far along and usable findings were available. Unfortunately, none of the IMEs tested a cash assistance plan that was combined with the provisions of public service jobs. Interest in such a combination was not, indeed, could not have been, foreseen when the IMEs were initiated. Thus, the experiments were not directly applicable to PBJI. Nonetheless, as will be seen, findings from the IMEs—or at least those from the Seattle-Denver experiment—played an important role in designing PBJI. However, they probably had little to do with the fate of the program in Congress. Before examining these topics, however, a bit of background information might be helpful.

Both DHEW and the Department of Labor (DOL) played important roles in shaping the Program for Better Jobs and Income. Within DHEW, the major responsibility was within OASPE, which was then headed by Henry Aaron. Aaron's major aide in this endeavor was Michael Barth, the deputy assistant secretary who headed the office that put together the details of the proposal. One of the persons with major responsibility for working out these details was John Todd, who was also in charge of DHEW's cost estimates for PBJI. Aaron's counterpart within DOL was Arnold Packer, who headed the Office of the Assistant Secretary for Policy, Evaluation, and Research (OASPER), while Barth's counterpart was Jody Allen, a deputy assistant secretary of labor.

These individuals, all of whom had extensive experience in working on welfare issues before the PBJI effort, held numerous meetings with one another and with relevant persons in other parts of the government, including the Treasury Department, the President's Council of Economic Advisers, the Congressional Budget Office, and congressional staff. These meetings provided an obvious forum for discussing findings from the IMEs and incorporating these findings into PBJI. However, the individuals mentioned in the previous paragraph, as well as most other persons whom we interviewed, suggested that the IME findings were, in fact, rarely directly discussed in meetings on the PBJI.[26] This is not to say that those present at these meetings were not knowledgeable of the IME findings. Some had detailed knowledge of them, and most of the others at least knew that the findings indicated that NITs cause hours of work and marital stability to decline.

Results from the Seattle-Denver experiment did play a significant indirect role in the development of the Program for Better Jobs and Income. The indirect role was somewhat complex. It began with the use of data from the Seattle-Denver experiment by SRI analysts to estimate income and substitution effects (see Keeley et al. 1978). Those estimates, in turn, were incorporated into microsimulation models[27] that were used to predict the costs, labor supply effects, number of persons taking public service jobs, and distributional implications of alternative welfare reform proposals.[28] The income and substitution effect estimates from the Seattle-Denver experiment provided a means by which the simulation models could predict adjustments in hours of work and, hence, earnings by potential beneficiaries of the proposals in response to the changes in their income levels, wage rates, and tax rates that would occur.[29] The predicted hours of work adjustments were, in turn, important because they affected the simulation predictions of the costs of proposed programs; in general, the larger the adjustment, the higher the cost of a proposed increase in transfer benefits. Thus, as the General Accounting Office (1981, 28) stated, "The Seattle-Denver experiment's work incentive results [were] an essential component of the [simulations]."

The simulation estimates of costs were prominent in discussions about the development of PBJI because, as Henry Aaron told us, "Everything was driven by costs." More specifically, the simulation models allowed different proposed versions of PBJI to be compared—for example, programs with different income guarantees and tax rates and programs that did and did not contain a public service jobs component. As a result of comparisons of simulation predictions of the costs, effects on earnings, and other implications of the alternatives, modifications in the developing plan were made. The simulation estimates were not, of course, the only consideration in choosing among different versions of PBJI—for example, political appeal was also important—but they were often a significant factor. Eventually, the Carter proposal emerged. After that, the simulation cost estimates became, as the General Accounting Office (1981, 28) notes, "an important input to the congressional debate on [PBJI] in 1977 and 1978. . . ."

Because of the emphasis placed on microsimulation predictions in developing PBJI, simple experimental-control comparisons from the IMEs received relatively little attention. Consequently, the Seattle-Denver experiment played a much more important (albeit indirect) role than the other three IMEs. As Robert Moffitt, who was the economist with major responsibility for estimating the effects of the Gary experiment on hours of work, told us, "I don't recall any specific findings from the Gary experiment that fed into PBJI." Moffitt went on to indicate that Gary was simply one of several income maintenance experiments and, hence, contributed "background information."

Use of the Seattle-Denver findings brought some credibility to the simulation estimates. John Todd related to us that at meetings he attended it was simply necessary to explain that the simulation estimates were based on the Seattle-Denver Income Maintenance Experiment. Todd indicated that further explanation was rarely necessary and the estimates were not challenged. However, the simulation estimates were apparently not fully accepted by all those involved in welfare reform at the time. For example, Robert Strauss, who performed staff work for a special committee that had been established in the House of Representatives to consider welfare reform, indicated to us that several staff economists in the House were reluctant to "depend on large databases and software that few understood, and which were prone to unintended programming glitches" and, instead, used administrative data that did not incorporate labor supply responses to obtain their own cost estimates (letter to David Greenberg dated October 23, 1995). This is not to suggest that these persons questioned the validity of the Seattle-Denver estimates that were used in the simulation models; rather, it was the models themselves that they distrusted.[30]

The Seattle-Denver experiment, as embodied in the simulation estimates, played an especially prominent role in a heated debate that took place between DHEW and DOL early in the process of developing PBJI. DHEW, especially the staff within OASPE, strongly favored a program that closely resembled a pure NIT. After all, the OASPE staff had developed just such a plan, the Income Supplement Program, just a few years earlier. DOL, in contrast, was already running a very large countercyclical public employment program at the time under the Comprehensive Employment and Training Program, and strongly favored incorporating a major public service jobs component into PBJI.

The role that microsimulation played in this debate can be illustrated through a few simulation predictions from the period.[31] The predictions, which are shown below, rely on income and substitution estimates based on the Seattle-Denver data. They apply to two-parent families only and are in billions of 1975 dollars. The two hypothetical simulated programs both provide an income guarantee equal to the poverty line and reduce benefits by 70 cents for each dollar of earnings. However, the first program does not require cash assistance recipients to take jobs and, hence, approximates a pure NIT. The second program, in contrast, does contain a job requirement and backs it up by providing public service jobs to those who cannot find regular employment.

	Program 1 [no jobs required] (in $billions)	Program 2 [jobs required] (in $billions)
Net increase in cash assistance	$3.25	$2.62
Decline in earnings from regular jobs	−.79	−1.62
Earnings from public service jobs	0.00	4.48
Net increase in family income	2.46	5.48

Turning first to Program 1, the program without a public service jobs component, it can be seen that nearly a quarter of the additional assistance provided two-parent families is predicted to be offset by reduced earnings that results from a reduction in hours of paid work. Simulations of other program configurations that did not have public service jobs components often predicted even larger earnings reductions relative to increases in transfer benefits (Aaron and Todd 1978, 50–51).

These simulation estimates, a product of findings from the Seattle-Denver Income Maintenance Experiment, undercut DHEW's argument for a program approximating a pure NIT. Indeed, they affected the way the labor supply findings from the IMEs were perceived by those developing PBJI. Earlier, when we discussed findings from the IMEs, we noted that the losses in hours from NITs were generally viewed as moderate. Certainly, Secretary Weinberger interpreted them this way when he signed off on the Income Supplement Program. Viewed now through the lens of a simulation model, however, these same reductions in hours seemed to cause pure cash assistance programs to be inefficient; each dollar of increased cash assistance translated into considerably less than one dollar in increased income for beneficiaries.

It should be pointed out that it was not necessary to use a simulation model to reach this conclusion. The example developed by Burtless, which was cited earlier, was also based on findings from the Seattle-Denver experiment but did not rely on simulations at all to make a very similar inference. Thus, the findings from the IMEs were key. The simulations, however, seemed to focus the attention of policymakers in DHEW and DOL on the possibility that even if the reduction in hours of work that would result from an NIT were modest, this reduction could nonetheless cause the ratio of income increases to transfer costs to be well under 1.

The simulations also implied that one way to address this problem was to combine cash assistance with public service jobs. As can be seen, the simulation findings for Program 2 indicate that when this is done, a dollar of cash assistance translates into more than one dollar of increased income. This is possible because the public service jobs component allows total net earnings (i.e., earnings from public service jobs less the reduction in earnings from regular jobs) to grow. Under a pure cash assistance program, in contrast, net earnings shrink.[32]

Public service jobs are fraught with problems of their own,[33] but this need not concern us here. The key point is that DOL won the debate: A decision was made to include a public service jobs component in PBJI. This decision was an important watershed in welfare policy. Since then reform proposals have all been jobs-oriented. Indeed, PBJI was the last seriously considered welfare reform plan that would have substantially expanded the welfare rolls and the amount of cash assistance provided. Subsequent proposals have been aimed at getting recipients into jobs and reducing the size of the rolls and the amount of assistance. Consequently, as will be seen, social experiments that tested NITs—the IMEs—were little used in later attempts to change the welfare system. They no longer provided pertinent information.

Did DOL win the debate because of simulation estimates based on findings from the Seattle-Denver experiment? There is no way to know with certainty. The simulation estimates were clearly part of the debate, but other factors were, perhaps, more important. Henry Aaron suggested to us that the IMEs demonstrated "yes, marginal tax rates were significant, but people care about work requirements as much for the message it sends and the stance that the government takes with respect to work versus passively accepting cash." One reason for this is that by the time PBJI was being designed, the participation of women in the labor force had greatly expanded and, as a result, public attitudes toward requiring single AFDC mothers with children to work had changed. As noted previously, even before this time, polls had showed that voters strongly preferred publicly provided jobs for the poor over expanded cash assistance. Moreover, Jimmy Carter entered office favorably disposed toward public service jobs. In addition, many of the persons participating in the public jobs component of the Comprehensive Employment and Training Act that DOL was then running were from the middle class. By tying public service jobs to cash assistance, it became possible to target these jobs better to the poor.

Aaron and Todd (1978, 52) state that although inclusion of the public service jobs component in PBJI "was not an inevitable result of the [simulation] findings . . . ," they were "a strong influence." When interviewed, Jody Allen suggested that the simulations demonstrated that work incentive effects mattered and, in that sense, were "useful weapons" for DOL in the debate. Thus, the IMEs "might" have been important in getting a jobs program into PBJI. She further asserted that over the past several decades there has been a "continuum" in a movement toward getting people off cash assistance and requiring them to take jobs. Thus, Allen claims that today "the conventional wisdom has turned strongly towards jobs. Did the experiments help turn that tide? Maybe." Somewhat similarly, Robert Spiegelman, who was the director of research on the Seattle-Denver experiment, believes that the experiments may have "influenced looking at more direct ways to influence work effort," such as requiring welfare recipients to participate in job-oriented programs.

The IMEs and the political response to PBJI. By combining cash assistance and jobs, the designers of PBJI hoped to appeal to a wide political spectrum. We now consider how successful this strategy was.

PBJI was not reported out of committee in the House of Representatives. Consequently, the House never voted on it and it never reached the Senate. There are a number of reasons why the program failed politically.[34] Congress was no closer to a consensus on welfare reform than it was in the FAP days. As in the FAP days, many members of Congress were still ideologically opposed to guaranteeing income and expanding the welfare rolls, even if those initiatives were combined with a job requirement. In addition, the need to administer the public service jobs component of PBJI for an estimated 1.4 million low-skilled assistance recipients raised serious concerns. Moreover, as Strauss (1978, 194) pointed out at the time, the fate of any welfare reform bill depends upon support from the states and this depended, in turn, on "the degree of fiscal relief provided the states." PBJI provided some fiscal relief, but apparently not enough. Furthermore, Proposition 13 had recently passed in California, inflation was high, and Congress was in a budget-cutting mood. There was not much sentiment for establishing a large, costly new program such as PBJI. Finally, there were issues about the credibility of the cost estimates the Carter administration provided Congress and concern that the public service jobs component and, hence, the cost of PBJI would be even larger than anticipated.

Given all this, it seems unlikely that PBJI could have succeeded in Congress no matter what the findings from the IMEs were.[35] This does not necessarily mean that the IMEs were not a factor, however, just that other considerations loomed larger. For example, if the experiments had indicated that NITs have no effect on hours of work, then this might have contributed positively to PBJI's chances of passage, but probably would have been overwhelmed by other considerations. On the other hand, if the IMEs had implied that NITs have large negative effects on hours of work, then this would have simply added to the forces already aligned against the program.

John Todd suggested to us that the moderate effects on hours that were actually found might, on balance, have had a positive political impact by reducing uncertainty about labor supply. Todd pointed out that in the absence of experimental evidence "if someone had made a speech claiming there would be a 60 percent labor supply reduction, we couldn't have disproved it." Thus, in his words, the findings from the IMEs took the issue of the magnitude of labor supply responses to welfare reform "off the table"—it was no longer an area of controversy. However, interviews with persons who were on relevant congressional staffs at the time PBJI was under consideration suggest that the simple fact that the labor supply findings from the IMEs implied that NITs cause hours of work to decline, regardless of evidence suggesting that the size of this decline would be modest, reduced the probability that the PBJI could pass. In other words, evidence on the existence of the effect tended to receive much more notice within political circles than evidence on the size of the effect.

Several of the persons we interviewed, though they felt that PBJI had only a small probability of passage under any circumstances, thought that the Seattle-Denver marital stability findings made certain that the proposal would fail. This position is well represented by Henry Aaron, who stated that the Seattle-Denver marital stability findings "destroyed what little chance there may have been. . . . Any proposal like [PBJI] which is controversial and has high ambitions to change a lot of stuff is going to be a close call. At best, you'll win by a few votes. So . . . any loss of 20 votes in the House or 5 votes in the Senate, you're dead." Aaron went on to say that a more important factor was "Proposition 13 in California, which suddenly was a wake-up call for members of Congress that there was a tax rebellion . . . a lot of them just hunkered down and pulled back and got very timid."

The only member of Congress known to have reacted strongly to the marital stability findings was Senator Patrick Moynihan of New York, who stated that they were "as important as anything I have seen in my lifetime to the formation of making judgments about a large social problem"[36] and held hearings on them. Moynihan is a social scientist and, as a senior White House aide under President Nixon, had played a major role in fashioning FAP. Now, he felt that the marital stability findings indicated that "we were wrong about a guaranteed income! Seemingly it is calamitous. It increases family dissolution by some 70%, decreases work, etc. Such is now the state of the science, and it seems to me we are honor-bound to abide by it for the moment."[37] Although Moynihan was still in his first Senate term at the time PBJI was considered, he was well known as an authority on welfare and a long-time champion of guaranteed income for the poor. Moreover, he was chairman of the Senate Finance Subcommittee on Public Assistance. Therefore, it is conceivable that had PBJI reached the Senate and that to ensure passage it needed only Senator Moynihan's vote and those of other senators he could influence, he might have blocked it in response to the Seattle-Denver findings.

As discussed earlier, however, numerous other factors kept the program from getting close to this point. Indeed, it is not even clear that Moynihan's own opposition to PBJI was primarily motivated by the Seattle-Denver marital stability findings. Instead the driving force may have been fiscal relief for New York State. New York paid among the highest AFDC benefits in the country. Moreover, Moynihan was concerned about a tax revolt similar to Proposition 13 in New York. In response to these factors, Moynihan was sponsoring his own bill at the time PBJI was on the policy agenda. That bill, the State and Local Welfare Reform and Fiscal Relief Act, combined welfare reform with fiscal relief for high-benefit states, such as New York and California, and was strongly opposed by the Carter administration (see Lynn and Whitman 1981, 245–49).

Perhaps the effect of the findings from the income maintenance experiments on the PBJI are best viewed as another nail in an already firmly closed coffin Even the modest effects on hours of work tended to be perceived negatively by noneconomists. For example, in an editorial that is fairly typical of news coverage that appeared at the time, the *Rocky Mountain News* (November 29, 1978) first commended the federal government for testing the negative income tax concept before implementing one and then stated that "the last thing the country needs is welfare revision that encourages people to work less and desert their families."

THE OMNIBUS BUDGET RECONCILIATION ACT OF 1981
With the election of Ronald Reagan as president in 1980, reducing the size of the existing welfare rolls came to the fore. The new administration developed various provisions that would modify the AFDC program to accomplish this. Many of those provisions were incorporated into the Omnibus Budget Reconciliation Act, which was passed by Congress in 1981. Findings from the IMEs do not appear to have had any influence on decisions about these provisions.

They were used, however, by the Congressional Budget Office to help predict the effects of one of the most important provisions. This provision, which was intended to lower the AFDC breakeven and, thereby, reduce the number of persons eligible for benefits, increased the AFDC program tax rate from 67 percent to 100 percent for recipients who have worked for at least four months. It was expected that those leaving the rolls would work more. However, by reducing AFDC benefits a dollar for each dollar of earnings, it was also anticipated that those still on the rolls would have little remaining incentive to work. Findings from the IMEs were used by the Congressional Budget Office to help predict the relative sizes of these effects and, hence, the net budgetary savings resulting from increasing the AFDC tax rate.

THE FAMILY SUPPORT ACT

In 1988, Congress passed the Family Support Act (FSA). This legislation resulted in significant changes in the nation's welfare system. For example, every state was required to operate a JOBS program that obligated AFDC recipients to participate in training, education, subsidized private sector jobs, public service jobs, or job search assistance in exchange for their welfare grant. These so-called welfare-to-work programs continued the trend that began with PBJI to move welfare recipients into employment. However, to a much greater extent than PBJI would have, JOBS focused on moving welfare recipients into regular jobs and on reducing the size of the welfare rolls. In addition to JOBS, the FSA extended the length of time families leaving the AFDC rolls could continue to remain eligible for Medicaid and child care subsidies,[38] once again to encourage recipients to leave welfare and take jobs. The FSA also tightened up federal provisions for the awarding and collection of child support for custodial single parents. Finally, the FSA required all states to participate in the AFDC-Unemployed Parent (AFDC-U) program. This program allowed two-parent families in which the father was unemployed to receive AFDC benefits under certain restrictive circumstances. Before the FSA mandate, state participation in the program was optional and only about half the states took part.

Social experiments played a major role in the design of the JOBS component of the FSA. However, as we will detail in chapter 8, the social experiments that performed this role were very different than the IMEs. The IMEs themselves had little to contribute. They simply were not designed to provide information that was germane to JOBS or, with the possible exception of the expansion of the AFDC-U program, the other provisions of the FSA. Ironically, by encouraging the incorporation of a public service jobs component in PBJI, the IMEs sowed the seeds of their own eventual obsolescence.

RECENT WELFARE REFORM EFFORTS

More recent welfare reform legislation has taken place at the state as well as the federal levels, and has continued the trend toward attempting to promote work and reduce the size of the welfare rolls. This legislation is discussed in some detail in chapter 8. Here we merely point out that, once again, the IMEs did not provide information that was germane to formulating this legislation. This is readily apparent from the nature of the legislation. For example, recent important federal legislation has limited the number of years welfare recipients can remain on the rolls and replaced the AFDC program with block grants to the states. Many of the modifications in the welfare system made by states—expanding the provision of education and training, requiring welfare recipients to work at either a regular job or a public service job, and further improving the collection of child support payments—can be viewed as extensions of the FSA. Some states have also prohibited increases in benefits for families in which an additional child is born while the family is on the AFDC rolls.

Assessing the Use of the Income Maintenance Experiments with the Conceptual Framework

In chapter 3, we described a conceptual framework that consists of four components. The first of these components concerns alternative explanations of the decision to undertake social experiments and was discussed earlier in this chapter. The remaining three components of the conceptual framework all concern the use made of information provided by social experiments. In this section, we use these three components to summarize our conclusions on the use of findings from the IMEs.

Taxonomy of Use

The eight-cell reformulation of Whiteman's taxonomy of the ways in which research is used is shown in table 6.2. As the individual entries that appear in the table have been previously described, only a few general points about the table need to be made here. First, the table indicates that findings from the IMEs were used in a variety of ways. One or more entries appear in six of the eight cells.

Second, possibly the most important entry in table 6.2 appears in the upper left-hand corner: the formative-concrete-substantive contribution of labor supply findings from the IMEs to the decision to include a jobs component in the Program for Better Jobs and Income and, more generally, to the increasing emphasis on moving welfare recipients into jobs. However, as previously emphasized, one can only speculate on how important this contribution really was; the same decision may have been made and the same trend may have developed regardless of the findings.

Third, the income maintenance experiments affected how welfare programs are administered by demonstrating the use of monthly reporting

Table 6.2. *Uses of the Income Maintenance Experiments*

	Substantive	Elaborative
Concrete		
Formative	Strengthened case of proponents of including a public service jobs component in PBJI and, hence, perhaps ultimately contributed to the increasing emphasis on moving welfare recipients into jobs.	Influenced design of PBJI through incorporation of labor supply findings into microsimulation models. Influenced adoption of more frequent reporting by welfare recipients and retrospective accounting. Resulted in estimates of behavioral parameters from the IMEs being incorporated into a variety of research and policy analyses. Popularized the use of random assignment social experiments and influenced the way in which such experiments are conducted.
Persuasive/ Advocacy	"Premature" findings from New Jersey experiment used to argue in favor of FAP. Completed New Jersey findings used to argue in favor of ISP. Simulation findings based on Seattle-Denver experiment used by DOL to argue for including public service jobs component in PBJI.	
Conceptual		
Formative	By focusing attention on the gap between transfer costs and the resulting increases in the incomes of transfer recipients, probably persuaded some long-time supporters of a "pure" NIT to relinquish their position. Altered view of some that extending cash assistance to intact families would cause massive withdrawals from the work-force and the view of others that the resulting labor supply effects would be inconsequential.	Refined understanding of the size of income and substitution effects. Emphasized role of independence effect in marital separation decisions. Altered view that extending cash assistance to intact families would enhance marital stability.
Persuasive/ Advocacy	Confirmed general expectations concerning the magnitude of labor supply responses to changes in wage rates and income.	

and retrospective accounting. Although we have listed this as a concrete use, doing so is not quite correct. As indicated earlier, a specific policy decision to use these two innovations in administering welfare was not made on the basis of findings from the IMEs. Instead, the findings from the IMEs first underwent further tests.

Fourth, the role of labor supply findings from the IMEs in altering views on the size of negative income tax effects on hours of work has been listed in table 6.2 as a substantive use, whereas the role of the marital stability findings on views pertaining to the effects of NITs on family separations has been listed as an elaborative use. This is a judgment call based on the fact that estimating labor supply effects, rather than marital stability effects, was the key reason the IMEs were launched.

The I-I-I Model

The IMEs failed to result in the specific formative-concrete-substantive use envisioned by its sponsors: national adoption of an NIT. Moreover, as suggested earlier, it is doubtful that they would have resulted in this use regardless of actual findings from the experiments.

This outcome is strongly consistent with Weiss's I-I-I framework. Neither the voting public nor Congress ever broadly supported NITs. Consequently, the IMEs could cause such a program to be adopted only if the major concern of large numbers of nonsupporters was the potential effect of NITs on hours of work. Instead, as will be discussed next, information from sources other than the IMEs, political interests, and (especially) the ideologies of nonsupporters all were aligned against the NIT concept. Thus, information provided by the IMEs—regardless of what it was—was likely to be of secondary importance. However, although the constellation of information from other sources, interests, and ideologies probably precluded the IMEs from being used in the manner originally intended by their sponsors, it did not—as table 6.2 attests, but in contrast to predictions from Weiss's model—keep findings from the IMEs from being used in many other ways.

INFORMATION FROM SOURCES OTHER THAN RESEARCH

Although there has been an enormous amount of research on welfare programs and welfare recipients,[39] this research often competes unsuccessfully with information from other sources. Especially important in this regard are unflattering (and sometimes unsubstantiated) anecdotes about individuals on welfare. Persons moved by such anecdotes were unlikely to support the expansion in the welfare rolls that would have resulted from an NIT.

POLITICAL INTERESTS

Welfare recipients do not form a natural constituency for members of Congress in the same sense that farmers or senior citizens often do, in part because many welfare recipients do not vote. However, middle- and higher income persons who are likely to vote would inevitably pay for any expansions in welfare benefits resulting from enactment of an NIT.

IDEOLOGIES

Welfare policy in the United States appears to be driven much more by ideology than by research. For example, Kenneth Bowler, who was staff director of the Public Assistance Subcommittee of the House Ways and Means Committee during the period in which the Program for Better Jobs and Income was being developed, asserted to us that "welfare is viewed with philosophical blinders and is resistant to policy analysis." Similarly, Michael Stern, the staffer on the Senate Finance Committee during the 1970s who was responsible for welfare issues, indicated to us that "welfare reform is a fundamental values issue."

The ideological views of most voters worked against enactment of an NIT. For example, the most fundamental ideological issue on NITs is its central concept: providing a guaranteed income for persons capable of working. That concept was unacceptable to many persons. As Henry Aaron (1990, 277) has written, "The public and their elected representatives have made clear in every way they know how that they think it is good for healthy working-age people to receive pay in return for work and bad for them to get pay without work." In addition, concern over the fact that an NIT would expand the welfare rolls and budget was partly ideologically based; taxes would be higher and the role of the government larger than otherwise.[40]

Use Factors

TIMELINESS

Compared with other types of research, social experiments tend to have especially long gestation periods, and the gestation periods for the IMEs were longer than for most social experiments. For example, the Seattle-

Denver experiment was initiated in 1970, preliminary results began to be available in 1976, the final report was published in 1983, and the Cain and Wissoker reanalysis of the marital stability findings was published in 1990. This caused problems both before and after the findings were available. On one hand, findings from the IMEs were not yet available at the time FAP, an NIT-type program, was being considered, although, as described earlier, premature findings from the New Jersey experiment were released in an attempt to circumvent this limitation. On the other hand, by the time the analyses of the IME data were complete, the policy agenda had moved on to welfare reform proposals that had little in common with the types of program tested. The lack of timeliness had dire implications for those who supported negative income taxes: At the time the IMEs were launched, the political climate was as favorably disposed toward NITs as at any time in the nation's history; by the time the findings finally became available, political support for such a program had severely eroded.

That lack of timeliness might have been even more dire had the income maintenance experiments delayed consideration of NIT-type programs. However, it seems apparent that the research clock for the IMEs and the policy clock for negative income taxes moved independently of one another. The fact that the Family Assistance Program was proposed before findings from the IMEs were available suggests that policymakers did not wait for the experiments to be completed before acting. On the other hand, there is also no evidence that findings from the IMEs influenced the policy agenda by causing NIT-type programs to be considered. Nonetheless, the accidental juxtaposition between President Carter's Program for Better Jobs and Income proposal in 1977 and the availability of findings from the IMEs was close to ideal. This vindicates one of the rationales for undertaking the IMEs that was mentioned earlier: that welfare reform was likely to be a long-term issue, one to which information from the experiments would ultimately contribute. However, by the time the Carter proposal was made, the IMEs already suffered from some obsolescence; the public service jobs component of PBJI was not tested in any of the IMEs.

Although the problem of obsolescence is obviously more important for concrete uses of experimental findings than for conceptual uses, it does occur for both types of utilization. For example, of 125 citations in an excellent 1992 review article by Robert Moffitt on the way the welfare system affects the behavior of recipients, only seven citations focus primarily on findings from the IMEs. As the analyst who was responsible for estimating the effects of the Gary experiment on work effort, Moffitt is more aware of findings from the IMEs than most social scientists. The IMEs simply do not provide information that is relevant to many topics of current concern.

COMMUNICATION AND VISIBILITY

The four income maintenance experiments were large and expensive, and they represented the nation's first effort at social experimentation. As a result, there appeared to be a general presumption on the part of those involved with the IMEs that findings from them would inevitably reach a large, receptive audience. Thus little, if any, careful thought seems to have been given to the way findings from the IMEs could most effectively be communicated to policymakers. Partially as a result of this passive attitude, the General Accounting Office strongly criticized DHEW in a report entitled *Income Maintenance Experiments: Need to Summarize Results and Communicate the Lessons Learned.* More specifically, GAO stated that "the needs of prospective users were apparently not fully considered" and "there were no results dissemination procedures, resulting in apparently untimely reports and inconsistent reporting practices" (1981, 10).

This is not to say that efforts at communicating findings from the IMEs were not made and that relevant individuals within the policy community were not aware of the findings. Communications of findings from the IMEs may be viewed as having taken place in two layers. The first layer consists of communication between the research teams and the sponsoring agency, initially OEO and later DHEW. The second layer consists of communication between the research teams or the sponsoring agency and the general policy community, including other governmental agencies, Congress, the administration, academics, and the general public.

Communication within the first layer mainly consisted of technical reports that the research teams transmitted to the research staffs of the sponsoring agencies, although there were also numerous meetings and briefings. As most members of the agency research staffs were social scientists, they could readily understand the technical papers. At the later stages of the analysis of data from the Gary and Seattle-Denver experiments, a system was instituted whereby members of the Office of the Assistant Secretary of Planning and Evaluation research staff wrote memos on each technical report assessing its strength and weaknesses and summarizing its findings. These memos were then transmitted to the deputy assistant secretary responsible for welfare policy and to the assistant secretary in charge of OASPE.

Communication within the second layer was considerably more sporadic. The research teams focused mainly on their peers, other social scientists. Consequently, although they produced books and numerous journal articles, those tended to be technical and methodologically oriented and not widely read by the general policy community. Robert Spiegelman, the director of research for the Seattle-Denver experiment, pointed out to us that during the course of the experiment, he rarely met with anyone at DHEW except those staff members directly responsible for monitoring the project contract and, until Senator Moynihan held hearings at the very end of the experiment, never gave a briefing outside of DHEW. He indicated that this was not due to intent on anyone's part but resulted because having the research team communicate with the broader policy community simply did not occur to either the researchers themselves or staffers at DHEW.

DHEW used a number of vehicles for communicating findings from the IMEs: press releases, occasional briefings of congressional staffers, congressional testimony, comments on the IMEs in its "Policy Research Report" (an annual report to Congress in which DHEW summarized all its research activities), and (possibly most important) summary reports written by OASPE staff on each experiment. Although state (and sometimes county) governments administer welfare programs, except for press releases, DHEW focused mainly on communicating findings from the IMEs to policymakers at the federal level. This is not surprising; at the time findings from the IMEs became available, state and local governments played a relatively minor role in welfare policymaking.

Although there was not a well-organized systematic effort to disseminate findings from the IMEs, this fact does not appear to have seriously impeded the use of findings from these experiments. Because the IMEs were large and among the first social experiments, they were highly publicized and well known.[41] Findings were accessible to the social science community through numerous reports, conference presentations, and published papers. The policy community obtained information about the experiments through summary reports produced by DHEW, although, as the General Accounting Office (1981) noted, the reports tended not to be timely, as they often were not made available until relatively long after the reported research was completed. Also, as previously described, labor supply findings from the Seattle-Denver experiment were indirectly communicated to policymakers through simulation predictions when PBJI was being considered. Key findings from the IMEs were communicated to the general public through fairly frequent stories that appeared in the popular media.

Although a general knowledge of the experimental findings existed among members of the policy community, that knowledge often seems not to be deep. This situation is exemplified by Michael Stern, the staffer on the Senate Finance Committee during the 1970s with responsibility for welfare issues. When interviewed, Stern recalled that findings from the Seattle-Denver experiment indicated that NIT payments and tax rates "dampened work incentives." He found this finding "intuitive," but thought it "gratifying" that in this instance intuition was verified by research. Stern did not mention either the other three IMEs or any IME findings other than those that pertain to hours of work.[42]

There was ample opportunity for confusion to occur in the communication of findings from the IMEs.[43] As was appropriate, given the complex nature of the IMEs, much of the analysis was highly technical (for example, the estimation of income and substitution effect elasticities and the use of hazard models in some of the marital stability work). Moreover, findings differed somewhat among the four IMEs; and there were a substantial number of different information sources, including DHEW, other government agencies, the different organizations hired to perform the research on data from each experiment, and independent analysts who conducted research with these data.[44]

There is not much evidence that serious confusion actually occurred, however. Perhaps the reason is that technicians were capable of sorting through the profusion of complex findings, whereas most nontechnicians received the findings in nontechnical form—for example, the newspapers and DHEW summary reports generally emphasized simple experimental-control differences—and probably did not follow the experiments closely enough to notice conflicts in findings. As Mundel (1985, 254) has asserted, the highly sophisticated analyses performed on the IME data could *potentially* have caused confusion among nontechnicians about what was tested and what was found. But this does not seem to have occurred in practice. Probably the more serious issue is that the understanding of the IME results among nontechnicians was incomplete. That understanding often did not go beyond knowledge that the findings implied negative effects of NITs on hours of work and on marital stability.

GENERALIZABILITY

As indicated in chapter 3, generalizability, as it pertains to social experiments, refers to the extent to which findings can be applied to different contexts—for example, different times and locations—and policies that differ to some extent from the ones directly tested. Virtually all social experiments, the IMEs included, are circumscribed in generalizability because of various design limitations that were necessary because of cost considerations. Several of those limitations are briefly discussed next.

Like most social experiments, the IMEs were located in only a few places and limited to only a few years. The extent to which the findings apply to other locations and other times is inherently problematic. However, the fact that the four IMEs took place in diverse locations, yet produced roughly similar results on the effects of NITs on hours of work, is reassuring.

Those who implemented the IMEs hoped to provide information that was generalizable to a national, ongoing NIT program. Like most social experiments, however, relatively few low-income families in each IME site were eligible to participate in the tested NITs and eligibility was for a limited period. As a consequence, certain effects that could result from a full-scale, ongoing NIT might have been missed. For example, if there were substantial reductions in hours worked under a full-scale NIT, employers might respond by increasing wage rates, and this increase might mitigate the fall in hours. Moreover, it might be easier to administer a small-scale NIT than a large-scale one. In addition, those eligible for NIT benefits might respond differently to a permanent program than they would to a program being tested in a temporary experiment.[45] It is also possible that social attitudes and tastes that are unaffected by a temporary, small-scale experimental NIT might change under a permanent, full-scale NIT.

Like the IMEs, most other social experiments are also subject to limitations of the sort listed above. However, the IMEs also have an important advantage over most other social experiments in generalizability. They are among the relatively few examples of "response surface" experiments ever conducted. That is, the IMEs were designed in a way that permitted estimation of the effects of variations in the basic parameters of the programs being tested, namely, changes in the income guarantee provided by an NIT and variations in the program's tax rate. Once obtained, estimates of those response surface parameters can, at least in principle, be used to project the effects of any program that had the basic features of an NIT, even if the guarantee levels and tax rates differed substantially from those tested in the experiments.

As described in some detail earlier in the chapter, response surface parameters (or, more specifically, income and substitution effects) were, in fact, estimated from data from the Seattle-Denver experiment. The parameters were then incorporated into a microsimulation model that was used in designing and costing out the Program for Better Jobs and Income. Thus, microsimulation helped facilitate the generalization of findings from the Seattle-Denver experiment to the nation as a whole and to transfer programs other than those directly tested in the experiment.

RELEVANCE

As emphasized earlier, the principal objective of the income maintenance experiments was to determine the effect of negative income taxes on work incentives. Even on its own terms, the relevance of the IMEs was somewhat limited because none of the tested programs included work requirements, and, at least in retrospect, it seems unlikely that the country would ever run a welfare program that did not incorporate some such requirement. Thus, findings from the experiments probably overstated the reduction in hours that would occur under an actual operating NIT. Moreover, whereas much was learned about running cash transfer programs, nothing was learned about issues arising in administering work requirements.

More important, although the work incentive issue is undoubtedly of relevance to welfare reform, it is not the only, or probably even the most important, concern of policymakers. For example, the effects of the reform on the size of the welfare rolls and on government budgetary cost may be more critical.[46] And for many lawmakers and their constituents, the very principle of providing a guaranteed income to persons who are able to work may be a more fundamental issue than behavioral responses to changes in welfare programs. In an article written shortly after Carter's Program for Better Jobs and Income failed to receive congressional support, Robert Strauss (1978), an economist on the staff of the Joint Committee on Taxation who was prominently involved in assessing the Carter proposal, listed "ten areas, which any welfare reform proposal must explicitly or implicitly address." Incentives are only one of these areas.

However, even here, he gives somewhat passing reference to work incentives and appears more concerned with the way welfare reform proposals would affect the incentives of those running welfare to improve the administration of a transfer program and the incentives of the government and employers to create jobs. In summary, the focus of the income maintenance experiments, although not irrelevant, was somewhat tangential to the central concerns of many policymakers.

Several other aspects of relevance are also worthy of mention in the context of the IMEs. For example, on one hand, the IMEs illustrate that the relevance of social experiments can be enhanced if they can be readily generalized to programs that differ somewhat from those directly tested, something made possible because the IMEs were response surface experiments. On the other hand, the IMEs also illustrate that social experiments are likely to become increasingly less relevant with the passage of time. As described earlier, this situation resulted for the IMEs because welfare reform proposals increasingly diverged from the NIT concept. Finally, the IMEs also illustrate one of the more important conclusions that Beyer and Trice (1982, 612–13) drew from their review of the utilization literature: In using research for postdecision purposes, users tend to find relevant those results that conform to their prior conclusions. For example, in the development phase of PBJI, representatives from DOL found especially relevant those simulation estimates that predicted that an appreciable fraction of increased income provided under pure cash assistance programs would be offset by reductions in the earnings of recipients caused by declines in hours of work.

DEFINITIVENESS
There were two sets of well-known findings from the IMEs: those on the effects of NITs on hours of work and those pertaining to the effects of NITs on marital stability. The definitiveness of these two sets of findings (that is, the certitude surrounding them) differs and will be discussed separately. As will be seen, both sets of findings provide useful tests of several of the hypotheses mentioned in chapter 3 about the perception of policymakers of the definitiveness of a given set of research findings. These hypotheses indicate that perceived definitiveness will be lower if

- there is debate among researchers on the validity of the findings;
- the findings are subject to scrutiny;
- the findings are ambiguous;

- the findings contradict other information sources or the intuition, values, experience, and expectations of potential users; or
- the findings are threatening to potential users' goals.

A number of factors could *potentially* have undermined the perception of policymakers as to the definitiveness of the labor supply findings from the IMEs. (1) Although the experiments consistently indicated that NITs caused hours of work to fall, the estimated magnitude of the findings varied across the four IMEs. (2) Because four separate research teams conducted the analyses of the experimental data, the statistical techniques used and the formats in which findings were reported varied.[47] Moreover, as previously mentioned, there were a number of alternative sources of information about the experimental findings, each of which reported the findings somewhat differently. (3) The microsimulation models, which were a major vehicle for the concrete utilization of IME findings on the effects of NITs on hours of work, were complex, easily subject to technical criticism, and difficult to describe in readily accessible form to policymakers.

Finally (4), as might be expected given their size and prominence, the IMEs were subject to considerable scrutiny by outside researchers. For example, the New Jersey and Rural experiments were thoroughly critiqued in papers presented at separate conferences the Brookings Institution held on each of the experiments (see Palmer and Pechman 1978 and Pechman and Timpane 1975). And the Russell Sage Foundation sponsored an additional book-length critique of the New Jersey experiment (Rossi and Lyall 1976). In addition, the Federal Reserve Bank of Boston and the Brookings Institution sponsored a conference and book on all four experiments that contained numerous criticisms of the IMEs (Munnell 1986). Moreover, toward the end of the 1970s, data from the income maintenance experiments began to be reanalyzed by economists who focused on certain methodological issues associated with the labor supply findings and purported to demonstrate that the initially estimated treatment effects on hours of work were either seriously understated or overstated (see, for example, Burtless and Greenberg 1982; Cogan 1978; and Greenberg, Moffitt, and Friedmann 1981).[48]

Given all this, it may be somewhat surprising that the perceived definitiveness of the IME findings on NIT work effort does not appear to have been seriously undermined among policymakers. Indeed, even most members of the social science community seemed to accept the basic conclusion that NITs would cause moderate reductions in hours of work among low-income families.

There are several reasons that policymakers viewed the IMEs' findings on hours of work as definitive. First, during the period of greatest policy use of the IME findings, the Program for Better Jobs and Income period, focus tended to be on findings from the Seattle-Denver experiment. Consequently, cross-experimental variation was not much noticed. Second, most policymakers either were not much aware of or did not wish to get involved in technical (and sometimes esoteric) controversies about the IME findings or to learn much about the inner workings of the micro-simulation models. Thus, experience with the IMEs does not support the first two hypotheses listed above. Third, and consistent with the fourth hypothesis, the labor supply findings generally conformed to the previous expectations of most policymakers. Fourth, and consistent with the fifth hypothesis, the findings were not really threatening to the goals of most policymakers.[49] If the findings had been more dramatic—for example, if they had implied that NITs would cause virtually no reduction in hours or that they would cause most low-wage males to cease working entirely—this might not have been the case. As previously discussed, however, the actual findings played only a tangential role in the debate over whether or not to enact an NIT.

In contrast to the findings on work hours, those on marital stability were counterintuitive and unexpected. As mentioned earlier, the expectation was that, relative to the existing welfare system, the experimental treatments would strengthen marital stability because the treatments appeared to provide much less of a financial incentive to separate. Thus, consistent with the fourth and fifth hypotheses, the findings were instantaneously controversial. Some persons used them to argue against the welfare reforms being considered by the Carter administration. Others suggested that because PBJI incorporated a public service jobs component, it would increase the probability that husbands in intact families would bring home earnings and thereby would be stabilizing. It was also argued by some that interpretation of the findings was ambiguous (the third hypothesis)—for example, if the experimental payments allowed women to leave an unhappy marriage, was this necessarily bad? Finally, some attempted to dismiss the findings by suggesting statistical reasons for not taking them seriously. Thus, some persons accepted the marital stability findings, whereas others questioned their definitiveness.[50] Whether the controversy about the definitiveness of the findings was a source of their apparent lack of influence in Congress on persons other than Senator Moynihan is unclear.

NOTES

1. An IME was also conducted in Canada (see Hum and Simpson 1991), one of the very few instances of social experimentation outside the United States. Discussion of that experiment, however, is beyond the scope of this book.

2. The New Jersey and the Rural experiments were transferred from OEO to OASPE when OEO was disbanded in the mid-1970s.

3. Like an NIT, Aid to Families with Dependent Children (AFDC), the major public assistance program at the time the IMEs were initiated, could also be described in terms of a guarantee, a program tax rate, and a breakeven point. Unlike a pure NIT, however, AFDC benefits did not depend solely on income; for example, households had to contain a child and, except under restrictive circumstances, benefits were limited to one-parent families.

4. After the New Jersey Income Maintenance Experiment began, considerable nonexperimental research was conducted on the relationship between hours of work and wage rates, tax rates, income, and other variables. (Many of these studies appear in Cain and Watts 1973.) Like the IMEs, much of this research, which mainly relied on data from household surveys and an econometric framework originally formulated by Lewis (1957), was stimulated by interest in NITs. However, little research of this sort had been conducted before the beginning of the New Jersey Income Maintenance Experiment, and that which existed was not well known to policymakers.

5. However, as Alice O'Connor (1995) has written, there were additional attractions to undertaking the IMEs: "Labor economists would get hard evidence to test theoretical models of labor supply; econometricians the chance to see if controlled experimentation could work on a large scale with human subjects; OEO the chance to prove its worth in policy innovation and scientific analysis. . . ."

6. In fact, combined, the four IMEs cost in excess of $100 million in 1972 dollars. However, the full cost of the IMEs seems to have been larger than was initially anticipated. For example, Robert Spiegelman, who headed the analysis effort for the Seattle-Denver Income Maintenance Experiment, told us that that experiment cost three or four times more than the original expected cost.

7. Demogrants, which are found in some Western European countries, provide income transfers to families based on family size or number of children. Unlike NITs, the size of the transfer is not conditioned on family income.

8. Although two-parent families were ineligible for AFDC in New Jersey at the time the experiment was initiated, New Jersey unexpectedly introduced an AFDC program for intact families shortly after the experiment began. As a result, a substantial fraction of treatment group families received AFDC at some point during the course of the New Jersey experiment. (See Rees and Watts 1977, 11; and Watts, Poirier, and Mallar 1977, tables 2.10 and 2.11.) This substantially complicated interpreting the experimental findings and was an important reason for testing NITs at other sites.

9. Perhaps the most complete sources of information on findings from the IMEs are the final reports produced by the research teams responsible for analyzing the data produced by each experiment (see Watts and Rees 1977 for the New Jersey Income Maintenance Experiment; Bawden and Harrar 1977 for the Rural Income Maintenance Experiment; Kehrer, McDonald, and Moffitt 1980 for the Gary Income Maintenance

Experiment; and SRI International 1983 for the Seattle-Denver Income Maintenance Experiment). Information in more summary form on findings from three of the IMEs can be found in reports produced by DHEW (see U.S. Department of Health, Education, and Welfare 1973 for the New Jersey Income Maintenance Experiment; U.S. Department of Health, Education, and Welfare 1976 for the Rural Income Maintenance Experiment; and U.S. Department of Health, Education, and Welfare 1983 for the Seattle-Denver Income Maintenance Experiment). In addition, conferences were held on findings from three of the experiments and the resulting papers were collected into published volumes (see Pechman and Timpane 1975 for the New Jersey Income Maintenance Experiment; Palmer and Pechman 1978 for the Rural Income Maintenance Experiment; and Robins, West, and Lohrer 1980 for the Seattle-Denver Income Maintenance Experiment). Three useful cross-experimental syntheses of effects on hours of work were conducted by Moffitt and Kehrer (1981), Robins (1985), and Burtless (1986). Finally, cross-experimental summaries of many of the non-labor-supply effects can be found in Hanushek (1986), Michael (1986), and Bradbury (1986).

10. The weighted averages for female family heads are from only the Gary and Seattle-Denver experiments as the sample in the New Jersey experiment excluded such persons and the sample in the Rural experiment included too few such persons to provide reliable estimates. For very similar summary estimates, also see Robins (1985) and Moffitt and Kehrer (1981).

11. Many economists would take exception to this statement because it emphasizes government budgetary costs rather than costs that result from reductions in economic efficiency and because it ignores the value of increased leisure that transfer recipients receive when they reduce the number of hours they work (for example, see the comments by Hall [1986] on Burtless's statement). However, these considerations are irrelevant to the way the implications of the Seattle-Denver findings suggested by Burtless's statement might play out in the policy arena. For example, legislators often resist increases in government budgetary expenditures, even if they would result in improvements in efficiency, and seem to place little, if any, value on increases in leisure received by the poor.

12. Both Moffitt and Kehrer (1981) and Burtless (1986) have made such comparisons. Our conclusions are based on their comparisons.

13. We thank Robert Moffitt for drawing this point to our attention.

14. For a summary of the Seattle-Denver findings on marital stability, see Groeneveld, Hannan, and Tuma (1983).

15. SRI reports on the marital stability findings began to appear as early as 1974 (Hannan, Beaver, and Tuma 1974) and articles were published in the *American Journal of Sociology* in 1977 and 1978 (Hannan, Beaver, and Tuma 1977 and Hannan, Tuma, and Groeneveld 1978). Cain first reported very preliminary results from a reanalysis at a 1986 conference (Cain and Watts 1986). However, the major reanalysis by Cain and Wissoker was not published until 1990 (Cain and Wissoker 1990).

16. The idea of retrospective accounting and monthly reporting did not originate solely from the IMEs. Governor Reagan's administration in California was also exploring similar modifications in welfare administration at roughly the same time.

17. For a discussion of lessons learned from the New Jersey experiment on how to field and operate a social experiment, see Kershaw and Fair (1976).

18. Empirical evidence of the existence of an independence effect preceded the Seattle-Denver findings, however. See, for example, Ross and Sawhill (1975).

19. FAP differed in only two major respects from a pure NIT. First, FAP benefits were limited to families in which there was at least one dependent child under 18. Under a pure NIT, eligibility would have depended solely on income. Hence, single individuals and childless couples would have been eligible for benefits. In addition, under FAP, adults were to be required to accept employment if a suitable job was available. A similar work test would not be required under a pure NIT. However, it was not at all clear that the FAP work test would be rigorously enforced.

20. For details on the demise of FAP, see Moynihan (1973) or Burke and Burke (1974).

21. Even some congressional supporters of the NIT approach were lukewarm to FAP, as Coyle and Wildavsky (1986) point out, because they thought its benefit level was set too low and because it excluded childless couples and single individuals.

22. Stern further suggested that those opposed to the NIT approach did not like the fact that it took away money as people earned more income. Thus, many members of Congress were much more enthusiastic about an Earned Income Tax Credit because it rewarded work effort, while NITs penalized work effort.

23. President Nixon's own enthusiasm for FAP also seems to have waned. For example, H. R. Haldeman (1994) wrote in his diary on July 13, 1970: "About Family Assistance Plan, [the president] wants to be sure it's killed by Democrats and that we make big play for it, but don't let it pass, can't afford it."

24. For details of this interesting episode, see Williams (1972, chapter 4).

25. When interviewed, Harold Watts, the author of the Institute for Research on Poverty report on the preliminary New Jersey Experiment findings, argued forcefully that, even in hindsight, issuing the report was appropriate. In his view, the information was relevant to considering FAP and, although preliminary, was the best information available at the time.

26. However, Kenneth Bowler, who headed the staff of a special House of Representatives subcommittee that was established to consider PBJI, told us that in conversations among people working on welfare issues, the IMEs were "part of the conversation; [they] always came up."

27. Microsimulation models are computer models that compare (1) the circumstances that a nationally representative sample of families currently face with (2) the circumstance these families would face under a proposed program such as the PBJI (see Citro and Hanushek 1991 for details). The incremental cost of the proposed program can be computed by subtracting each family's transfer benefits without the proposed program from the family's benefits under the program and then multiplying by the family's sample weight and summing across all the families in the sample.

28. In fact, three separate microsimulation models were used for these purposes. All three models incorporated estimates of income and substitution effects that were obtained from data from the Seattle-Denver experiment. One of them, the KGB model, was developed in-house at DHEW specifically to simulate PBJI and was used in obtaining the cost estimates for the program that DHEW reported to Congress (see Betson, Greenberg, and Kasten 1980). The second model, MATH, had existed at Mathematica for some time but did not allow for labor supply adjustments to simulate changes in transfer programs until substitution and income effect estimates from the Seattle-Denver experiment became available. That model was used by both DHEW and DOL to obtain cost estimates of PBJI that could then be used to check the validity of the cost estimates

produced by KGB. The third model, TATSIM, was developed at SRI International. This model, which was based on extensions and refinements of the MATH model, was used by the Seattle-Denver research team to examine the implications of their labor supply findings for national policy (Robins et al. 1980).

29. Data from the other IMEs could have been used instead of the Seattle-Denver data to estimate income and substitution effects that could have been incorporated into simulation models. In fact, income and substitution effect estimates were available from the Gary experiment. However, the Seattle-Denver experiment had a larger sample than the other three experiments combined and, hence, seemed best suited to the task. Income and substitution effect estimates that were based on nonexperimental data could also have been used instead of estimates from the Seattle-Denver experiment. Indeed, crude simulation estimates that used income and substitution effects that were estimated with nonexperimental data had been computed for FAP (Greenberg and Kosters 1973) and brought to the attention of then-Secretary of the Department of Health, Education, and Welfare Elliot Richardson.

30. Use of estimates based on the behavior of low-income families in Seattle and Denver to make projections for low-income families throughout the entire nation could, in fact, have been questioned.

31. These estimates are taken from Aaron and Todd 1978, table 2.

32. Another advantage of combining cash assistance with public service jobs that was made apparent by the simulations was that the incomes of very poor families could be increased without adding moderately better off families to the welfare rolls. To increase the incomes of poor families under a pure cash assistance program, in contrast, it is necessary either to raise the income guarantee level or to reduce the program tax rate. Either approach raises the program breakeven level and makes large numbers of additional families with relatively high incomes eligible for benefits.

33. For example, as a comparison of Programs 1 and 2 implies, the availability of guaranteed public service jobs would cause earnings at regular jobs to decline by more than they would under a pure cash assistance plan. This occurs because some persons would prefer minimum wage public service jobs to low wage, disagreeable private sector jobs.

34. For a detailed discussion, see Lynn and Whitman (1981).

35. Of course, PBJI might have been difficult to resist had the findings from the four IMEs consistently indicated that the program increased *both* hours of work and marital stability. However, both economic theory and common sense suggest that it is highly unlikely that the IMEs could ever have implied that an NIT would increase hours of work. Indeed, such findings would have been highly controversial and probably greatly reduced the credibility of the experiments.

36. Quoted in Demkovich (1978, 2063).

37. Letter to William Buckley published in the *National Review*, September 29, 1978.

38. This continued eligibility for Medicaid and child care subsidies is commonly referred to as "transitional benefits."

39. For example, see Moffitt (1992) and the references cited therein.

40. Interestingly, opposition to the public service jobs component of PBJI was also partly ideological: the number of public sector jobs would expand, in part, at the expense of private sector jobs.

41. Indeed, the New Jersey and the Seattle-Denver experiments, the first and the largest of the IMEs, respectively, seem by far the best remembered of the four experiments.

42. In fairness, it is important to recognize that Stern probably had not thought about findings from the IMEs for 15 or more years before he was interviewed.

43. Neuberg (1988) has argued that the information communicated to policy-makers and to the general public about findings from the income maintenance experiments highly "distorted" what the experiments could actually say about the policies that were under consideration.

44. In a democracy, having a number of alternative sources of information is, of course, advantageous. It means that no single individual or agency has a monopoly over the information and can use it for its own ends.

45. This possibility was directly tested in the Seattle-Denver experiment by randomly assigning members of the experimental group to three different treatment duration groups—3, 5, and 20 years—and observing whether the groups do, in fact, respond differently to the treatment.

46. As pointed out earlier, the effect of an NIT on hours of work would influence the total cost of such a program. This issue was examined by incorporating income and substitution effect estimates into microsimulation models. However, even in the absence of any effects on work incentives, adoption of a national NIT would still have increased the cost of public assistance and the number of persons on the welfare rolls. It was this possibility that concerned many policymakers.

47. The differences among the research teams in methodology partially result from the fact that research on the four experiments did not all take place at the same time. Researchers on the later IMEs learned from the research conducted on the earlier IMEs, and the methodology evolved over time.

48. Cogan argued the estimated treatment effects were understated because they incorporated the labor supply responses of all households, both those who actually received the experimental NIT payments and presumably might have responded to the program work incentives and those who did not receive the experimental payments and were presumably unlikely to have responded to NIT work incentives. Greenberg, Moffitt, and Friedmann empirically examined the effect of underreporting in the Gary experiment and found evidence that some households in the experimental sample underreported their hours of work to those collecting the experimental data, whereas households in the control sample did not. Consequently, findings that failed to take underreporting into account overstated the experimental impact on hours of work. Burtless and Greenberg used data from the Seattle-Denver experiment to examine whether labor supply responses to short duration experiments are likely to understate responses to a permanent NIT program. Contrary to earlier findings that also relied on data from the Seattle-Denver experiment, they concluded that this would not necessarily occur.

49. The one possible exception to this statement concerns bureaucrats at DHEW during the Carter administration who, as described earlier, found their support for a pure NIT undermined by simulation predictions that were based on labor supply findings from the Seattle-Denver Experiment. As DHEW sponsored the Seattle-Denver Experiment and the microsimulation model that produced the predictions was developed in-house at DHEW, those persons were in an especially poor position to question the definitiveness of the predictions and, to their credit, remained honest research brokers and did not.

50. For a very brief summary of this controversy, see General Accounting Office (1981, 20–22).

7

The Unemployment Insurance Bonus Experiments

S everal current programs are designed to assist unemployed workers. The unemployment insurance system (UI) provides income for those who have lost their jobs, whereas the Employment Service (ES) provides work search assistance. With technological advances and increasing trade and competition in many blue-collar industries, worker dislocation and displacement are seen as societal problems to be addressed. Congress has responded with the Job Training Partnership Act (JTPA). Its goal is to provide services to teach the unemployed skills and assist them in finding employment. For those workers who have been displaced or dislocated from their jobs because of trade adjustments, Trade Adjustment Assistance (TAA) provides additional job search assistance and training. Those programs are usually coordinated at the state and local level.

The UI system provides an income maintenance entitlement for workers who lose their jobs through no fault of their own. It has a work search requirement that is designed to overcome the work disincentive that such an entitlement might cause. During the 1980s the system was under considerable stress, which caused much concern at the state and federal levels. However, there was no interest in increasing taxes to improve the solvency of the UI trust funds. The adequacy of the UI trust fund was of particular concern to states, as they administer the UI program within their boundaries. As unemployment rose during the 1970s and 1980s with recession and economic restructuring, state funds were stressed to the degree that federal assistance was needed. This remained a concern, and any proposal that might relieve pressure on those funds by reducing the overall costs and length of unemployment spells was viewed as potentially beneficial to the states (USDOL 1989b, 190).

The four UI bonus experiments examined in this chapter were initiated through the U.S. Department of Labor and state employment departments. Their objective was to determine if offering a bonus to program participants for finding a job before the expiration of their payments would promote more vigorous job search, cause earlier exits from the UI rolls, reduce payments from the UI trust funds, and bring in new tax revenues to the government. These experiments addressed the following question: Could the incentive of a bonus be a cost-effective way of changing behavior in the UI system?

Description of the Four Experiments

Table 7.1 provides a summary description of the four UI bonus experiments.

New Jersey Unemployment Insurance Reemployment Demonstration Project

The U.S. Department of Labor (DOL) initiated the New Jersey Unemployment Insurance Reemployment Demonstration Project in cooperation with the New Jersey Department of Labor to provide displaced workers with additional services and incentives that would hasten their exit from the unemployment rolls. The agencies were particularly interested in which UI claimants would benefit most from the tested services and incentives.

Beginning in July 1986 and continuing through the fall of 1987, the project offered 8,675 UI claimants one of three treatments. Eligible claimants were randomly assigned to job search assistance (JSA) only, JSA with training or relocation, or JSA plus a bonus for early reemployment. A randomly assigned group of 2,385 UI claimants received existing services and served as a control group. Participation in the various tested interventions began at about the fifth week after the initial UI claim. Participation orientation, testing, attendance at a job search workshop, and a counseling/assessment session were mandatory for all UI

Table 7.1. *Description of the UI Bonus Experiments*

	New Jersey[a]	Illinois	Pennsylvania	Washington
Bonus Levels	Declining	$500 to claimants $500 to employers	3× weekly UI benefit 6× weekly benefit	2× weekly UI benefit 4× weekly benefit 6× weekly benefit
Qualifying Period		11 weeks	6 weeks 12 weeks	20% UI entitlement period 40% UI entitlement period
Data Collection Period	1986–87	1984–85	1988–89	1988–90
# Sites	10	22	12	21
Target Group	Displaced or dislocated workers	New UI claimants & Job Service registrants	New UI claimants	New UI claimants

a. New Jersey tested other treatments besides a bonus: job search assistance, training, and relocation assistance.

claimants who received a first payment, with noncooperation leading to a denial of UI benefits (USDOL 1989a, 4). A process evaluation of the experiment determined that the requirement was enforced "reasonably well" (342).

To enhance generalizability of results, at least across New Jersey, the experiment was conducted in 10 sites that had state UI offices. The sites were chosen randomly (after a geographic stratification), but with the probability of selection proportional to the size of the UI population at the site (USDOL 1989a, 31).

The experiment in New Jersey was targeted at claimants who were experienced workers but were classified as displaced or dislocated permanently from their former jobs and thus likely to have difficulty in becoming reemployed. JTPA had been enacted to address the needs of that clientele. Hence, the experiment sought to tie the services provided through ES and the UI system to the needs of the unemployed targeted by JTPA.

Earlier in the 1980s research had shown that reemployment services might aid displaced workers in obtaining jobs (USDOL 1989a, 191). Concern over the solvency of the state UI trust funds also provided motivation to target those workers, as their likelihood of collecting UI for long periods was great. Upon becoming unemployed, those workers typically found that the type of job that they had held was no longer available, that their skills did not match available jobs, or that they lacked job-finding skills.

To be eligible for the bonus, claimants had to have received a first UI payment, be 25 years of age or older, have previously worked at the same job for at least three years (the Department of Labor's requirement for a dislocated worker), not been part of a temporary layoff, and not been subject to hiring through a union hiring hall. All those requirements were aimed at eliminating workers with limited or unique attachments to the labor market (USDOL 1989a, 3).

The bonus was designed to promote rapid reemployment of displaced workers by providing an economic incentive to seek work before the expiration of UI benefits. Thus, the bonus was at a maximum when first offered and declined thereafter, reaching zero well before the expiration of UI benefits.[1]

The size of the bonus payment was determined by the length of time that a worker had been unemployed. At the initial assessment interview, the maximum bonus was offered, equal to half the remaining UI entitlement. That amount would be paid if the claimant found work within two weeks of the interview. After that, the bonus declined by 10 percent of the maximum per week until it reached zero at the 11th week of the offer. Workers accepting certain types of jobs—for example, employment by a former employer or relative or temporary, seasonal, or part-time employment—were not eligible for bonus payments. Sixty percent of the bonus was paid after 4 weeks of work and the remainder after 12 weeks (USDOL 1989a, 4–5). The average bonus offered was $1,644 (33).

Illinois Unemployment Insurance Incentive Experiment

In contrast to the New Jersey experiment, the Illinois experiment involved only cash bonuses aimed at reducing the length of unemployment by inducing UI claimants to search actively for a job. Two treatments were tested at 22 sites in northern and central Illinois. The first treatment (the Claimant Experiment) offered a bonus of $500 to claimants if they could find a job within 11 weeks of filing for unemployment insurance and keep that job for at least four months. The second treatment (the Employer Experiment) offered $500 bonuses to employers hiring UI claimants if claimants were hired within 11 weeks of filing for UI and kept their jobs for at least four months.

The 11-week eligibility period was chosen arbitrarily. The four-month job-holding requirement was designed to avoid payments for seasonal work (Woodbury and Spiegelman 1987, 515). The $500 bonus payment was determined by the size of the budget for the experiment ($750,000 was available for bonuses) and a judgment about the size of the bonus needed to evoke a response.[2] For employers, the Targeted Jobs Tax Credit, a program that provided credits of up to $3,000 to employers who hired disadvantaged workers, guided the decision. The designers of the Illinois experiment believed that unemployed workers were more attractive to employers than the disadvantaged. Hence, the bonus for hiring unemployed workers could be smaller (514).

The Illinois experiment was targeted at claimants who were filing initial UI claims and were Job Service registrants. As in the case of the New Jersey experiment, this eliminated unemployed workers who had layoff recall dates or who were usually hired through a union hall. Claimants also had to be between 20 and 55 years old. This last requirement helped eliminate workers who were part of special programs for youth or who had retired.

From mid-1984 to 1985, the project assigned 17,306 UI claimants to the experiment. Of these, 3,952 were randomly assigned to the control group; 4,186 were assigned to the claimant treatment; and 3,963 were assigned to the employer treatment. Claimants in the treatment groups were asked to agree to participate, and many did not (Woodbury and Spiegelman 1987, 517). This was especially true in the employer portion of the experiment because of the stigma attached to workers' identifying themselves as being in the program (telephone interview with Robert Spiegelman, October 27, 1995). Hence, although 14 percent of those assigned to the claimant experiment claimed bonuses, the claimant rate in the employer experiment was only 3 percent.[3]

Subsequent analysis by Carl Davidson and Stephen Woodbury (1990) of the data from the claimant experiment separated claimants according to their eligibility for Federal Supplemental Compensation (FSC), which at the time of the Illinois experiment extended eligibility for UI for certain claimants from 26 weeks to 38 weeks. The analysis demonstrated that those eligible for FSC were more likely to take advantage of the bonus offer; thus, the bonus had "a greater impact on workers with greater potential duration of benefits" (5).

Pennsylvania Reemployment Bonus Demonstration

After the results of the New Jersey and Illinois experiments began filtering in, the U.S. Department of Labor decided to conduct further tests of the bonus concept. In cooperation with the Pennsylvania Department of Labor and Industry, it initiated an experiment in Pennsylvania to determine the relative effects of alternative bonuses on UI receipt and on reemployment. The experiment also tested the effectiveness of job search assistance in conjunction with the bonus.

Four different treatments tested combinations of two different bonus offers (a low offer of three times the weekly UI benefit amount and a high offer of three times the weekly UI benefit amount) and two different qualification periods (a short period of 6 weeks and a long period of 12 weeks). The two time periods were selected so that the researchers could determine whether a longer period promoted greater participation in the bonus plan, while also examining the effect that this longer period had on the costs of the program. A fifth treatment coupled the 12-week qualification period with a declining bonus—that is, the bonus amount remained constant for the first 3 weeks and then declined by 10 percent each week for the remaining 9 weeks (USDOL 1992b, 7). The qualification periods tested in Pennsylvania were compatible with those in the Illinois and New Jersey experiments and similar to those tested in Washington. This arrangement allowed for comparison across experiments and, hence, was intended to enlighten the subsequent policy discussion.

The small bonus amount averaged $500 and the large bonus amount averaged $997 (USDOL 1992b, 7); these amounts were set using findings from the Illinois and New Jersey experiences. Their determination was based on a multiple of the weekly UI benefits so that all claimants would have a similar incentive to take advantage of the bonus offer, even though their UI benefit amount varied. Doing this also allowed for comparison across experiments (a similar decision was made in Washington). Moreover, it was believed to be the likely basis for permanent adoption of a bonus system. An additional consideration was the need to set the bonus amount high enough to induce a response without setting it so high that the costs of the program became prohibitive. A range of bonuses was proposed to help determine the relationship between the size of the bonus and the behavioral response.

All five of the treatments described above included a job search assistance (JSA) component. A sixth treatment sought to isolate the effects of the JSA activities and, consequently, offered only the high bonus for the long qualification period. Attendance at the JSA sessions was voluntary. As it turned out, participation in the JSA activities was extremely low because of a lack of interest. The researchers also conjectured that the presence of the bonus offer might have been a disincentive to JSA participation, although they did not indicate why they thought this. Because of the low participation rate, the researchers concluded that voluntary JSA workshops were probably not feasible, at least in Pennsylvania (USDOL 1992b, 69–70).

The Pennsylvania experiment was targeted at new UI claimants who neither exclusively sought employment through union halls nor were likely to be recalled by their former employer. From July 1988 to October 1989, the project randomly assigned 15,005 eligible UI claimants to one of the six treatments or to a control group. There were 3,000 control group members and 10,120 treatment group members who were drawn from 12 sites that were randomly selected throughout the state. So that claimants who were representative of various unemployment conditions throughout the state could be chosen, UI offices were clustered on the basis of the size of their caseload. One UI office was randomly selected from each cluster. The claimants for the experiment were then chosen randomly from those offices.

Washington Reemployment Bonus Experiment

The U.S. Department of Labor conducted a further test of bonuses in collaboration with the Washington State Employment Security Department and the W. E. Upjohn Institute for Employment Research. This reemployment bonus demonstration was conducted as an expanded version of the experiments previously conducted in Illinois and New Jersey. The project was designed to validate the results of the previous experiments, test a range of bonus plans, and determine the most cost-effective bonus plan (USDOL 1992c, xiii).

Six different treatments tested three combinations of different bonus offers ranging from twice the weekly UI benefit amount to six times the weekly UI benefit amount and two different qualification periods (one-fifth of the claimant's UI entitlement period and two-fifths of the entitlement period). To receive a bonus, claimants had to remain employed for four months. As in Pennsylvania, the bonuses were multiples of the weekly UI benefit amounts. Thus, while the actual amounts varied, the relative amounts remained the same among claimants within a treatment group. The three levels were twice, four times, and six times the weekly UI benefit amount, with the middle level chosen to approximate the bonus offered in the Illinois experiment (USDOL 1992c, 11–12). The bonuses offered ranged from $110 to $1,254 (O'Leary, Spiegelman, and Kline 1993, 10). The average bonuses paid were $304, $608, and $912 (USDOL 1992c, 12).

In the other UI bonus experiments, the qualification period, the time during which the claimant was eligible to receive a bonus, was of fixed duration. In Washington, as indicated above, the qualification period varied. It was set at a fixed proportion of the claimant's period of entitlement. A long period of qualification would increase the opportunity to receive a bonus but not necessarily change work search behavior greatly. A short period of qualification would reduce the probability of receiving a bonus but should increase work search activity during the period. To balance this trade-off and to determine an optimal qualification period, two levels were chosen, one at 20 percent of the claimant's period of entitlement and the other at 40 percent. Effectively, this varied from 3 to 13 weeks, depending on the UI claimant (USDOL 1992c, 13–14).

The experiment in Washington was targeted at UI claimants whose job search activities could be increased by the bonus offer and for whom the state would incur UI costs. Thus, as in the other UI bonus experiments, newly discharged veterans and federal employees were ineligible. Only new claimants eligible to receive UI benefits were targeted, as it was believed that if a bonus system were permanently implemented, only new claimants would be eligible. Because the offer of a bonus was unlikely to affect their work searches, claimants likely to be recalled by their previous employer and those usually hired through union halls were ineligible for bonuses.

From 1988 until January 1990, when the last bonus was paid, the project randomly assigned 15,534 eligible claimants to treatment or control groups at 21 sites throughout the state. Having a variety of sites was consistent with a federal requirement that mandated that the research sample be representative of the demographics of the state (O'Leary et al. 1993, 3). To avoid claimants eligible for bonuses at these sites displacing claimants in the control group from jobs, enrollment occurred over an eight-month period. For similar reasons, bonus eligibility was limited to 20 percent of the caseload at the treatment sites.[4]

Like the other UI experiments, the Washington experiment was designed using power analysis—that is, the sample size for each treatment was determined using the expected effect size, the desired level of statistical significance, and the desired power. This, in turn, determined the budget request (which was accepted). The sample size for each treatment was set large enough to detect a reduction of the number of weeks in the UI system equal to the size of the one in Illinois. A budget limitation of $1.2 million available for bonus payments resulted in sample sizes varying between 1,535 and 2,353 for the six treatment groups, with the larger samples in the less expensive treatments, and 3,082 for the control group (O'Leary et al. 1993, 12–13, 46).

As with the other UI experiments, the Washington experiment relied on financial incentives to change job-seeking behavior. Thus, the Washington experiment was designed with the intention of obtaining a higher participation rate than the relatively low one that occurred in Illinois. The enrollment agreement was eliminated; and more information, including questionnaires, was given to the participants to make sure that they understood the program. However, as it turned out, a significant improvement did not occur, although perhaps it would have improved over time had the program been longer in duration and exposure to it greater. As might be expected, the proportion of eligible claimants collecting bonuses increased with the size of the bonus and the length of the qualification period (USDOL 1992c, 173–76). Although this was expected, it also resulted in additional costs for the program. Thus, estimates of the extent to which the collection of bonuses varies with the size of the bonuses and the length of the qualification period are needed as parameters for planning the implementation of a permanent bonus program.

Origin of the Experiments

The four UI bonus experiments, although conducted in different states at different times, were all primarily concerned with two parameters of interest: the size of the bonus and the length of the qualifying period. The four experimental states were considered "leading edge states,"[5] although each was chosen for different reasons. Illinois elected itself as an experimental site, using special funds provided by the federal government from the Wagner-Peyser Act and set aside by the governor. Illinois then chose Upjohn to evaluate the experiment. Robert Spiegelman, who headed Upjohn's evaluation team, suggested that the following factors motivated Illinois to conduct the experiment: "Experiments were hot, federal money available, and giving bonuses to employers sounded like a good Republican program" (telephone interview, October 27, 1995).

The other three states conducted experiments under the auspices of the U.S. Department of Labor. According to Walter Corson and Steve Wandner, Secretary of Labor William Brock wanted to do something for dislocated workers (telephone interviews with Walter Corson, May 28, 1996, and Steve Wandner, April 17, 1996). At the end of FY 1985, the Department of Labor scrambled to initiate a research project, and New Jersey was willing to do it. The window of opportunity opened, and New Jersey used it. Later, the Department of Labor decided to run more experiments and asked other states to volunteer. Desiring to replicate New Jersey and Illinois results in two additional states, the Department of Labor wanted a western state. According to Spiegelman, Washington was chosen because California had too many requirements at the state level and Washington had good, eager research people. Pennsylvania, the fourth site, was selected because it was large enough to have diverse labor markets, according to Corson.

The scientific objectives of the experiments flowed from the behavioral issues of interest. The UI system is designed to provide short-term financial assistance with promotion of early reemployment through required work search activities and referral to the employment service. However, because UI guaranteed income for a specified period (usually 26 weeks), it had the effect of discouraging active searching for work early in the unemployment period.

Before the experiments, it was hypothesized that more intensive job search activities would shorten the unemployment spell of those workers who were displaced or otherwise expected to have difficulty in finding employment. The New Jersey experiment was initiated to test this hypothesis and to determine if such workers could be identified early enough to benefit from those services (USDOL 1989a, 29). The experiment also aimed to strengthen the links between the UI system, ES, and JTPA providers. The bonus portion of the experiment aimed at mitigating the behavior disincentive for active job search that is inherent in the UI system. Thus "this treatment was designed to simulate a UI benefit cash-out program to the extent possible, whereby claimants receive at least part of their remaining entitlement as a reward for not exhausting it" (121).

Although providing extra services and bonus payments to unemployed workers could prove costly, the New Jersey experiment was designed to determine "if reemployment assistance were provided early in the UI claim period the savings in UI benefit payments could potentially outweigh the costs of providing these services." However, the designers of the experiment believed that "even if paying for reemployment services for these workers does not prove cost-effective from the standpoint of UI, the UI system may play an important role by identifying a broad population of displaced workers *early* in their unemployment spells who could benefit from receiving the services" (USDOL 1989a, 29).

Thus, the New Jersey experiment was designed to address concerns about providing extra services for those with reemployment difficulty, overcoming work search disincentives, promoting linkages among agencies helping these claimants, identifying claimants, and safeguarding the solvency of the state UI trust funds.

The Illinois experiment sought to respond to criticism of the UI system that, rather than encourage job search, it subsidized leisure and, consequently, lengthened the period of unemployment. The experiment sought to change the behavior of claimants through the use of economic incentives (Woodbury and Spiegelman 1987, 514). Like the New Jersey experiment, it provided bonuses intended to offset the behavioral disincentive inherent in UI, which, as previously noted, provided a guaranteed income that was thought to discourage active job search during the early stages of the unemployment period. Of particular political interest in Illinois was whether the payment of bonuses to claimants or to their employers would reduce the length of unemployment.

The behavioral issues of interest in the Pennsylvania experiment were the same as for the New Jersey and Illinois experiments: motivating people to find work and exit the UI system. However, the Pennsylvania experiment was designed to fine-tune the specifics of the bonus offer to determine the optimal policy for accelerating exit from the UI rolls. Thus, six treatment plans were tested. Not only could the impact of each of the plans be tested by comparison with the control group, but each of the treatments could be compared with the others to obtain a range of impacts, a range of costs for the treatments, and the relative cost-effectiveness of each treatment.

Like the Pennsylvania experiment, the Washington experiment was designed to fine-tune findings from the Illinois and New Jersey experiments. As with the Pennsylvania experiment, a variety of bonus plans was tested to provide policymakers with information about a range of alternatives. Political concerns in Washington State centered on costs to the taxpayer and solvency of the state UI trust funds. Thus, the experiment was designed with the intent of finding a way to provide income support during a period of unemployment, while reducing the work disincentive engendered by that income entitlement. The bonus was seen as a way to create economic incentives for individuals that would relieve pressure on the UI system and would keep taxes from rising.

The experiments were not intended to examine policy alternatives that fundamentally changed the policy of providing unemployment insurance. Rather, they sought to promote rapid reemployment within the structure of the UI system, that is, Lindblom's incremental changes around the margins of existing policy. In keeping with the incremental approach, one of the survey respondents noted, "The design of Texas UI programs has changed only marginally over the years. With few exceptions, Texas legislators have not sought creative ways for unemployed workers to have access to their benefits or ways to shorten the period of UI benefit payments."

Decisionmaking Models

The rational model of decisionmaking suggests that the unemployment insurance bonus experiments were conducted to gather information that would aid in the selection of those policy alternatives that maximize the decisionmaker's utility function. Further, the cost of collecting the information should be less than the value of the evidence obtained. In hindsight, everyone associated with the four UI experiments seems to agree that the motivation behind initiating these experiments, especially those in Pennsylvania and Washington, was just that: to gather useful information that would provide for the assessment of future policy choices. Concerns had been developing about the disincentives in the UI system that result from paying people who do not work. The need to change to incentives to encourage employment was perceived as necessary (see Moffitt and Nicholson 1982).

Secretary of Labor William Brock wanted demonstration projects to collect information about specific alternatives to submit in future proposed legislation and put money in his FY 1987 budget for that purpose. The normal budget approval process meant that the request was not approved quickly (the monies were ultimately used to fund the Washington and Pennsylvania experiments). Consequently, because of Brock's strong interest in running such a project, already available FY 1985 funds were used for the New Jersey experiment (telephone interviews with Steve Wandner, April 17, 1996, and Walter Corson, May 28, 1996). Testimony before the Subcommittee on Public Assistance and Unemployment Compensation of the House Ways and Means Committee in 1987 further reinforced the notion that the Department of Labor was interested in "seeking funds . . . to carry on adequate demonstration projects out of general revenue funds" (70). As Dunstan and Kerachsky (1988, 1) put it, the Department of Labor wanted to use the experiments to "test the feasibility and cost-effectiveness [of bonuses]."

Because the Illinois and New Jersey experiments were limited to just one bonus level and qualifying period, the subsequent experiments in Washington and Pennsylvania used varying levels of bonuses and qualifying periods. The Department of Labor specifically funded the latter two experiments to confirm the results of the first two and to extend the information they provided by determining the effects of various combinations of bonus levels and qualifying periods (O'Leary et al. 1993, 2). More specifically, the Washington and Pennsylvania experiments were expected to provide the structural information needed to estimate the response surface of values required for modeling revisions to the unemployment insurance program. As O'Leary, Spiegelman, and Kline suggest, the Department of Labor decided to use the experiments as "part of an effort to find ways to reduce the cost of unemployment insurance" (39) by collecting the information needed to decide among policy parameters.

Although the literature suggests that the rational model is inadequate for explaining the way available knowledge is used, it may, nevertheless, be adequate as a model for explaining why the knowledge is gathered in the first place. The people at the Department of Labor and the researchers who designed and ran the UI experiments made assumptions about the policy process that included presumptions about rational behavior, albeit bounded. They presumed bonuses would be an alternative on the policy agenda when the findings were available. Especially after the success of the first two experiments, proceeding to expand the knowledge base they had already established seemed both rational and appropriate:

> Because only limited information is currently available on most new policy options, important questions remain about how they can be operationalized, their ability to respond to current problems, and their benefits relative to their costs. A powerful and widely used method for generalizing the information is a demonstration of one or a combination of policy options operated directly within the context of a state program. With careful design and implementation, a demonstration can yield reliable information to weed out unpromising options and to show the way toward successful policies and programs in the future. (USDOL 1989b, 9)

Social experimentation is by its nature a rational way of looking at the world, of collecting information. According to Spiegelman, when Illinois wanted to conduct a demonstration to examine alternatives for the UI system, he talked state officials into an experiment: "There was nothing like it to provide data, so a demonstration or experiment was needed." He taught them about random assignment, and they went along. When state officials in Washington wanted to do research in this area, they were familiar with experimentation from having previously conducted social experiments, and "never thought of anything else" (telephone interview, October 27, 1995). Steve Wandner of the Department of Labor also indicated that previous work in nonrandomized design research for other Department of Labor projects had led to dissatisfaction over the validity of the results. It was "clear" to him that experiments were needed "if [they] were serious" (telephone interview, April 17, 1996). Corson noted that it was easy to implement random assignment under UI conditions because the state had control of the intake process and could direct people to the Employment Service for treatment (telephone interview, May 28, 1996).

What starts as a rational decisionmaking process, however, may not end that way. For the rational model to hold, some assumption must be made on the mechanism by which the information generated by the experiment(s) will be used at the end of the experiment. DOL's assumption on this became manifest when its representatives argued before Congress that action should be postponed until the findings were in. Therefore, they assumed that reforming UI would be on the policy agenda when the findings became available or that the findings would be compelling enough to put UI reform on the agenda.

When the findings did become available, the Department of Labor included bonuses in its legislative package. However, as described later in the chapter, growing fiscal conservatism, strains on the UI trust funds due to a recession, and other issues such as welfare reform and health care reform moved the policy agenda away from bonuses. Consequently, they never became an authorized option for state UI programs. An originally rational approach that envisioned the concrete use of findings from the experiments once they became available ended up providing information that DOL now suggests might be incorporated into legislation sometime in the future, a much more modest form of use.

An alternative to the rational model arises from Feldman's (1989) suggestion that policy research creates an inventory of information that can be used in future circumstances, if and when policy discussions relate to that information. In the case of the UI experiments, concern about costs of the program led to a search for ways to modify the system to get people back to work. The bonuses were viewed as one of those ways. The experiments were conducted to test the efficacy and efficiency of that proposal. Thus, they were not designed merely to accumulate knowledge but specifically to enlighten the policy deliberations at the time. As a practical matter nonetheless, they ended up adding to the Department of Labor's inventory of information. The reason that this happened is discussed later in the chapter.

Summary of Findings

This section describes the major findings from each of the UI bonus experiments. Table 7.2 provides a summary of these findings. The findings are discussed in greater detail below.

Table 7.2. *Findings of the UI Bonus Experiments*

	New Jersey	Illinois	Pennsylvania	Washington
Exit rates and weeks in UI	Rates for those receiving bonus > rates for control group Weeks decreased by almost 1	Claimant group: 5.5% reemployment gain for bonus recipients Employer group: Gain but small n Weeks decreased by over 1	Increase for all groups; greatest for largest bonus Depended on qualifying period	Greatest increase for larger bonus Weeks decreased by about 0.5
Exhaustion of UI benefits	Rate decreased by 4% for treatment group	Rate decreased by 3% for claimants Employer group results not significant	Only large bonus groups had reduction in rate of exhaustion	Only long qualification period groups showed reduction in rate of exhaustion
Cost	Reduction of $170 in benefits Benefits − costs > 0	Reduction of $194 in benefits Reduction of $61 for employer group	Large bonus, long qualifying period reduced benefits by $130 Other treatments showed $80 reduction Benefits − costs > 0	Large bonus, long qualifying period produced $141 reduction Across all treatments average reduction = $65

New Jersey

It was expected that the experiment would show that the period before reemployment occurs would be shorter for the treatment group receiving reemployment bonuses than for the control group; indeed, the bonus did appear to increase the rate of leaving the New Jersey Unemployment Insurance system during the early parts of the unemployment period. Rates of reemployment among the bonus treatment group exceeded those for both the control group and the treatment group that received special job search assistance services but were not eligible for bonuses. Moreover, these impacts were statistically significant. The treatments were most successful for those workers with marketable skills. Those who faced structural dislocations had more severe reemployment problems, which may have needed different and more intensive services (USDOL 1989a, xi).

The rate of exit increased early in the UI spell as a result of the bonus offer, indicating that the length of the spell decreased. Specifically, time spent in the UI system during the benefit year decreased by almost one full week (USDOL 1989a, 12). Consequently, the rate of exhaustion of UI benefits for the bonus treatment group decreased by almost 4 percent (13), whereas the percentage of time employed during the benefit year increased. A follow-up study was conducted to determine if the results held over longer periods of time than the benefit year, the period used in the original study. It found that the bonuses reduced time collecting UI by 1.6 weeks during the year following the treatment year, a statistically significant reduction (USDOL 1991, ix–x).

The bonus treatment was estimated to reduce UI benefits collected during the benefit year by $170 (USDOL 1989a, xi). Earnings rose relative to the control group during the benefit year, as did the hourly wage obtained post-UI. However, a follow-up study that examined the participants' earnings the year after the treatment year found that the JSA reemployment bonus treatment did not have long-term effects on earnings (USDOL 1991, 26).

The maximum costs of basic services provided by the combined JSA/bonus treatment of the New Jersey UI experiment were estimated to be $169, whereas the estimated cost of bonus payments themselves was $125 per claimant. However, sensitivity analysis reduced the estimates by up to 11 percent.

The benefits and costs that were associated with the programs tested in New Jersey were analyzed from the points of view of society, the claimants, and the Department of Labor. From the first two perspectives, benefits exceeded costs. From the Department of Labor perspective, the costs exceeded benefits. This last result is understandable since the Department of Labor paid for all of the services. However, when all government revenues are balanced against costs, benefits were estimated to exceed costs by $138 (USDOL 1989a, 333; 1991, 66). The follow-up study concluded that the JSA plus reemployment bonus treatment could lead to "modest net benefits for the Labor Department" (USDOL 1991, x).

In addition to impact and benefit-cost analyses, evaluations of process and implementation were also undertaken. According to these analyses, the goal of forming linkages among the UI system, JTPA, and the ES was, by and large, successfully accomplished (USDOL 1989a, 15). Because the success of the treatment depended on those linkages (and the use of a computerized tracking system), this suggests that the program can only succeed elsewhere if similar linkages can be established.

Illinois

Similar to that of New Jersey, the claimant experiment in Illinois showed a gain in the rate of reemployment of 5.5 percent during the first 11 weeks. In addition, the time spent in the UI system during the benefit year decreased by more than 1 week (Woodbury and Spiegelman 1987, 521). Weeks spent in the UI system after the initial spell of unemployment decreased even further—to more than 1.37 weeks. Hence, the rate of exhaustion of benefits decreased for the claimant treatment group by 3.2 percent.

The results of the employer experiment were far less dramatic than the results of the claimant experiment. The gain in reemployment was statistically significant only over the entire benefit year, not for the 11-week treatment period. This weak finding is attributable to the fact that only 3 percent of the members of the treatment group chose to use the bonus option in the employer experiment, whereas the results are based on all persons assigned to the treatment group. Thus the effect was diluted. The number of weeks spent in the UI system during the benefit year did not show a statistically significant reduction, but the number of weeks in the initial unemployment spell did decrease significantly—by about two-thirds of a week (Woodbury and Spiegelman 1987, 521). About 3 percent more treatment group than control group members ended their unemployment within the 11 weeks of the treatment period. The effect on the exhaustion of benefits, although in the expected direction, was not statistically significant.

UI benefits paid over the benefit year were estimated to fall by $194 as a result of the claimant treatment. That estimate was statistically significant (Woodbury and Spiegelman 1987, 521). However, earnings for the claimant group did not change significantly (522). This implies that claimants did not reduce their reservation wages to receive bonuses.

For the employer treatment, the estimated impact was a reduction of $61 in UI benefits paid over the entire benefit year. Although this figure was not statistically significant, it was in the anticipated direction. Moreover, the reduction of $112 in UI benefits paid during the first unemployment spell was statistically significant (Woodbury and Spiegelman 1987, 521).

In addition to an impact evaluation, a benefit-cost analysis was conducted from the perspective of the state budget. For the claimant experiment, the ratio of the benefit payment reduction to the cost of the bonus was 2.32 and for the employer experiment the ratio was 4.29 (Woodbury and Spiegelman 1987, 525). The higher utilization of the bonus in the claimant experiment resulted in higher costs. This limited benefit-cost analysis did not consider other perspectives. However, a more recent and comprehensive benefit-cost analysis of the claimant experiment in Illinois (Spiegelman 1992) indicates that benefits exceeded costs from the perspectives of society as a whole, the government, and the UI system.

Pennsylvania

As with the previous experiments, the Pennsylvania experiment resulted in a reduction in length of receipt of unemployment insurance benefits. The most generous bonus offer (i.e., the one with the large bonus and long qualification period) reduced the average length of receipt by 0.8 weeks. The offers with a smaller bonus, a shorter qualification period, or a declining bonus caused a half-week reduction. Exit rates from UI were increased for all treatment groups (USDOL 1992b, 87). The most generous bonus treatment significantly reduced the likelihood that recipients would exhaust their benefits, whereas the treatments with the smaller bonus, the shorter qualification period, and the declining bonus did not have this effect.

The most generous treatment reduced UI receipts by $130, whereas the other treatments resulted in an $80 reduction. The small bonus payments averaged $561, while the large bonus payments averaged $1,124 (USDOL 1992b, 78). The data collected during the experiment indicate that there were no significant increases in earnings, but post-treatment interviews indicated that earnings increased—from $200 to $500, depending on the treatment—in the following year. The likelihood of full-time employment also increased according to the post-treatment interviews. Moreover, there seemed to be no negative impact on the desirability of jobs obtained as a result of the bonus offers (118).

From the perspective of the claimants and society, there seems to have been a net gain in benefits over costs for most of the plans tested. Claimants received a bonus and wages gained from employment that exceeded their loss in UI benefits. The government costs included the bonus payments and administrative costs, but these costs were more than offset by the reduction in UI payments and the gain in taxes collected from UI recipients who obtained jobs. The UI system more or less broke even, however, as the reduction in UI benefits was roughly offset by the administrative and bonus payment costs that the system incurred (Spiegelman 1992).

A process evaluation indicated that the experiment was generally implemented as designed. The experiments succeeded in accurately identifying eligible claimants, randomly assigning them, and offering them the appropriate treatment in a timely manner. Moreover, the claimants understood the bonus offer, an important outcome when examining the feasibility of implementing such a program permanently.

Washington

Like the other UI bonus experiments, the treatment under the Washington experiment also appeared to engender a reduction in length of stay in the UI system, with the most substantial reductions occurring for the treatments with the highest bonuses. Those treatments produced a statistically significant reduction of about three-quarters of a week. Only one of the four smaller bonus treatments resulted in a statistically significant reduction in length of stay on UI. For all treatments combined, there was a statistically significant reduction of 0.41 weeks (USDOL 1992c, xv). However, there was not a statistically significant decrease in the proportion of claimants who exhausted benefits for the combined treatments, although there was a statistically significant decrease for the two treatments with the long qualification period.

As previously mentioned, the Washington experiment was designed to test various combinations of bonus size and qualification period length to find the best combination. The researchers determined that raising the bonus rate from twice the weekly UI benefit level to four times the weekly level had no significant effect in reducing weeks on UI, but raising it to six times the weekly UI benefit level did. Increasing the length of the qualification period was also found to have an effect on reducing compensation (USDOL 1992c, xvi).

Only the large bonus treatments significantly reduced the UI compensation paid—from $107 to $141, depending on the length of the qualification period. Across all bonus treatments, the total compensation paid by the Unemployment Insurance system for the benefit year was reduced an average of $65. The researchers estimated the effect to be "a reduction in compensation in the benefit year of $6.51 for each $100 increase in bonus amount offered and $5.48 for each additional week in the qualification period" (USDOL 1992c, xvi).

The most recent cost-benefit analysis of the Washington experiment (Spiegelman 1992) implies that because of low administrative costs and positive earnings gains, the two high-bonus plans resulted in positive net benefits for society as a whole. The other plans tested in Washington State did not, however. Moreover, the UI system appears to have suffered a net loss under all but one of the tested plans, as any reductions in the payment of UI benefits as a result of the plans were insufficient to offset the costs of administration and bonuses that the system had to bear.

Pooled Findings

Because of similarities between the demonstrations in Washington State and Pennsylvania, the data could be pooled to create a larger sample with which to estimate the impacts. Researchers from Mathematica Policy Research and the W. E. Upjohn Institute for Employment Research concluded that the combined treatments from both experiments reduced the time receiving UI benefits by about half a week; the amount of benefits received in a year by $85; the rate of benefit exhaustion by 1 percent; and the duration of the initial spell on UI by over one-third of a week (Decker and O'Leary 1995, 542; USDOL 1992a, 42). The data were also used to estimate the parameters of a simulation model that could be used to predict the effects of the size of bonus and the length of qualifying time on the UI claimant population as a whole and on specific subgroups of claimants (USDOL 1992a).

Spiegelman (1992) used the pooled data for the Washington and Pennsylvania experiments and the simulation model to analyze the benefits and costs of several hypothetical bonus plans. These hypothetical plans provide for bonus offers of either $500 or $1,000 and qualification periods of either 6 weeks or 12 weeks. In addition, Spiegelman tested the sensitivity of his findings to the possibility that conditions under bonus plans that were actually adopted could differ from those that existed under experimental tests of bonus plans. For example, he looked at the effects on benefits and costs if either the proportion of eligible unemployed workers who apply for UI benefits or the proportion of eligible claimants who apply for bonuses was higher under a real program than under the experimental programs. In addition, he examined the possibility that unemployed workers who respond to the bonus program by finding jobs more quickly would make it more difficult for unemployed workers who are ineligible for bonuses to find employment. This so-called "displacement" or "crowding-out" effect was not tested directly under any of the experiments, but has been extensively examined by Carl Davidson and Stephen Woodbury (1993), and Spiegelman relied on their findings in conducting his analysis.

On one hand, Spiegelman finds that it is quite feasible to design a bonus plan that would make society better-off—that is, a plan in which the benefits that would be received by society exceed the costs that would be borne by society. On the other hand, his results suggest that virtually any conceivable plan would require the UI system to pay out at least as much in bonuses as it would save as a result of reductions in UI payments.

These findings, which persist under a variety of different assumptions and are generally consistent with earlier findings from the UI bonus experiments, are important. As suggested in chapter 2 and discussed at some length in Boardman et al. (2000, ch. 2), benefit-cost analysts usually argue that any policy that makes society better-off should be adopted. However, because the experiments imply that bonuses are unlikely to result in cost savings for the UI system and in fact could increase costs, they are unlikely to be attractive to either Congress or those responsible for administering the system in the states. As will be discussed, this has important implications for the way the bonus experiments were used in the policy process.

Policy Effects of the Experiments

A tally of examples of use of the UI experiments appears below. This tally is based on documents, hearings, interviews, and a survey mailed to state UI officials. The examples are tallied in accordance with the cells in the utilization framework described in chapter 3. The individual cell entries are tabulated below and described in the following subsections.

	Concrete	Conceptual
Formative		
Elaborative	2	20[a]
Substantive	10[a]	4
Persuasive/advocacy		
Elaborative	1	2
Substantive	1	0

a. Includes uses listed by state UI officials in response to our mailed survey. Similar responses from different states are each counted once.

The counts appearing in the tally are not exhaustive. However, they do suggest the relative importance of each type of use. Assignment of elements to cells is a subjective process; the descriptions of those elements should make it possible, however, for readers to ascertain for themselves how well each entry fits into the cells of the typology.

Conceptual use of the UI experiments dominated. Although the rational model of decisionmaking predicted that the UI experiments would result in concrete utilization, and in fact they did, such instances involve the instigation of further experiments, model building, and legislation to promote flexibility in state UI policies, worker profiling, and self-employment allowances. In no case did they involve the implementation of bonuses within the UI system. Rather, bonuses are now part of a policy universe, where they provide a policy idea that *might* some day be adopted.

Formative-Concrete-Elaborative

Entries in this cell pertain to instances in which the UI bonus demonstrations directly influenced specific actions preceding policy decisions by clarifying or extending existing positions or policy solutions. A prime example occurred when results from the New Jersey and Illinois experiments influenced the decision by the Department of Labor (DOL) to fund the Washington and Pennsylvania experiments. This decision was the direct result of the perceived usefulness of findings from the experiments in New Jersey and Illinois. DOL wanted to examine the range of possible bonus configurations before advocating changes in the UI system (Spiegelman, telephone interview, October 27, 1995, among others). Moreover, as Steve Wandner of DOL stressed, the success of the reemployment bonus experiments provided the motivation to run other types of experiments such as the Life-Long Learning experiment in Baltimore (telephone interview, April 17, 1996). Secretary Brock wanted more experiments, and Congress was willing to fund them. In this instance, it is not the experimental results per se that were used. Instead, because the findings were viewed as useful, experimentation was made a part of decisionmaking at DOL.

Since 1987, congressional testimony before subcommittees of the House Ways and Means Committee has provided many examples of formative-concrete-elaborative use of the UI bonus experiments. For instance, at a 1987 Ways and Means Committee hearing, while the experiments were still being proposed and run, Robert Jones, who was then the assistant secretary for employment and training, requested that passage of the proposed legislation to reform the UI system be postponed until the experimental findings could be assessed. He believed that the experiment would yield "useful information . . . which we ought to assess before acting on such proposals" (42). At the same hearings, the deputy administrator for the Ohio Bureau of Employment Services testified in support of legislation that provided funding for demonstration projects in the UI system. And Sally Ward of the Illinois Department of Employment Security (who was directly involved in the Illinois experiment) testified in favor of both using future results to determine action and funding additional demonstrations. The deputy director of the Massachusetts Division of Employment Security reiterated this support for demonstration funding. Representative Sander Levin of Michigan testified at the 1987 hearings in favor of policy that provided the sorts of bonuses then being tested. Whereas public officials used the existence of the experiments to argue for concrete action, others such as Mark Levinson of the United Auto Workers argued against the reemployment bonuses in the proposed Unemployment Insurance Reemployment Demonstration Projects Act. The union was against public policy that would provide incentives for "workers to take unsuitable work" (209). Similarly at the 1987 hearings, the National Federation of Independent Business argued against "expansion into alternative areas" (265), specifically reemployment bonuses. Thus, the 1987 hearings of the House Ways and Means Committee provide numerous examples of formative-concrete-(policy action to run experiments and offer bonuses)-elaborative use.

Formative-Concrete-Substantive

This cell includes instances of use in which findings result in specific policy decisions at the core of policy.[6] The most important example of formative-concrete-substantive use of the UI bonus experiments occurred when results from the experiments were used as the basis of one component of a DOL legislative proposal. Specifically, the 1994 workforce bill contained "flexibility provisions," which encouraged states to tailor their UI programs to their needs by permitting them to select from a menu of policy options. Among the different options contained in this bill was a reemployment bonus. However, the bill failed to pass.[7] This is the closest reemployment bonuses have come to becoming part of national policy. They have not been incorporated into subsequent legislation, although according to Steve Wandner of DOL they remain in the Department of Labor's hopper of ideas for possible inclusion in future legislative proposals (telephone interview, April 17, 1996). We could find no evidence that findings from the UI bonus experiments have directly affected the lack of legislative success of reemployment bonuses. Nevertheless, the experimental results imply that bonuses would not result in budgetary cost savings for the UI system. Hence, there has been little enthusiasm to adopt them.

Our interviews revealed several additional, if less important, examples of formative-concrete-substantive use of the UI bonus experiments at the federal level. For instance, Steve Wandner, who was the staff person in charge of overseeing the experiments, noted that portions of the New Jersey findings were incorporated into the Economic Dislocation and Worker Adjustment Assistance Act (Greenberg and Shroder 1997, 330). In addition, several persons we interviewed indicated that results of the New Jersey experiment that profiled those recipients most likely to benefit directly from the treatments in the experiment led to 1993 legislation establishing the worker profiling system. The experiment also was the basis for technical assistance that DOL provided states that were implementing profiling.

As just indicated, DOL has made considerable effort to encourage the use of the findings from the UI bonus experiments. This is also suggested by testimony by Mary Ann Wyrsch, who was then director of the Unemployment Insurance Service, before the Subcommittee on Human Resources of the House Ways and Means Committee in 1991. As part of her testimony, she assured Congressman Downey of New York that the Department of Labor was working to facilitate state decisions on UI by disseminating the New Jersey implementation model and thereby encouraging specific action based on what worked in the experiment.[8] Downey responded to Wyrsch by noting that it is "troubling that we spend money to find out a program works and then decide not to do it or to have it be implemented through the auspices of another program [rather than through a Department of Labor mandate]" (U.S. Congress, House Committee on Ways and Means 1991, 25–26).

Responses to the survey of state UI directors include several additional examples of formative-concrete-substantive use. For instance, a respondent from Maryland indicated that, based on results of the New Jersey experiment, legislation in his state was proposed in 1990 to pay for a training program out of the UI trust fund. However, this legislation did not pass because of concern over the solvency of the trust fund during the recession that was then occurring. A representative in the Washington State legislature used results from the experiment there in testimony to support inclusion of bonuses in legislation proposed in 1994. However, that legislation did not pass. In 1992, Connecticut implemented a program that uses reemployment bonuses to help general assistance (welfare) recipients obtain full-time unsubsidized employment. Whereas the Connecticut respondent was unsure whether there was a connection between this program and the UI bonus experiments, DOL has made extensive efforts to disseminate results from the experiments. Thus, it is reasonable to assume that someone in the Connecticut policy deliberations had heard of UI bonuses being successfully tested. According to the respondent from the Washington State Employment Security Department, Canada asked for the results of the Washington experiment and considered implementing such a system but ultimately did not.

Finally, use of the results in Texas represented an example of formative-concrete-substantive use in which a state UI agency would have proposed legislation to create bonuses "if the bonus payments had indicated great savings to the UI program." But inasmuch as, in their judgment, such savings were not realized, the legislation was ultimately not proposed.

Persuasive/Advocacy-Concrete-Elaborative

This category consists of use that occurs after the decision to propose or enact policy, where research influences the periphery, rather than the core, of specific proposals. The only instance that we found of this form of use occurred when the Department of Labor decided to disseminate the New Jersey implementation model. The department decided that the results showed that it "is extremely difficult to do the identification and tracking of people across [the UI, ES, and JTPA] systems" (Mary Ann Wyrsch's testimony, House Ways and Means Committee 1991). Consequently, they issued technical assistance guides to help states if they chose to adopt the model.

Persuasive/Advocacy-Concrete-Substantive

This category consists of use that occurs after the decision to propose or enact policy, where research is used to justify the core of specific policy. In 1994, the Subcommittee on Human Resources and the Subcommittee on Trade of the House Ways and Means Committee held hearings on unemployment compensation reform. The subcommittees' press release announcing these hearings specifically mentioned the use of reemployment bonuses. The experiments themselves were brought up in testimony, but it is clear from the press release that the notion of bonuses was already part of the policy environment. The press release informed the public that reemployment bonuses were a "main component of the [a]dministration's reemployment proposal" (6). Thus, the administration had decided before the press release to include bonuses as a specific policy response to reform the UI system. In his testimony, Secretary of Labor Reich referred to the experimental results as the justification for the administration's proposal (80, 87–88, 91).

Formative-Conceptual-Elaborative

This category consists of use in which the opinions and views of policymakers are influenced or the policy community generally enlightened prior to policy decisions being made. As previously noted, testimony at legislative hearings can be both formative and persuasive. If people making proposals for legislation are using information to justify their actions, it is persuasive usage. If those testifying are using information as the basis of requesting action, it is formative use.

Many instances of formative-conceptual-elaborative use of the UI bonus experiments occurred in hearings. Representative Sander Levin of Michigan referred to the notion of reemployment bonuses and discussed the UI experiments that were then being conducted, at a 1987 hearing before the Subcommittee on Public Assistance and Unemployment Compensation of the House Ways and Means Committee on reform of the unemployment compensation program. For him, the bonuses were an example of using the UI trust funds for nontraditional purposes. He did not specifically advocate changing UI policy to include bonuses (concrete use), but instead used the notion of bonuses to influence thinking about using the trust fund monies in a flexible manner (a conceptual, elaborative use). In 1994 testimony on the Unemployment Reform and Unemployment Assistance Proposal before the Subcommittee on Trade of the House Ways and Means Committee, Frank Doyle of General Electric used the experiments in much the same way to advocate flexibility in promoting reemployment among unemployment insurance recipients.

David Stevens of the University of Maryland, Baltimore County, testified in 1990 before the Subcommittee on Human Resources of the House Ways and Means Committee at a hearing on the Unemployment Compensation Reform Act of 1990. In advocating "caution in further erosion of state autonomy," he used results from the New Jersey experiment as evidence. Stevens suggested that requiring states to make training mandatory, as was done in the New Jersey experiment, would take away state autonomy to decide how similar outcomes could be achieved. No specific policy was suggested; research findings were presented to advocate state autonomy.

During a 1991 hearing before the Subcommittee on Human Resources (U.S. Congress, House Ways and Means Committee 1991), Mary Ann Wyrsch, then-director of the Unemployment Insurance Service at the Department of Labor, and Representative Moody of Wisconsin engaged in a dialogue in which they used benefit-cost results from the New Jersey experiment to examine the solvency of the trust fund and policy alternatives that could affect that solvency. The experiment was used as a means of clarifying and influencing the views of the policymakers.

Ron Haskins, the staff director for the Human Resources Subcommittee of Ways and Means, reiterated that the committee had heard testimony about the experiments, especially the New Jersey experiment, and that the findings "reinforced welfare issues . . . [specifically], getting people back to work" (telephone interview, May 28, 1996). Thus the results supported the views of the committee and added to their store of knowledge. In discussing findings from the UI bonus experiments, as well as other social experiments, Haskins made an important observation about the use of such studies by Congress (telephone interview, May 28, 1996):

> It takes a stream of studies brought by people who are trusted by Congress with a consistent message. Changes won't occur overnight, especially for entitlements. . . . It can't be an isolated study. The message must be brought back repeatedly to the committee over the years by someone or some organization that is trusted. The best example is Judy Gueron and MDRC [Manpower Demonstration Research Corporation]. Then the results become part of the general view.

Surveys mailed to the UI directors in every state provided many examples of state-level formative-conceptual-elaborative use of the findings from one or more of the UI bonus experiments. Indeed this seemed to be the dominant form of use among state UI directors. Many indicated that the results had been circulated to staff and become part of informal discussions and "legislative brainstorming" about reemployment strategies, claimant profiling, initial planning to determine whether to apply for a demonstration grant, consideration of enabling legislation for self-employment allowances,[9] providing services to claimants, cost-effective options, and work-search policy. No states indicated that they decided to implement a bonus scheme. Thus, it seems reasonable to presume that the experimental results provided a contribution to the policy environment and influenced the views of policymakers, but in an elaborative rather than substantive way.

Formative-Conceptual-Substantive

This cell contains instances of use that influence the policy environment and the core of policymakers' views. In 1987, Robert Jones, deputy assistant secretary for employment and training, testified before the Subcommittee on Public Assistance and Unemployment Compensation (U.S. Congress, House Ways and Means Committee 1987) on reform of the unemployment compensation program. He spoke about the initiation of experiments to test activities that would enhance reemployment, thereby laying the groundwork for using the results for substantive reform proposals once they became available.

In 1988, the Congressional Research Service prepared a study on the unemployment compensation system (U.S. Congressional Research Service 1988). It included a section on alternative uses of the trust funds.

Reemployment bonuses were listed as the first option. The preliminary results from the New Jersey experiment provided the bulk of the analysis, but the other experiments were also described (it was too early for results from those experiments to be available). The report noted that whereas training is always a concern, "Quick reemployment of those most able to obtain jobs is healthy for the economy overall, results in greater tax receipts, promotes solvency in State [UI] accounts, and can help provide resources to design more targeted assistance for people with long-term problems" (388). Thus, this is yet another way in which bonuses were introduced into the policy environment by those seeking ways to promote quick reemployment.

In 1991, at a Subcommittee on Human Resources (U.S. Congress, House Ways and Means Committee 1991) hearing on unemployment insurance and the recession, Mary Ann Wyrsch testified on job search assistance at the request of the committee chair. She described the New Jersey experiment results, informing the committee of a variety of reemployment service options that had been tested and their costs and savings for the trust fund. Although she discussed specific options, she mainly used the testimony as a means of enlightening general policy perspectives.

As part of its effort to promote use of the results of the reemployment bonus experiments, the Department of Labor issued reports and technical assistance to the states and conducted a series of seminars involving representatives of business, labor, and the general public. *The Secretary's Seminars on Unemployment Insurance* (USDOL 1989b), issued as a result of the seminars, included the suggestion that one specific policy option for promoting reemployment is a bonus similar to those previously tested in Illinois and New Jersey (the experiments in Pennsylvania and Washington were still in progress). Thus, the Department of Labor seminars and the related publications disseminated information to provide substantive suggestions intended to enlighten the general policy perspective.

As previously mentioned, the inclusion of reemployment bonuses in the 1994 proposed workforce legislation was the result of the UI experiments. Steve Wandner noted that although that portion of the bill was removed, the Department of Labor and the administration had "gone public with the notion" of bonuses as part of their labor proposals (telephone interview, April 17, 1996). Thus, what began as a form of formative-concrete-substantive use later became an example of formative-conceptual-substantive use.

Persuasive/Advocacy-Conceptual-Elaborative

This cell pertains to examples of use in which those already holding a particular conceptual view use research findings to argue in favor of it. In testimony before the Subcommittee on Human Resources of the House Ways and Means Committee on unemployment compensation amendments in 1992, Louis Jacobson of the W.E. Upjohn Institute for Employment Research (which evaluated the Illinois and Washington experiments) used findings from the Illinois experiment to advocate reemployment bonuses as a cost-effective policy for countering the work disincentives inherent in the UI program. Jacobson also noted that the employer bonus portion of the Illinois experiment did not work and thus such an option should not be part of public policy. His testimony was reinforced by that of Mark Bendick, an economic consultant, who used the experimental results to advocate adding reemployment bonuses to the list of allowable reemployment services. They used the findings as justification for their advocacy of use of the bonuses in this legislation to amend the UI system, not at its core but as an addition to a list of options.

Summary

The typology provides a workable classification scheme for instances of use of the UI bonus experiments (see table 7.3). It allows for a variety of types of use. Indeed, all the cells but one have entries. However, most of the instances of use are indirect. Although the rational model of decision-making predicts that use should be direct—taking the form of formative-concrete-substantive use that leads to an explicit decision to adopt or not adopt reemployment bonuses—no such outcome appeared to occur in the case of these experiments. We found no evidence that explicit up-or-down decisions have been made for bonuses. However, findings from the experiments that implied that reemployment bonuses would not result in cost savings for the UI system clearly did little to generate political support for bonuses. Consequently, conceptual use of the experiments dominated, and no UI policy involving bonuses has yet been enacted.[10]

Almost all the state UI directors indicated that they knew of the experimental results and that those results had entered their discussions. The substance of the results appeared in many discussions influencing deliberations (formal and informal) about the UI trust funds, UI policy alternatives, and job search behavior. In most states bonuses appear to be

Table 7.3. *Summary of Cell Entries*

Formative-Concrete-Elaborative
1. Promotion of further experimentation in Pennsylvania and Washington
2. Postponement of action until findings available

Formative-Concrete-Substantive
1. Distribution of implementation model from New Jersey
2. U.S. Department of Labor incorporation of New Jersey findings into Economic Dislocation and Worker Adjustment Act
3. New Jersey findings leading to worker profiling
4. New Jersey findings providing technical assistance for worker profiling
5. Department of Labor proposals for flexibility provisions for states to tailor their programs
6. Legislation proposed in Maryland, Washington, Connecticut, Canada, based on New Jersey findings
7. Negative example—no legislation in Texas because findings not strong enough

Formative-Conceptual-Elaborative
1. Testimony by congressman advocating idea of bonuses for flexibility in use of unemployment (UI) monies
2. Similar testimony at three other hearings
3. Dominant form of utilization among the states—16 instances on surveys

Formative-Conceptual-Substantive
1. Testimony to introduce idea of using findings from experiments to reform UI after they become available
2. Congressional Research Service study detailed the experiments
3. Testimony to introduce options to UI—New Jersey findings used as an example
4. Department of Labor seminars

Persuasive/Advocacy-Concrete-Elaborative
1. Distribution of technical guides using New Jersey results

Persuasive/Advocacy-Concrete-Substantive
1. Hearing on administration proposal on reemployment

Persuasive/Advocacy-Conceptual-Elaborative
1. Justification for advocacy of bonuses for UI

---

part of the policy universe. However, concrete use was limited to the instigation of further experimentation; model building; and legislation proposed to promote flexibility in state UI policies, worker profiling, and self-employment allowances. Worker profiling and self-employment allowances were enacted nationally and were influenced by the experiments. However, the legislation that provided for those policies did not include bonuses.

The originally proposed concrete use of the findings to institute bonuses became instead a form of conceptual use, a policy idea that has not yet been adopted. The originally intended substantive use changed to elaborative use as the policy agenda became dominated by the idea of allowing flexibility at the state level. Bonuses became merely one possible means of contributing to that flexibility. But even that form of use did not occur. More specifically, when federal legislation allowing states the option of using bonuses was not enacted, states were essentially precluded from offering them.[11]

This may not be the end of the story, however. The Department of Labor has kept the notion of bonuses in its tool kit. Perhaps more direct use of the experimental findings will be made the next time UI reform reaches the policy agenda.

Utilization Factors

The conceptual framework described in chapter 3 includes two sets of factors that affect the type and amount of influence that the results of social experiments have on policy decisions. The first of these is the characteristics of the research itself; the second is the characteristics of the policy environment.

Definitiveness

Results of a classical random assignment experiment should have a built-in advantage to their credibility for policymakers. The methodology more closely matches that used in the natural sciences, which has long had great credibility in Western thought. The UI experiments had the additional advantage of replication of results in a series of experiments, which was not the case for the singular nursing home experiment discussed in an earlier chapter.

The knowledge utilization literature contains hypotheses that definitiveness will be reduced if certain conditions are met:

- Debate occurs among researchers about the validity of the findings;
- The findings are ambiguous;
- The findings are scrutinized;
- The findings contradict other information sources, intuition, values, or experiences of users; and
- The findings threaten users' goals or interests.

The UI experiments fared well in these hypotheses. First, the researchers themselves have indicated that the experiments were carried out with only small deviations in their designs. Internal validity questions were addressed in the government reports detailing the experiments and were satisfactorily resolved.[12] At the Secretary's Seminars on UI (USDOL 1989b, 139), several participants commented that only an experimental design would suffice for credibility. Meyer (1995, 126) echoed those comments by stating that only experimental evidence would satisfactorily convince economists of the validity of the results.

Second, the findings varied across the experiments, but only when considered in detail. Frequently, all that policymakers remember is that the treatments worked—for example, that bonuses put people back to work quicker. In that sense, the findings were unambiguous. Moreover, variation in findings did not seem to be a source of confusion. Most policymakers recalled findings in a simple way (e.g., reduced duration) so that any complexity or confusion about the results did not seem to impede understanding. There is no evidence the results were too technical to be understood.

Third, the findings were scrutinized in articles, at hearings, and at conferences. They were discussed in many published papers and were the source for parameter estimates used in several simulation models. They were followed in congressional hearings over a six-year period. That extensive attention only served to spread information about the experiments and to reinforce their definitiveness.

Finally, the results did not contradict long-held beliefs that economic incentives work. They instead filled out the contours of specifics for the optimal size of bonuses and the optimal length of the qualifying period and allowed estimates of costs and information on administrative issues to be obtained.

There were, however, three indications from the survey that at least a few state officials did not get the message. One respondent indicated that the experiments indicated that the treatment "didn't work." A second respondent said that the results were "ambiguous." And a third respondent stated that the findings "must prove better cost/benefit than [the] pilot . . . to consider [the] project . . . feasible and 'sellable' to our state legislature and employers." Nonetheless, such comments were rare among all those received in response to the survey.

Timeliness

Although the definitiveness of the experiments may not have been a problem, the time when the findings from the experiments became available was. The early 1980s had seen a period of high rates of unemployment, including many dislocated workers, a situation that resulted in a drain on many state UI trust funds. Thus, interest was high in revising the UI system to promote rapid reemployment. The experiments were designed to test one policy option (offering bonus incentives) to do that. However, by the end of the decade, when the experimental findings started to become available, the issues on the policy agenda had changed. Welfare reform and related issues of job training overshadowed other un-employment issues. Moreover, fiscal conservatism was gripping Congress. Thus, offering UI bonuses was no longer a politically feasible policy option. Cutting taxes and reducing the deficit precluded policies that involved increased short-term spending, even if long-term savings could be demonstrated.

Exhaustion rates of UI benefits were high during the recession in the early 1990s. Nevertheless, results from the experiments implying that the length of time over which benefits were collected could be reduced with bonuses were too new to be compelling. Indeed, the experiments in Washington and Pennsylvania were not yet finished. Consequently, there was a tendency to postpone acting on the earlier experimental findings until all the remaining results were in. Although results from the Illinois and New Jersey experiments were used in hearings to request action, the extended period of experimentation provided an excuse to delay action. By the time all the results were in, the pressure on the UI trust funds that resulted from the recession had been reduced. Worker profiling to determine who was most likely to exhaust benefits and need extra reemployment assistance took center stage as the policy option of choice.

Communication and Visibility

There was a concerted effort to publicize information about the experiments and findings from them. Thus, communication occurred within the research community through numerous journal articles, government reports, and conference papers. Selected examples of those publications are listed in table 7.4.

The articles and government reports, as well as a series of seminars conducted under the auspices of the secretary of labor, also spread word to the policy community about the experiments and their findings. In addition, the individual experiments were the subjects of presentations at APPAM (Association for Public Policy Analysis and Management) conferences, where preliminary results were distributed. Thus, the results were accessible throughout the policy community, and there is every indication that they were well known. For example, all but nine of the respondents to the survey mailed to the states indicated that they had heard of at least one of the experiments and could list (although not always accurately) some of the findings.

The Department of Labor took pains to ensure that the results were communicated. Researchers and representatives of the four states participating in the experiments were brought to Washington, D.C., to testify before Congress[13] or to participate in presentations at the Interstate Conference of Employment Security Administrators. In at least two cases, Department of Labor staff briefed state legislators. Representatives of the Department of Labor kept Congress informed through frequent testimony while the experiments were still being run (to remind legislators) and later described the results in testimony. At most congressional hearings on unemployment insurance, at least one member of Congress responded to references to the experiments with either questions or comments indicating knowledge of the findings. Moreover, results from the experiments seemed to be a part of running conversations on Capitol Hill. At one hearing in 1991, the director of the Unemployment Insurance Service even referred to the Department of Labor's dissemination efforts. There is no question that the results of the experiments found their way into policy deliberations through the efforts of policy brokers.

Generalizability

Generalizability is the degree to which findings of the policy tested apply to differing policies, places, time periods, or populations. The UI

Table 7.4. *Selected Publications Resulting
from the UI Bonus Experiments*

Anderson, Patricia. 1992. "Time-varying Effects of Recall Expectation, a Reemployment Bonus, and Job Counseling on Unemployment Durations." *Journal of Labor Economics* 10(1): 99–115.

Davidson, Carl, and Stephen Woodbury. 1993. "The Displacement Effect of Reemployment Bonus Programs." *Journal of Labor Economics* 11(4): 575–605.

———. 1996. *Unemployment Insurance and Unemployment: Implications of the Reemployment Bonus Experiments.* Kalamazoo, Mich.: W. E. Upjohn Institute for Employment Research, Occasional Paper 96-44.

Decker, Paul. 1994. "The Impact of Reemployment Bonuses on Insured Unemployment in the New Jersey and Illinois Reemployment Bonus Experiments." *The Journal of Human Resources* 29(3): 718–41.

Decker, Paul, and Christopher O'Leary. 1995. "Evaluating Pooled Evidence from the Reemployment Bonus Experiments." *The Journal of Human Resources* 30(3): 534–50.

Levine, Phillip B. 1993. "Testing Search Theory with Reemployment Bonus Experiments: Cross-validation of Results from New Jersey and Illinois." *Eastern Economic Journal* 19(2): 125–41.

Meyer, Bruce. 1995. "Lessons from the U.S. Unemployment Insurance Experiments." *Journal of Economic Literature* 33: 91–131.

O'Leary, Christopher, Robert G. Spiegelman, and Kenneth J. Kline. 1993. *Reemployment Incentives for Unemployment Insurance Beneficiaries: Results from the Washington Reemployment Bonus Experiment.* Kalamazoo, Mich.: W. E. Upjohn Institute for Employment Research, Occasional Paper 93-22.

———. 1995. "Do Bonus Offers Shorten Unemployment Insurance Spells? Results from the Washington Experiment." *Journal of Policy Analysis and Management* 14(2): 245–69.

U.S. Department of Labor, Employment and Training Administration, Unemployment Insurance Service. 1989a. *The New Jersey Unemployment Insurance Reemployment Demonstration Project,* by Walter Corson, P. T. Decker, S. M. Dunstan, and A. R. Gordon. Unemployment Insurance Occasional Paper 89-3. Washington, D.C.: Government Printing Office.

———. 1989b. *The Secretary's Seminars on Unemployment Insurance,* by Walter Corson, Walter Nicholson, and S. Kerachsky. Unemployment Insurance Occasional Paper 89-1. Washington, D.C.: Government Printing Office.

———. 1991. *The New Jersey Unemployment Insurance Reemployment Demonstration Project, Follow-up Report,* by P. Anderson, Walter Corson, and P. Decker. Unemployment Insurance Occasional Paper 91-1. Washington, D.C.: Government Printing Office.

(continued)

Table 7.4. *Continued*

————. 1992a. *An Analysis of Pooled Evidence from the Pennsylvania and Washington Reemployment Bonus Demonstrations*, by P. T. Decker and C. J. O'Leary. Unemployment Insurance Occasional Paper 92-7. Washington, D.C.: Government Printing Office.

————. 1992b. *Pennsylvania Reemployment Bonus Demonstration Final Report*, by Walter Corson, P. Decker, S. Dunstan, and S. Kerachsky. Unemployment Insurance Occasional Paper 92-1. Washington, D.C.: Government Printing Office.

————. 1992c. *The Washington Reemployment Bonus Experiment Final Report*, by R. G. Spiegelman, C. J. O'Leary, and K. J. Kline. Unemployment Insurance Occasional Paper 92-6. Washington D.C.: Government Printing Office.

Woodbury, Stephen A., and Robert G. Spiegelman. 1987. "Bonuses to Workers and Employers to Reduce Unemployment: Randomized Trials in Illinois." *The American Economic Review* 77(4): 513–30.

bonus experiments are especially suited to generalization because they tested several different bonus sizes and qualifying period lengths, "bracket[ing] the policy-relevant range of reemployment bonus options" (USDOL 1992b, xv). Indeed, taken together, the experiments are appropriately viewed as response surface experiments. Their generalizability is further enhanced because they were used to estimate parameters that were incorporated into simulation models that predicted job search behavior and job-finding rates (Anderson 1992; Davidson and Woodbury 1990).

Nevertheless, taken individually, the experiments do present some problems for generalizing to a fully implemented program. For example, the New Jersey and Illinois experiments tested only one bonus level. In addition, the New Jersey, Pennsylvania, and Illinois experiments restricted participation to a relatively homogeneous group, a more restrictive group than would be eligible for bonuses in a fully implemented program. New Jersey targeted displaced workers,[14] and Illinois restricted eligibility to first-time registrants from the Job Service between the ages of 20 and 55. Pennsylvania used a group that was younger and less subject to recall than the overall UI-eligible population (USDOL 1992b, 27). On the other hand, Pennsylvania and Illinois used a demographic and industrial cross-section of the state to increase generalizability. The Washington experiment did not allow eligibility of union placements through a union hiring hall (USDOL 1992c).

Although the unions agreed to these restrictions, they would be unlikely to do so in a permanent program.

Generalizability is always an open question in going from small-scale experiments to full-scale implementation. Permanent programs are likely to be implemented with less care or control than experimental ones and are likely to target less homogeneous populations. Consequently, generalizing should be done carefully. More specifically, participation rates in an ongoing program are likely to vary from those in an experiment, as are take-up rates for the various bonus levels. For example, participants in New Jersey did not know of the existence of a bonus until after their initial interview (and after their initial filing for UI). With full-scale implementation, the existence of bonuses would become general knowledge and might induce participants to postpone finding a job until after the bonus was offered. Exposure and more widespread information and knowledge about a permanent program might alter take-up rates from those predicted in the experiments. The Washington experiment made a special effort to examine the problem and offered all claimants information about the bonuses at the time that they initially filed for UI. In New Jersey, receipt of a bonus did not preclude further UI receipt for that year. If bonus receipt were to preclude further UI receipt in a permanent program (which is a reasonable assumption), the take-up rates for both UI and bonuses might be different from those found in the New Jersey experiment (USDOL 1989a).

Conditions that exist in an experiment may differ from those at subsequent implementation. For example, differences in economic conditions over time will probably affect take-up rates. The experiments were run for too short a period to allow for estimating the differences such fluctuations could make.

Yet another generalizability issue arises because the UI bonus experiments measured effects for only those persons who were eligible to receive bonuses. As mentioned earlier in the chapter, displacement or crowding-out effects would occur if UI claimants who are eligible for reemployment bonuses respond to them by finding jobs more quickly and, as a result, it becomes more difficult for unemployed workers who are ineligible for bonuses to find employment. The experimental findings provide no direct information on the size of this effect, but a nonexperimental analysis conducted by Davidson and Woodbury (1993) suggests it could be large. For example, based on fairly realistic assumptions, they find that if a claimant returns to work two weeks earlier in response to the incentives provided by reemployment bonuses, an unemployed worker who is ineligible for reemployment bonuses would return to work more than a week later.

In general, the take-up rates exhibited in the experiments may be poor predictors of take-up rates in a fully functioning program. Such a program would be subject to conditions beyond the control of the experiments—for example, different economic conditions, increased participation in a fully implemented program, and increased willingness of unemployed workers to claim UI if a bonus were available. Thus the estimates of the costs to the UI of a real program may be understated by experimental cost estimates. Moreover, although the experiments measure the benefits that unemployed workers who are eligible for bonuses receive, they do not estimate the costs that unemployed workers who are not eligible bear as a result of the crowding-out effect. Nonetheless, there were four UI bonus experiments that at least partially replicate one another. As a result, the external validity of findings from these experiments is higher than for experiments without such replication. In this sense, the UI experiments rate relatively high in generalizability.

Relevance

Results from policy research are relevant if they meet the needs of policymakers. At the time the UI bonus experiments were conceived and conducted, policymakers were concerned about an appropriate government response to increased unemployment. Consequently, they were attentive to exhaustion of the UI trust funds, provision of tax relief for employers supporting the UI system, and extension of UI benefits to workers affected by the recession. Thus, reducing program costs was paramount. The results fit nicely into these concerns as they included benefit-cost analyses from various accounting perspectives. Depending on whose ox was to be gored, policymakers could use the results to show that bonuses are not cost-effective from the point of view of the state UI trust funds or that they are cost-effective from the point of view of society as a whole.

In a 1988 hearing before the Subcommittee on Public Assistance and Unemployment Compensation of the House Ways and Means Committee, the National Governors Association advocated that the experiments be used to determine if the costs of the UI system could be reduced (U.S. Congress, House Ways and Means 1988, 66). Even earlier (1987), before the same subcommittee, the Illinois director of employment security emphasized the cost savings that were demonstrated in the Illinois experiment.[15] In her testimony to the same subcommittee, Mary Ann Wyrsch, the director of the Unemployment Service, emphasized that the results indicated that incentive bonuses are a net benefit to society and to claimants (Ways and Means 1991). In questioning Wyrsch, Representatives Downey of New York and Moody of Wisconsin both discussed the relevance of the results to "achieving [financial] gains" (25, 34–35). Louis Jacobson of the W. E. Upjohn Institute for Employment Research and Marc Bendick, an economic consultant, reiterated the same points in testimony before the House Ways and Means Subcommittee on Human Resources in 1992.

Surveys of state UI directors revealed a different list of concerns, which were not as well addressed by the experiments. Whereas the directors all cared about costs and the solvency of the trust funds, they were also very much concerned with job search assistance, skills development and training, workfare, UI profiling,[16] integration of services to the unemployed, automating the processing of those services, experience rating, and access to UI benefits. Moreover, they reported that federal law was specific about ways that UI trust funds could be used and that they did not have the flexibility to adopt bonuses. In addition, the absence of evidence from the UI experiments that bonuses would result in cost savings for the UI system did not motivate the UI directors to mount the effort needed to change UI policy. Thus, the results were of limited relevance to them.

As discussed earlier, by the time results from the UI experiments were available for incorporation into policy, much of the public policy debate centered on health care reform, welfare reform, and deficit reduction. UI policy changes were not on the policy agenda, and offering bonuses was not perceived to result in deficit reductions.

Ideology, Interests, and other Information in the Policy Environment

The UI bonus experiments did not have the effects on social policy originally envisioned for them. There has been no formative concrete substantive use resulting in implementation of a national (or even state) system of bonuses offered to UI recipients. In hindsight, this is not surprising. Indeed, it is entirely consistent with Weiss's I-I-I framework.

In Weiss's framework, research results are only one, and perhaps the weakest, form of information. Moreover, the influence of research findings on policymaking also depends on whether they are compatible with self-interest and ideology. The results of the UI experiments were as expected: The tested economic incentives got people off unemployment compensation and back to work earlier. As such, these findings were compatible with prior knowledge and experience. On the other hand, Weiss posits that research that results in what are perceived as obvious conclusions has relatively little impact. Although the UI findings were not in conflict with other knowledge, they also did little to motivate policymakers to agitate for adoption of reemployment bonuses. The positive effects were modest. Moreover, the results indicated bonuses fail to produce cost savings for the UI system.

From an ideological standpoint, the findings are consistent with the almost universal view of policymakers that it is desirable to get the unemployed back to work. From testimony before subcommittees of Ways and Means considering unemployment remedies, however, it is clear that there was an ongoing debate in Congress over possible ways of improving the UI program, each with its proponents. UI bonuses were only one of several options being considered. Worker profiling legislation was passed in 1993 as a direct result of the conclusive results of the New Jersey experiment, but that legislation did not include bonuses (telephone interview with Steve Wandner, April 17, 1996). As mentioned previously, the bonus option was put into the 1994 federal workforce bill to provide states with flexibility in their UI programs, but the bill failed to pass.

Reemployment bonuses conflicted with the perceived self-interest of unions and small businesses. Bonuses were considered anti-union because those hired through a union hiring hall could not receive them. Spiegelman believes that although the unions allowed the experiments to proceed, they probably would object if persons hired through union halls were excluded in a real program (telephone interview, October 27, 1996). A representative of the UAW testified as early as 1987 that his union was opposed to unemployment bonuses "because we question whether it is wise public policy to provide incentives for workers to take unsuitable work" (U.S. Congress, House Ways and Means Committee 1987, 204). Although there was no experimental evidence that workers accepting bonuses took less productive or less-well-paying jobs just to get a bonus payment, the union obviously did not feel that UI bonuses were in the interests of its members.

Reemployment bonuses also conflicted with the interests of employers who recalled workers from layoff, as such workers were ineligible for bonuses. Moreover, employers were concerned that the use of bonuses would increase the taxes employers pay to support the UI system. For example, in testifying against bonuses, the National Federation of Independent Business stated that "To say it [i.e., unemployment] is solely an employer problem, or that it is a societal problem but employers should bear the whole burden for the solution, is poor policy at best" (U.S. Congress, House Ways and Means Committee 1987, 265).

Thus, other interests and beliefs came into play and provided a counterweight to the experimental results. The findings that bonuses worked but that their effects were moderate had insufficient impact to overcome the interests of unions and small businesses. Moreover, the finding that bonuses would not result in cost savings for the UI system failed to elicit the support of others.

In the survey, state UI directors were directly asked about the extent to which the experimental findings corroborated their other information sources, such as intuition, experience in the field, and knowledge of the field. Their answers indicate that the experimental findings generally fit into their existing knowledge base.

Results corroborate intuition (%): $n = 26$[a]	
Not at all	15
Very little	12
Somewhat	54
Very much	19
Results corroborate experience (%): $n = 26$	
Not at all	15
Very little	27
Somewhat	38
Very much	19
Results corroborate knowledge of the field (%): $n = 24$	
Not at all	4
Very little	21
Somewhat	67
Very much	8

a. Although the response rate for the survey was 98 percent, not everyone responded to all the questions.

The UI directors were also asked about the degree to which the experimental results corroborated their previously held views or changed these views. Only six respondents indicated that their views about UI had been changed by the experiments.

Weiss states that there should be little resistance to using the results of research if they do not conflict with information from other sources, ideology, and interest. The survey seems to suggest little conflict with information from other sources where the UI directors are concerned. However, there was some conflict with their interests and (to a lesser degree) their ideology. In particular, the benefit-cost findings suggested that adopting bonuses would probably not result in cost savings for the UI system and might even increase costs. Moreover, some survey respondents (Maine, Minnesota, and South Dakota) believed that offering bonuses to reward people to do something they are supposed to do anyway—search for work—is inappropriate. Others were unenthusiastic about bonuses, believing that they are not needed because most layoffs are seasonal (Idaho) or of short duration (New Hampshire). Still other respondents believed that "broader cost issues" (Michigan) and employers' strong feelings in favor of traditional use of the state trust fund (Washington State) overrode any reason to adopt reemployment bonuses.

In summary, at the time findings from the UI experiments became available, power rested with the ideology of fiscal conservatism. Thus, although the experiments indicated that reemployment bonuses would help get claimants back to work sooner and would benefit society as a whole, the evidence that they would be unlikely to produce cost savings for the UI system excluded the possibility of adopting them.

Policy Concerns That Overshadowed the Experimental Results

During the period when the results of the UI bonus experiments could have been used in policymaking, other UI-related issues tended to receive greater attention: welfare reform, UI trust fund solvency and administrative costs, extended UI benefits and what unemployment rate should trigger their availability, recessionary effects on the UI system, veterans' eligibility for UI, the ever-present necessity for deficit reduction, and worker profiling. Policymakers, as indicated in congressional hearings, typically focused on those issues to the exclusion of bonuses.

NOTES

1. At the time the New Jersey experiment was designed, a plan was considered that would have increased the size of the bonus as the gap between pre-unemployment and post-unemployment wages grew. The idea was to encourage workers to take lower paying jobs more quickly. However, even though this might have led to workers accepting more realistic wages than otherwise, the plan was deemed impractical (USDOL 1989a, 121). In fact, complicated bonus schemes were eliminated from consideration because of concern that their complexity would interfere with implementation and with client understanding of the purpose of the bonus.

2. For claimants, the $500 represented about 5 percent of their annual wages and about four weeks of UI benefits. Again, the experimenters believed, or at least hoped, that the bonus was large enough to induce a response. As it turned out, however, they spent less than their budget as fewer people applied for bonuses than was initially expected (telephone interview with Robert Spiegelman, October 27, 1995).

3. However, findings from the experiment are based on the entire treatment group to avoid the self-selection bias that would result from analyzing only those who agreed to participate.

4. At one site (Rainier) a 40 percent, rather than 20 percent, sample was chosen to increase African-American participation in the experiment and, thereby, compensate for the fact that another site with a similar racial breakdown had been eliminated because it was participating in another experiment.

5. Telephone interview with Mary Vrany of the Governor's Work Force Investment Board, State of Maryland, March 10, 1995.

6. The results could be incorporated into specific policy proposals through the use of models. Because the Washington and Pennsylvania unemployment insurance bonus experiments were response surface experiments, the results could be (and were) used to estimate parameters to create models for predicting policy effects. Carl Davidson and Stephen Woodbury (1990, 1993) modeled the displacement effect using the results of the Illinois experiment. Paul Decker and Christopher O'Leary (USDOL 1992a) used pooled results of the Pennsylvania and Washington experiments to model the price and duration effects. Patricia Anderson (1992) used the New Jersey results to model the job search process. Bruce Meyer (1988) also used the Illinois results to model unemployment behavior. And finally, Philip Levine (1993) modeled job search behavior using the New Jersey and the Illinois results. The Department of Labor distributed the Decker and O'Leary model as part of their UI series, and the other models were presented at conferences or through journal articles. Unfortunately, it was not possible to document whether any of those models translated into concrete impacts on policy.

7. An additional option included in the bill was subsidized self-employment for UI recipients. After the 1994 workforce bill failed, this option was reintroduced as separate legislation by then-Representative (now Senator) Wyden of Oregon and passed.

8. As an example of this effort, see USDOL (1989b).

9. The UI director in Iowa said that the results dealing with exit rates and overall costs were a "key factor" leading to discussions about self-employment allowances. Respondents from New Jersey and Missouri reiterated this notion, even though the UI bonus experiments did not test self-employment allowances.

10. Although reemployment bonuses have been adopted in Connecticut, as described earlier, they are available to welfare recipients, not UI recipients.

11. To offer bonuses, states would have faced the nearly impossible task of obtaining a waiver to do so. According to John Peterson, a program specialist in the Maryland Office of Unemployment Insurance, waivers are granted only for experiments, and the experiments were already done (telephone interview, December 19, 1996).

12. Although displacement effects and Hawthorne effects are of concern in experiments of this type, the researchers addressed these issues specifically.

13. According to Corson they testified "quite a lot."

14. The results for this group were not strong even though they were targeted. Results were strongest for those workers who had the strongest marketable skills and thus were already the most employable.

15. As discussed earlier, while there was evidence of cost savings from the Illinois experiments, findings from the later experiments in Washington and Pennsylvania implied that cost savings would not occur.

16. The New Jersey experiment did provide guidance in implementing this federally mandated effort.

8

The Welfare-to-Work
Experiments

During the 1980s, a number of states began to explore techniques for increasing the earnings of welfare recipients and decreasing their dependence upon transfer payments. Many of these efforts were subject to formal evaluations. The best known of those evaluations were a series of random assignment experiments that were evaluated by the Manpower Demonstration Research Corporation (MDRC). MDRC is a New York City–based nonprofit research firm, and the experiments were known as the "work/welfare demonstrations" or the "welfare-to-work experiments." Those demonstrations and their role in policymaking are the subject of this chapter.

A Description of the Experiments

The specific welfare-to-work experiments that we consider in the chapter are listed below, along with a brief description of the tested programs:[1]

Arkansas WORK Program
Sequence of group job search followed by individual job search and (for a few) unpaid work experience

Baltimore Options Program
Choice of services, including individual or group job search, unpaid work experience, education, job skills training, and on-the-job training

California GAIN (Greater Avenues for Independence) Program
Adult basic education and job search followed by assessment and further education, unpaid work experience, job skills training, or on-the-job training

Cook County (Illinois) WIN (Work Incentive) Demonstration
Tests of two alternative programs: (1) individual job search; and (2) sequence of individual job search and (for a few) unpaid work experience

Maine On-the-Job Training (OJT) Program
Sequence of employability training, unpaid work experience, and subsidized on-the-job training at private sector firms

New Jersey On-the-Job Training (OJT) Program
Subsidized on-the-job training at private sector firms

San Diego I (Employment Preparation Program/Experimental Work Experience Program)
Test of two alternative programs: (1) group job search; and (2) sequence of group job search followed by unpaid work experience

San Diego SWIM (Saturation Work Incentive Model)
Sequence of group job search, unpaid work experience, and education and job skills training; emphasis on maximizing participation

Virginia Employment Services Program (ESP)
Sequence of individual or group search, unpaid work experience, and some education or job skills training (but only slightly more than controls received on their own)

West Virginia Community Work Experience Program (CWEP)
Open-ended unpaid work experience; for AFDC-U applicants and recipients, emphasis on maximizing participation

The number of state welfare reform efforts initiated during the 1980s far exceeded the number of demonstrations and programs listed above. However, the 10 listed demonstrations and programs have several common features that distinguish them from the others and cause researchers and policymakers to tend to view them collectively. (1) They all provided services to applicants for or participants in state AFDC programs[2] that were intended to increase the employment of these persons. (2) They were all evaluated experimentally.[3] (3) As previously indicated, all of the evaluations were conducted by MDRC. (4) With one important exception, California's Greater Avenues for Independence program (GAIN), they were all initiated between 1982 and 1985. Moreover, all but GAIN and San Diego's Saturation Work Incentive Model (SWIM) were stimulated in large measure by the Omnibus Budget Reconciliation Act of 1981. As discussed later, findings from evaluations of the nine initial welfare-to-work experiments were usually used together. GAIN is included in our list because, as will be seen, it is intricately connected to the two experiments that preceded it in California—San Diego I and SWIM. Hence, our report would be incomplete if GAIN were ignored.

As the brief program descriptions make clear, most programs tested by the welfare-to-work experiments incorporated several components. This is important because it means that the separate effects of the individual components could not be distinguished and, hence, the welfare-to-work experiments are of the black box type mentioned in chapter 2.

The programs tested in two of the welfare-to-work experiments, those in New Jersey and Maine, were limited to AFDC recipients who volunteered to participate. Those two programs placed the volunteers into private sector jobs in which AFDC grant funds were used to subsidize employers.

Eligible AFDC applicants and recipients were required to participate in the remaining eight programs. Although the specific combination of components varied among the eight programs, they included one or more of the following: assessment of basic skills, structured job search, job skills training, adult basic education or other forms of education, and unpaid community service employment at government or nonprofit agencies in exchange for receiving AFDC grants (the latter is sometimes called "unpaid work experience" or "workfare"). Of the eight programs, only two, the Baltimore Options program and California's GAIN, provided members of treatment groups with appreciably more training and education than members of control groups. The major emphasis of the other six programs was on job search and community service employment, although in some instances very modest use was made of education and training.

Background information about the welfare-to-work experiments appears in table 8.1. As the table indicates, all of the tested programs and demonstrations were targeted at the AFDC-R population (that is, low-income one-parent households in the regular AFDC program that make up the bulk of households receiving AFDC). In addition, half were also targeted at the AFDC-U population (two-parent households in which the head is unemployed). The remaining information in table 8.1 should be self-explanatory.[4]

The welfare-to-work experiments had certain characteristics that strongly influenced future trends in social experimentation. Although those features were not necessarily first introduced by these experiments, as will be seen, the welfare-to-work experiments were large and very prominent and, hence, they certainly helped popularize them. Thus, the welfare-to-work experiments can be appropriately viewed as a watershed in social experimentation. Four characteristics stand out.

1. As described in the following section, the tested programs were designed by state and (sometimes) local welfare agencies and operated through local welfare offices. Most policies that were previously tested experimentally, in contrast, were developed at the national level and often administered through separate field offices set up specifically for that purpose. The welfare-to-work experiments avoided those somewhat artificial "hothouse" arrangements.

2. As indicated in table 8.1, all but the New Jersey and Maine experiments were at least nominally mandatory. That is, AFDC participants were threatened with grant reductions if they refused to participate, although the extent to which the mandate was enforced varied greatly among the experiments. Participation in most previous social experiments had been entirely voluntary. As will be discussed later, this mandatory feature had important implications not only for social experimentation but for the future of welfare policy as well.

3. Before the welfare-to-work experiments, social experiments had been used almost entirely to evaluate pilot tests of proposed policies. Thus, the treatment group consisted of only a small subset of

Table 8.1. *Background Information on the Welfare-to-Work Experiments*

Tested program	Mandatory or voluntary	Evaluation sites	Sample size (including controls)	Year sample intake began	Net cost per participant ($)	Target group
Arkansas WORK	Mandatory	2 counties	1,153	1983	118	AFDC-R applicants and recipients with children 3 and older
Baltimore Options	Mandatory	10 of the 18 city welfare offices	AFDC-R: 2,775 AFDC-U: 337	1982	953	AFDC-R applicants and recipients with children 6 and older; AFDC-U applicants and recipients
California GAIN	Mandatory	6 counties	AFDC-R: 22,800 AFDC-U: 10,200	1988	3,422	AFDC-R applicants and recipients with children 6 and older; AFDC-U applicants and recipients
Cook County WIN Demonstration	Mandatory	countywide, including Chicago	11,919	1985	157	AFDC-R applicants and recipients with children 6 and older
Maine OJT	Voluntary	statewide	444	1983	2,019	Unemployed AFDC recipients on rolls for over 6 months
New Jersey REACH	Voluntary	statewide	1,943	1984	787	AFDC-R recipients with children 2 years and older

(*continued*)

Table 8.1. *Continued*

Tested program	Mandatory or voluntary	Evaluation sites	Sample size (including controls)	Year sample intake began	Net cost per participant ($)	Target group
San Diego I	Mandatory	countywide	AFDC-R: 3,231 AFDC-U: 3,020	1982	636	AFDC-R applicants with children 6 and older; AFDC-U applicants
San Diego SWIM	Mandatory	2 of the 7 county welfare offices	AFDC-R: 3,211 AFDC-U: 1,341	1985	919	AFDC-R applicants and recipients with children 6 and older; AFDC-U applicants and recipients
Virginia ESP	Mandatory	11 counties	3,184	1983	430	AFDC-R applicants and recipients with children 6 and older
West Virginia CWEP	Mandatory	AFDC-R: 9 administrative areas AFDC-U: 8 administrative areas	AFDC-R: 3,694 AFDC-U: 5,630	1983	260	AFDC-R applicants and recipients with children 6 and older; AFDC-U applicants and recipients

Sources: Adopted from Gueron and Pauly (1991), tables 3.1 and 3.2, and from Greenberg and Shroder (1997).

Notes: AFDC-R = AFDC payments for single-parent households with children; AFDC-U = AFDC for two-parent families in which the primary wage earner is unemployed; CWEP = Community Work Experience Program; ESP = Employment Services Program; GAIN = Greater Avenues for Independence; OJT = on-the-job training; SWIM = Saturation Work Incentive Model; WIN = Work Incentive.

the target population, with the remaining population ineligible to participate in the tested program. In contrast, several of the welfare-to-work experiments—Virginia ESP, West Virginia CWEP, and California GAIN—were used to assess programs that had been recently adopted by entire states. Thus, in those states the entire target population, except for a small randomly selected control group confined to specific geographic areas, was eligible to participate in the program being evaluated. That fact set an important precedent in using random assignment experiments to evaluate previously adopted programs, not just small pilot tests of proposed programs.

4. As indicated by table 8.1, the experimental sample sizes were generally large. The large sample sizes were deemed necessary because the treatment effects were expected to be small. Given the limited funds available for evaluation, the large samples were feasible only because the evaluations of the welfare-to-work experiments were based mainly on data that were already being routinely collected by state administrative agencies.[5] This arrangement contrasts with the evaluations of most previous social experiments, which relied on the collection of expensive survey data.

Origin of the Experiments

An Overview

The origin of the welfare-to-work experiments can be traced to the Reagan administration's (1981–89) desire to alter the welfare system. As two-term governor of California before he became president, Ronald Reagan had implemented a state welfare reform package that included a work requirement, the California Work Experience Program (CWEP), which attempted to link AFDC payments to mandatory community service without pay. Although CWEP was never fully implemented in California and had not been rigorously evaluated, upon assuming the presidency Reagan and his associates proposed a similar requirement for the nation as a whole. As part of a political compromise, the then-Democratic-controlled Congress instead passed legislation that permitted states desiring to do so to implement welfare-to-work programs of their own design. That legislation, which was incorporated into the

Omnibus Budget Reconciliation Act of 1981 (OBRA) as part of a more comprehensive welfare reform package, permitted states to select from the various program components listed earlier, including mandatory community service.

Many states responded to the new flexibility permitted by OBRA by developing welfare-to-work plans. In response, the federal government issued a request for proposals (RFP) to study the implementation of the plans. The Manpower Development Research Corporation responded by writing a proposal to measure the impacts and benefit-costs of state welfare-to-work programs, as well as to study their implementation. Because the federal government did not fund MDRC's proposed study or any other study, MDRC submitted a proposal with similar objectives to the Ford Foundation and in the spring of 1982 received a challenge grant of $3.5 million.

It was that grant that permitted the welfare-to-work experiments to be undertaken, but not until after a number of other hurdles were cleared. Under the terms of Ford's challenge grant, MDRC had to find funds to match dollar for dollar the money provided by the Ford Foundation. Moreover, MDRC had originally been established in the 1970s to administer a large-scale random assignment experiment, the National Supported Work Demonstration, and remained strongly committed to experimental methodology because of an ardent belief in the superior rigor of the approach. Thus, it was necessary for MDRC to find states that were implementing interesting welfare-to-work programs and were willing to submit to random assignment and then have their programs evaluated by outsiders. Those states also had to be routinely collecting the administrative data on welfare payments and earnings that were required for the evaluation. Moreover, the program had to be of sufficient scale to generate a large enough sample for evaluation purposes.

Many, although not all, of the changes states initiated in response to OBRA required approval under federal waiver requirements before they could be implemented. Although obtaining federal waivers required an evaluation plan, during the early post-OBRA period states were not usually obligated to conduct either rigorous or independent evaluations of the sort MDRC contemplated. Indeed, some of the evaluations of state welfare-to-work programs were cursory (see Greenberg and Wiseman 1992). Thus, as Gordon Berlin, who in 1984 became Ford's project officer for the welfare-to-work experiments, suggested, MDRC had to do a strong "selling job . . . to convince states to do a random assignment design [and] to let outsiders in to look at what they were going to do. . . ."

After receiving the challenge grant from Ford, MDRC visited about 30 states. Some of those states were not running welfare-to-work programs that were worthy of evaluation, in MDRC's judgment, and others did not have the necessary administrative data. In addition, a few states resisted evaluation, especially random assignment evaluation.

However, according to Judith Gueron, who led the MDRC effort to initiate the welfare-to-work experiments and is now the organization's president, the idea of being part of a Ford Foundation project and the resulting status appealed to a number of states. Furthermore, welfare directors in states that were testing welfare-to-work innovations on a pilot basis liked being able to hold off state legislatures until they could learn about the effectiveness of the innovation. Although there was some resistance to random assignment in the selected states, MDRC was often able to convince the states of the value of obtaining rigorous knowledge about the efficacy of innovations of their own choosing. Moreover, states typically did not have sufficient funds to provide welfare-to-work services to everyone on AFDC, and random assignment often appeared to be a fair allocative mechanism.

The Ford Foundation's support allowed the welfare-to-work experiments to go forward. With the Ford grant, MDRC could approach states with half the funding required for a rigorous experimental evaluation already in place. The sources of the remaining funds varied. The states themselves often provided all or part of the needed funding. Some states (for example, West Virginia and Arkansas) obtained funds from foundations. Finally, several states (New Jersey, Maine, and California [in the case of San Diego I]) won federal funding by responding to requests for proposals.

Thus, four different institutions were involved in initiating the welfare-to-work experiments: the federal government, state and (sometimes) local governments, the Ford Foundation, and MDRC. It is useful to consider briefly the role of each.

As previously discussed, in passing the 1981 OBRA legislation, Congress encouraged states to innovate. In general, at the time the first 9 of the 10 experiments considered in this chapter were initiated (1982–85), the executive branch of the federal government appears to have generally taken a hands-off attitude on the evaluation of state welfare reform initiatives. However, initially, there was some resistance by Reagan administration officials to random assignment. But by the mid-1980s, the executive branch of the federal government had become a strong supporter of using random assignment in evaluating welfare program innovations. As described later, this was particularly true of the office within the Department of Health and Human Services responsible for evaluating research demonstrations.

Although MDRC had to obtain the Ford Foundation's approval for each project that it helped fund and the foundation provided critical reviews of MDRC's research plans, Ford's role was mainly limited to funding. As Gordon Berlin expressed it, "MDRC did the work, Ford provided the money." There was great uncertainty on whether large-scale social experiments could be successfully run through state and local welfare agencies when Ford awarded MDRC the challenge grant in 1982— as Berlin put it, Ford "made a bet." However, Ford was sufficiently pleased with MDRC's initial effort that it issued a second challenge grant in 1991 so MDRC could continue its work.

The line of division between the role of state and local governments and that of MDRC was fairly clear, at least in principle. The state and local governments designed, implemented, and operated the innovative programs that were to be evaluated, and MDRC developed the evaluation design and conducted the actual evaluation. At first, MDRC was somewhat uncomfortable with this situation because in previous large-scale social experiments, evaluators had enjoyed considerable control over the tested program, as well as over the evaluation. As Judith Gueron told us, MDRC "traded off control for ownership by the states." That is, the states were testing their own programs, rather than programs designed elsewhere. Gueron went on to say, "Ultimately I came to believe that ownership, if you were interested in research affecting social policy, was more important than control."

It should be pointed out that, in practice, the line between program design and evaluation design is sometimes murky because the two can affect one another. Consider just one example. In the San Diego I experiment, two separate programs were tested. The first program provided group job search; the second program also provided group job search, but in addition those who did not find employment could then be assigned to an unpaid work experience job. Consequently, members of the target population were randomly assigned to one of three groups— one of the two alternative programs or control status. The motivation behind this innovative evaluation design was to determine if job search in combination with community service employment was more effective than job search alone. Thus, the evaluation design was very much influenced by what California wished to test in San Diego.

The California Experiments

California has a special role in the history of experimentally based evaluations of welfare-to-work programs. Not only were 3 of the 10 experiments conducted there but, as will be discussed later, those experiments have also played a prominent role in policymaking outside the state. Thus it is useful to examine the evolution of the three California evaluations in some detail. Moreover, the progression among the three California experiments—San Diego I, SWIM, and GAIN—provides an interesting case study of the reason experiments are undertaken and how one social experiment can influence the next.

The San Diego I experiment was a direct result of the failure of earlier attempts within California to evaluate welfare-to-work programs nonexperimentally. In reaction to OBRA, a number of bills were introduced in the state legislature in the early 1980s to implement welfare-to-work programs. The California Employment Development Department (EDD) was asked by the legislature to assess the efficacy of the proposed programs. In reaction, EDD decided to run some demonstration programs and evaluate their effects in-house. To do this, they first considered an experimental design but, according to Virginia Hamilton, who worked for EDD at the time, dismissed it because it seemed "too hard" and "we were all too scared to do it." They then decided on a design in which matched treatment and control counties were to be compared, but could not find counties that they considered sufficiently similar. They finally settled on comparing treatment and control offices within counties. However, they found that even the offices they were trying to compare were too dissimilar. As Hamilton put it, "different things were happening in different offices."

At about this juncture, EDD responded to a U.S. Department of Health and Human Services request for proposals to run and evaluate welfare-to-work demonstrations. Using the funding provided under the resulting grant, EDD decided to run demonstration programs in San Mateo and San Diego counties but to hire an outside contractor to perform the evaluation. MDRC competed successfully against other firms for the project.[6]

Given their previous problems with attempting to conduct a non-experimental evaluation, EDD was receptive to the idea of a random assignment design, an approach strongly favored by MDRC. The details of program and evaluation designs were worked out during a number of meetings attended by state and county officials and by MDRC. San Mateo County had already been running a job search program on a demonstration basis for some time, while San Diego County initially wanted to test a pure mandatory work experience program. This combination of factors motivated the idea of combining job search and a mandatory work experience requirement into a single program. It also resulted in the three-group evaluation design described earlier.

Interestingly, the San Diego County and the San Mateo County Welfare Offices were both initially resistant to random assignment because they did not want to deny program services to people who they thought could benefit from them. After a series of meetings, San Diego eventually agreed to random assignment and to allowing MDRC to control the process. MDRC did not win similar control in San Mateo. Instead, a compromise was reached: Controls would consist of AFDC applicants with 0 or 5 as the last digit of their social security number and all other AFDC applicants would be assigned to treatment status. According to Virginia Hamilton, staff at the San Mateo County Welfare Office believed so strongly in the program they were testing that they allowed some of those assigned to control status to receive services. As a result, the San Mateo data could not be used for analysis and was useless for policy purposes. Thus, the experiment was effectively limited to San Diego.

As will be discussed in greater detail later, the results from the San Diego I experiment were generally encouraging. Impacts were fairly small, but in the hoped-for direction—welfare receipts fell and earnings increased. However, the treatment group was limited to new AFDC applicants, excluding those on the rolls at the time the demonstration was initiated. Moreover, fewer than half of those who were assigned to the treatment group actually received any program services, even though the program was mandatory. There were a number of reasons for the disparity between the label "mandatory" and actual practice—for example, some persons were excused because of such factors as ill health and family responsibilities and others left the AFDC rolls before service slots became available. This raised two obvious questions:

- What is the maximum feasible participation rate for a welfare-to-work program?
- How would program impacts be affected if current AFDC recipients, as well as new AFDC applicants, were required to participate and if participation rates were increased to their maximum feasible level?

The city, the state, and the U.S. Department of Health and Human Services (HHS) were all interested in the answers to these questions. Indeed, HHS was interested sufficiently to issue a request for proposals for an evaluation project that would examine the questions directly. San Diego was one of the cities that submitted a proposal in response and was one of the two sites selected by HHS (Philadelphia was the other). The result was a second experiment in San Diego—SWIM, the *Saturation* Work Initiative Model (emphasis added). As designed, SWIM included current AFDC recipients as well as new applicants, and placed great emphasis on obtaining the highest feasible participation rate among persons assigned to the treatment group. Thus, in this particular instance, questions raised by findings from one experiment led directly to the initiation of a second experiment. San Diego County operated SWIM, with the state having only minimal involvement.

The third California experiment, GAIN, differed from the first two because it was intended to evaluate legislation that established a statewide welfare-to-work program, rather than demonstration programs operating in only one or two counties. Although results from SWIM were not yet available at the time the Greater Avenues for Independence Program legislation was passed, findings from San Diego I were. The role San Diego I played in the design of the GAIN program will be discussed later. Here, we consider the GAIN evaluation design and the effect of San Diego I on it.

Most of the persons involved in developing the GAIN legislation were aware of the San Diego I findings and considered them useful.[7] For example, David Maxwell-Jolly, who at the time the legislation was being developed worked for the California Legislative Analyst's Office, told us that those involved in designing GAIN "were tickled pink with the kinds of information [they] got out of San Diego." He went on to say that the GAIN designers were especially concerned with whether GAIN (which, as table 8.1 indicates, is a relatively expensive welfare-to-work program) would be cost-effective, and to find out they needed to know what would happen in the absence of the program. Therefore, according to Maxwell-Jolly, including a random assignment research component in GAIN seemed like "a natural thing to do."[8]

The GAIN legislation gave each of California's 57 counties considerable freedom to design its own welfare-to-work program within the basic framework specified by the legislation. This resulted in a key evaluation design issue: Should the evaluation focus on obtaining estimates of the overall statewide impact of GAIN or on obtaining estimates of the impact in individual counties? The first approach would necessitate a daunting management task. AFDC recipients throughout the state would have to be randomly assigned and mechanisms would have to be put in place in welfare offices scattered about the state to ensure that members of the control group were denied services under GAIN. The second approach meant that the experiment would be limited to only a selected subset of counties, which would considerably reduce the management burden imposed by the evaluation. However, it also meant that the evaluation sample in each of the selected counties would have to be large, so that statistically significant impact estimates could be obtained. An important potential advantage of the second approach was that it offered the possibility of relating causes to effects. That is, according to Paul Warren, who headed the staff of the GAIN Oversight Committee established by the state legislature, it was hoped that it would be possible to examine "the different treatments that the counties chose and how that affected the success of the program."

The decision was to adopt the second approach. As discussed later, this decision had profound implications for the way GAIN has been used in the policy process. Because of cost considerations and because some counties were resistant to evaluation or to random assignment, the experimental sites were limited to six counties. As the selection of counties did not occur until 18 months after the legislation was passed, information existed about the details of the GAIN program model adopted by each county. Thus, there was an attempt to obtain a sample of counties that differed in the programs they were operating. There was also an attempt to obtain a mixture of urban and rural counties. However, it was considered essential to include Los Angeles County, because 40 percent of the state's AFDC caseload was located there, and San Diego County, so that GAIN could be compared with the earlier programs run there.

There was relatively little controversy within California over the research design, in part because the state deferred to MDRC on technical questions (for example, sample size). Nonetheless, in California, as elsewhere, some administrators resisted random assignment because they did not want to deny services to members of control groups.[9] However, counties that were adamantly opposed to the evaluation or random assignment were excluded from the evaluation. Other counties had to be convinced to accept random assignment. Random assignment usually became more acceptable to those counties once they recognized that they did not have sufficient funding to serve their entire caseload and, hence, that some mechanism was needed to determine who would be denied services.

Why Were the Welfare-to-Work Experiments Undertaken?

The motivation for undertaking the welfare-to-work demonstrations differed somewhat among the various institutions involved. Among the states that were operating the programs being evaluated and the federal government that helped fund most of the programs, there was an obvious interest in determining whether the programs had the desired effects and whether they made effective use of government funds. Those objectives are particularly understandable in the context of the time. The welfare-to-work experiments were launched in 1982, halfway through President Reagan's first term, at a time when there was widespread pessimism over whether any positive benefits at all resulted from government expenditures on social programs.

The interests of MDRC and the Ford Foundation were somewhat broader than those of the states operating the welfare-to-work experiments. To them, the 1981 OBRA legislation represented a major change in welfare policy. Thus, the welfare-to-work experiments were viewed, in Gordon Berlin's words, as an attempt to "systematically . . . build knowledge . . . to learn about what states do and what difference it makes." It is apparent that this statement is consistent with Feldman's (1989) hypothesis that research is undertaken to build an inventory of information in case the need for the information eventually arises.

The states that served as experimental sites were clearly following a variant of the rational paradigm in deciding to participate in undertaking the experiments. On the one hand, states that were running demonstration programs (for example, Arkansas's WORK Program) desired to know whether to adopt the tested programs statewide, possibly in modified form. On the other hand, states that had already adopted a program statewide (for example, California's GAIN) wanted information on whether they had made a good decision and on how the program might be improved. For instance, California hoped to learn which of the GAIN models in the six experimental counties was most effective. In at least some of the states conducting the experiments, there seemed to be a presumption that once the findings were available, there would be an appropriate policy response to them.[10]

At first glance, it might appear that Feldman's inventory model provides the best explanation of Ford's and MDRC's desire to initiate the welfare-to-work experiments. The model implies that social experiments will be initiated to create an inventory of information for future, but unspecified, policymaking situations. Consistent with this prediction, Gordon Berlin told us that there was little discussion at Ford about what would be done with the findings. There was just an assumption that MDRC would distribute them and they would be used. However, Feldman's model further implies that whether research information gets used is more or less a random event. Ford and MDRC, in contrast, felt certain that the inventory of information that they were creating would be used—certainly in the states in which the experiments were being conducted, probably by other states, and possibly by federal agencies and Congress.[11] The reason for believing that findings from the welfare-to-work experiments would be used by states that did not serve as experimental sites is that once OBRA was passed, it seemed apparent that many of those states would consider implementing welfare-to-work programs of their own. It seemed reasonable to anticipate that those states would want information on whether such programs were effective and, if they were, what sort of program design might work best. Moreover, as discussed later in this chapter and in chapter 9, MDRC decided to make an active effort to disseminate findings from the welfare-to-work experiments and thereby promote their use. If the inventory were created, it was expected that policymakers would surely draw upon it. Thus, the rational paradigm appears to provide an appropriate explanation of the decision by Ford and MDRC to initiate the welfare-to-work experiments, as well as the decision by certain states to serve as sites.

Findings from the Welfare-to-Work Experiments

As one might imagine, the 10 welfare-to-work experiments produced an enormous volume of findings, although reports of the findings came in waves due to different evaluation schedules for the different experiments. In this section, we attempt to summarize only the more important of those findings, particularly those that were likely to attract the notice of policymakers. We focus on providing an overview of results from the 10 experiments, discussing an experiment individually only when it produced a finding that was especially noteworthy. The most complete sources of information about the individual experiments are the reports that MDRC produced on each one, especially the final report.[12] In addition, there have been a number of very useful syntheses of findings from welfare-to-work experiments that go into much greater detail than we do here.[13]

In discussing findings from the welfare-to-work experiments, we distinguish between those that rely on comparisons between individuals who were randomly assigned to experimental and control status and those that are not based on such comparisons. As will be discussed later, both types of findings influenced the policy process.

Experimental Findings

Table 8.2 presents a number of the key experimentally estimated effects of the welfare-to-work demonstrations. Those estimates are averaged across members of the treatment group in each experiment, and therefore they should be viewed as estimates of program effects on a typical member of each treatment group. This is important to keep in mind in considering the estimates in the table because, for a variety of reasons, many members of the treatment groups received little or no actual service under the tested programs. Thus, the programs may have had little or no impact on them.[14] If so, the lack of program participation by and impact on an important segment of the treatment group pulled down the average estimated effect for the group as a whole.

Estimates in table 8.2 are reported for each of the 10 experiments and, in addition, are reported separately for one of the six GAIN experimental sites—Riverside County. As discussed later in this and the next chapter, findings for this one county have received a great deal of attention among policymakers. The findings are also reported separately for one-parent

Table 8.2. Selected Estimates of the Impacts of the Welfare-to-Work Experiments

Tested programs	Earnings[a] ($)		Percent receiving AFDC[b]		Quarters of observation	Net benefit by perspective[c] ($)		
	Control group	Program impact[d]	Control group[e]	Program impact[d]		Participant	Nonparticipant	Societal
AFDC-R								
Arkansas WORK	321	51	41.0	-5.6	20	-499	944	494
Baltimore Options	731	99	62.1	-1.1	13	1,739	74	1,813
Cook County WIN	409	9	79.0	-1.5	4	-227	419	192
Maine OJT	590	207	68.6	1.9	9	3,182	-418	2,764
New Jersey REACH	988	109	60.7	-3.5	5	1,262	1,069	2,331
San Diego I	683	95	45.9	-2.4	4	733	860	1,593
San Diego SWIM	702	104	48.7	-4.8	19	96	1,673	1,769
Virginia ESP	627	62	37.8	-1.2	18	800	383	1,183
West Virginia CWEP	154	-2	68.6	-1.8	4	-84	731	647
California GAIN	631	154	56.9	-2.6	16	923	-990	-67
Riverside	625	271	51.7	-5.5	16	1,900	2,559	4,458

AFDC-U

Baltimore Options	1,499	−416	43.0	4.8	3	−1,233	−1,856	−3,089
San Diego I	1,580	38	40.4	−4.9	4	−1,337	1,335	−2
San Diego SWIM	759	110	64.1	1.2	8	−347	2,130	1,783
West Virginia CWEP	608	−38	59.0	−5.3	4	—	—	—
California GAIN	842	100	59.3	−0.9	16	−186	−652	−838
Riverside	905	106	47.5	−2.0	16	−714	1,180	466

Sources: The estimates for California GAIN are from Lin, Freedman, and Friedlander (1995). The earnings and AFDC receipt estimates for AFDC-Rs for Arkansas WORK, Baltimore Options, San Diego SWIM, and Virginia ESP are from Friedlander and Burtless (1995). The remaining earnings and AFDC receipt estimates are from Greenberg and Wiseman (1992), who obtained them from various MDRC research reports. The remaining net benefit estimates are from Greenberg (1992), who obtained them from various MDRC research reports.

Notes: AFDC-R = AFDC payments for single-parent households with children; AFDC-U = AFDC for two-parent families in which the primary wage earner is unemployed; CWEP = Community Work Experience Program; ESP = Employment Services Program; GAIN = Greater Avenues for Independence; MDRC = Manpower Demonstration Research Corporation; OJT = on-the-job training; SWIM = Saturation Work Incentive Model; WIN = Work Incentive; — = not available.

a. Average per calendar quarter in current dollars (averaged from quarter 3 through last available quarter).

b. Percent receiving AFDC per calendar quarter (averaged from quarter 3 through last available quarter).

c. The present value of benefits minus the present value of costs.

d. Treatment group average minus control group average.

e. Average in absence of the evaluated program.

AFDC-R and two-parent AFDC-U households. Three types of program impact estimates are reported in table 8.2: the effect of the tested programs on earnings, their effect on whether AFDC was received, and their net benefits (that is, the amount by which their benefits exceeded their costs).

The first two measures directly reflect key goals of most of the tested programs: improving the labor market performance and reducing the welfare dependence of the target population. The earnings and AFDC receipt estimates are averaged over all the calendar quarters for which they are available except the first two. The number of calendar quarters on which the estimates are based, which varies considerably among the experiments, is reported in the fifth column of the table. The first two quarters were omitted in computing the estimates because many members of the treatment group were still receiving program services during that period. Thus, it may have been too early for the full effect of the program to manifest itself. The earnings of members of the control group and the percentage of the control group receiving AFDC are also reported in table 8.2 to provide a benchmark, an estimate of what would have happened in the absence of the program. For example, the first row of the table implies that, based on the last 20 of the 22 quarters for which estimates were available, a typical member of the Arkansas WORK program AFDC-R treatment group would have received earnings of $321 per quarter in the absence of the program. As a result of the program, however, the individual instead received earnings of $372. Similarly, over the 20 calendar quarters, 41.0 percent of the controls received AFDC during a typical quarter, while only 35.4 percent of the experimental group did so.

The net benefit estimates in table 8.2 were obtained from MDRC's cost-benefit studies of the welfare-to-work experiments. The objective of those studies was to determine whether benefits generated by each of the welfare-to-work programs exceeded costs incurred as a result of the program, and if so, by how much. In computing net benefits, MDRC summed benefits and costs over a five-year period, which began with enrollment into the programs.[15] As the table implies, there are three different ways to view net benefits: the participant perspective, the nonparticipant perspective, and the societal perspective. From the perspective of program participants, net benefits consist of gains from employment (that is, increases in earnings and fringe benefits less increases in taxes and work-related expenditures such as day care) less any reductions in government transfer benefits such as AFDC payments. The nonparticipant group includes persons who pay taxes that fund welfare and the operation of welfare-to-work programs.

From their point of view, net benefits consist of reductions in transfer benefits paid to and increases in taxes paid by participants plus the value of any output participants produce while working at unpaid community service jobs less the cost of operating the welfare-to-work programs. Finally, society as a whole consists of both participants and nonparticipants, two mutually exclusive subgroups that encompass the entire population. Thus, net societal benefits are the sum of the net benefits received by participants and nonparticipants.

The estimates of program effects that are reported in table 8.2 vary considerably among the experiments. This is not surprising given the variety of treatments offered, differences in the target groups covered by the tested programs, differences in the proportion of treatment group members who actually received services under the programs, and variations in the economic, political, and institutional environments in which the experiments were conducted. Nonetheless, it is possible to draw two important general conclusions from the estimates reported in the table.

CONCLUSION 1

Most of the estimates imply that the tested programs increased earnings and reduced the size of the welfare rolls. This is particularly true for one-parent households receiving AFDC-R, who constitute about 90 percent of the total AFDC population. Moreover, at least in the case of AFDC-R households, the estimates indicated that the benefits to society as a whole of most of the programs exceeded the social costs of the programs. And, perhaps more important from a political point of view, the programs usually resulted in net savings for taxpayers. In other words, they generally succeeded in more than paying for themselves from a taxpayer perspective. Indeed, in the case of AFDC-R households, the programs often had a positive payoff for both participants and taxpayers. Viewed in the political context that existed at the time most of the findings became available, a situation in which many persons believed that expenditures on social programs were a waste of resources, these generally positive findings were potentially galvanizing. Furthermore, the positive effects were found for a variety of program designs and in diverse geographic settings, suggesting that favorable effects could be obtained for various specific combinations of program components and in other geographic locations than those in which the experiments were conducted. In addition, the programs were operated by typical government agencies, not special hothouse units.

CONCLUSION 2

Most of the impact estimates appearing in table 8.2 imply that the effects of the experimental programs were relatively small. For example, almost all of the earnings impact estimates, although positive, are well below $200 in a calendar quarter. On an annual basis, only the Riverside GAIN program for AFDC-R households raised average earnings by as much as $1,000 a year. Few families were pulled above the poverty line.[16] Similarly, although the tested programs were generally successful in reducing the incidence of welfare receipt, none of the impact estimates exceeded six percentage points.[17] The net benefit estimates are also modest, although usually positive for at least one-parent households. For example, the estimates were computed over a five-year period; in only a few instances do either participants or nonparticipants enjoy a total net gain of more than $2,000 per treatment group member during this period.

Taken together, these modest but typically positive effects would seem to imply that welfare-to-work programs are well worth undertaking. The best of them are cost-effective, increasing the incomes of participants while reducing the burden on taxpayers. The fact that program effects are modest in absolute value is hardly surprising. As table 8.1 indicates, the government's expenditures on the programs were also modest. Except for the California GAIN and the Maine OJT programs, they were below $1,000 per participant.

Nonetheless, it is evident from the findings that even the best welfare-to-work programs are no panacea. At the time the welfare-to-work experiments were conducted, many persons were convinced that the existing welfare system was broken. That is, they believed that it burdened taxpayers but did not really help those who participated in it. As clearly implied by findings from the experiments, welfare-to-work programs could not fix a welfare system that many viewed as broken; they merely comprised a small move in the right direction. As will be seen later, both the fact that most of the welfare-to-work experiments produced positive effects and the fact that the effects were modest had important implications for the way that the findings were used in the policy process.

One additional implication of table 8.2 deserves emphasis. The table, as well as considerable additional evidence (see Riccio, Friedlander, and Freedman 1994), strongly suggests that the GAIN program in Riverside County was the most successful welfare-to-work program ever run, especially for AFDC-R households. The finding is of particular importance because in administering GAIN, Riverside County placed emphasis on moving members of the treatment group into the workforce as quickly as possible. As part of that approach (which has become variously known as the "Riverside model," the "work first model," and the "labor force attachment model"), a strong message was consistently communicated to those enrolled in GAIN that employment, even at poorly paying jobs, should be sought expeditiously. The other five counties that participated in the GAIN experiment, in contrast, relied to varying degrees more on a "human capital model" in which education (particularly adult basic education) and training were used to upgrade the skills of welfare recipients before they sought work. Although Riverside varied from the other five counties in numerous respects in addition to differing in terms of program models, it became widely accepted among state welfare system administrators that the GAIN experiment demonstrated that the work-first approach is superior to the human capital approach.

Nonexperimental Findings

Several nonexperimental findings from the welfare-to-work experiments were of considerable policy importance. It is important to recognize, however, that had the findings that relied on experimental/control comparisons not been generally favorable, those nonexperimental findings would have been of little consequence. The most important of the nonexperimental findings are listed below:

- It was apparent that states could design and implement successful welfare-to-work programs, and that they could do so in a variety of typical welfare settings. This finding was important because the freedom provided the states under the 1981 OBRA legislation was controversial. The success of several state welfare-to-work programs suggested to some that the states be given even more flexibility in operating welfare programs.
- The welfare-to-work experiments demonstrated that it was administratively feasible to require AFDC recipients to participate in mandatory programs in exchange for the receipt of transfer benefits. Moreover, surveys that MDRC conducted of participants in several of those programs indicated that AFDC recipients themselves generally thought that mandatory participation in job search

and community service jobs was fair.[18] This undermined arguments by liberals in the 1980s that mandatory programs for AFDC recipients, especially those that had community service components, constituted "slave labor."

- Two of the welfare-to-work demonstrations were explicitly designed to determine the maximum feasible rates of participation among the target population in activities that met program objectives. The SWIM evaluation found that during a typical month in the program's second year, 52 percent of the AFDC-R and AFDC-U recipients that were registered in the program either participated in program activities or worked part-time or participated in self-initiated education and training. The West Virginia CWEP program for AFDC-U recipients achieved monthly participation rates that averaged around 60 percent (Gueron and Pauly 1991).[19] Because these two programs attempted to maximize participation and had sufficient funding to do so, the estimated participation rates suggest upper bound limits on what is feasible.

Use of Findings from the Welfare-to-Work Demonstrations

The welfare-to-work experiments have influenced the policy process in a variety of ways. In addition, they have also influenced the direction of social experimentation itself.

Influence on Social Experimentation

As discussed earlier, the welfare-to-work experiments had several defining characteristics.

1. The treatments were designed by state (and sometimes local) governments and operated through typical government administrative agencies.
2. Most of the treatments were mandatory.
3. Several of the experiments were used to evaluate already adopted programs, rather than to test proposed policy changes on a demonstration basis.
4. The evaluations relied mainly on available administrative data, rather than on survey data collected especially for the purpose.

The welfare-to-work experiments were the first large, prominent social experiments to exhibit these characteristics. As a result, they influenced subsequent social experiments. For example, chapter 2 documents the increasing number of experimental tests of mandatory programs in recent years, the increasing tendency to administer experimental treatments through existing administrative offices, and the increasing role of state governments in social experimentation. That chapter also indicates that the sample sizes used in social experiments have substantially increased, something that has been possible financially only because evaluations of experiments have relied increasingly on administrative data. Finally, although there have been relatively few random assignment evaluations of ongoing programs, several recent ones have been of important programs—the Job Corps and the programs run under the Job Training Partnership Act.

Obviously, any or even all of these trends might have occurred had the welfare-to-work experiments never been conducted. However, the fact that those experiments were generally thought to have been successfully conducted and to have produced useful information almost certainly contributed to the trends. For example, had MDRC been unable to establish viable working relationships with state government agencies or make effective use of administrative data, attempts by research firms to do so in the future would surely have been discouraged.

Influence on Conceptual Views

In contrast with, say, the income maintenance experiments or the health insurance experiment, the welfare-to-work experiments were not direct tests of behavioral parameters that were grounded within theoretical frameworks. Hence, they were unlikely to either modify or reinforce the theories of social scientists (although they did provide many social scientists with a better idea of how welfare-to-work programs actually operate than they previously had). Nevertheless, they did influence conceptual views of policymakers in several important respects.

First, when the welfare-to-work experiments were initiated, many persons were pessimistic that government social programs could be beneficial. The positive, albeit modest, effects displayed by almost all the tested programs suggested that, at least under certain circumstances, government intervention could have a positive payoff in reducing welfare dependency and increasing earnings, and thus may have mitigated the prevailing pessimism to some degree.

Second, before the welfare-to-work experiments, there was strong opposition on the part of many liberals to mandatory programs for welfare recipients, especially those that imposed mandatory work requirements. By showing that such programs were administratively feasible, could be effective and, most importantly, were not opposed by welfare recipients themselves, the experiments forced liberals to relinquish that position.

Third, by demonstrating that states could design and implement modestly effective welfare-to-work programs, the experiments probably strengthened the confidence of state decisionmakers in their ability to manage welfare programs on their own. Equally important, they probably also increased the willingness of decisionmakers in Congress and the executive branch of the federal government to provide the states with greater freedom in running their programs. Ultimately, this probably encouraged the devolution of welfare programs to the states.

Fourth, considerable debate existed among state decisionmakers on the relative merits of the human capital and work-first approaches to improving the labor market performance of welfare recipients. The theory behind the more expensive human capital approach is that by investing program resources up front in enhancing the skills of recipients, they will be able to obtain sufficiently high-quality jobs. Consequently, not only will they be induced to leave the welfare rolls, they will remain off the rolls. Supporters of the work-first approach emphasize the fact that getting recipients into jobs and off the welfare rolls quickly will reduce expenditures to the government. Moreover, they theorize that even if the initial jobs that recipients take are not attractive, over time the recipients will build work habits and develop skills that allow them to obtain better jobs—and that this will keep them off the welfare rolls. Before the GAIN experiment, there was little evidence on the relative merits of these arguments. As discussed in some detail in the following chapter, the Riverside findings greatly weakened the arguments of those who favored the human capital approach and caused at least some of them to change their position.

Finally, in its briefings and reports, MDRC has consistently emphasized the distinction between program "outcomes" (for example, the number of program participants obtaining employment or leaving the welfare rolls) and program "impacts" (the *additional* number of program participants obtaining employment or leaving the welfare rolls *because of the program*). Obtaining an impact estimate requires measuring differences between treatment and comparison groups, whereas obtaining an outcome estimate does not. Indeed, an improved outcome, such as a reduction in the size of the welfare rolls, could be due to an improved economy rather than to receiving, say, job search assistance or training. Based on our interviews, the conceptual distinction between outcomes and impacts seems to have become increasingly clear to many (but far from all) persons involved in administering job search and training programs. This is potentially important because historically job search and training programs have typically been inappropriately assessed on the basis of the outcomes they produce, rather than on the basis of their impacts. This misunderstanding, in turn, has encouraged "creaming" in which program personnel seek program participation by persons who are easiest to place in a job (for example, relatively well educated persons who are likely to find a job even without the program), rather than by those who will benefit most from the services provided (poorly educated persons who may not find a job without receiving program services).

Influence on the Federal Waiver Process

As previously mentioned, states desiring to test a welfare-to-work program often first had to obtain a federal waiver. According to Howard Rolston, who is responsible for AFDC waivers at the U.S. Department of Health and Human Services, two important changes in the way the waivers were administered occurred in 1987, a time by which findings from most of the welfare-to-work experiments had become widely available. First, before 1987, the Reagan administration would not allow states to test policies that they did not want tested. Then in 1987, as Rolston put it, federal policy changed "from willing to let states test what we want them to test to willing to let states have the flexibility to test what they would like to test." Second, to obtain federal waivers to test changes in their welfare programs, states were required to submit an evaluation plan, but were not required to conduct a random assignment experiment. Beginning in 1987 there developed, in Rolston's words, "some expression of preference for random assignment," although the policy was administered in a "hit and miss" manner.[20] It seems unlikely that either of these policy decisions would have been made if the welfare-to-work experiments had not been available as a model. The experiments were perceived by federal government administrators as convincingly demonstrating both that states could develop successful programs on their own and that the information provided by experimental designs was often superior to that obtained by non-experimental methods.

Federal waiver policy was modified again in 1992. In that year, a call was made by the George H. W. Bush administration to use the "states as labs" to test various alternatives to existing welfare policy.[21] Many states responded by seeking waivers to modify their AFDC programs. However, Howard Rolston told us that a number of federal officials were convinced by 1992 that nonrandom assignment evaluations of changes in welfare policy had been unreliable and, hence, that states should receive waiver approval only if they agree to evaluate the new changes they proposed by random assignment. Moreover, waivers usually require cost neutrality (that is, the policy change must not increase cost to the federal government) and a comparison of randomly assigned experimental and control groups came to be viewed as the most reliable way of determining whether this requirement was met. Hence, federal administrators came to believe that random assignment was well worth any added costs and complexity that it might engender.

Thus, beginning in 1992, whether a state could obtain a waiver without first agreeing to an experimental evaluation was no longer "hit or miss." In Rolston's words, random assignment "became the rule of thumb." This was important because many administrators in state and local government had resisted random assignment. In addition, some liberals felt that it was unethical to deny control group members services provided by the tested programs and some academics believed that other evaluation designs were superior (for example, see Heckman and Smith 1995). Again, it seems unlikely that this policy decision would have been made had the welfare-to-work experiments not been viewed as providing reliable information on whether the tested programs had the intended effects and on whether they were cost neutral.

Influence on Welfare Reform Initiatives

Possibly more than any other social experiments, the welfare-to-work experiments have played an important role in policymaking. At the national level, this role was especially important in contributing to the design and passage of the Family Support Act of 1988. After 1988, however, the role of the experiments in national policymaking waned considerably. As will be seen, however, it did not disappear. Moreover, the experiments continued to play a part in policymaking at the state level.

THE FAMILY SUPPORT ACT OF 1988

As briefly described in the previous chapter, in 1988, Congress passed and President Reagan signed the Family Support Act (FSA), which marked an important shift in national welfare policy. The centerpiece of this legislation was the Job Opportunities and Basic Skills Training (JOBS) program. Under JOBS, states were to be provided with additional federal funds to operate education, training, work-readiness, and job-seeking programs, which by 1995 were to maintain a minimum participation rate of 20 percent for AFDC-R recipients who were not exempt.[22] The minimum participation rate for AFDC-U recipients was to reach 75 percent by 1997, and there were considerably fewer exemptions than for AFDC-R recipients. Within broad guidelines, the states were given considerable freedom to design a JOBS program of their own choosing. Thus, activities could include job search, training, education, subsidized private sector employment, and unpaid community work service jobs. States, however, were required to target 55 percent of their JOBS spending on a group consisting of long-time users of AFDC and young parents who had dropped out of high school and had little or no work experience.

At the time the FSA was being considered by Congress, findings had been obtained from all of MDRC's welfare-to-work experiments except GAIN, although not all these results were in final form. By the end of 1986, MDRC had published evaluation reports on all the experiments except the SWIM, GAIN, and New Jersey REACH programs. A summary of many of MDRC's findings was available in February 1987 in the form of a monograph by Judith Gueron entitled *Reforming Welfare with Work*.

As most of the features of JOBS are similar to those tested by the welfare-to-work experiments—the major new ingredients were the participation rate and target group requirements—one might anticipate that the experiments played an important role in the legislation. In fact, there is considerable evidence that they did. For example, in an article the Ford Foundation commissioned to examine MDRC's role in the development and passage of the Family Support Act, Peter Szanton wrote:

> In interviewing House and Senate staffers, lobbyists, reporters, and others in the months following passage of the bill, I found a surprising consensus. The central players in the bargaining that produced the legislation believe that without the

findings of a timely set of analyses, the bill could not have retained its most significant elements—its employment and training provisions. A major shift in the
nation's social policy, in short, seems to have been largely shaped by research and
analysis. (1991, 591)

Similarly, Erica Baum (1991) has written:

Research made a difference for FSA. The education, training, and work requirements in the legislation were substantially influenced by the evaluations of
welfare-to-work programs conducted by the Manpower Demonstration Research
Corporation and the conduct of MDRC in the dissemination of these results
contributed significantly to the effort's political success. (603)

Our own interviews with various knowledgeable individuals also uni-
formly suggested that the FSA was significantly affected by the welfare-
to-work experiments. For example, when asked how findings from the
experiments influenced FSA, Larry Mead, a well-known academic writer
on welfare issues, stated, "They mandated state efforts. They persuaded
Congress that employment strategies work. Now, there was firm information that such policies would generate an impact." One congressional
staff member with long-term experience on welfare program issues
made an even stronger statement: "The JOBS program was based on
MDRC findings. The framework for the 1988 legislation was determined
by the MDRC findings." Although that statement certainly suggests the
importance attached to the welfare-to-work experiments by congressional staffers, it probably exaggerates to some degree their role in the
designing of JOBS. As will be seen, various political considerations also
had important effects on the design of JOBS.

In the remainder of our discussion of FSA, we shall examine some of
the specific ways in which the welfare-to-work experiments influenced
the legislation and discuss some of the factors constraining this influence. For purposes of this discussion, we rely heavily on articles by Erica
Baum (1991) and Ron Haskins (1991) that detail the role of the experiments in Congress, supplemented by our own interviews. The Family
Support Act was developed within Congress, rather than being submitted to Congress by the executive branch,[23] and Baum and Haskins were
key committee staffers involved in that effort. As a senior legislative assistant for domestic policy for Senator Daniel Patrick Moynihan, a Democrat who chaired the subcommittee of the Senate Finance Committee
with primary responsibility for welfare policy, Baum drafted much of
the Senate bill from which the Family Support Act was derived. Haskins
was a Republican staff member on the Ways and Means Committee in

the House of Representatives, the committee with primary jurisdiction over welfare policy in the House.

Baum (1991, 608) notes that MDRC's findings were used at several key junctures in the legislative process on the Senate side:

- in early 1987, when the legislation was still being developed;
- in April 1988, when the Finance Committee marked up the bill;
- in June 1988, during floor debates in the Senate when MDRC findings were cited;
- in September 1988, when the House-Senate conference committee was meeting; and
- in May 1989, after the FSA became law, to help the Department of Health and Human Services in drafting regulations needed in implementing the law.

Haskins (1991, 620) states that in 1986 MDRC testified four times before congressional or other governmental bodies and gave two briefings to congressional staff about findings from the welfare-to-work experiments. In 1987, MDRC testified five times and gave 10 briefings. Haskins (620–26) also examined the number of times research studies were mentioned at each successive stage at which welfare reform was being considered in the House of Representatives: during hearings, in marking up the House version of FSA, and when the bill was considered on the House floor. He found that research was referred to considerably more frequently during the hearings than when the bill was marked up and during the floor debate. At each step, however, when research studies did come up, the welfare-to-work experiments were by far the most frequently mentioned. Finally, Haskins (628–29) points out that, even if members of Congress refer to research relatively infrequently, congressional staff also influenced specific provisions of FSA, they were familiar with pertinent research in general and findings from the welfare-to-work experiments in particular, and they made use of this knowledge.

The MDRC findings were clearly used at important junctures during the legislative process. However, Baum indicates that Judith Gueron's monograph, *Reforming Welfare with Work,* which she relied upon heavily, did not reach Senator Moynihan's office until February 1987, *after* "most of the key provisions of the JOBS program had already been worked out" (1991, 610). When we interviewed her, Baum indicated that what was important was that MDRC's findings "supported what had already been drafted." Thus, according to Baum, although the findings were used in fine-tuning the provisions, they were not used to develop them in the first place.[24] For example, as previously mentioned, states were required to target 55 percent of their JOBS spending on a target group consisting of long-time users of AFDC and young parents who had dropped out of high school and had little or no work experience. Moynihan's staff had initially wanted to target 100 percent of the JOBS spending on such persons. They were persuaded, however, to adopt a lower targeting standard by evidence from the welfare-to-work experiments that seemed to suggest that neither the least skilled AFDC recipients nor the most skilled benefit as much from welfare-to-work programs as a group somewhere in the middle.[25]

Although findings from the welfare-to-work experiments caused those designing FSA to modify some provisions, they also encouraged them to hold to the course for other features of the draft legislation. For example, Baum (1991) writes, "MDRC found that variously structured work-training programs produced favorable outcomes, so we were comfortable with our decision to permit states wide latitude in designing programs to respond to local conditions" (611). However, she goes on to state that this decision was also influenced by pressure from state officials who wanted control over program design and national political figures (including President Reagan) who desired to decentralize welfare program administration. Nonetheless, it seems apparent that if findings from the welfare-to-work experiments had implied that states did not have the ability to design successful programs, FSA would not have provided them with the "wide latitude" that Baum mentions.

Although the welfare-to-work experiments clearly did play a role in the design of the JOBS program, its role was inherently limited for two different reasons. First, those designing the JOBS program thought that it should incorporate certain features on which the experiments provided little useful evidence one way or the other. For example, there was a decision in designing the JOBS program to encourage states to use remedial, basic, and even postsecondary education. However, with the exception of the Baltimore Options program, the programs for which evaluation findings were available at the time FSA was developed made little use of education.[26,27]

Second, in some instances political considerations were more important than research evidence. This was particularly true when the interpretation of the evidence was ambiguous. The most important example of this occurred during debate over the participation rate requirements in FSA. Those who supported setting the standards low argued that high participation rates would simply spread the limited resources available for JOBS too thin. To make this point, they suggested that the very low level of expenditure on each participant in the Cook County WIN demonstration resulted in the very small effects produced by this program (see tables 8.1 and 8.2). Those promoting high participation rates argued, in contrast, that moderate-cost welfare-to-work programs such as those in San Diego, Virginia, and Arkansas had proved successful and that JOBS would provide sufficient funds to support that level of effort. They further argued that the most costly of the programs tested by the welfare-to-work experiments, those in Baltimore and Maine, did not save taxpayers and the government money (see table 8.2).[28] Overall, arguments and counterarguments that were based on evidence from the welfare-to-work experiments tended to neutralize one another (see Baum 1991, 612–13; and Haskins 1991, 626–28). Ultimately, those favoring high participation rates prevailed, but their key argument was ethical, rather than empirical—that citizens who accepted public money had an obligation to return something to the public.

The results of the welfare-to-work experiments clearly played an important, if somewhat limited, role in designing the JOBS component of the FSA. However, they were probably more important in securing passage of JOBS in a form that was fairly close to that developed by Senator Moynihan's subcommittee. Baum (1991, 611) specifically mentions the evidence from the experiments that mandatory community service jobs were workable and viewed as fair by participants. That evidence was useful in fending off the efforts of liberals to curtail or eliminate allowing such jobs as a state option.

More important, it seems evident that had the experiments not consistently indicated that welfare-to-work programs can produce positive, if modest, effects and that they would more than pay for themselves, it is unlikely that the JOBS component of the Family Support Act would have been enacted. The findings created the positive climate needed for passage. For example, Peter Szanton (1991, 597) quotes a House Republican staff member as stating, "MDRC gave respectability to the idea that training programs had some promise. . . . Without MDRC we either would have had no bill, or simply an [AFDC] benefit increase bill—and then probably a veto."

The welfare-to-work experiments not only influenced the Family Support Act. They also influenced how the law was to be assessed. After the legislation was enacted, a decision was made to evaluate its JOBS component using a seven-city random assignment evaluation design that in many respects was modeled after the one used in the welfare-to-work experiments. For example, in addition to being based on random assignment and conducted at a variety of sites, the evaluation assesses programs that were designed by and administered through state and local welfare agencies. Particular emphasis was placed on helping to resolve the controversy over the comparative merits of work-first and human capital approaches. To do this, welfare recipients were randomly assigned to programs based on the two approaches that were simultaneously operated at the same sites. By funding this new evaluation, the federal government, in effect, paid homage to the usefulness of the information previously provided by the welfare-to-work experiments.

CLINTON WELFARE REFORM EFFORT

In running for his first term as president, perhaps Bill Clinton's best-known campaign promise was to "end welfare as we know it." Thus, when he assumed office in 1993, several nationally known welfare experts were appointed to key positions at the U.S. Department of Health and Human Services. Among them were David Ellwood and Mary Jo Bane, two academics from Harvard University who have written extensively on welfare issues, and Wendell Primus, who had been a staff expert on welfare matters for the Ways and Means Committee of the U.S. House of Representatives. Those persons, along with many others, set about to design a plan to radically overhaul the welfare system.

The welfare reform legislation that the Clinton administration ultimately proposed in 1994, the Work and Responsibility Act, was a clear departure from the existing system. Because the legislation was extremely detailed and complex, it is only sketched here. Its key provision was a two-year lifetime time limit on AFDC, after which the heads of AFDC families would be required to participate in a newly established WORK program to receive any additional assistance. Under the legislation, WORK would provide temporary employment paying at least the minimum wage. If, after taking account of any earnings received from employment, the household remained eligible for AFDC, it could continue to receive whatever payments it was due. However, if individuals assigned to a WORK position failed to work the number of hours provided by the position, their AFDC grant would not be adjusted to reflect their reduced earnings. Moreover, to ensure that WORK positions were less attractive than regular employment, earnings from WORK would not qualify for the Earned Income Tax Credit. The legislation also would have increased participation in the JOBS program among those who had not reached the two-year time limit in an attempt to minimize the number of AFDC households that reached the limit. JOBS was also to focus more strongly on immediate job entry. Moreover, to encourage employment among those below the two-year limit, any months in which the head of the household worked at least 20 hours at a regular job would not be counted against the limit.

With its emphasis on work, this legislation was clearly a marked departure from welfare policy of the past. Indeed, the centerpiece of the legislation, the two-year time limit, was an idea that had been promoted by David Ellwood in his writings but never been tested. It is important to recognize that this feature set a time limit on when AFDC recipients must begin to work; it did not set a time limit on the receipt of assistance. Yet, as discussed in the following subsection, it set the nation on the road to adopting legislation that would do exactly that.

The Work and Responsibility Act attempted to fulfill President Clinton's promise to "end welfare as we know it." The welfare-to-work experiments, however, were designed to meet much more modest goals, and none tested time limits. Therefore it was inevitable that they would play a limited role in designing the legislation. Nonetheless, the experiments did play an important role, particularly in the legislation's employment and training provisions. In part, this occurred because those who developed the legislation were already familiar with findings from the experiments when they began their efforts and had considerable respect for the research. Moreover, MDRC researchers presented numerous briefings to those designing the legislation. In addition, some of those designing the legislation visited Riverside and Alameda counties in California to view GAIN first hand.

The general effect of findings from the experiments on the legislation is apparent in the decision to increase participation in the JOBS program for AFDC recipients who had not yet reached the time limit and to use JOBS to promote early job entry. Ellwood had stressed that "the best time-limited welfare program is one in which no one hits the limit."[29] The evidence from the welfare-to-work experiments suggests that one way to at least reduce the number hitting the limit is to use welfare-to-work programs. Moreover, the accomplishments of the Riverside version of GAIN suggested to those developing the legislation that JOBS could be made more effective if it incorporated a work-first approach. On the other hand, the experiments also sounded a cautionary note by demonstrating that welfare-to-work services would have only limited success in keeping AFDC recipients from reaching the time limit.

Findings from the welfare-to-work experiment were also used in developing some of the details of the legislation. For example, the experiments that had job search components were examined to decide between requiring job search at application for AFDC or after approval for benefits. (The decision was in favor of the latter.) Findings from the experiments that incorporated work components (for example, Arkansas, SWIM, and GAIN) were examined in assessing the capacity of states to create WORK positions and put large numbers of people into these jobs. Perhaps most important, the SWIM experiment in San Diego had attempted to maximize participation. The resulting monthly participation rate of around 50 percent was viewed as suggestive of the maximum that was feasible. Thus, the legislation would have used federal funds to reward a state if its JOBS participation rate exceeded 55 percent and to penalize it if its rate fell below 45 percent.[30]

As part of developing the legislation, special computer runs were conducted at both MDRC and the Department of Health and Human Services with data from some of the welfare-to-work experiments. These runs were used to determine exit rates from and recidivism rates to the AFDC rolls for different age groups of recipients and to learn how participation in welfare-to-work programs affected these rates. That information was critical for determining the proportion of AFDC recipients in different age groups who would actually reach time limits of various lengths. Thus, it was used to help determine where to set the time limit. It was also the basis of a decision to phase in the time limit gradually, beginning with parents in their teens and early 20s. In addition, it was incorporated into microsimulation models that were used to predict the cost of the legislation and its effects on AFDC recipients. The microsimulation models also incorporated information from the experiments on the impact of welfare-to-work programs on earnings and AFDC benefits. In addition, the microsimulation model developed at the Congressional Budget Office used data from some of the welfare-to-work experiments.

Congress never seriously considered the Work and Responsibility Act. Although the legislation embodied findings from the welfare-to-work experiments, the experiments played no role in its lack of success, which instead was at least partially attributable to the fact that during his first two years in office President Clinton's energies and political capital went into a failed attempt at health care reform. By the time he was ready to focus on welfare reform, it was too late. The Democrats lost their majorities in both the Senate and the House in the November 1994 elections and, as discussed in the next subsection, the Republicans wanted to pass welfare reform legislation of their own crafting.

THE PERSONAL RESPONSIBILITY AND WORK OPPORTUNITY RECONCILIATION ACT OF 1996

In 1995 Congress, which was at the time Republican dominated, passed major welfare reform legislation, the Personal Responsibility Act. President Clinton then vetoed this legislation. The next year similar legislation was again passed by Congress, but this time with sufficient modifications to win the votes of many Democrats in Congress, as well as presidential approval. This 1996 legislation, the Personal Responsibility and Work Opportunity Reconciliation Act (PRWORA), completely replaced the AFDC program with block grants to the states called Temporary Assistance for Needy Families (TANF). In addition, the law denied most federal benefits to illegal aliens and to legal aliens granted temporary residency, denied access to Supplemental Security Income and Food Stamps to large numbers of permanent legal aliens, and made important changes affecting child care and the Food Stamp program. PRWORA also placed restrictions on the eligibility of children for disability benefits under the Supplemental Security Income program.

Although states are given great leeway under PRWORA to run their TANF programs as they see fit, they are subject to reductions in their block grants if they fail to meet a specified schedule of minimum work participation rates. The required work participation rate ranged from 25 percent of all families in FY 1997 to 50 percent in FY 2002 and beyond. The required work participation rate for two-parent families ranged from 75 percent in FY 1997 to 90 percent in FY 1999 and beyond. A variety of activities satisfy the work participation requirement, including subsidized or unsubsidized employment, job training and vocational education, and job search. To count toward the participation requirement, single parents must have participated in allowable work activities for at least 20 hours per week in FY 1997 and 30 hours per week in FY 2000 and beyond.[31] Two-parent families must participate in allowable work activities for at least 35 hours per week to count toward the participation requirement. In addition, the law mandates that unmarried teen parents must live in an adult-supervised setting and attend school to be eligible for TANF benefits. It also requires that individuals applying for assistance provide information about the noncustodial parent and requires states to reduce the TANF grants of unwed mothers who refuse to cooperate in establishing paternity.

Finally, the legislation carries the Clinton administration's earlier thrust toward time limits considerably further by setting three separate limits. First, states must require recipients who have received TANF for two months and who are not engaged in work to participate in community service employment. Second, states must require TANF recipients to engage in work once they have received assistance for 24 months. However, each state is allowed to use its own definition of "work." Moreover, there is not a specific penalty if a state fails to meet these requirements. Third, and most important, states are prohibited from using federal block grant funds to provide cash benefits to families who have accumulated a lifetime total of five years of TANF assistance, whether or not consecutive. However, states are permitted to exempt up to 20 percent of their caseloads from this provision. States are allowed to reduce the length of each of the three time limits if they so choose.

The Personal Responsibility and Work Opportunity Reconciliation Act represents a clear break with previous welfare policy. As both the name of the legislation and the law's provisions, especially the five-year limit on TANF benefits, imply, the intent of PRWORA was to reduce drastically the number of persons receiving welfare and, as a consequence, substantially shrink federal expenditures on welfare. In addition, Congress wanted to impose work-related obligations on welfare recipients in exchange for their grants and to minimize federal control over state welfare programs.

Given these goals, it is not surprising that the welfare-to-work experiments played little role in establishing the law's provisions. The experiments had already demonstrated that the tested programs would only have modest effects on the size of the welfare rolls. Moreover, findings from the experiments were simply not relevant to some of the key provisions of the Act, such as state block grants and restrictions on the receipt of federal benefits by aliens. The experiments, as well as other research, also provided no information on what would happen to welfare households once they reached the time limit on receipt of benefits. The findings were germane to other provisions of the legislation, but those results tended to be ignored. For example, evidence from the experiments suggested that meeting the law's stringent work participation requirements would be difficult for states because they exceeded the level of participation achieved in any of the experimental programs. The evidence also strongly implied that requiring participation in work-related activities would only modestly reduce the number of households reaching the five-year time limit on benefits.

Rather than being research-driven, PRWORA appears instead to have been largely politically driven. The newly empowered Republicans desired to appeal to a core constituency that disliked tax expenditures on welfare and favored greater state control over welfare, and many Democrats felt a need to appear "tough" on welfare issues. Although Judith Gueron, the president of MDRC, had testified before the various congressional subcommittees concerned with welfare reform, she believed that the staff of the Senate and House subcommittees, although aware of pertinent findings from the experiments, were too "constrained by the politics of the process" to make much use of them in drafting the legislation. Indeed, Gueron asserted to us that the legislation "is an extremely un–research-driven bill. The big picture here is the political picture . . . you wouldn't have gotten there from research or from the history of incremental welfare reform in the past." Gueron went on to say that research is usually conservative in the sense that "when people claim that they have silver bullets, research usually shoots down those bullets. The strategy then might be to pluck at those things you don't know anything about [for example, time limits and block grants]. . . . In the past, one couldn't get away with this because there was a serious discussion. There was never a serious discussion of this bill. There just wasn't a reasoned discourse. It is a shouting match of slogans . . . winning power politically."

Nonetheless, the welfare-to-work experiments did play a small role when PRWORA was being drafted. First, as in the case of the earlier Clinton welfare reform legislation, information from the experiments was used in developing estimates of the cost to operate welfare-to-work programs. Second, an MDRC analyst used data from welfare-to-work experiments to demonstrate that participation rates for welfare-to-work programs are highly sensitive to the way the numerator and denominator of the rates are defined (Hamilton 1995). As a result, "participation rate" was defined in the legislation in a way that makes meeting the PRWORA participation requirement somewhat more feasible, although still difficult.

CHANGES IN WELFARE AT THE STATE AND LOCAL LEVELS

The preceding sections discuss in some detail the effect of the welfare-to-work experiments on policymaking at the national level. However, those experiments also were used in welfare program policymaking in a number of states. Indeed, Wendell Primus suggested to us that "a lot of what MDRC puts on the table should guide what a local administrator does in running a welfare-to-work program," rather than influence national legislation. In his view, it is simply not necessary for national legislation to specify many of the details on how these programs should be run.

States were sometimes influenced by experiments that they themselves conducted and sometimes by experiments run in other states. The next chapter examines the use of findings from welfare-to-work experiments in states other than the ones in which they were conducted. Here, we examine how the three experiments that were conducted in California influenced policymaking in that state.

As described earlier in this chapter, the first two California experiments, San Diego I and SWIM, were demonstration programs run by a county government in one city. However, the third experiment was a six-county random assignment evaluation of a major welfare reform initiative that was implemented throughout the state. As will be discussed next, there is little question that findings from San Diego I were important in developing the GAIN legislation. Results from SWIM were not yet available at the time the legislation was developed, however, and thus played little role in designing GAIN.

To understand the influence of San Diego I on the GAIN legislation, a bit of background is necessary.[32] The legislation resulted from a laboriously negotiated compromise between conservatives and liberals. The leading negotiator on the conservative side was David Swoap, who had previously held welfare positions under Ronald Reagan in both California and Washington and who as then-secretary of the California Health and Welfare Agency represented Governor George Deukmejian. The leading negotiator on the liberal side was Art Agnos, a former San Francisco social worker who was chairman of the Health and Welfare Subcommittee of the State Assembly's Ways and Means Committee. At the beginning of the discussions over GAIN, Swoap favored a simple workfare program in which welfare recipients would be required to work in public service jobs in exchange for their benefits. Agnos, in contrast, favored a nonmandatory program in which those who elected to participate could receive education, training, and support services such as child care and transportation. A key event in the development of GAIN was a trip that Swoap and Agnos took in early 1985. During their travels, they visited West Virginia and Pennsylvania, which were running workfare programs of the sort that Swoap favored, and Massachusetts, which was operating a voluntary program of the type Agnos supported. Although the trip did not resolve Swoap' and Agnos's differences, it did give them a set of common experiences that they could take to the negotiating table.

In many respects, the design of the Greater Avenues for Independence legislation can be viewed as the result of a political compromise between conservatives and liberals. Nevertheless, the San Diego I findings were important. As one California official told us, before the San Diego I evaluation "people just sort of took grabs at what might work and it was all anecdotal." As indicated below, that was less the case once the findings were available.[33]

1. The San Diego I findings demonstrated that sanctions could be used to compel participation in welfare-to-work programs; thus, mandatory programs were administratively feasible. Nevertheless, making GAIN mandatory was strongly resisted by many liberals throughout the GAIN negotiations, particularly liberal social workers and case managers working in the welfare system. Ironically, however, Agnos's views on this issue were changed by his visit to the voluntary program in Massachusetts, where he became convinced that unless welfare-to-work programs were mandatory, creaming would result and welfare recipients who could potentially benefit from program services would not receive them. Thus, Agnos, although a liberal, supported making GAIN mandatory.

2. The evaluation indicated that the San Diego I treatment had more positive effects on single mothers than on the male heads of two-parent families. The explanation suggested for this finding was that the male family heads were more "job ready" than single mothers and, as a result, could more readily find and keep jobs on their own. Thus, they had less to gain from the services provided by the tested programs. Information about welfare-to-work programs in other

states, as well as other types of research, reinforced the view that program resources should be focused on persons who, although potentially employable, were not yet job ready. As a consequence, the GAIN program included a test to determine whether participants were job ready. In addition, a decision was made to put a priority on serving long-term recipients—that is, those who were presumably least job ready.

3. San Diego I tested workfare and surveys of participants indicated that they did not object to being required to participate in workfare. That information greatly reduced the resistance of liberals to including a workfare component in GAIN.

4. San Diego I also tested group job search, called job clubs, and the findings suggested that job clubs are cost-effective. As a result, the GAIN legislation channeled recipients into job clubs first if they appeared to be job ready. That provision represented a compromise between the conservatives who wanted to put GAIN participants into workfare immediately and liberals who wanted to put them into education or job training immediately.

5. The results from San Diego I were modest. That outcome allowed conservatives to contend that workfare should last longer than the 13-week maximum tested in San Diego and liberals to argue that education and training were needed in addition to job search. As part of the political compromise, the GAIN legislation provided resources for both longer workfare and education and training.

Like the evaluation of San Diego I, the evaluation of GAIN has also influenced welfare policy in California. Indeed, state officials waited to modify GAIN until results from the evaluation were available. Once the generally favorable early findings, particularly those in Riverside County, were in, they might have helped to protect the program. In fact, Paul Warren, who headed the staff of California's GAIN Oversight Committee, asserts, "GAIN wouldn't be alive if we hadn't had the evaluation." He relates that, because of pressures on the state's budget, members of Governor Deukmejian's administration wanted substantial reductions in the amount of education and training provided by GAIN, but "the preliminary [evaluation] results that came out were so good that they had to back off."

A key effect of the GAIN evaluation on welfare policy in California ensued from the very favorable early findings for Riverside County. That result caused other counties in California to adopt the "Riverside model," partly of their own volition and partly because of pressure from the state.[34] It is worth noting that there have been important differences of opinion in California (as well as elsewhere) on exactly what the Riverside model is. To some it is a work-first model that emphasizes quick place-ment into jobs and, hence, allows resources allotted to education and training to be minimized. Others believe that education and training must be available for those who do not quickly obtain jobs. Riverside did, in fact, provide such services. Still others attributed Riverside's success to the dynamic and aggressive administrator who headed the county's wel-fare office. The evaluation, however, does not allow one to determine the relative contribution of those factors to Riverside's success.

Assessing the Use of the Welfare-to-Work Demonstrations with the Conceptual Framework

Taxonomy of Use

Table 8.3 uses the three-dimensional taxonomy of the ways in which research findings are used, as described in chapter 3, to summarize the previous section. It is apparent from the table that the experiments were used in a variety of ways; entries appear in all but two of the eight cells.

Table 8.3 is, in fact, incomplete; additional entries almost certainly exist. However, because the welfare-to-work experiments produced a large number of findings, many of which were used both nationally and in different states, it simply was not possible for us to learn of every instance of utilization. Consequently, no attempt is made to list every instance in the table. Instead, we often resort to broad categories. For example, we indicate that information from the welfare-to-work exper-iments has frequently been used in making cost estimates of welfare reform proposals; we do not list the individual proposals. Similarly, we indicate that the welfare-to-work experiments influenced subsequent experiments without listing the individual experiments. We also suggest that the experiments affected the design of welfare-to-work programs without mentioning all the different ways in which those program designs were influenced.

We do, however, list a few specific instances of use that we consider espe-cially important—for example, the role of the experiments in fostering a

Table 8.3. *Uses of the Welfare-to-Work Experiments*

	Substantive	Elaborative
Concrete Formative	By demonstrating that welfare-to-work programs are cost-effective, contributed to the adoption of these programs in the states and to the passage of the JOBS program. *May* have contributed to the devolution of welfare to the states by demonstrating the capability of states to manage welfare programs. By showing that welfare-to-work programs produce positive but only modest effects, the experiment *may* have helped pave the way for the more radical changes in the welfare system embodied in PRWORA.	Exerted influence on the design of various welfare-to-work programs, including the JOBS program. Both federal and state decisionmakers were influenced. The Riverside findings contributed to the increased emphasis on the work-first approach in welfare-to-work programs and the decreased emphasis on the human capital approach. Influenced the design of subsequent social experiments, which are now more likely to be mandatory, to use administrative data, and to be run out of existing government offices. For example, served as a model for the JOBS evaluation.

Persuasive/Advocacy	Used to argue in favor of making GAIN and JOBS mandatory.	Encouraged the federal government to require random assignment evaluations in exchange for granting waivers to states.
		The experimental findings were used in developing cost estimates of various welfare reform proposals.
		Sometimes used to argue in favor of program provisions (e.g., the work-first approach) that were already favored for other reasons.
		Findings used to argue both for and against requiring high participation rates in the JOBS program.
Conceptual		
Formative	Caused liberals to drop opposition to mandatory programs for transfer recipients.	Refined the understanding of some policymakers as to the conceptual distinction between outcomes and impacts.
Persuasive/Advocacy	Persuaded some that there are social programs that have positive, if modest, effects.	Persuaded some that the work-first approach is superior to the human capital approach.

Notes: GAIN = Greater Avenues for Independence; JOBS = Job Opportunities and Basic Skills Training Program; PRWORA = Personal Responsibility and Work Opportunity Reconciliation Act.

greater acceptance of making welfare-to-work programs mandatory and the role of findings from the GAIN experiment in Riverside in promoting the work-first approach. This last utilization example will be discussed in greater detail in chapter 9, where we examine the extent to which experiments conducted in one state are used in other states.

Two of the items listed in the formative-concrete-substantive cell are best viewed as speculative. The welfare-to-work experiments *might* have contributed to the devolution of control over welfare to the states and helped pave the way for such radical changes as time limits on how long welfare recipients can remain on the rolls. However, there is no clear evidence whether they actually did. The other items listed in the table are less speculative. Nevertheless, it is important to recognize that although they point to ways in which findings from the experiments contributed to different decisions—for example, the decision to make the Greater Avenues for Independence program mandatory—political and ideological considerations were also often important, perhaps even more so.

Utilization Factors

DEFINITIVENESS

As has been discussed previously, the key findings from the welfare-to-work experiments were that most of the tested programs resulted in modest increases in the earnings of welfare recipients and modest decreases in transfer program expenditures. There was little to undermine the perception of policymakers about the definitiveness (that is, the certitude) of those findings. To the contrary, there was ample reason for policymakers to feel confident in them.

1. They were viewed as consistent with expectations and as non-controversial and nonthreatening. There was sometimes controversy on the appropriate interpretation of the findings, however, as their role in the dispute over how high participation rates should be set in the JOBS program illustrates. The Riverside findings, which seemed to support a work-first approach, also engendered some contention, as some policymakers preferred a human capital approach. Those controversies were relatively technical and narrow in scope, however, and did little to undermine confidence in the key findings from the welfare-to-work experiments.

2. There were 10 welfare-to-work experiments and, although the estimates of their effects varied considerably, they generally pointed in the same direction, indicating that earnings increase and welfare dependence decreases. The fact that those key findings were replicated a number of times increased confidence in them. And because the findings were usually based on large samples, they were often statistically significant. Even greater confidence resulted because the experiments varied from one another in important dimensions—for example, their components differed and they were administered in different ways in different places at different times—but nonetheless consistently produced positive findings, suggesting that welfare-to-work programs are effective under a variety of conditions.

3. The welfare-to-work experiments were evaluated by a single organization, the Manpower Demonstration Research Corporation (MDRC), which used a virtually identical methodology in all its analyses and followed a similar format. That procedure allowed the results from the different experiments to cumulate and reinforce one another. Moreover, because a single organization evaluated the experiments, a single internally consistent interpretation of findings from them tended to emerge. In addition, MDRC's findings were unchallenged because there has been virtually no reanalysis of the data from the experiments by non-MDRC researchers. Indeed, MDRC's basic findings appear to be generally accepted by the research community.

4. Finally, as suggested by many respondents to our interviews and in various publications, MDRC enjoys a widespread reputation for technical excellence and integrity.[35] As a result, policymakers are usually willing to accept findings with the MDRC stamp on them. The fact that the evaluations of the welfare-to-work experiments were based on random assignment also contributed to acceptance, especially at the national level;[36] whereas the fact that the experiments were administered through existing state agencies, giving them an aura of realism, was important in obtaining acceptance from state officials.[37]

TIMELINESS

The welfare-to-work experiments had a gestation period of three to five years between selecting the research sample and publishing the final report. Although that period is fairly long, there is little evidence that the length of the gestation period diminished the use of the research findings to any significant degree. One reason is that MDRC issued interim findings only a couple of years after many of the experiments began. More important, the ferment over welfare policy that began in the late 1960s continued over the next three decades. Although findings from the experiments did not exist during the first half of that period, they were available by the second half, while they were still pertinent to policy.

It is clear, however, that findings from the welfare-to-work experiments suffered from obsolescence over time, especially at the federal level. They simply did not provide information about some of the major federal policy thrusts of the 1990s such as time limits and state block grants.

Obsolescence appears to be much less of a factor at the state level. Almost all states are still operating welfare-to-work programs, and the experiments provide information that is potentially useful in considering changes in these programs. In fact, if anything, welfare-to-work programs have increased in importance to the states as they provide a key means of meeting the stringent participation requirements set by the Personal Responsibility and Work Opportunity Reconciliation Act of 1996. Yet some obsolescence has occurred at even the state level. During the 1990s, for example, states increasingly used various financial incentives to attempt to encourage welfare recipients to seek employment, but the welfare-to-work experiments that were initiated during the 1980s provide little information about these incentives.[38]

COMMUNICATION AND VISIBILITY

The welfare-to-work experiments had considerable visibility among policymakers. There were 10 of them and each was fairly large. Moreover, findings from those experiments were effectively communicated. Indeed, some dissemination at the subnational level was virtually automatic as eight different states ran them.

More important, there was only one initial source of information about findings from the welfare-to-work experiment: MDRC. As demonstrated in chapter 9, MDRC has a well-deserved reputation for its skills and efforts in disseminating its research findings. MDRC's reports on the different experiments that it evaluates are all written in a similar format. And the emphasis is on simple, readily understood comparisons of differences between program groups and control groups. Moreover, MDRC has a lengthy mailing list of state and national officials to which it mails its reports. MDRC also puts considerable effort into writing executive summaries of each of its research reports. Although the summaries are often lengthy, they are written in nontechnical language. Furthermore, MDRC sends its research reports to organizations such as the National Governors Association, the Center for Law and Social Policy, and the American Public Human Services Association, which serve as research brokers by sending to their membership their own brief summaries of MDRC's executive summaries. MDRC itself has also disseminated several brief, nontechnical summaries of overall findings from the welfare-to-work experiments (Gueron 1986, 1987, and 1990). Baum (1991, 607) asserts that the 1987 summary, the appearance of which she calls a "scintillating omen," was especially important in the development of the 1988 Family Support Act: "Finding out whether the [welfare-to-work] demonstrations worked better than what we had before was important. Having data in time to help shape and promote our legislative efforts was nothing short of amazing."

MDRC's efforts at dissemination do not stop with articles and reports. It often writes press releases. It also frequently presents briefings before interest and advocacy groups, federal agencies, congressional staffers, and interested state officials. Judith Gueron has also often testified in congressional hearings. Further, MDRC puts considerable effort into maintaining the integrity of the research to help ensure that it will continue to be used. For example, MDRC attempts to correct policy advocates when they believe that their findings are being misused.

RELEVANCE
The welfare-to-work experiments were used to investigate program effects that were of direct concern to policymakers at both federal and state levels. For example, information provided on the effects of the tested programs on the probability of receiving welfare and on government budgetary expenditures are central to the interest of many legislators. In addition, MDRC's evaluations of the experiments provided considerable information on administering welfare-to-work programs, a topic of considerable importance to state officials. Yet, as indicated earlier in discussing the timeliness of information from the experiments, by the 1990s the results of the experiments had clearly become less relevant than they were during the 1980s as issues such as block granting, time limits, and fiscal incentives took center stage.

On occasion during the 1980s, individuals who occupied key positions at the time important welfare reform legislation was being considered facilitated the utilization of findings from the welfare-to-work experiments. Those persons believed so strongly in the relevance and usefulness of the findings that they practically guaranteed that they would be used. One important example of this, the use of the findings by Ron Haskins, Erica Baum, and other congressional staffers in the legislative process involving the Family Support Act, was described earlier in the chapter. A second example involved Julia Lopez, a former key staff person on welfare issues in the California state legislature, who played a role similar to that of Haskins and Baum in development of the GAIN legislation. As was discussed earlier, the San Diego I experiment had an important influence on that legislation. Lopez told us that at the beginning of the GAIN negotiations, MDRC's report on San Diego I had been written but not yet released by the state agency sponsoring the experiment. Because she thought the report was pertinent to the negotiation, Lopez first managed to obtain a smuggled copy of it and then prevailed upon the agency to release it.

GENERALIZABILITY

While the four use factors just discussed all tended to work in favor of the welfare-to-work experiments being used, the fifth factor, generalizability, did not. The welfare-to-work experiments were classical black box experiments. Each tested the effects of a particular set of program components on a particular group of welfare recipients in a particular place and at a particular time. Findings from such experiments are not well suited for extrapolation to programs, populations, places, and times that differ substantially from those that were the subject of the experiments.

The lack of generalizability of the welfare-to-work experiments probably reduced the extent to which they were used in the policy process, at least in state policymaking. For instance, in conducting a telephone survey of state welfare officials,[39] we were often told by respondents that evaluations of programs that were conducted in another state did not apply to their state, particularly if the evaluations were conducted in states that differed substantially from the respondent's state. (For example, if the respondent was from a rural state in the South and the evaluated programs were in urban states in the West.)

The generalizability problem probably did not seriously impair the utilization of the welfare-to-work experiments in national policymaking.

One reason for this, as previously mentioned, is that the 10 experiments tested diverse programs in varied locations. Yet key findings from most of them pointed in the same general direction, suggesting that welfare-to-work programs result in tax savings and increases in the earnings of those assigned to programs. A second reason is that for certain purposes, such as cost projections and simulations of proposed policy changes, findings from the experiments sometimes provided the best, or the only, information available. Consequently, they were used for these purposes even though they were inappropriate.

Many of those who used information from the experiments were well aware of their lack of generalizability. For example, although Baum (1991) attests to the considerable use that she and others made of the experiments in developing the Family Support Act, she qualifies the use by stating, "Only certain strategies had been tested [by the experiments] at a limited number of sites. Whether the same outcomes would occur in a national program with different requirements and a broader population of AFDC recipients was impossible to say" (610).

Ideology, Interests, and Other Information in the Policy Environment

Findings from the welfare-to-work experiments became available at a time at which the policy environment was especially receptive to them. In terms of Weiss's I-I-I framework, there was considerable internal consistency among information from sources other than the experiments (including other research, articles in the public media, anecdotes, and personal experiences), political interests, and ideology. In particular, as will be discussed next, all were supportive of the same social goals for welfare policy. These goals included increasing employment among welfare recipients, reducing tax expenditures on welfare and the size of the welfare rolls, and requiring welfare recipients to meet obligations in exchange for their benefits. Thus, it is hardly surprising that if it could be demonstrated that welfare-to-work programs help meet those goals, that information would be used in policy process. However, information from other sources, political interests, and (especially) ideology also tended to limit the influence of the use of the welfare-to-work experiments. When those forces were strong, the opportunity for the experiments to play a role in decisionmaking diminished.

INFORMATION FROM OTHER SOURCES

Two publications at the time the welfare-to-work experiments were being initiated had considerable influence on thinking about welfare policy, and still do. The first of these, *The Dynamics of Dependence: The Routes to Self-Sufficiency,* by Mary Jo Bane and David T. Ellwood, which appeared in 1983, focused on how long AFDC recipients remain on the rolls. Bane and Ellwood used longitudinal data to demonstrate that the welfare system is fluid: Some recipients remain in the system for a relatively short time; some move off and on the rolls several times; and relatively few remain continuously in the system for many years. For example, Bane and Ellwood found that only 17 percent of all welfare recipients stayed eight years or more. However, those very long-term recipients constitute the majority of recipients at any point in time and receive over half of all welfare expenditures.

These findings implied to many that welfare policy should attempt to dislodge long-term recipients from the rolls. One way to help accomplish that goal is to target a disproportionate share of expenditures on welfare-to-work programs for long-term users, a notion that was incorporated into both GAIN and the Family Support Act. A second possible approach is to impose time limits on welfare recipients. As previously discussed, this was originally proposed by David Ellwood and is now an integral part of the nation's welfare policy.

The second publication that influenced thinking about welfare policy, particularly among conservatives, is Charles Murray's polemic *Losing Ground,* a book that was published in 1984. Murray argues that welfare *causes* poverty by, among other things, providing perverse incentives that cause welfare recipients to avoid training for work and to avoid work itself.[40] One obvious antidote for that situation is a *mandatory* welfare-to-work program. Murray himself does not appear to support government funded training and jobs programs of any sort, arguing that their effects are simply too small to lift families out of poverty and cause unintended side effects. Instead, he favors abolishing the welfare system, the source of the perverse incentives. However, other conservatives who are convinced that Murray is correct about the perverse incentives but not ready to eliminate the welfare system, view mandatory welfare-to-work programs as at least a step in the direction of overcoming those incentives.

Information about welfare recipients was not, of course, limited to books. Anecdotes about individuals on welfare also played a role. Many of them concerned able-bodied individuals who refused to seek employment. Others involved "welfare cheaters" who work while on the rolls, but fail to report their earnings. One attraction of mandatory welfare-to-work programs to persons who are disturbed by such anecdotes is that those programs require recipients not only to engage in work-related activities, but to do so at a time when they might otherwise be employed at unreported jobs.

POLITICAL INTERESTS

Welfare-to-work programs will be in the self-interest of middle- and upper-income persons if the tax savings from reductions in welfare payments exceed tax expenditures on the programs themselves. Thus, such persons are likely to support welfare-to-work programs if they believe this to be the case. Findings from the welfare-to-work experiments indicate that it almost always is.

The experiments are less clear on whether welfare-to-work programs are in the interests of recipients. On the positive side, earnings and, perhaps, self-respect may increase. On the negative side, the programs impose obligations on recipients where none previously existed and usually result in reductions in welfare receipts.

Regardless of whether the interests of welfare recipients are served, however, the interests likely to be more influential in the political arena are those of middle- and upper-income taxpayers. There are more of them. They make larger political contributions. And they are more likely to vote.

IDEOLOGIES

Americans have always believed strongly in the value of work. Nevertheless, for many years, there was also general acceptance of the view that it was important that mothers remain home with their children, especially while they are still young. That view underwent a dramatic change after the Second World War as increasing numbers of mothers began to work. Between 1960 and 1990, for example, the labor force participation rate of married women with children under 18 increased from 28 percent to 66 percent (U.S. Bureau of the Census 1995, table 638). Consequently, an increasing number of voters came to believe that public funds should not be used to subsidize mothers who are able to work, but choose not to. A quote from an article by Henry Aaron that appears

in chapter 6 bears repetition here: "The public and their elected representatives have made clear in every way they know how that they think it
is good for healthy working-age people to receive pay in return for work
and bad for them to get pay without work" (1990, 277).

This widely held value, as well as the view that families that receive
public funds have a reciprocal obligation to the public, strongly implies
that welfare-to-work programs should be mandatory. For a number of
years, however, that idea was resisted by the belief of many liberals that
mandatory programs, especially those that assigned welfare recipients to
government or nonprofit agencies to work off their payments, were a
form of slave labor. However, because MDRC conducted surveys of
participants in some welfare-to-work experiments that indicated most
welfare recipients felt that such an obligation was fair, that view was
difficult to maintain.

IMPLICATIONS OF I-I-I FOR UTILIZATION OF THE EXPERIMENTS
An important hypothesis that Weiss develops from her I-I-I framework
is that the greater the internal consistency among ideologies, interests,
and information from other sources, the less likely it is that a particular
piece of research will be used (1983, 243). As was just discussed, internal
I-I-I consistency for welfare policy was strong during the 1980s and
1990s. Yet findings from the welfare-to-work experiments were used in
a variety of ways. This fact would appear to contradict Weiss's hypothesis. Still, the hypothesis provides valuable insights into the role of the
findings in the policy process.

For example, as was discussed in detail earlier in the chapter, the most
important instance of use of the welfare-to-work experiments is their
contribution to the design and passage of the Family Support Act of
1988. As indicated previously, findings from the experiments were used
to support passage of the JOBS component of the legislation. In addition, although the major provisions of the draft legislation had been formulated independently of the experimental findings, the findings were
used to fine-tune some of the provisions and to defend others from
modification or elimination.

One interpretation of the way in which the experimental findings
were used in the policy process surrounding the Family Support Act is
that they provided added information to a policy environment that
already strongly supported legislation promoting welfare-to-work programs. Because the added information also supported such legislation,

it enhanced the legislation's already promising chances for passage. In other words, findings from the experiments were additive to ideologies, interests, and information from other sources because they all pointed in the same general direction.[41] In addition, the experiments provided technical information that was useful in improving the legislation without fundamentally altering it.

Thus, because of the internal consistency among ideologies, interests, and information from other sources, findings from the welfare-to-work experiments played a limited, but still important, role in the design and passage of the Family Support Act. As was previously discussed, however, after that legislation was enacted, the role of the experiments in the policy process, although it did not disappear, was substantially diminished. In retrospect, this is not surprising. Four years after the legislation was passed, Arkansas Governor Bill Clinton was elected president on a pledge to "end welfare as we know it" and two years after that the Republicans gained control of both branches of Congress. Because the experiments indicated that welfare-to-work programs resulted in modest effects, meeting Clinton's pledge obviously required much greater change to the welfare system than welfare-to-work programs could provide. Upon obtaining power in Congress, Republicans had a political need and ability to top Clinton. Moreover, many had long had an ideological commitment to a fundamental restructuring of the welfare system, one that would require even larger changes than those proposed by President Clinton. Thus, by the 1990s, the welfare-to-work experiments had lost much of their relevance. The welfare reform process was instead mainly driven by political and ideological considerations and, consequently, legislative proposals incorporated provisions, such as time limits and block grants, that went well beyond what the experiments tested.

NOTES

1. The program descriptions are taken with slight modification from Gueron and Pauly (1991), tables 3.1 and 3.2.

2. AFDC (Aid to Families with Dependent Children) is now known as TANF (Temporary Assistance for Needy Families). Because this name change resulted from legislation passed by Congress in 1996, well after the evaluations of the welfare-to-work demonstrations were complete, we shall usually use the AFDC, rather than the TANF, designation.

3. There is one partial exception to this. An experimental design was used in evaluating the effects of the West Virginia Community Work Experience Demonstration on single-parent households that participated in the AFDC program, but a quasi-experimental design was used to evaluate the effects of the demonstration on two-parent AFDC households. In that design, counties were first matched to one another on the basis of various statistical criteria to create four pairs of similar counties. Then, one member of each pair was randomly assigned to treatment status and the other to control status.

4. A possible exception is the estimates of net costs per participant. Those figures, which are expressed in nominal dollars, include estimates of program operating costs, allowances paid to program participants (mainly for day care and transportation expenditures), and, in the case of the New Jersey and Maine experiments, roughly $350 in wage subsidies paid to private sector employers. The estimates are net of similar expenditures on comparison group members. Thus, they represent additional costs engendered by the evaluated programs.

5. Reliance on administrative data meant, of course, that the analysis had to be limited to information available in those data—mainly information about earnings, transfer payments, and program services received and the cost of running the programs being evaluated. Other potentially useful information—for example, on wage rates and the quality of jobs—was not available. Moreover, the data on services received were usually not as detailed as desirable, a situation that made it difficult to characterize accurately the treatment actually received. To overcome these limitations, survey data were collected on 3,000 members of the treatment and control groups in GAIN, the last of the welfare-to-work experiments listed in table 8.1.

6. Of the 10 evaluations of welfare-to-work experiments discussed in this chapter, San Diego I is the only one in which MDRC competed against other firms for the right to conduct the evaluation.

7. Although most of the individuals who were involved in developing GAIN appear to have been familiar with the two preceding San Diego experiments, one key person we interviewed, Carl Williams, was not. Williams was deputy director of the California Department of Social Services and played a major role in negotiations about GAIN and in implementing the program. As a deputy director of welfare programs in the U.S. Department of Health and Human Services during the Nixon administration, Williams was familiar with the income maintenance experiments, which he considered very useful. Moreover, he had been trained as an experimental psychologist. As a result, even though he was not familiar with San Diego I or SWIM, he strongly supported both evaluating GAIN and using random assignment to do so.

8. However, although the original GAIN legislation required that an evaluation be conducted, it did not specify random assignment. Nevertheless, the statute was interpreted as providing the authority to do random assignment. Thus, about a year after the initial GAIN legislation in 1986, MDRC presented the reasons to use random assignment to a meeting of legislative aides, who readily agreed with MDRC's arguments. Language was then put into a budget bill specifying that GAIN would be evaluated through random assignment.

9. About two years after the decision to use random assignment in conducting the GAIN evaluation, a key California legislator, Bill Green, who headed the State Senate com-

mittee with authority over GAIN, stated that he was opposed to the approach because he did not want controls excluded from the program. However, MDRC talked with Green and was ultimately able to convince him of the merits of random assignment.

10. While the GAIN experiment was running, a severe recession took place in California that considerably reduced the state's tax revenues. Consequently, there was strong pressure to modify GAIN in ways that would reduce its costs. However, an explicit decision was made to wait until findings from the experiment were available before taking any action.

11. As it turned out, and as will be discussed later, federal agencies and Congress drew extensively upon the information created by the welfare-to-work experiments. However, at the time the experiments were first initiated in 1982, there was no way that this outcome could be anticipated with any assurance.

12. Friedlander and Burtless (1995) considerably extend the findings in the MDRC final reports for four of the welfare-to-work experiments—Arkansas WORK, Baltimore Options, San Diego SWIM, and Virginia ESP—in a number of useful ways. Their study, however, is limited to the AFDC-R population and thus excludes the AFDC-U population.

13. See, for example, Bloom (1997), Burtless (1989), Greenberg (1992), Greenberg and Wiseman (1992), and Gueron and Pauly (1991).

14. However, as discussed in some detail in Friedlander, Greenberg, and Robins (1997), a mandatory welfare-to-work program may have an impact on even those persons who receive no services. For example, some individuals could decide to leave the welfare rolls to avoid having to participate in program activities.

15. More specifically, MDRC attempted to measure the present value of benefits minus the present value of costs over the five-year period, using a 5 percent discount rate. Because the programs could potentially affect some benefits and costs (for example, earnings and transfer benefits) over the entire five-year period, but program impacts were typically observed for only the first part of the five-year period, extrapolations, which were based on various assumptions, were usually required.

16. Many government officials did not believe, however, that raising welfare families above the poverty level was a major goal of the demonstrations. Instead, the primary goals were reducing dependence, increasing incomes, and decreasing welfare expenditures.

17. Program success in reducing the size of the welfare rolls was less than even these estimates might make it appear. The reason is that the target populations of these programs always excluded a substantial fraction of AFDC recipients—for example, unmarried mothers with very young children. For instance, 38 percent of those in the Arkansas AFDC-R caseload had children under the age of 3 and, hence, were not required to participate in that state's WORK program. Those persons were excluded in estimating the impact of the programs on welfare status. And presumably there was no impact on their welfare status.

18. Except for West Virginia, mandatory participation in those activities was limited to only a few months. Had the requirements been more onerous, the survey responses by AFDC recipients might have been less positive.

19. To count as participating in a program activity during a month in either SWIM or CWEP, an individual needed to be active for at least one hour.

20. During the late 1980s and the 1990s, Rolston himself was influential in encouraging the use of experimental design evaluations of state-initiated changes in welfare programs.

21. The tested policy changes included, but were not limited to, welfare-to-work programs.

22. The exempt included those AFDC-R recipients who were "ill, incapacitated or of advanced age; needed in the home because of the illness or incapacity of another member of the family; parents caring for a young child under age 3 . . . ; employed 30 hours or more a week; . . . under age 16 or attending, full time, an elementary, secondary or vocational school; a woman who is at least in the second trimester of pregnancy . . ." (U.S. Congress, House Ways and Means 1993, 608).

23. However, President Reagan, who expressed a desire for welfare reform in his 1986 and 1987 State of the Union addresses and in 1986 established a group to study the issue, stimulated this effort.

24. As previously indicated, MDRC gave briefings and testimony on findings from the welfare-to-work experiments in 1986, before the drafting of the legislation. Thus, the findings may have at least served as background material during the drafting process. However, Baum's point is that they were not explicitly taken into account until after the initial outline of the legislation had already taken shape. When we interviewed her, Judith Gueron, the president of MDRC, agreed with this account.

25. Greenberg and Wiseman (1992, 59–60) have taken serious issue with this particular interpretation of the findings.

26. Although the GAIN program also made considerable use of education, as previously indicated, findings from the GAIN evaluation were not available before the passage of FSA.

27. Haskins (1991, 621) writes that some liberals misinterpreted findings from the welfare-to-work experiments by suggesting that they indicated that education and training were essential to producing favorable effects. He points out that programs without much reliance on training and education, such as those in Arkansas and San Diego, produced favorable effects, while programs that did stress either training or education, such as those in Baltimore and Maine, were relatively expensive and did not result in savings for taxpayers (see tables 8.1 and 8.2).

28. It could be counter-argued that both these programs resulted in substantial net benefits for AFDC-R recipients and, hence, for society as a whole. However, that argument does not appear to have been made in debate over the FSA.

29. Quoted in Vobejda (1993).

30. These standards actually went beyond the participation rates achieved by SWIM because relatively few SWIM participants were engaged in program activities for 20 hours a week, which was the minimum required to count as a participant in JOBS.

31. Single parents with children under age 6 are required to participate in an allowable work activity for only 20 hours per week in FY 2000 and beyond.

32. The discussion in this paragraph relies heavily on a case study by David M. Kennedy (1987).

33. The following list is based on interviews with individuals who held policy-making positions in California at the time that GAIN was negotiated. Julia Lopez, who was Agnos's key welfare aide at the time, was especially helpful.

34. Particularly notable among those counties is Los Angeles County, which accounts for more than a third of the state's caseload and which had the least favorable findings of the six evaluation counties. A random assignment evaluation of Los Angeles's revamped GAIN program was conducted to see if the Riverside findings can be replicated in a more difficult environment. Los Angeles's version of the Riverside model was found to be more successful than the city's previous welfare-to-work approach (Freedman et al. 2000).

35. For example, in her keynote address at the 21st Annual Conference of the Eastern Evaluation Research Society on April 27, 1998, Debra J. Rog said that MDRC has "produced a legacy of reliable findings. On the basis of their expertise as well as credibility as evaluators, MDRC investigators have participated extensively in policy debates over the years and have attained a high degree of success in effecting change through their results."

36. According to Wendell Primus, within Congress, evidence based on random assignment tends to be taken seriously by some of the staff, but not by most lawmakers, "who don't really understand it."

37. As discussed in detail in the following chapter, most decisionmakers in the states seem less concerned than those at the national level with the type of research design used to obtain a set of findings. Indeed, they are typically less interested in estimates of program effects themselves, and more in whether particular programs are administratively feasible to implement and design.

38. They are being examined in more recent experiments, however (see Greenberg et al. 1995).

39. For a description of this survey, see chapter 9.

40. Murray also argued that welfare encouraged illegitimacy, the formation of single-parent families, and a host of other social ills.

41. This point is nicely summarized by Mark Greenberg, a welfare reform expert at the Center for Law and Social Policy, who told us that "Research findings ultimately only resonate when they suggest a conclusion that people wanted to reach for other reasons."

PART III:
Conclusions

9

The Dissemination and Use of Experiments in State Policymaking

This chapter continues the examination of the use of welfare-to-work experiments that we began in chapter 8. However, chapter 8 focused on the use of welfare-to-work experiments at the national level and, to a lesser degree, on use within the states in which they were conducted. In this chapter, in contrast, we examine the dissemination to and the use of welfare-to-work experiments in states other than the ones in which they were conducted.

The States as Policy Laboratories

It is often suggested that because the United States has 50 separate states, it has exceptional opportunities for learning what social service policies are most effective. To wit, it is said that each state can serve as a laboratory by testing its own approach toward delivering social services, and then the best of the various approaches can be adopted elsewhere.

In welfare policy, each state has been allowed to function as a laboratory since 1981. As discussed in chapter 8, in passing the Omnibus Budget Reconciliation Act (OBRA) of that year, Congress permitted states to implement innovations of their own choosing in administering Aid to Families with Dependent Children (AFDC). Although the innovations could not be implemented without clearing waivers from the national government, in practice, states were given considerable leeway in what they could try.[1]

If the laboratories established by the states are to serve a useful function in the policy process, three critical links must exist: (1) the effectiveness of the innovations introduced by different states must be reliably assessed; (2) mechanisms must exist to disseminate information from assessments to appropriate policymakers; and (3) the information must be used in decisionmaking. As described in chapter 8, all three links were present when Congress passed the Family Support Act (FSA) in 1988. First, in part because of encouragement by (and sometimes the insistence of) the federal government, many of the early innovations under OBRA had been subjected to rigorous evaluations based on random assignment experiments by 1988. Second, the major evaluation firm involved in this effort, the Manpower Demonstration Research Corporation (MDRC), effectively disseminated its findings to the relevant congressional committees through written reports, briefings, and testimony. Third, that information played an important role in crafting the legislation.

As a consequence of the passage of the Personal Responsibility and Work Opportunity Reconciliation Act (PRWORA) in August 1996, all three links are now subject to considerable stress. As indicated in chapter 8, that legislation provides states with funds for the AFDC program, which is now called Temporary Assistance for Needy Families (TANF), in the form of block grants and gives them enormous flexibility to design and manage their own programs. Because states no longer need federal waivers to introduce innovations, on one hand they have considerably greater freedom to experiment in their laboratories under the new legislation. On the other hand, however, the federal government can do little to require them to evaluate the innovations. In addition, unlike the situation in 1988, when the federal government could use information from evaluations of state programs to make important changes in welfare policy, if such information is to be used in the future, it will have to be mainly by the individual state governments. Consequently, evaluative information about the effectiveness of innovations in one state must now be disseminated to the other states, a considerably greater challenge than disseminating such information only to the federal government. Moreover, it is the individual states that choose whether to use the information, not the central government.

A survey that we conducted with the help of Matt Onstott in 1996 provides considerable insight into whether the second and third links described earlier—dissemination to the states and state use of the dis-seminated information—are likely to function adequately in the decen-tralized environment that PRWORA created. In that survey we examined whether states learned of findings from evaluations of welfare innovations in other states and, if they did, what use they made of that information. To examine this, we first selected random assignment evalu-ations of welfare-to-work programs in three populous states: California's Greater Avenues for Independence (GAIN), New York's Child Assistance Program (CAP), and Florida's Project Independence. We then tele-phoned officials with responsibilities for welfare policy in every state in the nation to determine whether they were familiar with the three eval-uations and, if they were, whether findings from them had influenced welfare policy within their states.[2]

In the remainder of the chapter, we first briefly describe both the three evaluations that formed the basis of our survey and the survey itself. We then discuss our major findings on the dissemination of eval-uation results to the states and the uses that state decisionmakers made of the information.

The Three Evaluations

GAIN, Project Independence, and CAP were selected as the focus of our state survey of evaluation dissemination and use for several reasons. First, evaluations of all three were based on a classical experimental design. As a result, questions about biases to findings from the evalua-tions, which could have impeded their use by state governments, were rarely raised. Moreover, the earliest reports on findings from the three evaluations became available between 1992 and 1994, well in advance of our survey, which was conducted during 1996. Thus, ample time existed for state decisionmakers to become familiar with the information and to have used it. Yet information on all three programs continued to be released through at least 1995. Thus, the programs should not have faded from memory by the time of our survey. Finally, the states in which the evaluations were conducted—California, Florida, and New York—were all large and visible, enhancing the chances that other states would learn of the evaluation findings.

As indicated in chapter 8, the evaluation of California's GAIN program, particularly in Riverside County, was especially notable. Consequently, findings from it were widely discussed in a number of different forums. Hence, if there was ever a welfare program evaluation that should be well known to state decisionmakers and have the potential to have been used by them, it is GAIN. The findings from the other two evaluations, although generally positive, are considerably less striking than those from GAIN. Thus, they provide a useful contrast. Two of the three evaluations, those of GAIN and Project Independence, were conducted by MDRC, a firm that makes a special effort to disseminate findings. The third evaluation, the one of CAP, was conducted by Abt Associates, a research firm that devotes far fewer resources than MDRC to dissemination, thereby providing another interesting contrast. GAIN is described in some detail in chapter 8. The Project Independence and CAP evaluations are briefly described next.

Project Independence

Florida's Project Independence was created in 1987. The program was implemented statewide and random-assignment evaluations of it were conducted in nine randomly selected counties. Except for individuals who were exempt, the program was mandatory for AFDC recipients. Indeed, sanctions were widely used to penalize those who failed to participate in program activities without good reason, and should therefore be considered a key program component. To keep program costs as low as possible, most participants were assigned to a relatively inexpensive "job-ready" track in which they were required to apply for a job with at least 12 employers. Those who did not find employment on their own were then assigned to a "job club"—a two- to three-week job search preparation course. A relatively small group of AFDC recipients who had very low levels of education and little previous job experience (as well as some of those who could not succeed in finding a job after participating in a job club) were deemed "not job ready" and assigned to a more costly second track. Participants in this track first developed an Employability Plan with the help of a case manager and were then assigned to education or training services.

The effects of Project Independence were small but generally positive. For example, over the two-year evaluation period, the average earnings of members of the program group increased by $227 relative to the average earnings of members of the randomly assigned control group, whereas their average AFDC payments fell by $265 (Kemple, Friedlander, and

Fellerath 1995). The first group of AFDC recipients who were assigned to Project Independence fared better than this, whereas the later groups did worse. A likely explanation for the difference is that funding reductions meant that the earliest program group received greater child care and other support services than the later groups. In terms of the government's budget, the program paid for itself. That is, the reduction in welfare costs to the government and the increase in tax revenues (because of earnings increases) exceeded the cost of providing services. However, welfare recipients were made worse off as a result of Project Independence because the reduction in their welfare receipts exceeded their increase in earnings.

Child Assistance Program

The Child Assistance Program (CAP) was initially implemented in seven New York counties in late 1988 and early 1989, with random assignment evaluations conducted in three of those counties. Unlike GAIN and Project Independence, CAP was not a mandatory program. Instead, it relied on financial incentives to induce AFDC recipients to obtain child support court orders and to work. For example, under regular AFDC, transfers were reduced by roughly a dollar for each dollar of earnings. Under CAP, in contrast, cash transfer benefits were reduced by only 10 cents for each dollar of earnings up to the poverty level and by 67 cents for each dollar of earnings above the poverty level. Thus, welfare recipients could substantially increase their incomes by working. In addition, CAP removed restrictions on the amount of assets program participants may hold and provided intensive case management. To qualify for the advantages offered by CAP, however, AFDC recipients had first to obtain child support court orders. If successful, this would reduce government expenditures because CAP's cash transfer benefits would be offset by a dollar for each dollar of child support payments collected.

CAP appears to have had substantial effects, even though only a minority of AFDC recipients met the requirements necessary to enroll. Over the first two years of the evaluation, for example, earnings averaged about $900 higher for members of the program group than for persons randomly assigned to the control group, although only around 10 percent of the former actually participated in CAP (Hamilton et al. 1993). In addition, members of the program group were 25 percent more likely to have established child support orders than were members of the control group. CAP resulted in both an increase in the average incomes of members of the program group and a reduction in overall government expenditures. Effects on public assistance receipts were small and statistically insignificant, however.[3]

Methodology

Our main data source for this study is a set of semistructured telephone interviews of 93 mid- to upper-level administrators within state welfare agencies, and the questions were tailored to such persons. Fifty-one of the respondents were obtained from a list provided to us by the American Public Welfare Association (APWA) (now the American Public Human Services Association) that contained the names of top-level administrators in the area of human and social services in all 50 states and the District of Columbia. The individuals listed were generally at the secretary or commissioner level within state departments of human or social services. We supplemented the list by asking the first set of respondents if they could think of another person who could provide additional information on the role of the three experiments in policy decisions in that state. Respondents from 41 states and the District of Columbia were able to provide at least one name and in each of these 42 cases we conducted a second round of interviews. Thus, we have 51 first-round interviews and 42 second-round interviews, for a total of 93.[4]

The interview protocol consisted of 12 qualitative questions.[5] We were interested in respondents' awareness and familiarity with each of the three evaluations and how they learned of them, if indeed they had.[6] Questions also asked about specific instances of use in decisionmaking processes. There was one question about the role of other sources of information in the processes and another on changes in opinion that could be attributed to the findings from the three evaluations. To focus on the agenda-setting process, as well as on the decisionmaking process, we also asked about specific welfare reform initiatives undertaken by the state, the role played by the three experiments in deliberations on those specific initiatives, and what led to the considerations of the initiatives. Many of the questions were open-ended. Hence, a variety of responses was possible.[7] However, most responses to most questions fell into relatively few categories and, consequently, could be readily coded.

Knowledge of the Experiments

All but two of the 93 respondents to our telephone survey were at least aware of GAIN. Indeed, several suggested that GAIN has become "common knowledge" in the field. Said one respondent: "It's cited frequently— it almost seems common knowledge in our field." And another told us, "I think everybody in the country is aware of their publicity." There was considerably less (but still high) familiarity with CAP and Florida's Project Independence, as 64 of our 93 respondents (69 percent) were familiar with CAP and 68 of them (73 percent) had knowledge of Project Independence.[8]

Many respondents who indicated they were aware of a particular experiment were familiar either with the experiment in name only or with the nature of the treatment, but not with the evaluation findings on program effects. That was particularly true in the case of CAP and Florida's Project Independence. Only 26 of the 64 respondents (41 percent) who were familiar with CAP were familiar with the evaluation findings from it. An even smaller fraction (18 of 68 or 26 percent) of the respondents familiar with Florida's Project Independence were familiar with the evaluation findings from it. There was considerably more knowledge of the evaluation findings from GAIN than from the other two experiments. Sixty-four of the 91 respondents (70 percent) who were familiar with GAIN knew about the evaluation findings, especially the finding that the effects of the variant of GAIN tested in Riverside were large.

The responses for the way the respondents became aware of the various experiments were coded into several categories. Table 9.1 allows for multiple information sources and summarizes the frequency with which the categories were identified. Four findings about the source of respondents' knowledge of the experiments warrant highlighting.

1. A number of potential sources of information about the three experiments played only a minor role in bringing them to the attention of our respondents. Those sources include persons in the respondent's home state,[9] interstate "networks" of associates in which they are involved,[10] and the news media. Conspicuously absent from the responses we received is the Internet, which was cited as a source of information only once.

Table 9.1. *Frequency with Which Sources of Knowledge Were Cited by Respondents*

| | Experiment | | | |
| | GAIN *n* (%) | CAP *n* (%) | Project independence *n* (%) | All *n* (%) |
Source				
The evaluation contractor (i.e., MDRC or Abt)	44 (52)	4 (7)	18 (30)	66 (32)
Intermediary organizations (e.g., APWA, National Governors Association)	31 (37)	25 (42)	27 (44)	83 (41)
Federal government (i.e., DHHS or the *Federal Register*)	16 (19)	9 (15)	14 (23)	39 (19)
State providing experimental site (i.e., Calif., N.Y., or Fla.)	12 (14)	23 (39)	7 (12)	42 (21)
Person in respondent's home state[a]	7 (8)	4 (7)	8 (13)	19 (9)
Media	5 (6)	0 (0)	1 (2)	6 (3)
Interstate networks	7 (8)	2 (3)	7 (12)	16 (8)
Other	24 (29)	17 (29)	10 (16)	51 (25)
Number of responses[b]	84	59	61	204

Notes: Columns sum to more than 100 percent because respondents often cited more than one source of information about the experiments. APWA = American Public Welfare Association; CAP = Child Assistance Program; DHHS = U.S. Department of Health and Human Services; GAIN = Greater Avenues for Independence; MDRC = Manpower Demonstration Research Corporation.

a. Such individuals include librarians, research office staff, individuals who formerly worked in the state in which the experiment in question was conducted, legislators in their home state, staff from the governor's office in their home state, and other members of their department.

b. Of the 91 respondents who indicated that they were familiar with GAIN, the 64 familiar with CAP, and the 68 familiar with Project Independence, all but 5, 3, and 5, respectively, could identify how they had learned of the experiment. These cases were excluded in computing the figures in this table, as were the 6 cases in which the respondent was from one of the three states in which the evaluations were conducted. Hence, this table pertains to the way 84 respondents learned about GAIN, 59 learned about CAP, and 61 learned about Project Independence.

2. "Intermediary organizations," such as the American Public Welfare Association, the National Governors Association, and the Center for Law and Social Policy, played a significant role in bringing the experiments to the attention of state policymakers through their publications and through meetings and conferences that they sponsor. The federal government (primarily the U.S. Department of Health and Human Services) also serves as an important intermediary organization. Reinforcing the point made earlier on the greater familiarity with the nature of the tested program than with the evaluation findings, our findings indicate that many of those who learned of the respective experiments through intermediary organizations cited "lists" provided by these organizations or the *Federal Register* as their source of knowledge.

3. Contact with individuals in New York State was an important source of knowledge about CAP,[11] whereas contact with individuals in California or Florida was cited much less frequently as a source of knowledge for GAIN and Project Independence, respectively.[12] Respondents who learned about CAP in this manner pointed to such sources as a report produced by New York State, a telephone conversation with someone from New York, or a conference presentation by someone from New York (for example, several respondents had attended a conference sponsored by New York State).[13]

4. Presentations made and reports produced by the evaluation firm were the most frequently cited sources of knowledge of GAIN, less important sources of knowledge for Project Independence, and rarely cited in connection with CAP.[14] As previously indicated, the first two of these experiments were evaluated by MDRC, whereas Abt Associates evaluated CAP.

The frequency with which respondents cited MDRC as a source of their knowledge on GAIN and, to a lesser extent, Florida's Project Independence, is not surprising. Conversations we had with staff at MDRC and Abt, as well as many of our respondents' comments, suggest that MDRC is both zealous and skillful in dissemination efforts. In the words of one of our respondents, for example: "My overall sense is that MDRC does good PR with their stuff. MDRC has a way of getting my attention. Their executive summaries have the right kind of triggers to get me to read them.

The presentation is not at all deadly." Another told us, "When MDRC does a study and issues a report, I make the assumption they go to all states. [My state] has received reports for years." A third respondent, when asked how she became aware of GAIN, replied, "Reports. Report after report. I'm sick of GAIN." Indeed, there is even somewhat of a "halo" effect associated with MDRC's dissemination efforts. A few of our respondents mentioned MDRC as their source of knowledge about CAP.[15]

In part, the greater effort and resources that MDRC puts into dissemination than Abt does occurs because Abt is a for-profit firm whereas MDRC is nonprofit. Consequently, although both organizations are interested in serving both their immediate clients and the public at large, Abt puts greater emphasis on the former and MDRC on the latter. Indeed, broad dissemination of findings is a formal component of MDRC's mission statement. Moreover, because of its nonprofit status, MDRC receives considerably more funding than does Abt from foundations. Foundations also view their mission as serving the general public, allow for the costs of dissemination in determining grant amounts, and put pressure on grant recipients to disseminate their research findings. In addition, much of MDRC's work focuses on welfare issues, whereas Abt works in many different areas. Consequently, MDRC can disseminate to a single audience, but Abt faces several different audiences. Organizational history also plays a role. MDRC was initially founded in the 1970s to administer the Supported Work Demonstration Project. Findings from that project were not widely disseminated and used. As a result, MDRC made a policy decision to put a greater effort into dissemination in the future. Finally, MDRC's president, Judith Gueron, is especially skilled at dissemination.[16]

Effects of the Evaluations on Policy

As has been discussed in chapter 3, one of the most significant conclusions to emerge from previous studies of the effects of evaluation on policymaking is that evaluation influences policymaking in diverse and, for the most part, subtle ways. Our findings on the effects of the three experiments we examined are consistent with these previous studies.

The potential was there to influence policy at the state level. As was seen in the previous section, the three experiments that we asked about, especially GAIN, were well known among welfare administrators within the states. Moreover, the programs examined in the three evaluations were certainly germane to policy.[17] For example, as was discussed in chapter 8, GAIN is widely viewed as a test of two competing alternative welfare-to-work program models: a human capital model versus a labor force attachment model. Virtually all our respondents said that there had recently been serious consideration within their states of moving the JOBS program from a human capital model to a labor force attachment model and, in fact, all but a few of these states ultimately made such a move. Similarly, all but three respondents indicated that their states had considered use of at least one of the three program components tested by Project Independence that we specifically asked about—sanctions for noncompliance, individual employment planning, and job clubs—and most had considered two or all three. Offering financial incentives to welfare recipients for establishing child support orders, a major component of CAP, was much less widely considered by the states. Still, 27 of our respondents (representing 22 of the 51 states[18]) said that it had been considered in their state.

Although the potential was clearly there for the three experiments to influence state welfare policy, our interviews suggest that they did not have dramatic, decisive effects on policymaking. For example, when asked directly if the Riverside findings played a role in decisions about welfare programs in their states, not one of our respondents told us that his or her state was so impressed by the unprecedented large earnings gains and reductions in welfare dependence attributed to the Riverside version of GAIN that, as a result, a decision was made to adopt this program.

Although the three experiments did not have dramatic, decisive effects on policymaking, there is evidence from our survey that GAIN and CAP nonetheless played some role in deliberations in many states over the tested policy. For example, 43 of our 93 survey respondents (46 percent)[19] recalled that GAIN was specifically mentioned at the time that their states were considering moving their JOBS programs toward a labor force attachment model. Of the 27 respondents who indicated that their states had considered using financial incentives to establish child support orders, 12 (44 percent) stated that CAP was mentioned in deliberations over this issue.[20] Although, as indicated above, the policy components tested by Project Independence were considered by most states, only five respondents stated that the evaluation of the program played a role in deliberations over those topics. The reason appears to be a matter of timing. Many states had considered sanctions for noncompliance, individual employment planning, and job clubs well before—indeed, often years before—the Project Independence evaluation was conducted. Thus, the evaluation of Project Independence tended to be perceived as focusing on issues that were old. Many viewed GAIN, in contrast, as a test of a critical major current issue: whether welfare-to-work programs should emphasize human capital development or immediate job placement. One obvious lesson here is that a condition for an evaluation to be used in the policy process is that it addresses questions that are currently important to policymakers.

The figures reported in the previous paragraph may understate the role of program evaluations in policy deliberations. Previous studies (e.g., Caplan, Morrison, and Stambaugh 1975; Weiss 1980) have found that policymakers receive information from a variety of sources and are frequently unable to disentangle information obtained from evaluations from information received from other sources. It is consistent with this previous research that our respondents were often uncertain where specific policies that were being considered in their states came from. For example, one respondent indicated that the three studies she was being asked about "become part of current thinking and things get blurred. Findings become part of your knowledge base." Another suggested, "You forget where the idea came from, but you end up promoting it. If you tell me about a program, it adds to the awareness. Frankly, I don't care where the study was done or who did it, only what works." Other respondents indicated that because other states were implementing similar policies, their states were also considering them. Although the states they were directly emulating may not have conducted an evaluation, it is possible that the original source of the policy idea, or at least one source, was a social experiment that formally tested it. Policymakers may be aware of particular ideas, but not be able to pinpoint their original source. For example, State B may adopt a policy that is tested experimentally in State A. Then, State C may adopt it from State B.

Other Information Sources

As suggested by Weiss (1983), among others, to contribute to state welfare policymaking, formal evaluations of programs must compete with other potential sources of information. We therefore asked our respondents specifically about which other sources of information were considered valuable in making decisions about the policies tested in CAP,

GAIN, and Project Independence. The responses we received appear in table 9.2. As is evident, many of our 93 respondents mentioned more than one information source.

As indicated in table 9.2, the single most important knowledge source about welfare issues is information on projects and programs taking place in other states. Some of this information comes from descriptions of formal evaluations, but more often it does not. Instead, as suggested by the director of an office with responsibility for state welfare program innovation, states often find out about what other states are doing by direct contact: "We've called all the states. I've got a filing cabinet full of stuff." A second important information source, called "specific national sources" in table 9.2, includes organizations and agencies such as the American Public Welfare Association, the National Governors Association, and the U.S. Department of Health and Human Services. Often it was brief summary information provided by these national sources that prompted state welfare administrators to contact a counterpart in a state running a program of interest so that more detailed information could be obtained. The third most important information source is internal analyses that states sometimes conduct on data they collect on their

Table 9.2. *Sources of Information about the Policy Issues Addressed by the Experiments*

	Number of responses[a]
External information	
Projects or programs in other states	59
Specific national sources	36
Nonspecific national sources[b]	21
Political debate	16
Internal information	
State data	26
Community input	19
Staff input	17

Notes: Policy issues addressed by the experiments include the possibility of adopting the labor force attachment model, using financial incentives to establish child support orders, toughening sanctions for noncompliance, engaging in individual employment planning, and assigning welfare recipients to job clubs.

a. Based on answers from 93 respondents. Respondents frequently cited more than one source of information.

b. Examples of this category of response include "the national debate" and "federal priorities."

welfare caseloads. States also sometimes solicit the views of the citizenry, welfare caseworkers, and even welfare recipients about welfare policy, occasionally by establishing special panels and commissions.

Factors Influencing State Welfare Policy

As suggested by Weiss (1983), forces other than information also influence state welfare policy, often strongly. For example, state policy is sometimes driven by attempts to meet the requirements of federal legislation. In addition, the ideology of the governor or a particular state legislator and the views of the citizenry are frequently influential. As the director of welfare policy development in one state told us, "Welfare policy is crafted on the personality of the governors . . . and the way people feel welfare should be."[21]

The various factors that influence changes in state welfare policy are usefully illustrated by the movement of JOBS programs in most states from a human capital model to a labor force attachment model, the very model that was tested in Riverside County, Calif., as part of the GAIN experiment. At first, it would appear that GAIN must have played an important role in this movement, as much of it took place shortly after the positive preliminary findings for Riverside became available. In addition, as indicated earlier, there was widespread awareness of the GAIN experiment and GAIN was frequently mentioned in deliberations over this issue.

Several other factors, however, probably had a more compelling influence on the movement toward the labor force attachment model.[22] First, at the time preliminary findings from GAIN were available, time-limited welfare had been proposed by the Clinton administration, and state policymakers believed that limiting the time that individuals can remain on welfare would soon become national policy, as in fact it has. Thus, it appeared important to move as many welfare recipients into jobs as quickly as possible. A labor force attachment model was viewed as more consistent with that effort than were long-term investments in the human capital of welfare recipients.

Second, policies that focused on getting welfare recipients into jobs often were viewed as politically expedient. As one survey respondent told us: "I just came from a meeting this week and someone from the governor's office said it's amazing how long it's taken to discover the gold mine of welfare reform. [The governor] has a two-piece agenda, tax cuts and welfare reform, and has an 80 percent approval rating."

Third, the labor force attachment model was also viewed as consistent with efforts that were being undertaken by many states at the time to minimize expenditures on welfare recipients. Those efforts, in turn, were almost surely stimulated by the existence of labor market conditions that made it relatively easy to find low-wage jobs for welfare recipients. The director of public assistance in one state suggested to us, for example, that there had been "changes in JOBS philosophy . . . [due to] a lack of money and society wanting people off welfare faster. A change in attitude—the political attitude is more conservative. . . . If we had more money, we'd like to give people more education, but. . . ."

Thus, the Riverside findings can be viewed as supportive of the movement toward a labor force attachment model for state JOBS programs, but other considerations may have been far more important. Indeed, the head of the office responsible for welfare reform planning in one state went so far as to assert, "My suspicion is that if we hadn't read the MDRC [GAIN] studies, we'd still have moved toward a labor force attachment model. A lot of this we don't really have a choice about. We'd probably have done it anyway."

Somewhat paradoxically, GAIN might have played a more critical role had the Riverside findings suggested, contrary to what was actually found, that a labor force attachment model was ineffective. In that case, they would have sounded a cautionary note and, perhaps, offset the other forces causing states to move toward the labor force attachment model. Instead, as the quotes below suggest—and they are typical of numerous others we heard—the Riverside findings reaffirmed the existing views of most survey respondents on welfare issues:

"I just don't recall any findings that were contrary to what we believed to be the case already."

"I don't think there were any findings that were surprising—kind of what you'd almost expect."

"[GAIN, Project Independence, and CAP] didn't change us so much, but help us feel comfortable in the way we're proceeding."

"I think that more than anything, the findings from [MDRC studies, including GAIN] reinforce thoughts and directions rather than give new information. They add to the knowledge base. . . . The findings reinforce what we already believed and had ideas about."

Hence, consistent with previous studies of knowledge use, movement toward the labor force attachment model occurred because numerous factors, including the GAIN findings, reinforced one another. Because the GAIN findings were consistent with already existing views and pressures to adopt a labor force attachment model, not surprisingly, they were sometimes used persuasively to help sell this policy:

> "Generally the usefulness of those studies [is in] confirmation or double-checking in terms of what we believe. We weren't all that surprised by the findings. We typically haven't used them in policy formation, but in the sales department—trying to convince others."

> "GAIN made our arguments more easily delivered because they were saying the same things as us."

> "[GAIN played a role] in how we're marketing [the labor force attachment model] . . . the buttons and slogans—we've used those as models. They seemed effective."

The Role of Evaluations in State Policy Formulation

In addition to being used persuasively, evaluations of the three welfare-to-work experiments that we examined were also used for elaborative purposes. Even then, however, findings about the effects of the tested programs on earnings or welfare receipts seemed to play relatively little role, except occasionally, as one state official with responsibility for welfare reform indicated, to sound a cautionary note: "GAIN was mentioned a lot [in discussions on welfare reform], but mainly it was 'Just remember that you're not going to have overnight success and you'll never get rid of your entire caseload.' " Consistent with that cautionary note, the head of a state social service office stressed, "The role of GAIN was it heightened our awareness of the enormity of the challenges. . . . GAIN gave us not specifics, but raised critical issues. Then, we started with a blank sheet of paper." As these statements imply, respondents to our survey rarely mentioned estimates of treatment effects specifically unless directly asked about them, and then they often could only vaguely recall them.[23]

Much more important to most states than empirical findings about the effects of tested programs was information about how these programs actually operated in the field.[24] For example, the director of a state welfare demonstration project told us that "as we have been making policy . . . [we] discussed the GAIN project, not for its results . . . but how they had achieved the cultural change, turning eligibility workers, who were used to writing checks, into case managers." The director of a state welfare office echoed this: "I know we used Riverside County and how they treated customers as they walked through the door. Copies of reports, quotes, percentages, I don't recall using at any of the meetings." Finally, the director of a state office of social services indicated, "The plan we have is the governor's vision, but the studies have helped us in smaller ways, defining our implementation and using their experience in our implementation process. We already had information from GAIN before we did that." Although evaluation reports obviously facilitated obtaining such information, they clearly were not required. Instead, the information could be, and often was, obtained directly from the agency operating the program: "We invited the Riverside director to come talk to us about cultural change as we were preparing training for our staff. It was about job development and working with employers."

As important as the "how to" information was evidence that the policies tested in welfare-to-work experiments were logically consistent (that is, there was no obvious reason to think that they would be unsuccessful), could clear federal waivers, and would not encounter major political resistance. For example, a staff member in a state research and planning office asserted that these experiments "probably haven't figured in a rational decisionmaking process. We've discussed them not as models of intervention, but as strategies of working the waiver process. You hear about what State X got away with doing their waivers."

A randomized experiment, or even a formal evaluation, is obviously not required to provide such information.[25] Indeed, only about half a dozen of the survey respondents mentioned randomization at all during the course of being interviewed and when they did, it was usually to protest randomization as being unnecessarily imposed on states by the federal government.[26]

More tellingly, perhaps, many respondents mentioned states that have well-known reputations for welfare policy innovation as having an important influence on policy in their own states. Particularly prominently mentioned were Wisconsin, Michigan, and Oregon. Whether the programs in those states had been subject to random assignment evaluations (and they typically had not been) had little bearing on their influence on policy in other states, as the following statements by respondents suggest:[27]

"We have looked at things that other states are doing, but I don't think we've gotten any evaluation results. . . . [The information we've obtained contains] summaries of the projects, but they're descriptive, not evaluative."

"They [state legislators] wanted to know what other states were doing, but they weren't looking at evaluation findings. Just, 'Well, there's an idea we could try.' "

"Other states—Michigan, Wisconsin—they're very important to us. They have high visibility at the national level. With our press, there's always questions about why aren't we doing it too."

"[A key piece of information is] knowing what other states have gotten away with under federal rules. I use this all the time. Tapping into others' wisdom."

Norris and Thompson (1995, especially p. 235) found similar evidence of such bandwagon effects in state welfare reform efforts, an effect that had little to do with whether a formal evaluation had taken place.

One respondent deplored the idea of adopting the policies of other states without evidence that the policies were effective and, in fact, viewed experimental evidence as an antidote against doing this:

We've used [well-done evaluations] to keep our legislature straight. There are a few states trying stuff and some people running them must have come from the marketing side of things in school. So you have to be kind of careful. GAIN has been studied. It's not bragging. That's why I have a lot of respect for what MDRC does, and those other [evaluation firms] also.

However, we received no other similar statements. Moreover, the individual quoted above is more familiar with evaluation than most of the state officials we interviewed, as MDRC was conducting a random assignment evaluation of a welfare-to-work program in her state. The key point here is that it is not typically evidence of treatment effects obtained through random assignment evaluations that is critical in determining whether a state adopts a particular policy, but rather evidence indicating that the proposed policy can be successfully implemented and meet various political and legislative tests. Consequently, in terms of contributing to the state-level policy process, the most important effect of a formal evaluation may be to help publicize a particular program and provide detailed information about its implementation. Thus, the fact that evaluation reports typically dispense detailed descriptions of program implementation may be more important than their presentation of treatment impact estimates.

The use of welfare-to-work evaluations at the state level sharply contrasts with experience at the federal level in developing the Family Support Act of 1988. In this instance, as discussed in chapter 8, treatment effect findings from evaluations of experimental tests of welfare-to-work programs are widely acknowledged to have played a major role in crafting the legislation (see Baum 1991; Haskins 1991; and Szanton 1991). In one respect, this contrast is not surprising. Some of the congressional staffers who helped craft the Family Support Act were trained social scientists with considerable knowledge of and interest in evaluation. Most persons in state welfare agencies, in contrast, are experts on the administration of welfare programs and many have practical field experience, but relatively few of them are knowledgeable about evaluation. Not surprisingly, these persons are often strongly process-oriented and thus concerned with whether a proposed policy seems logically coherent, is legally and politically acceptable, and can be implemented.[28] The situation is well summarized by one respondent who is, in fact, knowledgeable about evaluation: "Before I was involved in [a random assignment welfare-to-work evaluation], I knew very little about experimental designs. I think there's a lack of knowledge among policy people as far as this goes. It's largely a lack of time, but there's not a strong enough linkage between the policy and research communities. They don't even speak the same language."

Conclusions

Virtually all the officials we interviewed knew of one of the experiments, GAIN, and many knew that the program tested in GAIN's Riverside site produced large effects. A substantial majority also knew of the other two, CAP and Project Independence, although they often had little or no knowledge of the estimates of the effects of the tested programs. Various national organizations and the government played important roles in the dissemination of this information, as did the evaluator (MDRC) in the case of GAIN and Project Independence and the state sponsoring the evaluation (New York) in the case of CAP. The greater awareness of GAIN than the other two evaluations was almost surely because Riverside tested a variant of the labor force attachment model, a program model that many states were considering at the time findings from GAIN became available. In general, state welfare officials seemed to learn what they felt they needed to know to perform their jobs. However, the information they want may often be generated by means other than a formal evaluation. For example, knowledge that another state has adopted a new policy that appears logical and politically appealing may be all that they feel is required.

The experiments did play a role in policymaking in states other than those in which they were conducted. This role was of some importance, but not critical and perhaps different from what many evaluators anticipated. Most important, although findings from the experiments were used in a wide variety of ways, we discovered no instances in which estimates of the effects of the tested programs, presumably the rationale for conducting random assignment experiments, were decisive in the decision to adopt or not to adopt a tested policy. One plausible interpretation of the reason is that other factors—for example, political appeal; ease of implementation; and consistency with current state objectives, the philosophy of the governor or voters, and federal policy—were considered more important in deciding whether to adopt them than effects measured by the evaluations. In short, political considerations seemed to dominate information from evaluations. This is not surprising; it is well documented by previous studies. Nonetheless, if available and reliable evaluation information about program effects is not used in making these decisions, then allowing each state to serve as a laboratory in which different policies and programs are tested will contribute substantially less to effective policymaking than it otherwise might.

NOTES

This chapter was adapted from Greenberg, Mandell, and Onstott (2000).

1. See Norris and Thompson (1995, 7) for a helpful list of the innovations.

2. Because the three evaluations, as well as the survey, were conducted before the passage of the Personal Responsibility and Work Opportunity Reconciliation Act, we usually use the acronym AFDC, rather than TANF, in this chapter.

3. We rely here on findings for the first two years of the evaluation, as these were available to our interview respondents. A later report (Hamilton et al. 1996) provided findings for a five-year evaluation period, but that report was not yet available to most of our respondents at the time they were interviewed. Findings from the five-year evaluation were generally consistent with those for the two-year evaluation, except that statistically significant reductions in public assistance receipts were found only by the five-year evaluation.

4. The second-round respondents were frequently closer to the daily management of the state's welfare programs or were persons responsible for the state's welfare reform efforts. Those individuals were typically more familiar with the way the three experimental programs actually ran, but they were not necessarily more familiar with the evaluations and their findings.

5. The actual interviews typically took 20 to 25 minutes. The interviewer used probing comments and questions to obtain more complete or clearer responses. Responses were written verbatim when possible, although some paraphrasing was used.

6. Each of the first three questions pertained to the respondents' familiarity with one of the three evaluations and how they had become aware of it. The order in which the three questions were asked was rotated approximately every 10 interviews. That is, we first asked about GAIN, then CAP, then Project Independence. Later interviews had CAP at the top of the list, and still later interviews had Project Independence at the top.

7. For example, to learn about the utilization of CAP, respondents were asked, "Has your state considered offering financial incentives to welfare recipients for the establishment of child support orders?" If they answered in the affirmative, they were asked, "What led to the consideration of the issue?" "Did CAP play a role in deliberations on the issue?" "What other sources of information were considered valuable in making the decisions?" and, finally, "Did the findings play a role in *any* decisions recently made concerning welfare programs in your state?"

8. It is possible that this figure may somewhat exaggerate the level of familiarity with Florida's Project Independence. At the time of our survey, other states were running demonstration programs with similar names. Moreover, Florida was running a second demonstration program, the Family Transition Program. Thus, persons who thought they knew of Project Independence could actually have been thinking of one of the other programs.

9. Such individuals include librarians, research office staff, and the like; individuals who formerly worked in the state in which the experiment in question was conducted; legislators in their home state; staff from the governor's office in their home state; and other members of their department.

10. Some of these networks are specific and relatively formal, such as JOBS directors. Others are more amorphous groups, which are sometimes, though far from always, based on geographic proximity.

11. Admittedly, hazy recall might have resulted in contact with Abt Associates being recalled as contact with New York State. Even if this were the case, however, the lack of clear identification of Abt is noteworthy.

12. In some cases, the contact was initiated by the respondent's state, often in connection with preparing its own welfare reform initiative. For example, one respondent told us, "When we were [developing] our demonstration, we solicited other states . . . starting with close-by states and they gave us further contacts." In other instances, especially in the case of CAP, the contact was initiated by the state in which the experiment was conducted.

13. New York State's efforts to disseminate information on CAP effectively ended in 1994 after the incumbent governor lost his bid for reelection. The new governor was not anxious to distribute information about a successful program that had been initiated under his former rival's administration and, in fact, held up the release of the final report on CAP for several months. Nonetheless, the report was ultimately released and could then be ordered from Abt. (This information is based on a telephone interview with William Hamilton of Abt, who led the CAP research team.) Moreover, as table 9.1 indicates, information on CAP could be obtained from other sources, such as intermediary organizations. Still, had New York continued to promote CAP, the program might have become better known than it did.

14. Also included in this category are six instances in which the respondent learned of the experiment through contact with the contractor that occurred in connection with an evaluation that was being conducted in the respondent's own state.

15. We did not, of course, count these responses in the "evaluation contractor" category in table 9.1.

16. The information in this paragraph is based on telephone interviews with staff at Abt and MDRC.

17. However, respondents in some rural states believed that programs tested in populous urban states were of limited relevance to them. For example, one such respondent stated, "California and [our state] are very different, as are New York and Florida, but it is helpful to look at other states." Similarly, another respondent from a rural state indicated, "We look at what's happening in California, Florida, and New York, but the situation is so much different there. So we look at the information, but. . . ."

18. Here and elsewhere in using states as the unit of analysis, we treat the District of Columbia as a state.

19. Using states as the unit of analysis, at least one respondent from 30 states (59 percent) indicated that GAIN was mentioned at the time that the state was considering moving its JOBS program toward a labor force attachment model.

20. These 12 respondents represented 10 of the 22 states (45 percent) in which at least one respondent indicated that that state had considered using financial incentives to establish child support orders.

21. The director of welfare reform in a second state indicated, "When we were trying to decide on our [welfare reform] program, we had a citizens group, the empowerment commission, set up town meetings and all walks of people aired their view. That, along with what other states were doing and a philosophical mind set by our governor and administration, went into our program."

22. Norris and Thompson (1995) provide separate case studies of welfare reform in six states. Consistent with the findings from our survey, factors of the sort discussed in this section frequently played a major role in welfare reform in these states, but information on program effects from formal evaluations was typically not important.

23. However, a few respondents did indicate that the estimates of program costs that are usually provided by evaluation studies of welfare-to-work programs are helpful: "We had two things: a major budget issue in our state with changing funding and there were MDRC studies showing that trying to fix problems before putting people to work was more costly than the work attachment model."

24. Similar information from social experiments has influenced policies at the federal level. For example, as discussed in chapter 8, the use of retrospective accounting and monthly reporting in administering the income maintenance experiments led to adoption of these procedures by the national AFDC program.

25. As previously suggested, findings from random assignment experiments of effects on earnings and welfare receipts may be more important to the policymaking process when they indicate that a tested policy is ineffective. In this case, they would be difficult to ignore by those who were interested in implementing the policy for other reasons, but by simply reinforcing other reasons for implementing a policy, they can be safely relegated to a minor role.

26. The following statement is typical of those who did mention random assignment: "If we were left to our own devices, we wouldn't choose a random assignment format. They're cumbersome administratively. You're operating two different programs. . . . Random assignment tends to be burdensome."

27. Interestingly, the Wisconsin Works (W2) program, which probably evoked the greatest interest in other states at the time of our survey, had not yet even been initiated at that time. For example, the director of income support in one state told us, "The model that has caught our eye is W2 in Wisconsin. Based on their successes, we've begun to build our initiatives to position the state from the potential of federal block grants."

28. The head of a state office of policy and program development argued that the way evaluations are used at the state level is determined more by state politicians than by state welfare administrators:

> You want my two cents? I think politicians have the memory of a gnat. It's a PR world—a sound bite. There's only interest in the up-front [i.e., in what was tested and how it was implemented]. They're no longer interested four to seven years down the road to see what happened. I think professionals do read these things. We like the idea of formal evaluation and random assignment, but. . . .

10

Lessons from the Case Studies

This book has examined five social experiments or sets of social experiments in considerable detail. In each of these five case studies, we addressed three key questions:

- Why are social experiments conducted?
- How are findings from social experiments used?
- How is the use of a particular social experiment affected by the characteristics of the experiment and by the policy environment that exists after it is completed?

In this chapter, we draw some general conclusions about our answers to these questions. In addition, we highlight some lessons from our case studies about when social experiments are most usefully conducted, how they should be designed, and what the sponsors and evaluators of social experiments should do with the findings once they are available.

Why Are Social Experiments Conducted?

In chapter 3, we considered several competing explanations of why social experiments are conducted. These include the rational paradigm; additions to the information inventory, just in case such information is eventually needed; replacement of real deeds with symbolic action; and the effort to keep a policy idea alive until sufficient political support to adopt it can be garnered.

Our case studies suggest that, with one exception (the Nursing Home Incentive Reimbursement Experiment, chapter 5), reasons for conducting experiments combine elements of both the rational model and the inventory model. We found no support for the idea that they are used as part of a strategy for either forestalling action or keeping a policy idea alive until adequate support to adopt it can be mustered.

The Nursing Home Incentive Reimbursement Experiment fits squarely with the inventory model. The program tested by that experiment was not on the policy agenda when the experiment was initiated, nor was it anticipated that it necessarily would be in the future. The remaining four case studies, however, suggest that the difference between the rational model and inventory model is primarily one of degree rather than kind. That is, in these cases (the RAND Health Insurance Experiment, Income Maintenance Experiments, UI Bonus Experiments, and Welfare-to-Work Experiments), there was an expectation that, at some point, the findings would contribute to policymaking. In that sense, an element of the rational model was present in each. At the same time, these four experiments differed in terms of the precision regarding when and how the findings would contribute to policymaking. At one extreme, it was clearly expected that the findings of the UI bonus experiments would be used to help decide whether or not to adopt unemployment insurance (UI) bonuses and, if adopted, to design the optimum plan. Similarly, at the time the income maintenance experiments were fielded, it was anticipated that the findings would support the adoption of a negative income tax plan, that as a result such a program would be adopted, and that the findings would also be used to improve the design of the adopted plan. In the case of the welfare-to-work experiments, it is useful to distinguish between the states that served as experimental sites, on one hand, and other states, as well as the federal government, on the other. Before the welfare-to-work experiments were conducted, relevant decisions were identified relatively precisely in the states that served as experimental sites. There was, however, considerably less precision on when and how the findings would contribute to policymaking in other states and in the federal government. Nonetheless, there was great certainty on the part of those evaluating and funding those experiments that they would be used outside the experimental states as well as within them. Finally, in the case of the RAND Health Insurance Experiment, the anticipation was that some form of national health insurance would be implemented well before any findings were available. However, the findings were expected to be used eventually to improve the design of whatever national health insurance policy was adopted. Exactly how and when that would occur was nonetheless quite vague.

Even to the extent that social experiments are motivated by the rational paradigm, with the possible exception of the welfare-to-work experiments, we found little evidence of much attention at the time they were planned to ways to meet the stringent requirements of the model. For example, there was little advanced planning about ways to ensure that findings from the experiments would be communicated to the appropriate policymakers so that they could, in fact, be used in making the decisions they were intended to aid. Even more serious, as documented in the case studies, are the long lags between the time experiments are initiated and the time their findings become available. Under the rational model, findings from a social experiment are intended to contribute to a specific policy decision. However, there is no way to predict in advance that the particular issue an experiment addresses will, in fact, be on the policy agenda after the findings are available. Indeed, the expectations of those initiating an experiment are often unmet. For example, unemployment insurance bonuses were not on the policy agenda at the time the UI bonus experiments were completed, and national health insurance was not adopted either before or after completion of the health insurance experiment. Findings from an experiment that are strongly supportive of the policy innovation that is tested may, of course, help to place it on the policy agenda, but this did not occur in any of our case studies. More generally, there is no way to know in advance that the findings from an experiment will, in fact, be supportive of the tested policy (in our case studies, they often were not) or, even if they are, to guarantee that the policy innovation will reach the policy agenda. Those who were motivated by the rational paradigm to initiate experiments do not appear to have given much thought to these constraints.

How Are Findings from Social Experiments Used?

In chapter 3, we developed a taxonomy that allows for eight distinct types of use of policy research, including policy findings from social experiments. Application of that taxonomy to the experiments studied in each of our case studies proved difficult for a variety of reasons discussed in earlier chapters and was not completely satisfactory. Although we experimented a bit with alternative taxonomies, we were unable to develop a set of categories that we consider better than the one we used, and we leave this effort to future researchers. Although our effort to apply the taxonomy to empirical data was not entirely satisfactory, we nonetheless believe that the exercise was illuminating.

We found no instances in any of our case studies in which findings from a social experiment were clearly pivotal to a decision to adopt or not adopt a particular social program. Other considerations always appeared more critical. For example, findings from the GAIN program tested in Riverside County, Calif., did directly contribute to the decision in many states to adopt the work-first approach in administering their welfare-to-work programs. However, as we discussed in chapter 9, other factors probably played a more important role in those decisions. In other instances, findings from social experiments seemed to undercut support for the tested policy. For example, to a greater or lesser degree, findings from the Nursing Home Incentive Reimbursement Experiment, income maintenance experiments, and UI bonus experiments weakened support for the programs they tested. This, however, is a type of use; negative, as well as positive, findings from social experiments can make an important contribution to decisionmaking. Nonetheless, the findings from these experiments did not seem to be the determining reason the tested programs were not implemented. Other factors again appeared to be more important.

Even though findings from social experiments are rarely decisive in determining whether or not a program is adopted, it is evident from our case studies that they are, in fact, used, often in a variety of ways and sometimes in quite important ways. Indeed, although use of the Nursing Home Incentive Reimbursement Experiment was minimal (only three minor instances of use were uncovered), the other experiments we studied were used extensively and in a variety of ways. Overall, we found examples of all eight types of use in our typology. Although the experiments we studied were often used persuasively to support arguments for policies that were already favored for other reasons, we also found many instances of pre-decision (formative) use.

Specifically, examples of most of the types of use in the taxonomy were uncovered by the case studies of the income maintenance experiments and the welfare-to-work experiments. Although the policy tested by the income maintenance experiments was never adopted, it does not appear that findings from the experiments played a critical role in this outcome. However, arguably, the experiments may have contributed importantly to subsequent policies intended to move welfare recipients off the rolls and into jobs by demonstrating that, even when the reductions in hours of work that result from transfer programs are modest, each dollar of cash assistance increases the incomes of beneficiaries by considerably less than a dollar. The findings of the welfare-to-work experiments were used at both the federal and the state levels. At the federal level, the findings had a strong influence on the design of the Family Support Act of 1988, but played only a minor role in the design of the more important legislation embodied in the Personal Responsibility and Work Opportunity Reconciliation Act of 1996. The findings lent support to state use of mandatory welfare-to-work programs and a work-first approach and played a role in the way various states designed the specifics of their welfare-to-work programs. They also may have contributed to the adoption of time limits and the devolution of welfare programs to the states. Other factors also played major roles in promoting these policies, however.

Although use of the UI bonus experiments was far less extensive than either the income maintenance or the welfare-to-work experiments, the UI bonus experiments did affect policy, albeit indirectly. For example, they contributed to the adoption of worker profiling and policies intended to encourage self-employment among the unemployed. Moreover, although the tested policy was never adopted by the UI system, bonuses have now become part of the policy universe as a result of the experiments.

A frequent mechanism through which social experiments influence the policy process is the incorporation of findings from social experiments into microsimulation models. In fact, experiments examined in four of our five case studies contributed to such models. These micro-simulation models are then used to help refine the design of policy proposals, which, of course, may or may not ultimately be accepted.

Findings from social experiments frequently end up being used in ways that are unforeseen by those initiating them. For example, the use of findings from social experiments in microsimulation models has rarely been anticipated. Other examples include the adaptation by the national AFDC program of retrospective accounting and recipient monthly reporting requirements, administrative procedures that were originally developed for purposes of conducting the New Jersey Income Maintenance Experiment, and the use of data from the UI bonus experiments to develop a worker profiling system for use in administering the UI program. Interestingly, the fact that social experiments rely on random assignment was not important in these particular instances of use, nor in many other instances.

A final form of use that is worth mentioning here is that one experiment often begets several others. For example, the Gary and Seattle-Denver Income Maintenance Experiments and several experimental tests of monthly reporting and retrospective accounting all received funding as a result of the New Jersey Income Maintenance Experiment. Similarly, findings from the New Jersey and Illinois UI bonus experiments resulted in a decision to fund more elaborate bonus experiments in Washington and Pennsylvania and also motivated the Department of Labor to test other types of policies through experiments (for example, the Life-Long Learning Experiment in Baltimore).

How Do the Characteristics of Social Experiments Affect Their Use?

Table 10.1 summarizes our major conclusions on the effects that five key characteristics of social experiments had on the manner and extent to which the experiments included in each of our case studies were used. The characteristics are drawn from those emphasized in the knowledge-utilization literature; each is discussed in some detail in chapter 3. The entries found in each cell in table 10.1 are discussed in detail in the case study chapters.

Because of the lag between initiating an experiment and obtaining findings from it, in certain respects timeliness may be viewed as the most important of the five utilization characteristics. If findings from an experiment do not become available in a timely manner, their use is likely to be seriously impeded. As mentioned earlier, we found no instances in which findings from social experiments placed a tested policy on the policy agenda. Unfortunately, an experiment is often initiated when an issue seems to be "hot," but findings from it do not become available until well after the issue has cooled down and the policy agenda has moved

Table 10.1. *Utilization Factors*

	Definitiveness	Timeliness	Communication and visibility	Generalizability	Relevance
RAND health insurance experiment (HIE)	Little controversy regarding the effect of cost sharing on use; somewhat more controversy (but still less than marital stability findings in IME) regarding impact of cost-sharing on health outcomes.	By the time results were available, national health policy had largely left the policy agenda. However, it returned at the start of the Clinton administration. HIE results were viewed as best available data at that time, despite their age.	Widely communicated through academic journals, as well as frequent congressional testimony.	Response surface experiment. Incorporated into microsimulation models. Multiple sites.	None of the different insurance plans corresponded directly to specific national health insurance plans that were being considered by policymakers.
Nursing home incentive reimbursement experiment	Definitiveness of findings was never in question, but findings weak and inconclusive. Didn't support adoption of tested policy.	Tested policy never has reached the policy agenda.	Little effort to publicize. Experiment small and almost invisible.	Black box experiment, no replication, one site.	Addressed some germane issues, but there was little interest in incentive schemes such as those tested (regulation preferred).
Income maintenance experiments (IMEs)	Findings didn't especially support adoption of NIT. Labor supply findings	Findings became dated over time; weren't available when political climate for NITs	Large, highly visible experiments. Communication of findings to	Response surface experiments. Microsimulation used to facilitate	Focus somewhat tangential to the major policy concerns, such as

(continued)

Table 10.1. *Utilization Factors (Continued)*

	Definitiveness	*Timeliness*	*Communication and visibility*	*Generalizability*	*Relevance*
	generally viewed as definite by policymakers. Marital stability findings highly controversial.	was best. Still, they were available in time for the Carter PBJI proposal.	policymakers non-systematic and sporadic. Yet key findings were widely known.	generalization. Multiple sites.	work requirements and reducing the size of the welfare rolls.
UI bonus experiment	Findings viewed as definitive, but did not strongly support adoption of UI bonuses.	Findings became available well after the political climate for bonuses was most favorable.	Experiments fairly visible. Well known among pertinent policymakers. Concerted effort made to publicize experiments and communicate their findings.	Response surface experiments (more or less). Findings incorporated into simulation models. Multiple sites.	Addressed important issues concerning UI costs and trust fund solvency. But tested only one policy instrument, which was of limited relevance to state UI policies.
Welfare-to-work experiments	Key findings viewed as definitive. Viewed as supportive of policies that have been adopted, except for time limits.	Findings became available while still highly pertinent to policy. But they have become outdated over time. Still, they were used even in the 1990s.	Highly visible and effectively communicated.	Tested diverse treatments. Were used to obtain cost projections and in stimulations. But black box design was important limitation to generalizability. Multiple sites.	Findings initially highly relevant. Became less relevant as block grants, time limits, and fiscal incentives became more important, but still remained germane.

elsewhere. As indicated in table 10.1, this is precisely what occurred in the case of the UI bonus experiments.

It seems to be largely a matter of luck whether findings from an experiment are available at a time the tested policy is still on the policy agenda. For example, findings from the RAND Health Insurance Experiment, the income maintenance experiments, and the welfare-to-work experiments were all used to help formulate policy. However, the RAND Health Insurance Experiment was fielded so that it could be used in developing national health insurance, but that topic was no longer on the policy agenda at the time the experiment was finished. Nonetheless, the experiment proved useful when the Clinton administration was formulating national health policy years later. Similarly, results from the income maintenance experiments were not available when the Nixon administration unsuccessfully introduced legislation for a national negative income tax (NIT) program, but they were used to help develop a quite different negative income tax plan during the Carter administration almost a decade later. The welfare-to-work experiments were completed at almost the perfect time for use in developing the Family Support Act. However, when the experiments were being fielded in the early 1980s, no one knew that legislation of this sort would be considered in 1988.

Even if a tested program does reach the policy agenda, the program being considered is likely to differ in important specifics from the one that was tested. For example, the negative income tax plan proposed by the Carter administration included a work requirement, a provision that was not tested by any of the four income maintenance experiments. Indeed, our case studies suggest that because of shifts in the policy agenda, as well as social and economic changes, even when findings from social experiments are initially timely, they become obsolete over time. As a result, the welfare-to-work experiments played a much more important role in helping formulate the Family Support Act of 1988 than the Personal Responsibility and Work Opportunity Reconciliation Act of 1996.

Timeliness also strongly influences perceived relevance, another of the utilization factors. As might be expected, findings from social experiments are most likely to be used in the policy process if they address what policymakers view as their central concerns. Those concerns, however, may change over time. For example, as findings from the welfare-to-work experiments became available during the 1980s, policymakers initially viewed them as relevant; but they became increasingly seen as less relevant during the 1990s, as new issues not addressed by the experiments (for example, time limits, block grants, and fiscal incentives for welfare recipients) began to take center stage. Consequently, new experiments were initiated to address some of these issues.

Perhaps the major constraint on the policy relevance of social experiments is that they can test only a limited number of policies, and the policies selected may not be the ones of greatest interest to policymakers or the general public. For example, one reason the Nursing Home Incentive Reimbursement Experiment attracted little attention was that direct regulation was viewed as a more appropriate policy tool for mitigating perceived problems at nursing homes than incentive schemes, such as the ones that were tested. Similarly, the UI bonus experiments tested a policy instrument that was appealing to economists but not necessarily attractive to policymakers responsible for operating state unemployment insurance systems. In hindsight, the goals of the negative income tax plans that were tested by the income maintenance experiments (i.e., to guarantee a minimum income for all households regardless of their work effort, while minimizing inefficiency) were very much out of sync with the sorts of programs implied by the objectives of much of the public (which was to reduce the welfare rolls by putting as many welfare recipients as possible into jobs).

Our case studies indicate that policymakers usually view findings from social experiments as definitive—that is, they accept them as valid—even if analysts quibble over them. Indeed, perhaps because of the use of random assignment, there seem to be relatively few instances in which findings from social experiments engender serious controversy among analysts. The only examples that we found in our case studies involved the marital stability findings from the Seattle-Denver Income Maintenance Experiment and (to a lesser degree) findings from the RAND Health Insurance Experiment on the impact of cost sharing on health outcomes. Consequently, perceived lack of definitiveness does not seem to affect whether findings from social experiments are used. The only possible exception that we found occurred at the time the Nixon Family Assistance Program was being considered by Congress, when preliminary findings from the New Jersey Income Maintenance Experiment were released "prematurely."

Even if findings from social experiments are viewed as definitive or valid, as already discussed, policymakers do not necessarily see the findings as supportive of the policies they test. Of the five experiments or sets of experiments listed in table 10.1, only the welfare-to-work experiments produced findings that actually encouraged adoption of the policies that were tested. The UI bonus experiments and the Nursing Home Incentive Reimbursement Experiment produced measured effects that policymakers did not view as sufficiently large and promising to warrant adoption of the tested programs. If anything, the labor supply and marital stability findings from the income maintenance experiments probably discouraged adoption of a negative income tax program, although the influence of these findings on policy appears to be modest.

Of the experiments examined in our five case studies, only the welfare-to-work and the UI bonus experiments appear to have benefited from systematic thought about communicating findings and a systematic effort to communicate them. Nonetheless, the appropriate policymakers also seem to have been well aware of findings from the RAND Health Insurance Experiment and the income maintenance experiments. Results from those large and prominent experiments appear to have been sufficiently, if not systematically, communicated through a combination of journal articles, evaluation reports, the media, briefing, meetings, congressional testimony, and word of mouth. Only findings from the Nursing Home Incentive Reimbursement Experiment appear to have been unknown to policymakers. This experiment was so small that it was scarcely visible. Had the experiment been replicated several times, however, its smallness might have been overcome. For example, findings from a series of very small experiments that tested job clubs (programs that used peer reinforcement to help disadvantaged persons find jobs) during the 1970s became quite well known.[1] However, unlike the first job club experiment, findings from the Nursing Home Incentive Reimbursement Experiment were not sufficiently promising to warrant replication.

By itself, a perception by policymakers of a lack of generalizability of experimental findings (like a perception of lack of definitiveness in the findings or a lack of effort at communicating them) does not seem to impede their use very much. Our case studies suggest that policymakers will use whatever information is at hand if they believe it is germane to their purposes. It is true that findings from response surface experiments (such as the RAND Health Insurance Experiment, the income maintenance experiments, and the UI bonus experiments) are more readily incorporated into microsimulation models than are black box experiments and that use of such models greatly facilitates applying the findings to new populations, time periods, and programs. Nonetheless, findings from a series of black box experiments that test policy variations in a number of different sites (for example, the welfare-to-work experiments) may be viewed by those who use them as at least as generalizable as response surface experiments.

How Does the Policy Environment Influence the Use of Social Experiments?

As discussed in chapter 3, Carol Weiss (1983) provides a useful framework for looking at the way the policy environment influences the use of social experiments. She hypothesizes that new information from policy research, such as that provided by a social experiment, is likely to be used only if it is compatible with prevailing ideologies, the self-interests of decisionmakers, and other sources of information on the topic examined. Table 10.2 summarizes our conclusions on the compatibility of findings from the experiments examined in each of the five case studies with the three dimensions of the policy environment emphasized by Weiss. Details on these conclusions for the individual experiments can be found in the case study chapters.

Only the programs tested and the findings from the welfare-to-work experiments seem to have been highly compatible with the existing policy environment at the time they became available. Specifically, those experiments tested programs that were intended to result in tax savings and reductions in welfare dependence by helping welfare recipients obtain employment, goals that appear consistent with the ideology of many policymakers and much of the public, as well as in the self-interests of middle-class taxpayers. Findings from these experiments indicated that, at least to some extent, the tested programs succeeded in meeting their objectives. These findings were generally consistent with findings from other sources—for example, nonexperimental evaluations and research, anecdotal information, and common sense.

Consistent with Weiss's hypothesis, of all the experiments we examined, the welfare-to-work experiments are the ones that appear to have had the greatest influence on the policy process. Ironically, however, even though these experiments did have important effects on policy, their role was nonetheless limited by their very compatibility with prevailing ideology, existing political interests, and information from other sources. In particular, many policymakers already viewed the programs tested by the welfare-to-work experiments as attractive on other grounds. Find-

Table 10.2. *Policy Environment*

	Ideology	Interests	Information
RAND health insurance experiment	Although ideology has played an important role in policy deliberations regarding health care financing reform, the HIE did not test specific proposals that might have been consistent or inconsistent with prevailing ideology.	Although interests have played an important role in retarding major changes in health care financing, the HIE did not test specific proposals that might have been consistent or inconsistent with particular interests.	Few, if any, alternative sources of information.
Nursing home incentive reimbursement experiment	Government regulation preferred to incentive schemes.	Majority interest was to decrease government spending, something the treatment was unlikely to accomplish.	No alternative source of information existed about the tested treatment.
Income maintenance experiments	Tested treatments inconsistent with the majority ideology of the voting public and Congress.	NITs inconsistent with interests of taxpayers because they would increase government expenditures.	Information from the experiments had to compete with anecdotal information.
UI bonus experiments	Treatment and findings generally consistent with the prevailing ideology. But viewed as inconsistent with fiscal conservatism.	Bonuses inconsistent with interests of unions and small businesses.	Findings consistent with other knowledge sources (but not strong enough to generate support for bonuses).
Welfare-to-work experiments	Findings highly consistent with prevailing ideology, which was to impose obligations on welfare recipients, get them into jobs, and reduce the welfare rolls.	Consistent with interests of taxpayers—result in tax savings.	Generally consistent with information from other sources. Findings were additive to I-I-I. Thus, helped promote welfare-to-work legislation and provided program design information.

Note: NIT = negative income tax.

ings from the experiments simply reinforced that view. Consequently, rather than being pivotal to whether the types of programs they tested were adopted, they were instead used persuasively and in designing these programs. In other words, they aided policymakers in doing what they already wanted to do.

The other experiments that we examined were not especially compatible with the policy environment and, possibly as a result, played a smaller role in the policy process than the welfare-to-work experiments. Nonetheless, it is important to emphasize once again that although they seem to have played a smaller role in the policy process than the welfare-to-work experiments, findings from the income maintenance experiments, the UI bonus experiments, and the RAND Health Insurance Experiment were used in a variety of ways, some of which were important.

The negative income tax plans tested under the income maintenance experiments would have increased the size of the welfare rolls and, hence, were inconsistent with the prevailing ideology that work is good and welfare dependence is bad. Somewhat similarly, the Nursing Home Incentive Reimbursement Experiment tested a policy that would have relied on incentive schemes to improve the management of nursing homes, whereas direct regulation was more consistent with the prevailing ideology. Both negative income tax programs and nursing home incentive schemes were also inconsistent with taxpayer self-interests because they would have increased government expenditures. The fact that the policies tested by the income maintenance experiments and the Nursing Home Incentive Reimbursement Experiment were incompatible with prevailing ideology and the interest of taxpayers probably played a role in the fact that these policies were not adopted. However, as previously discussed, the characteristics of the experiments themselves were probably also important. Moreover, their findings were not especially supportive of the policies they tested.

Weiss's framework is probably less useful for examining the policy use of the RAND Health Insurance Experiment and the UI bonus experiments. The RAND Health Insurance Experiment was, of course, never intended as a test of a specific program or policy that could or could not be adopted, but instead had the objective of providing information useful to designing health insurance policies. However, there appears to be nothing inherently incompatible with prevailing ideology or the interest of the middle class that kept information from the RAND Health Insurance Experiment from being used once it became available. Moreover, its use was also encouraged because there was little information from other sources to compete with it.

Neither the treatment tested by nor the findings from the UI bonus experiments strongly conflicted with prevailing ideology, middle-class interests, or information from other sources. As indicated in table 10.2, there were some inconsistencies with the interests of unions and small businesses, but they certainly were not enough by themselves to keep the tested programs from being adopted. Much more important is the fact that although findings from these experiments indicated that reemployment bonuses would help get claimants back to work sooner and would benefit society as a whole, the experimental evidence also suggested that they would be unlikely to produce cost savings for the UI system. If fiscal conservatism is viewed as an ideology that has prevailed in the United States since the 1980s, then the finding is in conflict with that ideology. In any event, the finding that adopting bonuses would probably not result in cost savings for the UI system greatly dampened any political support that bonuses might otherwise have been able to muster.

Some Lessons for Conducting Social Experiments

Several lessons about the way social experiments should be designed and conducted flow rather naturally from the stated conclusions. First, the people included in the experiment target groups typically were disadvantaged in some way—for example, they were poor, unemployed, or in bad health. Yet the ideology and interests of the middle class play a crucial role in whether and how findings from social experiments are used. This fact suggests there is little point in testing a program or policy in a social experiment that is obviously inconsistent with the ideology and interests of the middle class. For example, a program that would greatly increase government expenditures is unlikely to be adopted regardless of the experimental findings.

A second important lesson follows from the conclusion that findings from social experiments are, perhaps, more likely than not to undercut political support for the policies they test (or at least to do little to promote those policies). Of course, whether findings from a specific experiment will do this cannot be known in advance. Indeed, providing information pertinent to policy decisions is the primary rationale for conducting social experiments. Still, this conclusion suggests that more thought should be given in advance of running an experiment to what its goals are and whether the findings are likely to advance those goals. In some cases, microsimulation can be used to help determine whether a particular experiment is likely to meet its goals.[2]

A third important lesson follows from the importance of timeliness in determining whether and how findings from an experiment will be used. Given the inevitable long delay in obtaining findings from social experiments, and the fact that after the findings become available, they become increasingly obsolete over time, social experiments should be used for examining issues that are likely to have a long shelf life.

One important way to extend the shelf life of experimental findings is to incorporate them into microsimulation models. Indeed, such models provided a key mechanism for using findings from social experiments in four of our five case studies. To the extent possible, then, experiments should be designed so that their findings can be readily incorporated into simulation models. Response surface experiments are especially valuable for this purpose.

Finally, our case studies highlight the importance of having a plan to enhance the visibility of social experiments and make the relevant policymakers aware of findings from them. Although this was rarely done in the case of the earlier social experiments, and many researchers are reluctant to promote the policy use of their findings, it does seem to be a lesson that many evaluators are learning over time.

NOTES

1. For brief summaries of each experiment, see David Greenberg and Mark Shroder (1997, 253–56, 267–70, 303–7, 309–11, and 401–4).

2. For an example of this, see Greenberg et al. (1995).

References

Aaron, Henry J. 1985. "Comment." In *Social Experimentation,* edited by Jerry A. Hausman and David A. Wise (1–10). Chicago: University of Chicago Press.

———. 1990. "Social Science Research and Policy." *Journal of Human Resources* 25(2): 276–80.

———. 1991. *Serious and Unstable Condition: Financing America's Health Care.* Washington, D.C.: Brookings Institution.

———. 1996. "The Problem That Won't Go Away." In *The Problem That Won't Go Away: Reforming U.S. Health Care Financing,* edited by Henry J. Aaron (1–12). Washington, D.C.: Brookings Institution.

Aaron, Henry J., and John E. Todd. 1978. "The Use of Income Maintenance Experiment Findings in Public Policy, 1977–1978." In *Proceedings of the 31st Annual Meeting* (46–56). Champaign, Ill.: Industrial Relations Research Association.

Anderson, Patricia. 1992. "Time-Varying Effects of Recall Expectation, a Reemployment Bonus, and Job Counseling on Unemployment Durations." *Journal of Labor Economics* 10(1): 99–115.

Bane, Mary Jo, and David T. Ellwood. 1983. *The Dynamics of Dependence: The Routes to Self-Sufficiency.* Cambridge, Mass.: Urban Systems Engineering, Inc.

Baum, Erica. 1991. "When the Witch Doctors Agree." *Journal of Policy Analysis and Management* 10:(4) 603–15.

Baumgartner, Frank R., and Bryan D. Jones. 1993. *Agendas and Instability in American Politics.* Chicago: University of Chicago Press.

Bawden, D. Lee, and William S. Harrar, eds. 1977. "Final Report of the Rural Income Maintenance Experiment." Madison: Institute for Research on Poverty, University of Wisconsin.

Berg, Mark R., Jeffrey L. Brudney, T. D. Fuller, Donald N. Michael, and B. K. Roth. 1978. *Factors Affecting Utilization of Technology Assessment Studies in Policy-Making.* Ann

Arbor: Center for Research on Utilization of Scientific Knowledge, University of Michigan.

Berlin, Gordon, Wendy Bancroft, David Card, Winston Lin, and Philip K. Robbins. 1998. *Do Work Incentives Have Unintended Consequences? Measuring "Entry Effects" in the Self-Sufficiency Project.* New York: Manpower Demonstration Research Corporation.

Betson, David, and David Greenberg. 1983. "Uses of Microsimulation in Applied Poverty Research." In *Applied Policy Research,* edited by Richard Goldstein and Stephen M. Sacks (175–90). Totowa, N.J.: Rowman and Allanheld.

Betson, David, David Greenberg, and Richard Kasten. 1980. "A Micro-Simulation Model for Analyzing Alternative Welfare Reform Proposals: An Application to the Program for Better Jobs and Income." In *Microeconomic Simulation Models for Public Policy Analysis,* edited by Robert H. Haveman and Kevin Hollenbeck (153–88). New York: Academic Press.

Beyer, Janice M., and Harrison M. Trice. 1982. "The Utilization Process: A Conceptual Framework and Synthesis of Empirical Findings." *Administrative Science Quarterly* 27(4): 591–622.

Bloom, Dan. 1997. *After AFDC: Welfare-to-Work Choices and Challenges for States.* New York: Manpower Demonstration Research Corporation.

Boardman, Anthony E., David H. Greenberg, Aidan R. Vining, and David L. Weimer. 2000. *Cost Benefit Analysis, Concepts and Practices,* 2d ed. Paramus, N.J.: Prentice Hall.

Boeckmann, Margaret E. 1976. "Policy Impacts of the New Jersey Income Maintenance Experiment." *Policy Sciences* 7(1): 53–76.

Boruch, Robert F. 1997. *Randomized Experiments for Planning and Evaluation.* Thousand Oaks, Calif.: Sage Publications.

Bowler, M. Kenneth, Robert T. Kudrle, and Theodore R. Marmor. 1977. "The Political Economy of National Health Insurance: Policy Analysis and Political Evaluation." *Journal of Health Politics, Policy and Law* 2(1): 100–33.

Bozeman, Barry. 1986. "The Credibility of Policy Analysis: Between Method and Use." *Policy Studies Journal* 14(4): 519–39.

Bradbury, Katherine L. 1986. "Discussion of 'Non–Labor-Supply Responses to the Income Maintenance Experiments' by Eric A. Hanushek." In *Lessons from the Income Maintenance Experiments,* edited by Alicia H. Munnell (122–25). Boston: Federal Reserve Bank of Boston.

Brandon, William P. 1995. "A Large-Scale Social Science Experiment in Health Finance: Findings, Significance, and Value." *Journal of Health Politics, Policy and Law* 20(4): 1051–61.

Brook, Robert H., John E. Ware Jr., William H. Rogers, Emmett B. Keeler, Allyson R. Davies, Cathy A. Donald, George A. Goldberg, Kathleen N. Lohr, Patricia C. Masthay, and Joseph P. Newhouse. 1983. "Does Free Care Improve Adults' Health? Results from a Randomized Controlled Trial." *New England Journal of Medicine* 309(23): 1426–34.

Bryk, Anthony, ed. 1983. *Stakeholder-based Evaluation.* San Francisco: Jossey-Bass.

Buchanan, Robert J., Peter R. Madel, and Dan Persons. 1991. "Medicaid Payment Policies for Nursing Home Care: A National Survey." *Health Care Financing Review* 13(1): 55–72.

Burghardt, John A. 1982. *Impact of a Monthly Retrospective Reporting Requirement on AFDC-Benefit Payment: Evidence from the Second Year of the Colorado Monthly Reporting Experiment.* Princeton, N.J.: Mathematica Policy Research, Inc.

Burke, Vincent J., and Vee Burke. 1974. *Nixon's Good Deed: Welfare Reform.* New York: Columbia University Press.

Burman, John M. 1994. "Judicial Review of Medicaid Hospital and Nursing Home Reimbursement Methodologies under the Boren Amendment." *Annals of Health Law* 3: 55–79.

Burtless, Gary. 1986. "The Work Response to a Guaranteed Income: A Survey of Experimental Evidence." In *Lessons from the Income Maintenance Experiments,* edited by Alicia H. Munnell (22–52). Boston: Federal Reserve Bank of Boston.

———. 1989. "The Effect of Welfare Reform on Employment, Earnings, and Income." In *Policy for the 1990s,* edited by Phoebe H. Cottingham and David T. Ellwood (103–40). Cambridge: Harvard University Press.

———. 1995. "The Case for Randomized Field Trials in Economic and Policy Research." *Journal of Economic Perspectives* 9(2): 63–84.

Burtless, Gary, and David Greenberg. 1982. "Inferences Concerning Labor Supply Behavior Based on Limited Duration Experiments." *American Economic Review* 72(3): 489–97.

Burtless, Gary, and Larry L. Orr. 1986. "Are Classical Experiments Needed for Manpower Policy?" *Journal of Human Resources* 21(4): 606–39.

Cain, Glen G., and Harold W. Watts, eds. 1973. *Income Maintenance and Labor Supply.* Chicago: Rand McNally.

———. 1986. "The Issues of Marital Stability and Family Composition and the Income Maintenance Experiments." In *Lessons from the Income Maintenance Experiments,* edited by Alicia H. Munnell (60–93). Boston: Federal Reserve Bank of Boston.

Cain, Glen G., and Douglas A. Wissoker. 1990. "A Reanalysis of Marital Stability in the Seattle-Denver Income Maintenance Experiment." *American Journal of Sociology* 95(5): 1235–69.

Caplan, Nathan, Andrea Morrison, and Russell J. Stambaugh. 1975. *The Use of Social Science Knowledge in Policy Decisions at the National Level: A Report to Respondents.* Ann Arbor: Center for Research on Utilization of Scientific Knowledge, Institute for Social Research, University of Michigan.

Card, David E., Philip K. Robins, and Winston Lin. 1997. *How Important Are "Entry Effects" in Financial Incentive Programs for Welfare Recipients?* Ottawa, Ontario: Social Research and Demonstration Corporation.

CBO. See U.S. Congressional Budget Office.

Chang, Fisher. 1996. "Evaluating the Impact of Mandatory Work Programs on Two-Parent Welfare Caseloads." Unpublished doctoral dissertation. Baltimore: University of Maryland, Baltimore County.

Citro, Constance F., and Eric A. Hanushek, eds. 1991. *Improving Information for Social Policy Decisions: The Uses of Microsimulation Modeling,* Vol. 1. Washington, D.C.: National Academy Press.

Cogan, John F. 1978. *Negative Income Taxation and Labor Supply: New Evidence from the New Jersey-Pennsylvania Experiment.* R-2155-HEW. Santa Monica, Calif.: The RAND Corporation.

Coleman, James. 1979. "The Uses of Social Science in the Development of Public Policy." Unpublished manuscript.

Coursey, David H. 1990. "Information, Credibility, and Decision Outcomes: An Experimental Examination of Credibility Logic." Ph.D. diss., Syracuse University, N.Y.

Cox, Gary B. 1977. "Managerial Style: Implications for the Utilization of Program Evaluation." *Evaluation Quarterly* 1(3): 499–508.

Coyle, Dennis J., and Aaron Wildavsky. 1986. "Social Experimentation in the Face of Formidable Fables." In *Lessons from the Income Maintenance Experiments,* edited by Alicia H. Munnell (167–93). Boston: Federal Reserve Bank of Boston.

Danziger, Sheldon. 2001. "Welfare Reform Policy from Nixon to Clinton: What Role for Social Science?" In *Social Science and Policy-Making,* edited by David L. Featherman and Maris A. Vinovskis (137–64). Ann Arbor: University of Michigan Press.

Davidson, Carl, and Stephen Woodbury. 1990. "Modelling the Effects of a Reemployment Bonus under Variable Potential Benefit Duration: New Results from the Illinois Claimant Bonus Experiment." Paper presented at annual conference of the Association for Public Policy Analysis and Management, San Francisco, Oct. 18–20.

———. 1993. "The Displacement Effect of Reemployment Bonus Programs." *Journal of Labor Economics* 11(4): 575–605.

———. 1996. "Unemployment Insurance and Unemployment: Implications of the Reemployment Bonus Experiments." W. E. Upjohn Institute for Employment Research Working Paper 96-44. Kalamazoo, Mich.: W. E. Upjohn Institute for Employment Research.

Decker, Paul T. 1994. "The Impact of Reemployment Bonuses on Insured Unemployment in the New Jersey and Illinois Reemployment Bonus Experiments." *Journal of Human Resources* 29(3): 718–41.

Decker, Paul T., and Christopher J. O'Leary. 1995. "Evaluating Pooled Evidence from the Reemployment Bonus Experiments." *Journal of Human Resources* 30(3): 534–50.

Dehejia, Rajeev H., and Sadek Wahba. 1999. "Causal Effects in Nonexperimental Studies: Re-Evaluating the Evaluation of Training Programs." *Journal of the American Statistical Association* 94(448): 1053–62.

Demkovich, Linda E. 1978. "Good News and Bad News for Welfare Reform." *National Journal* 10(4): 2061–63.

Dickinson, Katherine P., and Richard W. West. 1983. "Impacts of Counseling and Education Subsidy Programs." *Final Report of the Seattle-Denver Income Maintenance Experiment,* Vol. 1, *Design and Report Part IV.* Menlo Park, Calif.: SRI International.

Dunstan, S. M., and S. Kerachsky. 1988. "Design of the Pennsylvania Reemployment Bonus Demonstration Program." Report prepared for U.S. Department of Labor, Employment and Training Administration, Unemployment Insurance Service. Unpublished manuscript. Princeton, N.J.: Mathematica Policy Research, Inc.

Eden, Jill. 1994. "From the Congressional Office of Technology Assessment." *Journal of the American Medical Association* 272(1): 12.

Feldman, Martha S. 1989. *Order without Design: Information Production and Policy Making.* Stanford, Calif.: Stanford University Press.

Fink, Gary M., and Hugh Davis Graham. 1998. "Introduction." In *The Carter Presidency: Policy Choices in the Post-New Deal Era,* edited by Gary M. Fink and Hugh David Graham (1–6). Lawrence: University Press of Kansas.

Fisher, Ronald. 1925. *Statistical Methods for Research Workers.* London: Oliver and Boyd.

———. 1935. *The Design of Experiments.* London: Oliver and Boyd.

Fox, Daniel M. 1990. "Health Policy and the Politics of Research in the United States." *Journal of Health Politics, Policy and Law* 15(3): 481–99.

Fraker, Thomas, and Rebecca Maynard. 1987. "The Adequacy of Comparison Group Designs for Evaluations of Employment-Related Programs." *Journal of Human Resources* 22(2): 194–227.

Freedman, Stephen, Jean Knab, Lisa Gennetian, David Navarro. 2000. *The Los Angeles Jobs-First GAIN Evaluation: Final Report on a Work First Program in a Major Urban Center.* New York: Manpower Demonstration Research Corporation.

Friedlander, Daniel, and Gary Burtless. 1995. *Five Years After: The Long-Term Effects of Welfare-to-Work Programs.* New York: Russell Sage Foundation.

Friedlander, Daniel, and Philip K. Robins. 1995. "Evaluating Program Evaluations: New Evidence on Commonly Used Nonexperimental Methods." *American Economic Review* 85(4): 923–37.

Friedlander, Daniel, David H. Greenberg, and Philip K. Robins. 1997. "Evaluating Government Training Programs for the Economically Disadvantaged." *Journal of Economic Literature* 35(4): 1809–55.

Friedman, Milton. 1962. *Capitalism and Freedom.* Chicago: University of Chicago Press.

Fuchs, Victor R. 1993. *The Future of Health Policy.* Cambridge, Mass.: Harvard University Press.

GAO. See U.S. General Accounting Office.

Garfinkel, Irwin, Charles F. Manski, and Charles Michalopoulos. 1992. "Micro Experiments and Macro Effects." In *Evaluating Welfare and Training Programs,* edited by Charles F. Manski and Irwin Garfinkel (253–73). Cambridge, Mass.: Harvard University Press.

Ginzburg, Eli, with Miriam Ostrow. 1994. *The Road to Reform: The Future of Health Care in America.* New York: Free Press.

Goode, William J. 1966. "Marital Satisfaction and Instability: A Cross-Cultural Class Analysis of Divorce Rates." In *Class, Status, and Power,* 2d ed., edited by Reinhard Bendix and Seymour Martin Lipset (377–87). New York: Free Press. (Originally published in 1962 in *International Social Science Journal* 14(3): 507–26.)

Gramlich, Edward M. 1981. *Benefit-Cost Analysis of Government Programs.* Englewood Cliffs, N.J.: Prentice Hall.

Greenberg, David H. 1992. "Conceptual Issues in Cost-Benefit Analysis of Welfare-to-Work Programs." *Contemporary Policy Issues* 10(4): 51–64.

Greenberg, David H., and Marvin Kosters. 1973. "Income Guarantees and the Working Poor: The Effect of Income-Maintenance Programs on the Hours of Work of Male Family Heads." In *Income Maintenance and Labor Supply,* edited by Glen G. Cain and Harold W. Watts (14–101). Chicago: Rand McNally.

Greenberg, David H., and Marvin B. Mandell. 1991. "Research Utilization in Policymaking: A Tale of Two Series of Social Experiments." *Journal of Policy Analysis and Management* 10(4): 633–56.

Greenberg, David H., and Philip K. Robins. 1986. "The Changing Role of Social Experiments in Policy Analysis." *Journal of Policy Analysis and Management* 5(2): 340–62.

Greenberg, David H., and Mark Shroder. 1997. *Digest of Social Experiments,* 2d ed. Washington, D.C.: Urban Institute Press.

Greenberg, David H., and Michael Wiseman. 1992. *What Did the Work-Welfare Demonstrations Do?* Institute for Research on Poverty Discussion Paper No. 969-92. Madison: Institute for Research on Poverty, University of Wisconsin.

Greenberg, David H., Marvin B. Mandell, and Matt Onstott. 2000. "Evaluation Research and Its Role in State Welfare Policy Formulation." *Journal of Policy Analysis and Management* 19(3): 367–82.

Greenberg, David H., Robert A. Moffitt, and John Friedmann. 1981. "Effects of Under-reporting on the Estimation of Work Effort in the Gary Income Maintenance Experiment." *Review of Economics and Statistics* 63(4): 581–89.

Greenberg, David H., Mark Shroder, and Matthew Onstott. 1999. "The Social Experiment Market." *Journal of Economic Perspectives* 13(3): 157–72.

Greenberg, David H., Charles Michalopoulos, Philip K. Robins, and Robert Wood. 1995. "Making Work Pay for Welfare Recipients." *Contemporary Economic Policy* 13(3): 39–52.

Groeneveld, Lyle P., Michael T. Hannan, and Nancy B. Tuma. 1983. "Marital Stability." In *Final Report of the Seattle-Denver Income Maintenance Experiment*, Vol. 1: *Design and Results Part 2* (259–386). Menlo Park, Calif.: SRI International.

Gueron, Judith M. 1986. *Work Initiatives for Welfare Recipients*. New York: Manpower Demonstration Research Corporation.

———. 1987. *Reforming Welfare with Work*. Ford Foundation Project on Social Welfare and the American Future Occasional Paper No. 2. New York: Ford Foundation.

———. 1990. "Work and Welfare: Lessons on Employment Programs." *Journal of Economic Perspectives* 4(1): 78–98.

Gueron, Judith M., and Edward Pauly. 1991. *From Welfare to Work*. New York: Russell Sage Foundation.

Hacker, Jacob S. 1997. *The Road to Nowhere: The Genesis of President Clinton's Plan for Health Security*. Princeton, N.J.: Princeton University Press.

Haldeman, H. R. 1994. *The Haldeman Diaries: Inside the White House*. New York: G. D. Putnam's Sons.

Hall, Robert E. 1986. "Discussion of 'The Work Response to a Guaranteed Income: A Survey of Experimental Evidence' by Gary Burtless." In *Lessons from the Income Maintenance Experiments*, edited by Alicia H. Munnell (56–59). Boston: Federal Reserve Bank of Boston.

Hamilton, Gayle. 1995. *The JOBS Evaluation: Monthly Participation Rates in Three Sites and Factors Affecting Participation Levels in Welfare-to-Work Programs*. Washington, D.C.: U.S. Department of Health and Human Services, Office of the Assistant Secretary for Planning and Evaluation.

Hamilton, William L. 1985. *Monthly Reporting in the AFDC Program: Executive Summary of Demonstration Results*. Cambridge, Mass.: Abt Associates, Inc.

Hamilton, William L., Nancy R. Burstein, Margaret Hargreaves, David A. Moss, and Michael Walker. 1993. *The New York State Child Assistance Program: Program Impacts, Costs, and Benefits*. Cambridge, Mass.: Abt Associates, Inc.

Hamilton, William L., Nancy R. Burstein, August J. Baker, Alison Earle, Stefanie Gluckman, Laura Peck, and Alan White. 1996. *The New York State Child Assistance Program: Five-Year Impacts, Costs, and Benefits*. Cambridge, Mass.: Abt Associates, Inc.

Hamm, Linda V., Thomas M. Kickham, and Dolores A. Cutler. 1985. "Chapter VI." In *Long-Term Care, Perspectives from Research and Demonstrations*, edited by Ronald J. Vogel and Hans C. Palmer (167–254). Rockville, Md.: Aspen Systems Corporation.

Hannan, Michael T., S. E. Beaver, and Nancy. B. Tuma. 1974. "Income Maintenance Effects on the Making and Breaking of Marriages: Preliminary Analysis of the First Eighteen Months of the Denver Income Maintenance Experiment." Research Memorandum draft. Menlo Park, Calif.: SRI International.

———. 1977. "Income and Marital Events: Evidence from an Income-Maintenance Experiment." *American Journal of Sociology* 82(6): 1186–211.

Hannan, Michael T., Nancy B. Tuma, and Lyle P. Groeneveld. 1978. "Income and Independence Effects on Marital Dissolution: Results from the Seattle and Denver Income Maintenance Experiments." *American Journal of Sociology* 84(10): 611–33.

Hanushek, Eric A. 1986. "Non–Labor-Supply Responses to the Income Maintenance Experiments." In *Lessons from the Income Maintenance Experiments*, edited by Alicia H. Munnell (106–21). Boston: Federal Reserve Bank of Boston.

Haskins, Ron. 1991. "Congress Writes a Law: Research and Welfare Reform." *Journal of Policy Analysis and Management* 10(4): 616–32.

Haveman, Robert H. 1987. *Poverty Policy and Poverty Research: The Great Society and the Social Sciences.* Madison: University of Wisconsin Press.

Heckman, James J. 1992. "Randomization and Social Policy Evaluation." In *Evaluating Welfare and Training Programs*, edited by Charles F. Manski and Irwin Garfinkel (201–30). Cambridge, Mass.: Harvard University Press.

Heckman, James J., and Joseph V. Hotz. 1989. "Choosing among Alternative Non-experimental Methods for Estimating the Impact of Social Programs." *Journal of the American Statistical Association* 84(408): 862–74.

Heckman, James J., and Jeffrey A. Smith. 1995. "Assessing the Case for Social Experiments." *Journal of Economic Perspectives* 9(2): 85–110.

Heckman, James J., Hidehiko Ichimura, and Petra Todd. 1998. "Characterizing Selection Bias Using Experimental Data." *Econometrica* 66(5): 1017–98.

Heclo, Hugh. 1978. "Issue Networks and the Executive Establishment." In *The New American Political System*, edited by Anthony King (87–124). Washington, D.C.: American Enterprise Institute.

HHS. See U.S. Department of Health and Human Services.

Hotz, Joseph V. 1992. "Designing an Evaluation of the Job Training Partnership Act." In *Evaluating Welfare and Training Programs*, edited by Charles F. Manski and Irwin Garfinkel (76–114). Cambridge, Mass.: Harvard University Press.

Hum, Derek, and Wayne Simpson. 1991. *Income Maintenance, Work Effort, and the Canadian Mincome Experiment.* Ottawa, Ontario: Economic Council of Canada.

Jenkins-Smith, Hank C. 1990. *Democratic Politics and Policy Analysis.* Pacific Grove, Calif.: Brooks/Cole Publishing Company.

Johnson, Haynes, and David S. Broder. 1996. *The System: The American Way of Politics at the Breaking Point.* Boston: Little, Brown and Company.

Johnson, Terry R., Daniel H. Klepinger, and Fred B. Dong. 1994. "Caseload Impacts of Welfare Reform." *Contemporary Economic Policy* 12(1): 89–101.

Jones, Brenda J., and Mark R. Meiners. 1986. "Nursing Home Discharges: The Results of an Incentive Reimbursement Experiment." *Long-Term Care Studies Program Research Report*, DHHS Publication No. PHS 86-3399. Bethesda, Md.: U.S. Department of Health and Human Services, National Information Center on Health Services Research and Health Care Technology.

Keeley, Michael C., Philip K. Robins, Robert G. Spiegelman, and Richard W. West. 1978. "The Estimation of Labor-Supply Models Using Experimental Data." *American Economic Review* 68(5): 873–87.

Kehrer, Kenneth C., John F. McDonald, and Robert A. Moffitt. 1980. *Final Report of the Gary Income Maintenance Experiment: Labor Supply*. Princeton, N.J.: Mathematica Policy Research, Inc.

Kemple, James J., Daniel Friedlander, and Veronica Fellerath. 1995. *Florida's Project Independence: Benefits, Costs, and Two-Year Impacts of Florida's JOBS Program*. New York: Manpower Demonstration Research Corporation.

Kennedy, David M. 1987. *California Welfare Reform, Case Study C16-87-782.0*. Cambridge, Mass.: John F. Kennedy School of Government, Harvard University.

Kershaw, David, and Jerilyn Fair. 1976. *The New Jersey Income Maintenance Experiment, Volume I: Operatings, Surveys, and Administration*. New York: Academic Press.

Kingdon, John W. 1984. *Agendas, Alternatives, and Public Policies*. New York: Harper-Collins.

LaLonde, Robert J. 1986. "Evaluating the Econometric Evaluations of Employment and Training Programs with Experimental Data." *American Economic Review* 76(4): 604–20.

LaLonde, Robert J., and Rebecca Maynard. 1987. "How Precise Are Evaluations of Employment and Training Programs? Evidence from a Field Experiment." *Evaluation Review* 11(4): 428–51.

Leuchtenburg, William E. 1998. "Jimmy Carter and the Post-New Deal Presidency." In *The Carter Presidency: Policy Choices in the Post-New Deal Era*, edited by Gary M. Fink and Hugh David Graham (7–28). Lawrence: University Press of Kansas.

Levine, Phillip B. 1993. "Testing Search Theory with Reemployment Bonus Experiments: Cross-Validation of Results from New Jersey and Illinois." *Eastern Economic Journal* 19(2): 125–41.

Leviton, Laura C., and Edward F. X. Hughes. 1981. "Research on the Utilization of Evaluations: A Review and Synthesis." *Evaluation Review* 5(4): 525–48.

Lewis, H. G. 1957. "Hours of Work and Hours of Leisure, in Industrial Relations Research Association." *Proceedings of the Ninth Annual Meeting of the Industrial Relations Research Association* (195–206). Madison, Wisc.: Industrial Relations Research Association.

Light, Paul C. 1999. *The President's Agenda: Domestic Policy Choice from Kennedy to Clinton*, 3d ed. Baltimore, Md.: Johns Hopkins University Press.

Lin, Winston, Stephen Freedman, and Daniel Friedlander. 1995. *GAIN: 4.5-Year Impacts on Employment, Earnings, and AFDC Receipt*. New York: Manpower Demonstration Research Corporation.

Lynn, Lawrence, and David Whitman. 1981. *The President as Policymaker: Jimmy Carter and Welfare Reform*. Philadelphia: Temple University Press.

Majone, Giandomenico. 1989. *Evidence, Argument, and Persuasion in the Policy Process*. New Haven, Conn.: Yale University Press.

Mandell, Marvin B. 1984. "The Design and Selection of Evaluation Studies: A User-Oriented Framework and Its Assessment." *Knowledge* 5(4): 419–45.

———. 1988. "The Consequences of Improving Dissemination in Garbage-Can Decision Processes: Insights from a Simulation Model." *Knowledge* 9(3): 343–61.

————. 1989. "A Simulation-Based Assessment of the Value of Enhancing the Credibility of Policy Analysis." *Knowledge in Society: The International Journal of Knowledge Transfer* 2(2): 39–56.

Mandell, Marvin B., and Vicki L. Sauter. 1984. "Approaches to the Study of Information Utilization in Public Agencies: Problems and Pitfalls." *Knowledge* 6(2): 145–64.

Manski, Charles F. 1995. *Learning about Social Programs from Experiments with Random Assignment of Treatments.* Institute for Research on Poverty Discussion Paper No. 1061-95. Madison: Institute for Research on Poverty, University of Wisconsin.

Manski, Charles F., and Irwin Garfinkel. 1992. "Introduction." In *Evaluating Welfare and Training Programs,* edited by Charles F. Manski and Irwin Garfinkel (1–22). Cambridge, Mass.: Harvard University Press.

March, James G., and Johan P. Olsen. 1976. *Ambiguity and Choice in Organizations.* Bergen, Norway: Universitetsforlaget.

McCall, W. A. 1923. *How to Experiment in Education.* New York: Macmillan.

Mechanic, David. 1993. "Social Research in Health and the American Sociopolitical Context: The Changing Fortunes of Medical Sociology." *Social Science and Medicine* 36(2): 95–102.

Meiners, Mark R., Phyllis Thorburn, Pamela C. Roddy, and Brenda J. Jones. 1985. *Nursing Home Admissions: The Results of an Incentive Reimbursement Experiment Long-Term Care Studies Program Research Report.* DHHS Publication No. PHS 86-3397. Bethesda, Md.: U.S. Department of Health and Human Services, National Information Center on Health Services Research and Health Care Technology.

Meyer, Bruce D. 1988. "Reemployment Bonuses for UI Recipients: Implications of the Illinois Experiments for Theories of Unemployment and Policy Design." NBER Working Paper No. 2783. Cambridge, Mass.: National Bureau of Economic Research.

————. 1995. "Lessons from the U.S. Unemployment Insurance Experiments." *Journal of Economic Literature* 33(1): 91–131.

Meyer, Jack A. 1986. "Social Programs and Social Policy." In *Perspectives on the Reagan Years,* edited by John L. Palmer (65–89). Washington, D.C.: Urban Institute Press.

Michael, Robert T. 1986. "Discussion of 'Non–Labor-Supply Responses to the Income Maintenance Experiments' by Eric A. Hanushek." In *Lessons from the Income Maintenance Experiments,* edited by Alicia H. Munnell (127–30). Boston: Federal Reserve Bank of Boston.

Mintzberg, Henry. 1971. "Managerial Work: Analysis from Observation." *Management Science* 18(2): B97–B110.

Moffitt, Robert A. 1992. "Incentive Effects of the U.S. Welfare System: A Review." *Journal of Economic Literature* 30(1): 1–61.

————. 1996. "The Effect of Employment and Training Programs on Entry and Exit from the Welfare Caseload." *Journal of Policy Analysis and Management* 15(1): 32–50.

Moffitt, Robert A., and Kenneth C. Kehrer. 1981. "The Effects of Tax and Transfer Programs on Labor Supply." In *Research in Labor Economics,* edited by R. Ehrenberg (103-50). Greenwich, Conn.: JAI Press.

Moffitt, Robert A., and Walter Nicholson. 1982. "The Effect of Unemployment Insurance on Unemployment: The Case of Federal Supplemental Benefits." *Review of Economics and Statistics* 64(1): 1–11.

Moynihan, Daniel P. 1973. *The Politics of a Guaranteed Income: The Nixon Administration and the Family Assistance Plan.* New York: Random House.

Mundel, David S. 1985. "The Use of Information in the Policy Process: Are Social-Policy Experiments Worthwhile?" In *Social Experimentation,* edited by Jerry A. Hausman and David A. Wise (251–56). Chicago: University of Chicago Press.

Munnell, Alicia H., ed. 1986. *Lessons from the Income Maintenance Experiments.* Boston: Federal Reserve Bank of Boston.

Murray, Charles. 1984. *Losing Ground.* New York: Basic Books.

Neuberg, Leland G. 1988. "Distorted Transmission: A Case Study in the Diffusion of Social 'Scientific' Research." *Theory and Society* 17(4): 487–525.

———. 1995. "Review of *Free for All?*" *Southern Economic Journal* 61(3): 893–95.

Newhouse, Joseph P., Willard G. Manning, Carl N. Morris, Larry L. Orr, Naihua Duan, Emmett B. Keeler, Arleen Leibowitz, Kent H. Marquis, M. Susan Marquis, Charles E. Phelps, and Robert H. Brook. 1981. "Some Interim Results from a Controlled Trial of Cost Sharing in Health Insurance." *New England Journal of Medicine* 305(25): 1501–7.

Newhouse, Joseph P., and the Insurance Experiment Group. 1993. *Free for All? Lessons from the RAND Health Insurance Experiment.* Cambridge, Mass.: Harvard University Press.

Norris, Donald F., and Lyke Thompson, eds. 1995. *The Politics of Welfare Reform.* Thousand Oaks, Calif.: Sage Publications.

Norton, Edward C. 1992. "Incentive Regulation of Nursing Homes." *Journal of Health Economics* 11(2): 105–28.

O'Connor, Alice. 1995. "Social Research as Social Policy: The New Jersey Negative Income Tax Experiment." Unpublished manuscript.

O'Leary, Christopher J., Robert G. Spiegelman, and Kenneth J. Kline. 1993. "Reemployment Incentives for Unemployment Insurance Beneficiaries, Results from the Washington Reemployment Bonus Experiment." Working Paper No. 93-22. Kalamazoo, Mich.: W. E. Upjohn Institute for Employment Research.

Orr, Larry L. 1998. *Social Experiments: Evaluating Public Programs with Experimental Methods.* Thousand Oaks, Calif.: Sage Publications.

Orr, Larry L., Robinson G. Hollister, and Myron J. Lefrowitz, with the assistance of Karen Hester. 1971. *Income Maintenance: Interdisciplinary Approaches to Research.* Chicago: Markham Publishing Company.

Palmer, John L., and Joseph A. Pechman, eds. 1978. *Welfare in Rural Areas: The North Carolina-Iowa Income Maintenance Experiment.* Washington, D.C.: Brookings Institution.

Patterson, James T. 1998. "Jimmy Carter and Welfare Reform." In *The Carter Presidency: Policy Choices in the Post-New Deal Era,* edited by Gary M. Fink and Hugh David Graham (117–36). Lawrence: University Press of Kansas.

Pechman, Joseph A., and Michael P. Timpane, eds. 1975. *Work Incentives and Income Guarantees: The New Jersey Negative Income Tax Experiment.* Washington, D.C.: Brookings Institution.

Pelz, Donald C. 1978. "Some Expanded Perspectives on Use of Social Science in Public Policy." In *Major Social Issues: A Multidisciplinary View,* edited by Milton Yinger and Stephen J. Cutler (346–57). New York: Free Press.

Rasell, M. Edith. 1995. "Cost Sharing in Health Insurance—A Reexamination." *New England Journal of Medicine* 332(17): 1164–68.

Rees, Albert, and Harold W. Watts, eds. 1977. "The Labor-Supply Responses to the Experiment: A Summary." In *The New Jersey Income Maintenance Experiment, Volume II Labor Supply Responses*, edited by Harold W. Watts and Albert Rees (5–32). New York: Academic Press.

Riccio, James, Daniel Friedlander, and Stephen Freedman. 1994. *GAIN: Benefits, Costs, and Three-Year Impacts of a Welfare-to-Work Program*. New York: Manpower Demonstration Research Corporation.

Robins, Philip K. 1985. "A Comparison of the Labor Supply Findings from the Four Negative Income Tax Experiments." *Journal of Human Resources* 20(4): 567–82.

Robins, Philip K., Richard W. West, and Michael G. Lohrer. 1980. *Labor Supply Response to a Nationwide Negative Income Tax: Evidence from the Seattle and Denver Income Maintenance Experiments*. Research Memorandum draft, Socioeconomic Research Center. Menlo Park, Calif.: SRI International.

Robins, Philip K., Robert G. Spiegelman, Samuel Weiner, and Joseph G. Bell. 1980. *A Guaranteed Annual Income: Evidence from a Social Experiment*. New York: Academic Press.

Rosko, Michael D., Robert W. Broyles, and William E. Aaronson. 1987. "Prospective Payment Based on Case Mix: Will It Work in Nursing Homes?" *Journal of Health Politics, Policy and Law* 12(4): 683–701.

Ross, Heather L., and Isabel V. Sawhill. 1975. *Time of Transition: The Growth of Families Headed by Women*. Washington, D.C.: The Urban Institute.

Rossi, Peter, and Katharine C. Lyall. 1976. *Reforming Public Welfare: A Critique of the Negative Income Tax Experiment*. New York: Russell Sage Foundation.

Sabatier, Paul. 1978. "The Acquisition and Utilization of Technical Information by Administrative Agencies." *Administrative Science Quarterly* 23(3): 396–417.

Schiller, Bradley R., and C. Nielsen Brasher. 1993. "Effects of Workfare Saturation on AFDC Caseloads." *Contemporary Policy Issues* 11(2): 39–49.

Spiegelman, Robert G. 1992. "Bonus Offers as a Policy Tool for Reducing Unemployment of Unemployment Insurance Recipients." Paper presented at annual conference of the Association for Public Policy Analysis and Management, Denver, Oct. 29–31.

Sproull, Lee, and Patrick Larkey. 1979. "Managerial Behavior and Evaluator Effectiveness." In *The Evaluator and Management*, edited by Herbert C. Schulberg and Jeanette M. Jerrell (89–104). Beverly Hills, Calif.: Sage Publications.

SRI International. 1983. *Final Report of the Seattle-Denver Income Maintenance Experiment, Volume I: Design and Results*. Washington, D.C.: U.S. Government Printing Office.

Stafford, Frank P. 1979. "A Decision Theoretic Approach to the Evaluation of Training Programs." In *Research in Labor Economics: Evaluating Manpower Training Programs*, edited by Farrell E. Block (9–35). Greenwich, Conn.: JAI Press.

Storey, James R. 1973. "Systems Analysis and Welfare Reform: A Case Study of the Family Assistance Plan." *Policy Sciences* 4(1): 1–11.

Strauss, Robert P. 1978. "Incremental Versus Comprehensive Welfare Reform." In *Models for Analysis of Social Policy*, edited by Ron Haskins and James Gallagher (174–202). Norwood, N.J.: Ablex Publishing Company.

Swan, James H., Charlene Harrington, Leslie Grant, John Luehrs, and Steve Preston. 1993. "Trends in Medicaid Nursing Home Reimbursement: 1978–89." *Health Care Financing Review* 14(4): 111–32.

Szanton, Peter. 1991. "The Remarkable Quango: Knowledge, Politics and Welfare Reform." *Journal of Policy Analysis and Management* 10(4): 590–602.

Thompson, Mark S. 1982. *Decision Analysis for Program Evaluation.* Cambridge, Mass.: Ballinger Publishing Company.

Thorburn, Phyllis, and Mark R. Meiners. 1986. *Nursing Home Patient Outcomes: The Results of an Incentive Reimbursement Experiment.* Long-Term Care Studies Program Research Report, DHHS Publication No. PHS 86-3400. Bethesda, Md.: U.S. Department of Health and Human Services, National Information Center on Health Services Research and Health Care Technology.

Thorpe, Kenneth. 1996. "Comments on 'Estimating the Effects of Reform.'" In *The Problem That Won't Go Away: Reforming U.S. Health Care Financing,* edited by Henry J. Aaron (174–81). Washington, D.C.: Brookings Institution.

Tobin, James. 1965. "Improving the Economic Status of the Negro." *Daedalus* 94(4): 78–98.

U.S. Bureau of the Census. 1995. *Statistical Abstract of the United States, 1995.* Washington, D.C.: U.S. Department of Commerce.

U.S. Congress, Congressional Budget Office. 1993. *Managed Competition and Its Potential to Reduce Health Spending.* Washington, D.C.: U.S. Government Printing Office.

U.S. Congress, Congressional Research Service. 1988. *Federal-State Unemployment Compensation System.* 100th cong., 2d sess., September 8.

U.S. Congress, House Committee on Ways and Means. 1987. *Reform of the Unemployment Compensation Program.* 100th cong., 1st sess., December 14.

————. 1988. *Reform of the Unemployment Compensation Program: Hearing before the Subcommittee on Public Assistance and Unemployment Compensation.* 100th cong., 2d sess., September 15.

————. 1991. *Unemployment Insurance and the Recession.* 102d cong., 1st sess., February 6.

————. 1992. *Unemployment Compensation Amendments of 1992.* 102d cong., 2d sess., April 9, 30.

————. 1993. *Health Care Reform.* 103d cong., 1st sess., November 2.

————. 1994. *Unemployment Compensation Reform and Unemployment Assistance Proposal.* 103d cong., 2d sess., March 8, July 12.

U.S. Congress. House Select Committee on Aging. 1986. *Institute of Medicine Study on Nursing Home Regulation.* 99th cong., 2d sess., March 25.

U.S. Congress, Office of Technology Assessment. 1994. *Understanding Estimates of National Health Expenditures Under Health Reform.* Washington, D.C.: U.S. Government Printing Office.

U.S. Congress, Senate Finance Committee. 1987. *Quality of Long-Term Care.* 100th cong., 1st sess., April 28.

————. 1990. *Improving Quality of Care in Nursing Homes.* 101st cong., 2d sess., Aug. 28.

U.S. Department of Health, Education, and Welfare. 1973. *Summary Report: New Jersey Graduated Work Incentive Experiment.* Washington, D.C.: U.S. Department of Health, Education, and Welfare.

————. 1974. *Income Supplement Program.* Washington, D.C.: U.S. Department of Health, Education, and Welfare.

————. 1976. *Summary Report: Rural Income Maintenance Experiment.* Washington, D.C.: U.S. Department of Health, Education, and Welfare.

————. 1983. Office of the Assistant Secretary for Planning and Evaluation, Office of Income Security Policy. *Overview of the Seattle-Denver Income Maintenance Experiment Final Report.* Washington, D.C.: U.S. Department of Health and Human Services.

U.S. Department of Health and Human Services, Office of the Assistant Secretary for Planning and Evaluation. 1981. *National Health Insurance Working Papers—Department of Health and Human Services.* Washington, D.C.: U.S. Department of Health and Human Services.

U.S. Department of Labor, Employment and Training Administration, Unemployment Insurance Service. 1989a. *The New Jersey Unemployment Insurance Reemployment Demonstration Project,* by Walter Corson, Paul T. Decker, S. M. Dunstan, and A. R. Gordon. Unemployment Insurance Occasional Paper 89-3. Washington, D.C.: Government Printing Office.

————. 1989b. *The Secretary's Seminars on Unemployment Insurance,* by Walter Corson, Walter Nicholson, and S. Kerachsky. Unemployment Occasional Paper 89-1. Washington, D.C.: Government Printing Office.

————. 1991. *The New Jersey Unemployment Insurance Reemployment Demonstration Project, Follow-up Report,* by P. Anderson, Walter Corson, and Paul T. Decker. Unemployment Insurance Occasional Paper 91-1. Washington, D.C.: Government Printing Office.

————. 1992a. *An Analysis of Pooled Evidence from the Pennsylvania and Washington Reemployment Bonus Demonstrations,* by Paul T. Decker, and Christopher J. O'Leary. Unemployment Insurance Occasional Paper 92-7. Washington, D.C.: Government Printing Office.

————. 1992b. *Pennsylvania Reemployment Bonus Demonstration Final Report,* by Walter Corson, Paul T. Decker, S. Dunstan, and S. Kerachsky. Unemployment Insurance Occasional Paper 92-1. Washington, D.C.: Government Printing Office.

————. 1992c. *The Washington Reemployment Bonus Experiment Final Report,* by Robert G. Spiegelman, Christopher J. O'Leary, and Kenneth J. Kline. Unemployment Insurance Occasional Paper 92-6. Washington, D.C.: Government Printing Office.

U.S. General Accounting Office. 1981. *Income Maintenance Experiments: Need to Summarize Results and Communicate the Lessons Learned.* Report Number HRD 81-46, April 17.

————. 1983. *Medicaid and Nursing Home Care: Cost Increases and the Need for Services Are Creating Problems for the States and the Elderly.* Report to the Chairman of the Subcommittee on Health and the Environment, Committee on Energy and Commerce, U.S. House of Representatives. Washington, D.C.: Government Printing Office, Oct. 21.

Vobejda, Barbara. 1993. "Welfare Plan Begins to Emerge." *Washington Post,* May 9.

Watts, Harold W. 1970. *Adjusted and Extended Preliminary Results from the Urban Graduated Work Incentive Experiment.* Madison: Institute for Research on Poverty, University of Wisconsin.

Watts, Harold W., Dale J. Poirier, and Charles Mallar. 1977. "Sample, Variables, and Concepts Used in the Analysis." In *The New Jersey Income Maintenance Experiment: Vol. II, Labor Supply Responses,* edited by Harold W. Watts and Albert Rees (33–56). New York: Academic Press.

Watts, Harold W., and Albert Rees, eds. 1977. *The New Jersey Income Maintenance Experiment: Vol. II, Labor Supply Responses; Vol. III, Expenditures, Health, and Social Behavior; and the Quality of the Evidence.* New York: Academic Press.

Weiss, Carol H. 1980. "Knowledge Creep and Decision Accretion." *Knowledge: Creation, Diffusion, Utilization* 1(3): 381–404.

———. 1983. "Ideology, Interests, and Information." In *Ethics, Social Science, and Policy Analysis,* edited by D. Callahan and B. Jennings (213–45). New York: Plenum Press.

———. 1984. "Increasing the Likelihood of Influencing Decisions." In *Evaluation Research Methods: A Basic Guide,* 2d ed., edited by L. Rutman (159–90). Beverly Hills, Calif.: Sage Publications.

———. 1987. "Congressional Committee Staffs (Do, Do Not) Use Analysis." In *Social Science Research and Government: Comparative Essays on Britain and the United States,* edited by Martin Bulmer (94–111). New York: Cambridge University Press.

Weissert, William G., William J. Scanlon, Thomas T. H. Wan, and Douglas E. Skinner. 1983. "Care for the Chronically Ill: Nursing Home Incentive Payment Experiment." *Health Care Financing Review* 5(2): 41–49.

Whiteman, David. 1985. "Reaffirming the Importance of Strategic Use." *Knowledge* 6(Mar.): 203–24.

Williams, Robert G. 1979. *Colorado Monthly Reporting Experiment and Pretest: First Year Research Results.* Denver, Colo.: Mathematica Policy Research, Inc.

Williams, Walter. 1972. *The Struggle for a Negative Income Tax: A Case Study, 1965–70.* Seattle: Institute of Governmental Research, University of Washington.

Wissoker, Douglas A., and Harold W. Watts. 1994. "The Impact of FIP on AFDC Caseloads." Washington, D.C.: The Urban Institute.

Woodbury, Stephen A., and Robert G. Spiegelman. 1987. "Bonuses to Workers and Employers to Reduce Unemployment: Randomized Trials in Illinois." *American Economic Review* 77(4): 513–30.

About the Authors

David Greenberg is a professor of economics at the University of Maryland, Baltimore County (UMBC). He is a labor economist who received his Ph.D. from the Massachusetts Institute of Technology in 1966. Before coming to UMBC in 1982, he worked for the RAND Corporation, SRI International, and the U.S. Department of Health and Human Services. He has spent several recent years working in England and Hungary. Much of his research focuses on the evaluation of government programs that are targeted at the low-income population, especially public assistance, employment, and training programs. He is the coauthor of a widely used textbook on cost-benefit analysis and the *Digest of Social Experiments*, a reference book published by the Urban Institute Press that provides summary information on all previous and ongoing social experiments. In addition, he is the coauthor of a recent article in the *Journal of Economic Perspectives* that examines trends in social experiments over the past three decades and an extensive review of evaluations of government-funded training programs for the disadvantaged, which was published in the *Journal of Economic Literature*.

Donna Linksz is currently the dean of mathematics, science, and engineering at the Community College of Baltimore County. She received her Ph.D. in policy sciences from the University of Maryland, Baltimore County, in 1997. Previously, she was a professor of mathematics with a focus on statistics and evaluation research. Her current research interests include learning outcomes assessment at the course and program levels. Her previous publications include institutional research articles and two college mathematics textbooks.

Marvin Mandell is director and professor in the policy sciences graduate program at the University of Maryland, Baltimore County. He received his Ph.D. from Northwestern University in 1979. His research and teaching center around program evaluation, the application of operations research to public policy and management, and the role of various forms of policy research in the policy process. His work has also appeared in such journals as the *Journal of Policy Analysis and Management, Management Science, Location Science,* the *Evaluation Review,* and *Socio-Economic Planning Sciences.* He is the coeditor of *Government and Policy,* an associate editor of *Management Science,* and a member of the editorial board of the *International Journal of Technology, Policy and Management.*

Index

activities of daily living (ADL), 109n.6
advocacy, 55, 56
advocacy utilization, 50
Agnos, Art, 250–251
AHSIM model, 77–80, 82
Aid to Families with Dependent Children
    (AFDC), 21–23, 126, 145–147, 213,
    214, 222–224, 244–247,
    265–266nn.2–3, 276–277
    AFDC-R, 214–216, 228–234, 239
    AFDC-Unemployed Parent (AFDC-U)
        program, 22, 146, 214–216, 229,
        230, 234, 239
Arkansas WORK Program, 211, 215, 228,
    244–245

Baltimore Options Program, 212, 215,
    228, 229
Bane, Mary Jo, 262
Baum, Erica, 240–243, 261
black box experiments, 16, 33, 307–308

California Employment Development
    Department (EDD), 221–222
California GAIN. *See* GAIN

California Work Experience Program
    (CWEP), 217
Carter, Jimmy, 20
Carter health plan, 20–21, 76–77
Child Assistance Program (CAP),
    275–279, 281, 283, 291, 293n.13
Clinton health care plan, 77–81
Clinton welfare reform effort, 22–23,
    244–247, 265
communication and visibility, 55–56. *See
    also under specific experiments*
conceptual-elaborative utilization, 49,
    255
conceptual-substantive utilization, 48,
    255
conceptual utilization, 48, 51
concrete-elaborative utilization, 49, 148,
    254–255
concrete-substantive utilization, 5–6, 48,
    148, 254–255
concrete utilization, 48, 51, 148
Cook County (Illinois) WIN (Work
    Incentive) Demonstration, 212, 215,
    228
core-periphery dimension, 48
cost-benefit analysis, 17
    use of, 36–37

329

counseling interventions, 29
counterfactuals, 12
crowding-out effect, 186

definitiveness, 52–54. *See also under specific experiments*
Digest of Social Experiments (Greenberg and Shroder), 24
displacement effect, 186
dissemination efforts, 55–56
document analysis, 60
Dynamics of Dependence, The (Bane and Ellwood), 262

education interventions, 28
elaborative utilization, 48–50
Ellwood, David T., 262
employment, interventions for obtaining, 28
Employment Development Department (EDD), California, 221–222
entry effects, 15–16
experimental designs, 33–36. *See also* methodology
external validity, 14–15

Family Assistance Plan (FAP), 20, 72, 116, 121, 133–147
Family Support Act of 1988 (FSA), 22, 146, 238–244, 264
Fisher, Ronald, 18
Food Stamps, 247
Ford, Gerald, 20
Ford Foundation, 219, 220, 226
formative-conceptual-elaborative utilization, 102, 148, 255
formative-conceptual-substantive utilization, 51, 102–103, 148, 255
formative-concrete-substantive utilization, 50, 51, 101–102, 147–149, 254–255
formative utilization, 49–51, 148, 254–255

funding sources for social experiments, 37–38, 53

GAIN (Greater Avenues for Independence) Program, 212, 213, 215, 223–224, 228, 229, 232–233, 250–253, 260, 266–267nn.7–10, 275–276, 279–289, 291
Gary Income Maintenance Experiment, 111–113, 122, 126–128, 137, 139
generalizability, 56–57. *See also under specific experiments*
government funding, 37, 38
Gueron, Judith, 240, 241, 249

Haskins, Ron, 192–193, 240, 241
Health, Education, and Welfare, Department of (HEW), 73–75, 120
health care plan
    Carter, 20–21, 76–77
    Clinton, 77–81
health care status and usage, interventions on, 28–30
health insurance, national, 19–22. *See also* RAND Health Insurance Experiment
human capital model, 233

I-I-I (Ideology-Interests-Information) model, 52, 57, 58, 108, 149, 261, 264–265, 309
ideology(ies), 58. *See also* I-I-I; policy environment, ideology
    defined, 57
Illinois Unemployment Insurance Incentive Experiment, 169–170. *See also* unemployment insurance (UI) bonus experiments
    findings, 182–183
impact analysis
    approach(es) to, 12
    social experiments as an, 11–16

defined, 11
income effect, 123–125
income maintenance experiments
    (IMEs), 111, 114–115
    assessing the use of, with conceptual
        framework, 147
    communication and visibility,
        152–155, 303–304
    definitiveness, 157–159, 303–304
    generalizability, 155–156, 303–304
    I-I-I model, 149–150, 309
    relevance, 156–157, 303–304
    taxonomy of use, 147–149
    timeliness, 150–152
    background data, 111–114
    findings from, 122, 128–130
        effects on conceptual views, 131–132
        effects on hours of work, 122–126
        effects on marital stability, 126–127,
            159
        effects on other social experiments,
            131
        effects on research and policy analy-
            ses, 131
        effects on welfare administration,
            133
        effects on welfare reform initiatives,
            133–147
        use of, 130–131
    origin, 118–122
    why they were undertaken, 115–118
Income Supplement Program (ISP), 136
income transfer interventions, 28
information. See also under policy
    environment
    defined, 57
    interests, 58. See also under policy
        environment
    defined, 57
internal validity, 13
    defined, 42n.3
interventions, types of, 27–30
interviews, 60–62
inventory (creation) model, 47, 74, 298
issue network, 55–56

job club, 276
Job Opportunities and Basic Skills Train-
    ing (JOBS) program, 146, 239–246,
    283
job search assistance (JSA), 166, 171
Jones, Ron, 188

labor force attachment model, 233
labor markets, 39
Levin, Sander, 188, 192
location of experimental sites, 38–40
Lopez, Julia, 260

Maine On-the-Job-Training (OJT) Pro-
    gram, 212, 215, 228
Manpower Demonstration Research Cor-
    poration (MDRC), 211, 213,
    218–222, 225–227, 230, 236,
    240–243, 257–259, 281–282
market shares, 40–41
maximum dollar expenditure (MDE),
    68–71
Medicaid, 72. See also Nursing Home
    Incentive Reimbursement Experi-
    ment
Meiners, Mark, 95–97, 100
methodology, 59–63. See also experimen-
    tal designs
microsimulation models, 56, 156, 158,
    301, 312
Moynihan, Patrick, 144–145, 240–242
Murray, Charles, 262

National Center for Health Services
    Research and Health Care Technol-
    ogy Assessment (NCHSR), 89, 94,
    96, 97, 105–107
negative income tax program (NIT), 305.
    See also income maintenance experi-
    ments
New Jersey Income Maintenance Experi-
    ment, 111–113, 119–123, 126–128,
    133–137, 151, 158

New Jersey On-the-Job-Training (OJT) Program, 212
New Jersey REACH, 215, 228
New Jersey Unemployment Insurance Reemployment Demonstration Project, 166, 168–169. *See also* unemployment insurance (UI) bonus experiments
findings, 181–182
Nixon administration, 20. *See also* Family Assistance Plan
nongovernmental organizations (NGOs), 37–39
Nursing Home Incentive Reimbursement Experiment, 89, 306
description, 90–91
admissions, 93
discharge rates, 94
incentive scheme, 91–93
patient health status, 93–94
design issues
barriers to participation, 98–99
choice of location, 96–97
period of treatment, 98
private-pay patients, 99–100
target group of interest, 97–98
and inventory model, 298
origins and purpose, 89–90, 94–96
policy effects, 101–103
utilization factors, 103
communication and visibility, 104–106, 303
definitiveness, 103, 303
generalizability, 106–107, 303
ideology, interests, and information, 108–109, 303, 309
relevance, 107–108, 303
timeliness, 103–104, 303

Office of Economic Opportunity (OEO), 19, 72–75, 119–121
Omnibus Budget Reconciliation Act of 1981 (OBRA 1981), 21–22, 145, 218, 219, 225

On-the-Job-Training (OJT) Program, New Jersey, 212
organizations evaluating social experiments, 40

Pasteur, Louis, 18
Pennsylvania Reemployment Bonus Demonstration, 170–172. *See also* unemployment insurance (UI) bonus experiments
findings, 183–184
Perry Preschool Project, 42n.12
Personal Responsibility and Work Opportunity Reconciliation Act (PRWORA), 23–24, 247–250
persuasive/advocacy utilization, 49, 50, 148, 255
policy decisions to conduct social experiment, 46–47
policy effects of experiments, 48–52. *See also* utilization factors
typology of research use, 101
typology of ways that findings can be used, 48–50, 101–102
policy environment
ideology, interests, and information, 57–58. *See also under specific experiments*
influence on use of social experiments, 308–311
policy formulation, state, 291–292
role of evaluations in, 288–291
policy impacts, 12
policy process, connection between social experiments and
aspects of, 5
importance of understanding, 5
policy windows, 54
policymakers, interviews of, 61
policymaking agenda, experiments as attempts to influence, 48
process analysis, 17
use of, 36–37
Program for Better Jobs and Income (PBJI), 136–147

programs tested, types of, 27–31
  tests of new programs *vs.* changes in
    existing ones, 31–32
  voluntary *vs.* mandatory, 30–31
Project Independence, 275–277, 279
Proposition 13, 144, 145

RAND Health Insurance Experiment
  (HIE), 67, 305, 310
  design, 67–71
  estimation methodology, 71
  key findings, 71–72
  origins, 72–75
  policy impacts, 75–81
  enlightenment, 81–83
  utilization factors
    communication and visibility, 85,
      303
    definitiveness, 86–87, 303
    generalizability, 85–86, 303
    ideology, interests, and information
      in policy environment, 87–88,
      303, 309
    relevance, 84, 303
    timeliness, 83–84, 303
random assignment, 4, 18, 53, 222, 237,
  238
rational model of decisionmaking, 46–47,
  177–179
REACH, New Jersey, 215, 228
Reagan administration, 21, 22
Reforming Welfare with Work (Gueron),
  240, 241
relevance, 57, 305–306. *See also under spe-*
  cific experiments
  defined, 58
research brokers, interviews of, 61
researchers, interviews of, 60
response surface experiments, 16, 33,
  155–156. *See also* RAND
Riverside model, 233, 253. *See also* GAIN
Rolston, Howard, 237
Ross, Heather, 18, 118–119
Rural Income Maintenance Experiment,
  111–113, 119–122, 126–128, 137

San Diego I (Employment Preparation
  Program/Experimental Work Experience Program), 212, 216, 221, 228,
  229, 250–252, 260
San Diego SWIM. *See* SWIM
Saturation Work Incentive Model
  (SWIM), 212, 213, 216, 223, 228,
  229, 246, 250
Seattle-Denver Income Maintenance
  Experiment, 111–113, 122, 124, 127,
  128, 137–142, 144, 148, 152–154,
  156, 159
selection bias, 13–14
social experimentation, 3, 12. *See also*
  specific topics
  advantages and disadvantages, 13–16
  historical context, 19–24
  history, 18–19, 24–25
    three eras, 25–41
social experiments, 4. *See also specific*
  topics
  characteristics of previously con-
    ducted, 24–25
  components of, 3–4
  conceptual framework for, 8–9
  decision to conduct, 46–47
  evaluators of, 40–41
  how findings are used, 299–302
  how their characteristics affect their
    use, 302–308
  lessons from conducting, 311–312
  one experiment often begets other, 302
  poorly implemented, 53
  size of, 33–36
  types of, 16–17
  when they are conducted, 46–48. *See*
    also timeliness
  why they are conducted, 297–299
SPAM (Special Policy Analysis Model),
  78–80
sponsors, interviews of, 60
Stevens, David, 192
substantive-elaborative utilization, 48
substantive utilization, 50, 149
substitution effect, 123–125
Supplemental Security Income (SSI), 247

survey(s), 62–63
SWIM (Saturation Work Incentive
    Model), 212, 213, 216, 223, 228, 229,
    246, 250
Swoap, David, 250–251
Szanton, Peter, 239–240

target groups, 25–27
Temporary Assistance for Needy Families
    (TANF), 23–24, 247, 248
Thorburn, Phyllis, 95, 97
timeliness, 54–55, 305, 312. *See also under
    specific experiments*
training interventions, 28

unemployment insurance (UI) bonus
    experiments, 63, 165–166, 298, 306,
    307, 310
    decisionmaking models, 177–179
    description, 166–174
    findings, 179–185
        policy concerns that overshadowed
            the, 208
        pooled, 185–186
    origin, 174–176
    policy effects, 187, 195–197
        formative-conceptual-elaborative,
            191–193, 196
        formative-conceptual-substantive,
            193–194, 196
        formative-concrete-elaborative,
            187–189, 196
        formative-concrete-substantive,
            189–190, 196
        persuasive/advocacy-conceptual-
            elaborative, 195, 196
        persuasive/advocacy-concrete-
            elaborative, 191, 196
        persuasive/advocacy-concrete-
            substantive, 191, 196
    publications resulting from, 200–202
    utilization factors, 197
        communication and visibility,
            200–202, 304

definitiveness, 197–199, 304
generalizability, 200, 202–204, 304
ideology, interests, and information
    in policy environment,
    205–208, 309
relevance, 204–205, 304
timeliness, 199, 304
utilization factors, 52, 58, 103. *See also
    specific factors*

Virginia Employment Services Program
    (ESP), 212, 216, 228
voluntary vs. mandatory policies, 30–31,
    98–99

Washington Reemployment Bonus
    Experiment, 172–174. *See also
    unemployment insurance (UI)
    bonus experiments*
    findings, 184–185
Weiss, Carol H., 308. *See also* I-I-I
Weissert, William, 93–94, 97
welfare (policy)
    changes in, 250–253
    effects of evaluations on, 282–286
    federal waiver policy, 237–238
    state, 250–253
        factors influencing, 286–288
        states as policy laboratories, 273–275
welfare policy issues, sources of informa-
    tion about, 284–286
welfare reform, 19–24. *See also* income
    maintenance experiments
welfare reform efforts, recent, 146–147
    Clinton's, 22–23, 244–247, 265
welfare-to-work demonstrations
    assessing the use of, with conceptual
        framework
        taxonomy of use, 253–256
        utilization factors, 256–261, 304, 309
    and social policy, 261–263
        ideologies, 263–264, 309
        implications of I-I-I for utilization
            of experiments, 264–265

political interests, 263
use of findings from, 234
   influence on conceptual views,
      235–237
   influence on federal waiver process,
      237–238
   influence on social experimentation,
      234–235
   influence on welfare reform initia-
      tives, 238–253
welfare-to-work experiments, 211
   characteristics and background infor-
      mation on, 214–217
   description, 211–217
   findings, 227
      experimental, 227–233
      nonexperimental, 233–234

   knowledge of the, 279, 281–282
      sources of, 279–281
   methodology, 278
   origin, 217–221
      California experiments, 221–225
   why they were undertaken, 225–226
West Virginia Community Work Experience Program (CWEP), 212, 216,
   228, 229
Whiteman, David, 48
Work and Responsibility Act, 244–246
work first model, 233
Work Incentive (WIN) Demonstration,
   212, 215, 228
work incentives, 156–157. *See also*
   income maintenance experiments
Wyrsch, Mary Ann, 190, 192, 194